CHICAGO PUBLIC LIBRARY

R00930 63584

D0948366

THE CHICAGO PUBLIC LIBRARY
LITERATURE & LANGUAGE DIVISION

OCT     1993

FORM 19

# Her Bread to Earn

# Her Bread to Earn

## Women, Money, and Society
## from Defoe to Austen

MONA SCHEUERMANN

THE UNIVERSITY PRESS OF KENTUCKY

PR 858 .W6 S34 1993
Scheuermann, Mona.
Her bread to earn

Copyright © 1993 by The University Press of Kentucky

Scholarly publisher for the Commonwealth,
serving Bellarmine College, Berea College, Centre
College of Kentucky, Eastern Kentucky University,
The Filson Club, Georgetown College, Kentucky
Historical Society, Kentucky State University,
Morehead State University, Murray State University,
Northern Kentucky University, Transylvania University,
University of Kentucky, University of Louisville,
and Western Kentucky University.

*Editorial and Sales Offices:* Lexington, Kentucky 40508-4008

**Library of Congress Cataloging-in-Publication Data**

Scheuermann, Mona.
    Her bread to earn : women, money, and society from Defoe to Austen
/ Mona Scheuermann.
        p.    cm.
    Includes bibliographical references and index.
    ISBN 0-8131-1817-4 (alk. paper)
    1. English fiction—18th century—History and criticism.   2. Women
and literature—England—History—18th century.   3. Literature and
society—England—History—18th century.   4. Social problems in
literature.   5. Money in literature.   I. Title.
PR858.W6S34   1993
823'.509352042—dc20                                              92-40912

This book is printed on recycled acid-free paper meeting
the requirements of the American National Standard
for Permanence of Paper for Printed Library Materials.

R00930 63584

LIT

for Peter

# Contents

# Acknowledgments

There are many pleasures in writing a book. Among the greatest of these has been the opportunity in good conscience to spend many hours (this was work, after all) in conversations with friends and colleagues who have shared with me their perceptions of eighteenth-century life, literature, and history. I especially want to thank Jerry Beasley, Syndy Conger, Paul Hunter, Leland E. Warren, and Simon Varey for giving me so many good ideas and for helping me to shape the concepts of this book.

My seminar students at the University of Hamburg in 1985, as I began this book, and at the University of Berne in 1991, when I brought it to closure, were delightful auditors and questioners. To Cary Fink, who arranged my University Professorship at Hamburg, and to Werner Senn, who brought me to Berne, I owe some of the most pleasant months of my professional life.

Judi Mayzel, Joan Cichon, Barbara Keeley, Susan Maltese, and Sandra Wittman always have been ready to track down research materials and to help me to formulate searches; their cheerful professionalism has made this work much easier than it would otherwise have been. Nancy Sherman, who can conjure books out of the inter-library loan system seemingly at will, is irreplaceable. Richard Tracz had the answer to any question I asked and always made the time to answer. Thanks are due too to the staffs of the Newberry Library and the Northwestern University Library.

Aspects of this research have been presented at national and regional meetings of the American Society for Eighteenth-Century

Studies. I am especially grateful for the insightful comments of the colleagues who participated in the "Work in Progress" session I presented at the 1990 MWASECS meeting at Macomb, Illinois. Parts of this work have been published in *Studies in the Novel, The Durham University Journal*, and *The Age of Johnson*, and I thank the editors of those journals for their kind permission to reprint the material here. Finally, I want to thank the two readers for the University Press of Kentucky for their careful readings and their many constructive comments. They caught many errors and helped me to sharpen important aspects of my argument. Whatever errors remain are of course my own, but the good points in this book owe much to all of the friends and colleagues acknowledged here.

My last debt is to my husband Peter, whose encouragement and advice have been part of this project from its inception. He is at the center of everything I do.

Miss Campbell, who by that chance, that luck which so often defies anticipation in matrimonial affairs, giving attraction to what is moderate rather than to what is superior, engaged the affections of Mr. Dixon, a young man, rich and agreeable, almost as soon as they were acquainted; and was eligibly and happily settled, while Jane Fairfax had yet her bread to earn.

*Emma*
Jane Austen

# ONE

# Introduction

The images of women in the eighteenth-century English novel are more positive than much recent discussion of women in the novel would suggest. Women are depicted as strong, capable, and responsible members of society in a surprising variety of works, and while these women are often young, they are not all so narrow in their scope as such widely discussed young ladies as Burney's Evelina and Austen's Emma. Many of the most positive depictions, as well as the most nasty, appear in the works of male novelists. I examine the representations of women in the work of some of the major novelists, both male and female, of the eighteenth century. This range is important because the recent critical emphasis on images of women in the works only of women novelists—this category has come to include Richardson as a sort of honorary member of the women's group—distorts the reality of how women are perceived in the eighteenth-century novel. For one thing, it overemphasizes the view of woman as victim; for another, it emphasizes the image of the woman as a nonfunctioning member of society, essentially excluded from any but the role of sufferer.[1] It is surely odd to look for our images of women only in the works of women, since the majority of the important novels in the eighteenth century were written by men. Whether we are interested in expanding the canon, redefining it, or simply accepting it as we found it, this fact stands. I have chosen, then, in this study to look at the images of women in the important novels of the eighteenth century, those works traditionally accepted as the core of the canon or those novels that define an important trend at a particular time, as do the politically radical novels of the 1790s. Among the canonical writers, I look at the work of Defoe, Richardson, Fielding, and Austen; each of these novelists specifically addresses the situation of women in society. For the sake of the schema it was tempting also to include Smollett and Sterne, but finally I omit their novels from this study because neither Smollett nor Sterne focuses significantly on depictions of women. On the other hand, the radical novelists of the Godwin circle, who as a group represent perhaps the most important movement in fiction at the end of the century, do take the situation of women as an important center of their work.

The kinds of images in these novels are enormously varied, ranging from the extraordinary potential inherent in Defoe's depictions of women to the extreme limitation of Richardson's. Defoe's women are capable of virtually any accomplishment that men can achieve; Richardson's women can die or, at best, marry. There are wide differences in the kinds of images even one novelist provides: Fielding's women run the gamut from wondrous (and long-suffering) wives to horrendously frightening harridans. Comparing the images of women presented by these novelists, surprising patterns emerge. Defoe, in comparison to just about anyone else, has the most positive view of woman and her capabilities, insisting in both *Moll Flanders* and *Roxana* that a woman's talent for productive work is limited only by society's definition of what avenues for earning money are available to her. He also is sharply aware of the legal and social stumbling blocks society places in her way, presenting convincing arguments against the restrictions that marriage places on a woman. Fielding, who generally has had a good press with relation to his images of women, and Richardson, who of late years has been seen as virtually a feminist author, both come away with amazingly low grades when we look more closely at what they are actually saying and showing about woman, her capabilities, and her place in society. Similar redefinitions are called for at the end of the eighteenth century. Austen, who along with Richardson lately has been claimed as an early feminist,[2] seems relatively more conservative when we compare her images of women with those of writers such as Wollstonecraft, Bage, and Holcroft whose works precede hers. Juxtaposing these authors' images of women thus not only helps to define the eighteenth-century perception of women, but it helps to refocus our perceptions of each author. Looking at Roxana saving, investing, and managing her money, we see a woman who is intensely capable, and we appreciate an author who can imagine a woman so whole. When Roxana says she is "become, from a Lady of Pleasure, a Woman of Business, and of great Business too," we see that she is neither androgynous nor mad, but decidedly fulfilled.[3] And when we count up the many female horrors in Fielding, from Mrs. Partridge to Blear-Eyed Moll, it becomes equally difficult to see Fielding as quite so good-natured about women, so chivalrous, as he has long been reputed to be.

The themes in novels that relate to women are quite similar throughout the period. The greatest surprise in this research has been that the ubiquitous concern in these novels is money. From Defoe to Austen, each novelist depicts women as directly concerned with financial matters, and in each novel women not only talk about money but have a clear understanding of their finances and of the ramifications of their financial status. We are all familiar by now with the centrality of money to Austen novels; money plays an even larger role—and it should be noted a very positive role—in Defoe's novels. Fielding's *Amelia* is a constant chronicle of (Amelia's) financial travails, and *Clarissa*, of course, is awash in financial detail; that Pamela, constantly adding up the value of the change in her pocket and the clothes in her cupboard, is fascinated by money needs no reminder. The women in the radical novels of the nineties constantly discuss the management of money, in terms of its social usefulness or, in the case of *Maria*, in terms of society's viciously unfair treatment of woman's right to her own earnings or inheritance. This emphasis on money suggests an orientation in the novels that places women in the real world, functioning within and dealing with practical daily problems. The emphasis in these novels is not on the woman as professional virgin, fending off those who would attempt to rape rather than marry her, a distorted emphasis that results from too much attention to Richardson's images. While Clarissa and Pamela spend much of their time in delaying or avoiding sexual confrontations, the vast majority of eighteenth-century female characters are very active in the living of their own lives. Actually, relatively few eighteenth-century female characters spend much time worrying about their virginity. There is much more concern with making a living—whether the woman is single, which means finding money to live, or married, which implies managing finances. The inability of a husband to manage money and the wife's need somehow to deal with this situation is a more frequent theme in these novels than virginity, appearing in, to name just some of the books under discussion, *Moll Flanders, Roxana, Amelia, St. Leon,* and *Maria or The Wrongs of Woman.* The financial base of *Pride and Prejudice* of course has long been recognized, and most of the plot of *Emma* can be said to revolve around financial—in Austen's work virtually syn-onymous with matrimonial—pairings. And while critics traditionally have seen Richardson's novels centered on the defense of virtue, I argue that both *Pamela* and *Clarissa* are money centered as well.

Themes that we might have expected to find, conversely, do not show up in these novels with any significant emphasis. Female educa-tion, for example, is almost a nonsubject, except in *Tom Jones* where Learned Ladies come in for a great deal of satirizing, but the "proper" education of women is ignored. Women from Moll and Roxana to Evelina to the Austen heroines learn their way in the world, but there is almost no discussion, not even conduct-book stuff, about anything like a system of education. Austen's comment in *Emma* about Mrs. Goddard's school, that it is a place where young ladies are not "for enormous pay . . . screwed out of health and into vanity"[4] is one of the most explicit comments in these novels—surely not much of an analy-sis. If girls are being "educated" for anything, it seems, they are being educated to snare husbands; but, no, to the credit of all these writers, even the novels that deal in large measure with courtship are in even larger measure about human development, about the moral growth of the initially immature woman. And these concerns are precisely the same ones set out for male characters: there is little in these novels about the subject of education—in the sense of learning in an explicitly structured manner—with regard to men either, even in children's books such as Henry Brooke's *The Fool of Quality* and Thomas Day's *Sandford and Merton* which do, indeed, focus on the "education" of young male children. A book like *Tom Jones* hardly ever touches on the subject of education in the formal sense although it is clearly about Tom's moral and worldly education. In precisely the same way, Aus-ten's novels deal with the moral and social education of Elizabeth and Emma. Interestingly, this particular female focus takes some time to happen; for Richardson and Fielding, the "good" female is born mor-ally formed and requires none of the moral shaping needed by the male. Sophia serves as a stable moral point throughout *Tom Jones*.

If the female is not educated into courtship, she is nevertheless most interested in it. It comes as no surprise that many of these novels are extensively concerned with courtship. But the model is not always the Burney and Austen one, where the female, no matter how wonder-ful, is fortunate to snare the male in marriage. In most of the novels I discuss, the woman is an equal prize in marriage with the man; even Fielding, in so many ways markedly the male chauvinist, draws both Sophia and Amelia as better catches than Tom and Booth. And Defoe, as so often, presents the most positive view of all: male-female relationships of absolute equality—Moll and most of her male "friends," and Roxana and all but her first husband. So that in discussing the theme of courtship in the eighteenth-century novel, to juxtapose images across the century is to see rather different patterns from those we might have assumed to be there. Although the theme of courtship shows up in a large proportion of the novels, it plays a relatively unimportant role in most of them. That is, the idea of courtship is generally attached to another, more compelling theme such as domination *(Clarissa)*, or, more usually, money and making a living *(Pride and Prejudice)*. Further, although we might have assumed that courtship is generally positive and that the end of courtship—marriage—is a positive denouement, this turns out not to be the case in many of the important novels of the period: *Moll Flanders, Roxana, Clarissa, The Wrongs of Woman,* for example. Defoe, who shows women as most "empowered," to risk an anachronism, has very little interest in courtship. Also, again somewhat surprisingly, there is quite a range of female responses to courtship in these novels, going from the essentially passive female who allows herself to be courted, to the woman who urgently attempts to avoid the courtship (Clarissa, of course) to the woman who is an active partner in the development of the relationship (Anna St. Ives).

As I have suggested, the Richardsonian model, with both Pamela and Clarissa always in danger, has been given far too much credence as the shaping conception of the eighteenth-century novel. Many recent commentators on women in the eighteenth-century novel have insisted on the centrality of virginity and chastity in the perception of the heroine, and where the heroine clearly is not drawn to that measure have simply dumped her into a different category from the presumably more mainstream novelistic pattern. Thus Janet Todd notes that "Virginity or chastity is part of the ideology of every eighteenth-century heroine. In the tragic novels, its loss is so heinous that the fallen women can only move from one bed to another, from love to death. . . . In the criminal and whore histories . . . *Fanny Hill, Moll Flanders,* and *Juliette*—it is an expensive but expendable commodity."[5] Keith May, in a generally perceptive book, notes that "Defoe alone widened [women's] possibilities virtually to the extent enjoyed by men," but hedges, "partly perhaps because of the immorality of his women . . . we can deduce that his advocacy was heeded least."[6] The number of important eighteenth-century novels where chastity is the woman's primary concern actually is quite small; to put this another way, there are so many "exceptions" to the Richardsonian rule that we must finally redefine the rule. Of the novels I discuss in this book, *Moll Flanders, Roxana, Tom Jones, Amelia, Caleb Williams, St. Leon, Anna St. Ives, Hermsprong, Maria or the Wrongs of Woman, Pride and Prejudice* and *Emma* all find their focus elsewere. To this list I could add Burney's *Evelina* as well. The distinction to be made here is, I think, between sentimental and nonsentimental fiction, for, with the exception of Richardson, most eighteenth-century serious novelists focus on other aspects of their female characters' lives. Perhaps not surprisingly, this particular pattern for the novel has not changed from the beginning to the present, with serious fiction indeed representing all aspects of a woman's life, and cheap romance emphasizing . . . cheap romance.[7]

What do eighteenth-century novels focus on when they view women? In addition to the concern with money, and the widespread and closely connected concern with courtship, they do also talk about marriage. It is true as critics so often have noted that many eighteenth-century heroines are quite young, but it is also true that they are not all so young and that there are many female characters in these novels in addition to the heroines. Defoe in both *Moll Flanders* and *Roxana* shows mature male-female relationships which, if they are not always strictly legal, are assuredly domestic. Fielding devotes *Amelia* to the trials of a married woman, and Richardson gives a long (if often neglected) section of *Pamela* to recounting Pamela's married life; there is also the marriage of the senior Harlowes in *Clarissa*. At the other end of the century, almost all the novels I discuss show marriages, good and bad, comic and tragic. Rather delightfully, the most rhapsodic depiction comes from that anarchist and nonbeliever in matrimony, William Godwin, who in *St. Leon* draws a very loving picture of Mary Wollstonecraft in the character of St. Leon's wife Marguerite.

While marriage is widely depicted, mother-child relationships are virtually ignored. Again, it is basically only Richardson who pays a great deal of attention to the relationship between a woman and her mother in the depiction of Clarissa and Mrs. Harlowe; it is very rare indeed for a novelist to talk much about the maternal relationship of a heroine to her own offspring. Of all the female protagonists in these novels, only one, Amelia, actually is seen in the act of mothering. Remarkably, *all* Fielding novels end with the heroines either pregnant or already mothers, but except for Amelia, we see little or nothing of these maternal relationships. The most discussed filial relationship is the father-daughter one.

The world of women in eighteenth-century English novels is not so restricted as our misemphasis on chastity has suggested.[8] In fact, women get away with quite a lot. First of all, women leave home quite often, and they are not always well chaperoned. Moll and Roxana of course have extraordinary adventures, but so does Sophia Western. It is not a lucky accident that no harm comes to Sophia as she travels the roads of England; we need only remember how many awkward situations other women—Evelina, Anna St. Ives, even Maria—get into. The world is not perceived as horribly dangerous for a young woman—if she comes to harm, it is generally at the hand of someone she knows: a Lovelace, a Coke Clifton, a Mr. Venables (Maria's husband). In this, it might be noted, the English eighteenth-century novel is very different from the American, where, in novel after novel, the very smallest mistake leads to irreparable loss and imminent death.[9] The psychic and physical space available to women in the English novel of this period is then relatively large; perceptions of women as entirely limited by their sex are perhaps more frequent in novels by women than by men, but by no means, as I suggest, so ubiquitous as critics sometimes have implied. There is much to argue against in a statement like "A woman has virtually no freedom of emotional expression. The sexual attitudes displayed in eighteenth-century fiction and autobiography by women—the obsession with innocence, the concern for the danger of imagination (or passion), the anger at men, the longing to *be* a man, or a child—emphasize that lack of freedom."[10] And it is especially hard to maintain such a limited view when we look at images of women in novels by both male and female authors, yet another instance where it seems to me a most necessary perspective is available to us if we do not arbitrarily limit our images of women to women authors.

Another, related perception about female characters that comes to seem increasingly inaccurate is the "truism" that women suffer alarming rates of mortality in these books—especially any woman who, deliberately or accidentally, ventures beyond the bounds of polite behavior. As one critic puts it, "Women fall ill in the eighteenth-century novel alarmingly often. . . . The ultimate symbol of female debility is death, and in the eighteenth-century novel women die in droves."[11] But women "die in droves" only in certain kinds of books. Again, in the American novels of the period, which model themselves on the weakest English models, women indeed die in virtually every novel, and as punishment for the very smallest of peccadilloes. In English novels, the mortality rates are fairly high in sentimental fiction. But in the majority of other fictions—including again most of the important novels of the period—women are quite robust. The one example of a slowly dying lily in my survey is Clarissa, whose death leaves such a tremendous impression on all readers, partially because it takes roughly a thousand pages to complete itself. But Richardson is not the only model for the eighteenth-century novel. Even Richardson only kills off Clarissa; Pamela, playing with fire at each step, arrives at great success. The model of Clarissa, however, has distorted our view of the period. Actually, in all of the novels I survey here, only in *Clarissa* does the heroine sicken and die. Virtually all of the female characters in these novels, from Defoe's works to Austen's and from protagonists to minor players, exhibit physical good health and admirable psychological resiliency. Moll and Roxana, for example, barely pause in their dealings even for childbirth; in both *Tom Jones* and *Amelia*, women continue actively with their lives no matter what the circumstance. Moving to the other end of our period, in the two Austen novels I discuss, the most serious illness is Jane's cold—from which, of course, she recovers nicely. Even Maria and Jemima in Wollstonecraft's *Maria or the Wrongs of Woman*, each of whom suffers emotional and physical blows sufficient one would think to break anyone, both recover repeatedly to go on fighting. The women in most of the novels surveyed in this study experience a wide variety of situations and, except for Clarissa, all are survivors.

The novels depict female characters in all social classes, from servant to aristocrat. Interestingly, although we have tended to think of the women in eighteenth-century English novels as middle or upper class, in fact there is a very even mix of types. Fielding, for example, presents an astonishing range of classes in *Tom Jones*, and while Sophia assuredly takes center stage, she is supported by a full and colorful cast of supporting female characters. Even in *Amelia*, which portrays a much smaller social range, there are women of several social classes in the novel. Generally, women in these novels are not limited in what they can do because of the fact that they are female; rather, the active part that they can take in society is defined by their class, and this role is largely defined the same way for women and men of a given class. In Bage's *Hermsprong*, for example, Caroline, Maria, and Hermsprong all engage in the same socially useful roles and assume the same responsibility for the well-being of those less fortunate. Similarly, in Austen novels, the small compass of action traced by the female characters is not greatly different from that of their male companions. One of the discoveries of this study has been that in all novels that talk about social responsibility, men and women are seen as having essentially equal duties. In some cases, as in Holcroft's *Anna St. Ives*, the author acknowledges the reality that in physical strength and the ability physically to go about doing good deeds a woman may find herself more limited than a man, but her moral and intellectual duties are no different from his. Social responsibility and making a living are of course quite different issues, and in the vast majority of novels women who are concerned with the first have that luxury because they are free from the second: or, simply put, social responsibility is the luxury of those whose basic needs have been met: this is one of the explicit points Mary Wollstonecraft makes in *Maria*. Not surprisingly, when authors show women working, they deal with lower-class women. This is true even for such a radical writer as Wollstonecraft; in fact, even among the male radical writers, Godwin, Bage, and Holcroft, no matter how capable a woman is seen to be, she generally is not pictured as working. (There is one exception to this pattern in one of the later Godwin novels.) Women who are pictured in the "act" of work are almost always servants; upper-class women who discuss going to work, like Jane Fairfax, usually are rescued before they must submit to this horrendous fate. The great—and grand—exception to these patterns is Defoe, whose women learn, and struggle and work, and who succeed admirably. His female characters begin life in various classes of society, and they inevitably progress beyond wherever it was they started. Defoe, as I will be suggesting throughout this book, in his images of women provides us with many remarkable perspectives.

Some comment needs to be made about the relationship between these novelistic patterns and the horrible real-life legal restrictions on women as well as the very restricted range of employment options available to them. In brief, a woman's legal rights over her own property depended on her marital status. While an unmarried (and not betrothed) or widowed woman had control of her property and of her money, the married woman had virtually no such rights; a betrothed woman, even before her marriage, could no longer make gifts from her own estate. Even over her own children, a woman had virtually no legal rights. And in terms of work, especially in the cities, the options were limited, and sometimes not honorable.[12] These realities are reflected in the works of each novelist who deals with such issues, especially Defoe and Wollstonecraft. And yet I have been suggesting that overall the novels, except for *Maria*, present a relatively optimistic view of women in society. The apparent contradiction between the gloomy legal truths and the life-images in the novels is resolved by remembering that the novels generally are showing women living in society and functioning within society's conditions: that is, people, women, living their everyday lives rarely spend most of their time lamenting their disadvantages before the law. Where these issues are relevant—a good example is Roxana's refusal to marry the merchant because she would lose control of her fortune—they do enter the novels.

The topic of women and the eighteenth-century English novel has received careful and disparate attention in recent years, with the current period yielding a plethora of well-crafted, often compelling studies. Anyone who works in this field builds on the basic foundations of Marilyn Butler, Margaret Anne Doody, and Janet Todd, whose work in the 1970s prepared the way for all of us. Some authors, especially Defoe, Richardson, and Austen, have received much critical attention in terms of their treatment of women, while others, Fielding in particular, have not been looked into much at all.[13] In almost all cases, studies of the depictions of women in eighteenth-century English novels have fallen into two categories, studies of women in the work of a particular author or depictions of women in the works of female writers. General studies by and large have ignored the fact that women significantly are depicted by both male and female writers, and that by studying these images across writers we can learn much about the period's perception of women: it is this omission that I address. The images of Defoe, of Fielding, of Richardson, are all true in their ways, but none presents the entire truth of the life of a woman early in the eighteenth century, just as neither Holcroft, Wollstonecraft, nor Austen provides the whole picture of life late in the century. This book grew out of my own curiosity to trace perceptions of women as they appear throughout the period, whether the novels were written by men or women. It is my hope that the juxtapositions I have suggested will add to our sense of what seemed possible for women in the social circumstances of eighteenth-century England. The images of women in novels by women are not obviously different from the images in novels by men. Surveying these works, it seems clear that differences in perception are much more closely linked to differences in philosophical or political standpoint than to the gender of the novelist.

Finally, a note on methodology. Much recent criticism has chosen to shunt aside the text, preferring to theorize about rather than to read closely the constructs given to readers by authors. The very idea that we can analyze texts in some quarters has come into disrepute, replaced by the notion that all we have in books is a kind of unstable, obtuse stew of perceptions. Aspects of novels may do things like dynamically evolve and of course they may be (indeed must be) embedded; text is, in these "readings," contradictory and susceptible to all kinds of disruptions.[14] Such criticism is offended by the assumption that a text is stable and transparent and that aspects of that text are indeed detachable from their narrative and comparable therefore with other texts—that is, that we can compare "images" from one text to another. The premise of my book clearly implies that such comparison not only is possible but is valuable. My study attempts to redefine perceptions of how women are seen in the eighteenth-century English novel. I would be pleased if, in the course of this reexamination, it also helps to reverse recent trends towards marginalizing the texts themselves.

# TWO

# Daniel Defoe:
# *Moll Flanders* and *Roxana*

Defoe begins *Moll Flanders* with the demurrer that "When a Woman debauch'd from her Youth, nay, even being the Off-spring of Debauchery and Vice, comes to give an Account of all her vicious Practises, and even to descend to the particular Occasions and Circumstances by which she first became wicked, and of all the progression of Crime which she run through in threescore Year, an Author must be hard put to it to wrap it up so clean, as not to give room, especially for vitious Readers to turn it to his Disadvantage."[1] The woman to whom Defoe refers is of course Moll, in many ways one of the eighteenth century's most attractive heroines. I will argue that she becomes so attractive to the reader as the novel goes on because she is not perceived as evil but rather as wonderfully capable—her "vicious" acts necessitated by circumstances and, in fact, often illegal but never abhorrent. Defoe creates in both his heroines, Moll Flanders and Roxana, human beings to whom nothing comes free. Each should be society's victim but creates instead her own means not only to survive but to prosper. Defoe claims in both novels to be telling cautionary tales, but the cautions he makes weigh heavily against acceptance of victimization. Defoe believes in the self-made man, as *Robinson Crusoe* exemplifies. What is wonderful is that, almost alone among novelists of his century, he believes equally in the self-made woman. Since the possibilities for her to work are obviously narrower, Defoe grants her less than entirely legal options. Aware that society victimizes woman by limiting her means of earning money, Defoe shows us the woman functioning within these constraints that she has not created. The achievements of Moll and Roxana form the core of each book; both women have the real potential literally of starving to death and both build their finances from scratch to not inconsequential fortunes. Financial detail in *Moll Flanders* and *Roxana* often runs on for several pages at a time.

The emphasis on money in the novels focuses the books on real-life concerns. At all times we are aware of Moll and Roxana actively participating in the day to day happenings of their environment. I contrast this kind of involvement with the state of someone like Clarissa, who lives far more in the reality of her mind than in the world outside. Defoe draws his female characters as if they were men—that is, simply as human beings, rather than as specifically female human beings. He is one of very few eighteenth-century novelists who attain this perspective. Fielding, for example, never could. Fielding's female characters always belong to one or another "type" of the female and, as I will show in chapter four, most often his portrayals are clichéd. Defoe, on the other hand, always breaks stereotypes.

Defoe insists in both *Moll Flanders* and *Roxana* that a woman's potential for productive work is limited only by society's definition of what means for earning money are available to her. He also acknowledges the legal and social barriers society places in her way, presenting convincing arguments, for example, against the restrictions that marriage places on a woman. Defoe's view of woman centers on her as an economically capable human being. Clearly, the options open to women for earning initial capital are severely limited: thus Moll eventually turns to thieving, and Roxana, having tried the socially prescribed course of marriage—a course that leaves her penniless and burdened with five children—becomes mistress to a series of men, accumulating a great fortune as she proceeds from relationship to relationship. Remarkable in each of these Defoe novels is what each woman does with her money after she has earned her initial stake. Both Moll and Roxana are excellent managers. These are human beings capable of living by themselves in a world that surely is not initially hospitable to them. Independent and intelligent, Moll and Roxana prosper on the basis of their own good sense.

From the earliest pages of *Moll Flanders*, we are aware of Moll's precarious financial situation. Even her infancy is colored by the need to support herself. As the child of a transported felon, Moll does not have the right to parish support. She is taken in by gypsies but becomes separated from them; this time she is lucky, and the town magistrates, although they too have no responsibility for such a child, put her in the house of a poor woman who cares for destitute children. "THIS Woman had also a little School, which she kept to teach Children to Read and to Work" (*M*, 9); from here, at the age of eight years, Moll already is supposed to "go to Service" (*M*, 10). Terrified by the thought of work beyond her eight-year-old capabilities and of the attendant beatings she expects, Moll begs her "Nurse" to let her stay: "I believ'd I could get my Living without going to Service if she pleas'd to let me; for she had taught me to Work with my Needle, and spin Worsted, which is the chief Trade of that City, and I told her that if she wou'd keep me, I wou'd Work for her, and I would Work very hard. I talk'd to her almost every Day of Working hard; And in short, I did nothing but Work and Cry all day" (*M*, 10). The child's fears are reasonable; she is not afraid to work—she seems to work straight through her early childhood—she is afraid of work that she cannot manage. Beginning with these early years, Moll always has the intention of supporting herself. She tells her "Nurse" that she can get "THREE-Pence" for spinning and "4d. when I Work plain Work" *M*, 11). The woman understands what the child does not: this amount of money cannot support Moll. It won't buy clothes, she tells Moll, and it won't buy food. "I will Work Harder, then" (*M*, 12) says Moll, and "I will have no Victuals" (*M*, 12).

Moll wants to be a gentlewoman, she tells everyone, and people are amused at the child's misperception of her future. Modern critics have been amused too, seeing Moll's early statements as implicitly suggesting her immorality: she wants not to do honest work but to be a gentlewoman. But this critical view is wrong. Defoe insists on quite another perspective when he has Moll explain her innocent misperception of what the word means: "Now all this while, my good old Nurse, Mrs. *Mayoress*, and all the rest of them did not understand me at all, for they meant one Sort of thing, by the Word Gentlewoman, and I meant quite another; for alas, all I understood by being a Gentlewoman, was to be able to Work for myself, and get enough to keep me without that terrible Bug-bear *going to Service*, whereas they meant to live Great, Rich, and High" (*M*, 13). I think that in these passages (this play on little Moll the gentlewoman goes on for some pages) the point Defoe makes has been overlooked by readers whose cultural biases have prevented them from taking him at his word. He insists that people need to be able to support themselves, and to support themselves with dignity and without the requirement of subservience to others. It is a point that Defoe makes repeatedly in *Moll Flanders* and in *Roxana*. There is no irony, intended or unintended, here.[2] All of *Moll Flanders* chronicles Moll's economic life. We look normally for a novel to chronicle a spiritual life—this is Ian Watt's argument why Richardson rather than Defoe begins the novel.[3] But I suggest that this perspective is a critical fallacy; Defoe's chronicling of Moll and Roxana's economic life is his depiction of character. The child Moll has precisely the ambition of the adult Moll: to live independently by means of her own exertion.

Moll stays with the old woman, making herself so useful that she indeed manages to support herself. A month spent with a local family gives Moll a taste of a different life, and she begins to understand other meanings of the word gentlewoman. When her nurse dies, the four-teen-year-old Moll panics, but again she is lucky. The family she had visited earlier invites her to live with them. This is the context for Moll's affairs with the two brothers, the elder of whom becomes her lover, and the younger of whom becomes her husband. From earliest childhood Moll consciously has been concerned with finding a place for herself. Her appreciation of the luxuries of middle-class life comes from its contrast with the barer life she has lived with her nurse, a lifestyle that itself never seemed to the child and adolescent something to be taken for granted. Moll is not yet eighteen when she allows herself to be seduced; she already has been struggling economically for many years. The luxury and social position that her lover represents— he always claims that he will become her husband—promises for Moll a stability that she has never experienced. But that stability, it turns out, is chimerical, for he has no intention of marrying her. His younger brother, however, does want to marry Moll, and it makes perfect sense, as her lover assures her, that Moll accept this opportunity. These episodes with the two brothers must be seen within the perspec-tive of Moll's earliest life. Moll makes the right decision here in choos-ing to marry Robin; there is no real moral issue involved, only a falsely pious position to be abandoned. Moll is not represented by Defoe as moving from one brother to the other with no pain; she does love the elder brother and desires him even after she has married the younger. But her infidelity after her marriage is only in thought, never in deed. Moll harms no one in accepting Robin, certainly not Robin himself, and they live amicably and well together for some years until he dies.[4]

Even before her relationship with the brothers, we have been aware of Moll casting up her accounts: so much given to her by "the Ladies of the Town" (*M*, 15) in money or old clothes, and all taken care of and kept for the child by "my old Nurse, [the] *honest Woman*" (*M*, 14), who would "lay out" the money for "Head-Dresses, and Linnen, and Gloves and Ribbons" (*M*, 14) or save it for Moll to use later. If as a child Moll was so much aware of her financial state, and Defoe has made it

clear that indeed she had to be, then surely it is normal that when after
five years of living "very agreeably together" her husband Robin dies,
Moll takes stock of her assets. She notes that her "Circumstances were
not great; nor was [she] much mended by the Match." She goes on:
"Indeed I had preserv'd the elder Brother's Bonds to me, to pay me
500 *l*. which he offer'd me for my Consent to Marry his Brother; and
this, with what I had saved of the Money he formerly gave me, and
about as much more by my Husband, left me a Widow with about
1200 *l*. in my Pocket" (*M*, 58). Moll's actions are reasonable. She has no
one to watch out for her if she herself is not careful. By now fully adult,
Moll has understood that having money makes her independent.
When she cares to marry again, she finds that she may be interested in
marriage, but the man has it in mind that she should be mistress rather
than wife. Moll's money stands her in good stead this time, for she
"kept true to this Notion, that a Woman should never be kept for a
Mistress, that had Money to keep herself. Thus . . . my Money, not my
Vertue, kept me Honest" (*M*, 61). It takes Moll some time to learn that
marriage is not as good a safeguard as money. When she ruins herself
"in the grossest Manner that ever Woman did," it is in marriage: "my
new Husband coming to a lump of Money at once, fell into such a pro-
fusion of Expence, that all I had, and all he had before . . . would not
have held it out above one Year" (*M*, 61). Having destroyed their
finances, he leaves. Moll finds that she is in a worse case than she was
before her marriage. Her financial luck with husbands is not good;
even when she marries for money—going through an elaborate charade to make it seem that she is rich so that she can find a suitably rich
husband—she comes up relatively empty-handed. We need to look
more closely at this episode, for I think it helps to explain a great deal
about the structure of Defoe's novel. Moll's profligate husband, having
wasted all their resources, escapes the bailiffs by running away to
France, leaving Moll hardly able to "muster up 500 *l*." (*M*, 64). She
knows that her husband could not come back to England even "if he
liv'd fifty Years" (*M*, 64); she has no one to provide for her. Moll wants
to find another man, but she has a more serious problem than her
nominally married state: men look for women of means.

> I found nothing present, except two or three Boatswains, or such Fellows
> but as for the Commanders they were generally of two sorts. 1. Such as
> having good Business, *that is to say*, a good Ship, resolv'd not to Marry but
> with Advantage, that is, with a good Fortune. 2. Such as being out of
> Employ, wanted a Wife to help them to a Ship, I mean. (1.). A Wife, who

having some Money could enable them to hold, as they call it, a good part of a Ship themselves, so to encourage Owners to come in; Or. (2.) A Wife who if she had not Money, had Friends who were concern'd in Shipping, and so could help to put the young Man into a good Ship, which to them is as good as a Portion, and neither of these was my Case; so I look'd like one that was to *lye on Hand.*

THIS Knowledge I soon learnt by experience, *(viz.)* That the State of things was altered, as to Matrimony, and that I was not to expect at *London,* what I had found in the Country; that Marriages were here the Consequences of politick Schemes, for forming Interests, and carrying on Business, and that LOVE had no share, or but very little in the Matter. [*M,* 66-67]

As Moll's "Sister in Law, at *Colchester*" told her, "Beauty, Wit, Manners . . . or any other Qualification, whether of Body or Mind, had no power to recommend: That Money only made a Woman agreeable: That Men chose Mistresses indeed by the gust of their Affection, and it was requisite to a Whore to be Handsome . . . but that for a Wife, no Deformity would shock the Fancy, no ill Qualities, the Judgement; the Money was the thing" (*M,* 67). The reference to the earlier comment reminds us that the theme of women needing money to be marriageable has been sounded in the novel from the beginning. "As the Market run very Unhappily on the Mens side" (*M,* 67), Moll knows, she must do what she can to help herself. She finds that "I began to be dropt in all the Discourses of Matrimony: Being well Bred, Handsome, Witty, Modest and Agreeable; all which I had allowed to my Character, whether justly or no is not to the Purpose; I say, all these would not do without the Dross, which was now become more valuable than Virtue itself. In short, the *Widow,* they said, *had no Money*" (*M,* 76). Moll decides that she will act the part of a rich woman and with the help of her friend puts on an elaborate charade. In the country, with Moll not known to the locals, Moll's friend allows it to be assumed that her guest is rich. Moll chooses her man and lets him court her. They play love games, scratching charming messages on the windows telling each other that money is unimportant; Moll plans to use this testimony when her soon-to-be husband finds out that in fact she is not wealthy. In the event, of course, they realize that the deception has been mutual. Regardless of the unsatisfactory outcome, the point is that Moll could not marry without at least the appearance of money. This man who loves her very much would never have become involved with her if she had not put on the appearance of a fortune. Moll practices deceit here not from meanness or depravity but from social necessity.

The combined resources of Moll and her husband are not enough to allow them to live in England. Moll travels with her new husband to his home in Virginia, where she discovers with horror that this kind man is her brother; she leaves him and returns alone to England. The ship with her goods runs into violent weather, spoiling much of her cargo, and Moll comes out of this affair with only "between two or three Hundred Pounds in the whole" (M, 105). Her next liaison, with a married man, lasts six years, during which Moll often thinks of breaking off the relationship, "yet I had the terrible prospect of Poverty and Starving which lay on me as a frightful Spectre, so that there was no looking behind me: But as Poverty brought me into it, so fear of Poverty kept me in it, and I frequently resolv'd to leave it quite off, if I could but come to lay up Money enough to maintain me" (M, 120). Finally he drops her—but not without paying a last fifty pounds for "a general Release" (M, 125). Moll takes stock, as we would expect her to:

> I was now a single Person again, *as I may call my self*, I was loos'd from all the Obligations either of Wedlock or Mistressship in the World; except my Husband the Linnen Draper, who I having not now heard from in almost Fifteen Year, no Body could blame me for thinking my self entirely freed from. . . . I NOW began to cast up my Accounts; I had . . . had a second return of some Goods from my Brother, *as I now call him*, in *Virginia*, to make up the Damage of the Cargo I brought away with me. . . . Including this Recruit, and before I got the last 50 *l*. I found my strength to amount, put all together, to about 400 *l*. so that with that I had above 450 *l*. [M, 126-27]

She plays the "fortune" once again, resulting in the marriage to her Lancashire husband. Jemmy has run himself into enormous expense in his courtship of Moll, thinking, of course, that the expenditure would catch him an heiress. Much to their mutual chagrin, since they really are in love, they find that their combined resources are not adequate for them to live on. They part with the intention to come together again when their financial outlook improves; if Moll should find someone else in the meantime, Jemmy releases her from her vows. Moll finds someone else. Actually, Moll is pregnant by Jemmy and so must wait to give birth and set the child out to nurse. Then she joins her very stable, middle-class suitor, and in marrying him at last attains the settled station in life that she has pursued since childhood. With this man, who is her husband until her forty-eighth year, she lives "in an uninterrupted course of Ease and Content for Five Years" (M, 189) until business reverses break his spirit and he dies.

Thus half the book chronicles Moll's vain attempts to gain security through marriage. She repeatedly tries the socially acceptable way to gain security, that is, by snaring husbands; husbands not only bring her no security in and of themselves, but in fact, as in the case of her profligate second husband, significantly deplete her resources. Moll leads a basically lawful life until the age of forty-eight, a fact that critics of the book often underestimate. She has not, of course, kept her relationships strictly legal, but up to that age her misdeeds have been essentially those of being seduced or seducing. Whatever the beginnings of the affair, she was not unkind to her first husband. And with each man between that first husband and the decent man who is her husband until she is widowed at forty-eight, she gives as much to the relationship as she gets. This is especially true in her last marriage. During this period of five years Moll regrets her past life, and after her husband dies she does her very best to make her resources last. But, unrenewed, they slowly disappear, and Moll can only wait in terror as poverty seems inevitably about to overtake her once again. Before we turn to Moll's first theft, some discussion of this husband is in order, for Moll's original relationship with him is important.

Moll loses some money by entrusting it to a goldsmith who goes bankrupt; she remarks that such a loss would not have happened to a man because, Moll says, a man would have had access to the information that this person's "Credit, it seems, was upon the Ebb before, but I that had no knowledge of things, and no Body to consult with, knew nothing of it, and so lost my Money" (*M*, 128). Moll feels acutely the lack of an adviser, someone "who cou'd advise and assist together . . . [someone] to whom I could in confidence commit the Secret of my Circumstances" (*M*, 128). She worries about keeping her resources safe; desiring to remove from London to a cheaper venue, Moll doesn't know what to do with her all-too-vulnerable cash and plate—the major part of her resources.

> And now I found my self in great Distress; what little I had in the World was all in Money, except as before, a little Plate, some Linnen, and my Cloaths; as for Houshold stuff I had little or none, for I had liv'd always in Lodgings; but I had not one Friend in the World with whom to trust that little I had, or to direct me how to dispose of it, and this perplex'd me Night and Day; I thought of the Bank, and of the other Companies in *London*, but I had no Friend to commit the Management of it to, and to keep and carry about with me Bank Bills, Talleys, Orders, and such things, I look'd upon it as unsafe; that if they were lost my Money was lost, and then I was undone; and on the other hand I might be robb'd, and perhaps murder'd in

a strange place for them; this perplex'd me strangely, and what to do I knew not. [*M*, 130]

She hits on the idea of asking for advice at her bank from a clerk who had been especially honest with her earlier.

I WENT to him, and represented my Case very plainly, *and ask'd if he would trouble himself to be my Adviser, who was a poor friendless Widow, and knew not what to do: He told me,* if I desir'd his Opinion of any thing within the reach of his Business, he would do his Endeavour that I should not be wrong'd, but that he would also help me to a good sober Person who was a grave Man of his Acquaintance, who was a Clark in such business too, tho' not in their House, whose Judgment was good, and whose Honesty I might depend upon. [*M*, 130-31]

And so Moll finds a financial adviser. The clerk sets up an appointment for Moll with his friend, and she gives him a brief—essentially accurate—account of her affairs. "*I told him* my Circumstances at large; . . . that I had a little Money, and but a little, and was almost distracted for fear of losing it, having no Friend in the World to trust with the management of it; that I was going into the North of *England* to live cheap, that my stock might not waste; that I would willingly Lodge my Money in the Bank, but that I durst not carry the Bills about me, and the like, as above; and how to Correspond about it, or with who, I knew not" (*M*, 132).

The clerk's response is remarkably detailed, presenting, in effect, Defoe's guide to investment. Note the caveat at the end of the passage. Moll recounts that the clerk

told me I might lodge the Money in the Bank as an Account, and its being entred in the Books would entitle me to the Money at any time, and if I was in the North I might draw Bills on the Cashire and receive it when I would; but that then it would be esteem'd as running Cash, and the Bank would give no Interest for it; that I might buy Stock with it, and so it would lye in store for me, but that then if I wanted to dispose of it, I must come up to Town on purpose to Transfer it, and even it would be with some difficulty I should receive the half yearly Dividend, unless I was here in Person, or had some Friend I could trust with having the Stock in his Name to do it for me, and that would have the same difficulty in it as before; and with that he look'd hard at me and *smil'd a little;* at last, *says he,* why do you not get a head Steward, Madam, that may take you and your Money together into keeping, and then you would have the trouble taken off of your Hands? Ay, Sir, and the Money too it may be, *said I,* for truly *I find the hazard that way is as much as 'tis t'other way;* but I remember, *I said,* secretly to my self, I wish you would ask me the Question fairly, I would consider very seriously on it before I said NO. [*M,* 132]

Moll obviously understands these possibilities and distinctions; Defoe makes it plain that he would expect a woman to do so. Running accounts and interest differences, stock, transfers, dividends, and the rest do not intimidate Moll. Her adviser presents possibilities—he does not tell her what to do but promises to act as her agent if she wants him to.[5] This discussion leads to the clerk's semi-joking comment that Moll should get herself a "head Steward." Moll's answer is sharp: she has no wish to have the trouble "and the money too" taken off her hands, although the forcefulness of Moll's statement is weakened by her aside that she wishes the proposal were in earnest. Both Moll's statement and her disclaimer are significant in an analysis of Defoe's images of women, for the statement, but *not* the disclaimer, appears again in *Roxana* in virtually precisely the same words, so that if here in *Moll Flanders* Defoe is not quite ready to let such an analysis of the situation stand unrestricted, by the time he writes *Roxana* he can say with no hedging that a woman's money is safest in her own hands. This antipaternalist perspective defines both *Moll Flanders* and *Roxana;* in *Moll Flanders* it becomes ever clearer as the book draws to its conclusion.

These investment explorations come during the period when Moll still is trying to husband her resources, both in keeping control of what she has and in searching for a renewable source of income—i.e., a spouse. Her friendly adviser unfortunately is married, and rather than wait for him to get a divorce, as we have seen, Moll marries Jemmy. By the time her affair with Jemmy breaks up, the adviser is free, and Moll marries him. They are together until he dies, and during this period Moll repents her past life. Only the change in circumstance to needing money for survival causes her to go on to overtly criminal acts. "Poverty . . . is the sure Bane of Virtue" (*M,* 188), she says, and "Poverty . . . is the worst of all Snares" (*M,* 188).

When the "utmost Tranquility" in which she lives with her "Quiet, Sensible, Sober" husband is shattered, she is left with few financial resources, and no way of augmenting them:

I WAS now left in a dismal and disconsolate Case indeed, and in several things worse than ever: First it was past the flourishing time with me when I might expect to be courted for a Mistress; that agreeable part had declin'd some time. . . . But my Case was indeed Deplorable, for I was left perfectly Friendless and Helpless, and the Loss my Husband had sustain'd had reduc'd his Circumstances so low, that tho' indeed I was not in Debt, yet I could easily foresee that what was left would not support me long; that while it wasted daily for Subsistence, I had no way to encrease it one Shilling, so that it would be soon all spent, and then I saw nothing before me but the utmost Distress, and this represented it self so lively to my Thoughts, that it seem'd as if it was come, before it was really very near; also my very Apprehensions doubl'd the Misery, for I fancied every Sixpence that I paid but for a Loaf of Bread, was the last that I had in the World, and that To-morrow I was to fast, and be starv'd to Death." [M, 189-90]

She moves out of her house and into lodgings; she sells off most of her possessions, and still all she can see is the imminent prospect of "Misery and Want."[6] In these circumstances, she is tempted to her first theft and her first truly criminal act. Moll lives two or three *years* on the remnants of her married affluence; no matter what efforts she makes to save and hoard, she sees that the case only can deteriorate. She does her best to survive within legal bounds—selling off her goods, moving to cheap quarters. Only after all this does she give in to the impulse to steal.

Roughly one quarter of the book is devoted to the criminal period of Moll's life, the time between her first theft and her capture and subsequent internment in Newgate. Thus, although we often think of Moll as "criminal,"[7] Defoe devotes fully three quarters of the novel to other areas of her life. Even these proportions do not adequately define the book since the descriptions of Moll's career as a thief are couched in precisely the same tone—even the same words—as the description of her subsequent endeavors as a legitimate planter in the colonies. Moll's thieving is her business, while she does it, just as planting is for the last period of her life.[8] She is a very good businessperson; her logic, good sense, and planning abilities are first-rate, and she applies them in the same way to all her endeavors. Moll describes in precise detail the beginning of her career as a thief. Her first theft is a matter almost of chance: when the occasion presents itself, her dire financial need prompts her to take an unattended packet. But "the prospect of my own Starving, which grew every Day more frightful to me" (M, 193), remains, and her next theft comes of an opportunity she looks for, in the sense of leaving home to "seek for what might happen" (M, 193). She steals a necklace from a child, taking care not to frighten the child herself. The next pages recount Moll's adventures in her new line.

Moll tells us how she came to each chance, exactly what happened, and how she escaped from each situation. These narrations are paralleled later in the book in Moll's accounts of her preparations for life in Virginia. Note in this passage the precise description of the action and the exact description of the goods.

> One Adventure I had which was very lucky to me; I was going thro' *Lombard-street* in the dusk of the Evening, just by the end of *Three King Court*, when on a sudden comes a Fellow running by me as swift as Lightning, and throws a Bundle that was in his Hand just behind me, as I stood up against the corner of the House at the turning into the Alley; just as he threw it in he said, God bless you Mistress let it lie there a little, and away he runs swift as the Wind: After him comes two more and immediately a young Fellow without his Hat, crying stop Thief, and after him two or three more, they pursued the two last Fellows so close, that they were forced to drop what they had got, and one of them was taken into the bargain, the other got off free.
>
> I STOOD stock still all this while till they came back, dragging the poor Fellow they had taken, and luging the things they had found, extremely well satisfied that they had recovered the Booty, and taken the Thief; and thus they pass'd by me, for I look'd only like one who stood up while the Crowd was gone.
>
> ONCE or twice I ask'd what was the matter, but the People neglected answering me, and I was not very importunate; but after the Crowd was wholly pass'd, I took my opportunity to turn about and take up what was behind me and walk away: This indeed I did with less Disturbance than I had done formerly, for these things I did not steal, but they were stolen to my Hand: I got safe to my Lodgings with this Cargo, which was a Peice of fine black Lustring Silk, and a Peice of Velvet; the latter was but part of a Peice of about 11 Yards; the former was a whole Peice of near 50 Yards; it seems it was a Mercer's shop that they had rifled, I say rifled, because the Goods were so considerable that they had Lost; for the Goods that they Recover'd were pretty many, and I believe came to about six or seven several Peices of Silk: How they came to get so many I could not tell; but as I had only robb'd the Thief I made no scruple at taking these Goods, and being very glad of them too. [M, 195- 96][9]

From this and other adventures Moll accrues something of a collection of valuables. She realizes that most "poor Unhappy Theives" sell their things for almost nothing; she has other plans. "I WAS now at a loss for a Market for my Goods, and especially for my two Peices of Silk, I was loth to dispose of them for a Trifle; as the poor unhappy Theives in general do, who after they have ventured their Lives for perhaps a thing of Value, are fain to sell it for a Song when they have done; but I was resolv'd I would not do thus whatever shift I made, unless I was driven to the last Extremity. . . . At last I resolv'd to go to my old Governess, and acquaint myself with her again" (*M*, 197). The "old Governess" has conveniently enough turned pawnbroker, and she gladly takes Moll's goods. Having found an outlet, Moll's next step is to improve her skills. She apprentices herself to a "School-Mistress" who teaches her the finer points of thieving. Moll works diligently and accrues a good stockpile. Occasionally her conscience bothers her, as when she takes advantage of the confusion of a fire to steal from its victim, but in general she spends most of her energy safeguarding herself. Just as she took care to find the best outlet for her merchandise, she takes every precaution to prevent being caught. Her peers know her only by the pseudonym Moll Flanders and have no idea where she lives. Moll's approach to thieving is simply to earn the greatest rewards with the least risk. When she sets out to make an honest living as a transported felon, she proceeds precisely the same way.

When Moll's luck finally runs out, she is apprehended and sent to Newgate, from there to be transported to America. Moll's arrangements for her passage and setting up in America are precise, well planned, and well executed. She leaves nothing that she can control to chance; as with her former career, she makes every effort to ensure her future prosperity. She arranges for Jemmy's transportation as well. The period from Moll's incarceration in Newgate to the end of the book shows Moll at her most remarkable. Not only does she raise her own life from its nadir, but she manages to bring Jemmy, whom she coincidentally finds imprisoned under much her own circumstances, up with her.

Jemmy does not want to be transported; he would rather be hanged than be a servant. Moll, much more in command of her feelings and her fears, argues with him that his attitude is wrong: with fortitude and common sense they will make out fine, she assures him, for they have between them some money, and "Money . . . was the only Friend in such a Condition" (*M*, 303). She explains explicitly how they can set up a new life based on the money they have. "I TOLD him he frighted and terify'd himself with that which had no Terror in it; that if he had Money, as I was glad to hear he had, he might not only avoid the Servitude, suppos'd to be the Consequence of Transportation; but begin the World upon a new Foundation, and that such a one as he cou'd not fail of Success in, with but the common Application usual in such Cases" (*M*, 303). Jemmy has not been tried because for the moment there is only one witness against him and two are required for a case; he is being held while search is made for further witnesses. He can wait, in the hope that no further witnesses will appear, or voluntarily transport himself; Moll prevails on him not to take the chance of being condemned for what is, after all, a capital offense. Moll herself had hoped to avoid transportation, rather than going and later coming back, but as Jemmy's case does not allow him to explore this option, Moll decides that she has no choice but to go too. This is, incidentally, rather a new side of Moll, for she makes her decision out of care for Jemmy, not convenience for herself. Moll also has the option of seeking a pardon (she could still voluntarily accompany Jemmy), but this option she finds simply impractical: "my Governess who continu'd my fast Friend, had try'd to obtain a Pardon, but it could not be done unless with an Expence too heavy for my Purse, considering that to be left naked and empty, unless I had resolv'd to return to my old Trade again, had been worse than my Transportation, because there I knew I could live, here I could not" (M, 306). The implications of these comments underscore Moll's brief exegesis of Jemmy's twenty-five-year career as a highwayman.

Money is the key to all transactions in Moll's society; she can be pardoned of her criminality but stripped by the necessary bribes of any way to live further. Just so, Jemmy has carried on his business of highwayman for twenty-five years; in context, this becomes no more than a statement of how Jemmy has made a living. In years when he had earned enough, Jemmy lived like anyone else: "he had carried on that desperate Trade full five and Twenty Year, and had never been taken, the Success he had met with, had been so very uncommon, and such, that sometimes he had liv'd handsomely and retir'd, in one Place for a Year or two at a time, keeping himself and a Man-Servant to wait on him, and has often sat in the Coffee-Houses, and heard the very People who he had robb'd give Accounts of their being robb'd, and of the Places and Circumstances, so that he coul'd easily remember that it was the same" (M, 304-5). And had Moll really had money, "he would then have taken up and liv'd honestly all his Days" (M, 305). The unfolding of their life in America and their subsequent respectability in their return to England support Moll's view. If there is a moral statement here, it is that society should not force the reprieved prisoner to return to crime. In Jemmy's case, no less than in Moll's, society has not provided honest means to labor.[10]

Moll already has taken things in hand, convincing Jemmy to accept transportation and agreeing not to seek a way to avoid her own transportation since he refuses to go by himself "altho' he were certain to go directly to the Gallows" (M, 306). Continuing to arrange matters, she assures not only their extraordinary comfort aboard ship but success in their new life. We must marvel, I think, at Defoe's faith in his character's abilities; certainly Jemmy, appreciating fully Moll's capabilities, leaves everything to her. She begins by sending a letter of instruction to her friend the governess. Moll, almost always a good judge of character, sends off the boatswain with a letter and a shilling for the cost of a messenger. "I TOOK care when I gave him the Shilling, to let him see that I had a little better Furniture about me, than the ordinary Prisoners, for he saw that I had a Purse, and in it a pretty deal of Money, and I found that the very sight of it, immediately furnish'd me with very different Treatment from what I should otherwise have met with in the Ship; for tho' he was very Courteous indeed before . . . yet he was more than ordinarily so, afterwards" (M, 308). The man comes back with a letter from the governess and returns Moll's shilling, saying that he had delivered her letter himself. He later becomes the go-between for Moll with the ship's captain. From the very beginning of the episode Moll uses her money to help herself and Jemmy. Just letting the boatswain see that her purse is full brings his respect; when he delivers her letter and returns her shilling, he opens the way to further dealings based on mutual respect and good will—an equality that an impoverished felon normally could not have hoped for.

One of the first things that Moll must do is get Jemmy on the same ship with her. Jemmy finds that even if he is to transport himself, he may not be able to choose his ship, and in fact he may be in quite the same condition as any involuntarily transported felon. Even worse, he worries that some disaster will overtake Moll on the long voyage, and that he will be alone when he arrives—then "he should be the most undone Creature there in the World" (M, 310). Moll and her governess finally manage Jemmy's sailing, "which at last was brought to pass tho' with great difficulty" (M, 311). Moll and the governess have arranged to get him out of prison in time to sail with her; they have arranged to have him on the same ship. And Jemmy? "[H]e was as much at a loss as a Child what to do with himself, or with what he had, but by Directions" (M, 311). Depressed at first because he must be transported in essentially the same character as any other prisoner, Jemmy later realizes that Moll's assessment of his situation was absolutely right: it becomes clear that he would have been in great danger of prosecution, and he tells Moll *"Thou hast twice sav'd my Life, from hence forward it shall be all employ'd for you, and I'll always take your Advice"* (M, 313). Defoe presents a relationship between a man and a woman in which the woman is the more adept manager, and the man accepts her ability without any sense that he is less of a man for her effectiveness.[11]

And Moll is effective. Cultivating her acquaintance with the boatswain, Moll asks him to see if he can help her with the captain.

> I told him he had befriended me in many things, and I had not made any suitable Return to him, and with that I put a Guinea into his Hands; I told him that my Husband was now come on Board, that tho' we were both under the present Misfortunes, yet we had been Persons of a differing Character from the wretched Crew that we came with, and desir'd to know of him, whether the Captain might not be mov'd, to admit us to some Conveniences in the Ship, for which we would make him what Satisfaction he pleas'd, and that we would gratifie him for his Pains in procuring this for us. He took the Guinea as I cou'd see with great Satisfaction, and assur'd me of his Assistance. [M, 313-14]

We remember that the boatswain earlier had returned to Moll the shilling she'd given him to deliver her letter, but he gladly takes the guinea she now proffers. The combination of a full purse and her good management procure for Moll and Jemmy all the comforts the other passengers may have. The captain leaves orders that Moll is to have her choice of cabin, that she may bring on board any provisions she wants, and that she and her husband are welcome to dine at the captain's table. Moll is well pleased with the captain and all the arrangements: "Nor were his Conditions exorbitant, or the Man craving and eager to make a Prey of us, but for fifteen Guineas we had our whole Passage and Provisions, and Cabbin, eat at the Captain's Table, and were very handsomely Entertain'd" (M, 316). She is fortunate that she has chanced upon a decent man whose terms are reasonable and just. But the captain's character would have been irrelevant had Moll not set up a situation in which she could meet him on terms of relative equality.

Moll has been careful throughout to appear respectable but not rich. She already has arranged with her governess so that she will be provisioned for the trip and well prepared for her new life in Virginia. The governess has brought her

> a Sea-Bed as they call it, and all its Furniture, such as was convenient, but not to let the People think it was extraordinary; she brought with her a Sea-Chest, that is a Chest, such as are made for Seamen with all the Conveniences in it, and fill'd with every thing almost that I could want; and in one of the corners of the Chest, where there was a Private Drawer was my

Bank of Money, *that is to say,* so much of it as I had resolv'd to carry with me; for I order'd a part of my Stock to be left behind me, to be sent afterwards in such Goods as I should want when I came to settle; for Money in that Country is not of much use where all things are bought for To-bacco. . . .

BUT my Case was particular; it was by no Means proper to me to go thither without Money or Goods, and for a poor Convict that was to be sold as soon as I came on Shore, to carry with me a Cargo of Goods would be to have Notice taken of it, and perhaps to have them seiz'd by the Publick; so that I took part of my Stock with me thus, and left the other part with my Governess.

My Governess brought me a great many other things, but it was not proper for me to look too well provided in the Ship, at least, till I knew what kind of Captain we should have. [*M,* 309]

Moll's plan is to "Plant, Settle, and in short, grow Rich without any more Adventures" (*M,* 310). As soon as Jemmy is on board, they compare resources. Everything is added up: he has "an Hundred and Eight Pounds" (*M,* 311) after his prison expenses; she has "two Hundred forty six Pounds, some odd Shillings, so that we had three Hundred and fifty four Pound between us" (*M,* 311-12). That is not exactly all, for Moll has left a certain amount "in reserve" (*M,* 311) with her governess, "that in case I should die, what I had with me was enough to give him, and that which was left in my Governess Hands would be her own" (*M,* 311).

Naturally, Moll plans for her arrival as carefully as she does for the voyage. She knows that they will need "all sorts of Tools for [planting] and [tools] for building; and all kinds of Furniture . . . which if to be bought in the Country, must necessarily cost double the Price" (*M,* 316). The governess is dispatched to ask the captain what will be wanted.

[H]e accordingly gave her a long particular of things Necessary for a Planter, which by his Account came to about fourscore, or an Hundred Pounds; and fl.⅔₁.2x34.1in short, she went about as dexterously to buy them, as if she had been an old *Virginia* Merchant; only that she bought by my Direction above twice as much of every thing as he had given her a List of.

THESE she put on Board in her own Name, took his Bills of Loading for them, and Endorst those Bills of Loading to my Husband, Ensuring the Cargo afterwards in her own Name, by our order; so that we were provided for all Events, and for all Disasters.

I SHOULD have told you that my Husband gave her all his whole Stock of 108 *l.* . . . he had about him in Gold, to lay out thus, and I gave her a good

Sum besides; so that I did not break into the Stock, which I had left in her Hands at all, but after we had sorted out our whole Cargo, we had up near 200 *l.* in Money, which was more than enough for our purpose. [*M*, 318]

Moll plots the entire strategy, deciding how much will be spent and on what it will be expended. The arrangements on the ship are her doing; the agent for all other arrangements, the governess, is her agent. And throughout, although Moll does not comment on this fact at any point, it is she rather than her husband who makes the decisions. Moll does not expect any help from Jemmy, and the reader, having long been accustomed to Moll's self-sufficiency, is not surprised that it is she, rather than the man, who takes the situation in hand. Like Roxana, Moll turns automatically to her female accomplice rather than her mate for advice and for active assistance.[12] The talents Moll brings to her situation as a transported felon are the same ones we have seen her employ throughout the book.

In her preparations for Virginia, Moll acts entirely within the law. But she acts no differently than she had earlier. If we must admire her good sense in dealing with the captain and in providing for herself in Virginia, we must admire Moll in other situations, where she had brought the same survival skills to bear. She must make provision for herself if she is not to be poor and miserable in Virginia; she had turned to thieving when, her goods sold off and she too old for the marriage market, she had had no other means of supporting herself. At each turning point Moll manages, both in the sense of getting along and of turning events her way. Defoe lingers over Moll's preparations for Virginia; he has given us her careful planning at each earlier stage, whore, wife, mistress, thief, as well. If at some points Moll has no choice but to be criminal, she brings her capabilities to bear on criminal pursuits. But Defoe's interest in Moll is on her ability to survive.[13]

In looking toward her arrival in Virginia, Moll realizes that she needs help with more than her shopping lists. Some plan must be made for winning freedom for herself and for Jemmy.

So I discours'd that Point with my Governess, and she went and waited upon the Captain, and told him, that she hop'd ways might be found out, for her two unfortunate Cousins, *as she call'd us*, to obtain our Freedom when we came into the Country; . . . she let him know, tho' we were unhappy in the Circumstance that occasion'd our going, yet that we were not unfurnish'd to set our selves to Work in the Country; and were resolv'd to settle, and live there as Planters, if we might be put in a way how to do it:

The Captain readily offer'd his Assistance, told her the Method of entering upon such Business, and how easy, nay, how certain it was for industrious People to recover their Fortunes in such a manner. [*M*, 317]

The captain expresses the sense of the novel as a whole: there is no question of morality in having failed to prosper in a given stage of life. A new context provides a new beginning: "tis no Reproach . . . provided they do but apply with diligence and good Judgment to the Business of that Place when they come there" (*M*, 317). This is precisely how Moll proceeds at every stage of her life.

The captain advises Moll's governess that "your Cousins in the first Place must procure some Body to buy them as Servants, in Conformity to the Conditions of their Transportation, and then in the Name of that Person, they may go about what they will" (*M*, 317). The governess asks the captain to make the necessary arrangements. When they arrive in Virginia, the captain finds a planter to buy Moll and Jemmy; they all go out for a pleasant drink and the planter provides "a Certificate of Discharge, and an Acknowledgement of having serv'd him faithfully" (*M*, 320). For his services the captain asks "6000 weight of Tobacco, which he said he was Accountable for to his Freighter" and Moll and Jemmy give him "a present of 20 Guineas, besides, with which he was abundantly satisfy'd" (*M*, 320).[14] And so the issue closes: "we were free . . . the next Morning, to go whither we would" (*M*, 320). Moll arrives in Virginia in very good shape indeed. Free, fully equipped to begin her new life, even paired with the man she loves, everything seems to have fallen in place for Moll. But there is no luck involved here, for everything has been carefully planned, from getting Jemmy on her ship to the last packet of goods that she has brought along.

Having led the expedition thus far, Moll does not relinquish her place when she and Jemmy arrive in Virginia. Even when she would like to leave Jemmy on his own for a while, he won't allow it. "I knew he would never part with me, and be left there to go on alone; the Case was plain; he was bred a Gentleman . . . and when we did Settle, would much rather go out into the Woods with his Gun . . . than attend the natural Business of his Plantation" (*M*, 328). But if Jemmy would rather hunt than run a plantation, Moll's inclination always is to attend to business. She wants to learn what provisions her mother made for her, but she does not want the whole story of her brother-husband to come out. She considers sending Jemmy to Carolina with their goods, "but this was impracticable, he would never stir without me, being himself perfectly unacquainted with the Country, and with the Methods of settling there, or any where else" (M, 328). Moll is really worried: if her brother dies before she can make herself known to her son, how will she prove to the son that she is in fact his mother? She fears that she may lose both "the assistance and comfort of the Relation, and the benefit of whatever it was my Mother had left me" (M, 328). Not only does Moll want to keep this part of her distant past from Jemmy, she also has no wish to uncover her recent past, that is, her transportation, to her son. Her solution is to go away and then, when she comes back, seem to be returning "as from another Place, and in another Figure" (M, 328).

Moll never doubts that she and Jemmy will be accepted graciously in any community they choose. She knows that "it was always agreeable to the Inhabitants to have Families come among them to Plant, who brought Substance with them, either to purchase Plantations, or begin New ones, so we should be sure of a kind agreeable Reception" (M, 329). Surely she and Jemmy bring "substance" enough with them. Moll never loses track of the relationship between her wealth and her security, and she never takes either one for granted. Thus when she remembers their voyage to Maryland in "a poor sorry Sloop," the "very thoughts" (M, 330) of the trip horrify her; Moll realizes that had the ship foundered, all her goods might have been lost. She does not tremble about the loss of their lives: "if any Accident had happened to us, we might at last have been very miserable; supposing we had lost our Goods and saved our Lives only, and had then been left naked and destitute, and in a wild strange Place, not having one Friend or Acquaintance in all that part of the World" (M, 330). Originally the plan had been to go to Carolina, but Moll learns that the ship for Carolina already has sailed. This circumstance is "a Disappointment" (M, 330), but no more than that. Moll is a person "that was to be discourag'd with nothing" (M, 330), and she finds more than adequate potential in the spot where they have landed.

"I that was to be discourag'd with nothing," Moll says. This is indeed the joy of Defoe's characterization. It is not that Moll is an unreasonable optimist, waiting hopefully for good fortune to come to her, but that she sets up her good fortune herself. And so in the last pages of the book, it is clear that Moll will succeed. She and Jemmy take up "a large peice of Land from the Government of that Country, in order to form our Plantation" (M, 331) and within a year, she notes proudly, "we had near fifty Acres of Land clear'd, part of it enclos'd, and some of it Planted with Tobacco, tho' not much; besides, we had

Garden ground, and Corn sufficient to help supply our Servants[15] with Roots, and Herbs, and Bread" (M, 331). They buy more land—for cash—so that they have a plantation sufficient to employ "between fifty and sixty servants" (M, 332). Good fortune and careful management in Maryland are matched in Virginia: Moll finally returns to her son to claim her inheritance and finds a fully stocked, well managed plantation. Thus to Moll's self-made wealth comes this pleasant addition. "This Plantation, tho' remote from him, he said he did not let out, but . . . went over himself three or four times a Year to look after it. . . . [He said that] seeing I was likely either to Settle on the other side the Bay, or might perhaps have a mind to go back to *England* again, if I would let him be my Steward he would manage it for me, as he had done for himself, and that he believ'd he should be able to send me as much Tobacco to *England* from it, as would yeild me about 100 *l.* a Year" (M, 336). Moll is so pleased with her situation, and the solicitude of her son, that just for a moment she "began secretly now to wish that I had not brought my *Lancashire* Husband from *England* at all" (M, 335). But just for a moment. "HOWEVER, that wish was not hearty neither, for I lov'd my *Lancashire* Husband entirely, as indeed I had ever done from the beginning; and he merited from me as much as it was possible for a Man to do" (M, 335).

Moll spends five lovely weeks near her son. The center of their happy domesticity, as so often in Defoe, is in the scenes of mutual accounting. Moll gives him one of her (stolen) gold watches. "HE stood a little while Hesitating, as if doubtful whether to take it or no; but I press'd it on him, and made him accept it, and it was not much less worth than his Leather-pouch full of Spanish Gold; no, tho' it were to be reckon'd, as if at London, whereas it was worth twice as much there, where I gave it him; at length he took it, kiss'd it, told me the Watch should be a Debt upon him, that he would be paying, as long as I liv'd" (M, 338). This delightful scene is followed "a few Days after" when

he brought the Writings of Gift, and the Scrivener with them, and I sign'd them very freely, and deliver'd them to him with a hundr'd Kisses; for sure nothing ever pass'd between a Mother, and a tender dutiful Child, with more Affection: The next Day he brings me an Obligation under his Hand and Seal, whereby he engag'd himself to Manage, and Improve the Plantation for my account, and with his utmost Skill, and to remit the Produce to my order where-ever I should be, and withal, to be oblig'd himself to make up the Produce a hundred Pound a year to me: When he had done so, he told me, that as I came to demand it before the Crop was off, I had a right to the Produce of the current Year, and so he paid me an hundred Pound in *Spanish* peices of Eight, and desir'd me to give him a Receipt for it as in full for that Year, ending at *Christmas* following; this being about the latter End of *August*. [*M*, 338]

The tender financial communion between mother and son is paralleled in the homecoming of the wife to the husband. Joy, warmth, piety, and money are completely intertwined.

I BROUGHT over with me for the use of our Plantation, three Horses with Harness, and Saddles; some Hogs, two Cows, and a thousand other things, the Gift of the kindest and tenderest Child that ever Woman had: I related to my Husband all the particulars of this Voyage, except that I called my Son my Cousin; . . . I told him how kind my Cousin had been, that my Mother had left me such a Plantation, and that he had preserv'd it for me; . . . I pull'd him out the hundred Pound in Silver, as the first Years produce. . . . My Husband . . . lifted up both his Hands, and with an extasy of Joy, *What is God a doing* says he, *for such an ungrateful Dog as I am!* [*M*, 339]

Moll and Jemmy continue to have

very good Success; for having a flourishing Stock to begin with, as *I have said*; and this being now encreas'd, by the Addition of a Hundred and fifty Pound *Sterling* in Money, we enlarg'd our Number of Servants, built us a very good House, and cur'd every Year a great deal of Land. The second Year I wrote to my old Governess, giving her part with us of the Joy of our Success, and order'd her how to lay out the Money I had left with her, which was 250 *l.* as above, and to send it to us in Goods, which she perform'd, with her usual Kindness and Fidelity, and all this arriv'd safe to us. [*M*, 340]

Her relationship with Jemmy, too, is entirely satisfactory. Moll takes pleasure in buying clothes for both of them, as well as implements for the plantation and ever more servants. "I took especial care to buy for him all those things that I knew he delighted to have; as two good long Wigs, two silver hilted Swords, three or four fine Fowling peices, a fine Saddle with Holsters and Pistoles very handsome, with a Scarlet Cloak; and in a Word, every thing I could think of to oblige him. . . . The rest of my Cargo consisted in Iron-Work, of all sorts, Harness for Horses, Tools, Cloaths for Servants, and Woollen-Cloth, stuffs, Serges, Stockings, Shoes, Hats and the like; . . . and all this Cargo arriv'd safe, and in good Condition, with three Women Servants, lusty Wenches, which my old Governess had pick'd up for me" (*M*, 340). Her husband, overwhelmed by all these goods, worries that Moll has run up an enormous debt. No, my dear, she tells him—it's all paid for. This leads, of course, to another tender scene.

> HE was amaz'd, and stood a while telling upon his Fingers, but said nothing, at last he began thus, Hold lets see, *says he, telling upon his Fingers still;* and first on his Thumb, there's 246 *l.* in Money at first, then two gold Watches, Diamond Rings, and Plate, says he, upon the fore Finger, then upon the next Finger, here's a Plantation on York River, a 100 *l.* a Year, then 150 in Money; then a Sloop load of Horses, Cows, Hogs and Stores, and so on to the Thumb again; and now, *says he,* a Cargo cost 250 *l.* in *England,* and worth here twice the Money; well, *says I,* What do you make of all that? make of it, *says he,* why who says I was deceiv'd, when I married a Wife in *Lancashire?* I think I have married a Fortune, and a very good Fortune too. [*M*, 341]

There is no irony here. Jemmy is genuinely grateful to Moll for what she brings him. Their affairs have come to extraordinary fruition: "we were now in very considerable Circumstances, and every Year encreasing, for our new Plantation grew upon our Hands insensibly, and in eight Year which we lived upon it, we brought it to such a pitch, that the Produce was, at least, 300 *l.* Sterling a Year; I mean, worth so much in *England*" (*M*, 341).

The novel ends happily ever after. Moll retains control at every step, and the reward for her care and planning is a smooth transition into prosperity, personal happiness and respectability. In the last sentence of the novel, Moll sums up: "we liv'd together with the greatest Kindness and Comfort imaginable; we are now grown Old: I am come back to *England,* being almost seventy Years of Age, my Husband sixty eight, having perform'd much more than the limited Terms of my Transportation: And now notwithstanding all the Fatigues, and all the Miseries we have both gone thro', we are both in good Heart and Health; my Husband remain'd there sometime after me to settle our Affairs, and at first I had intended to go back to him, but at his desire I alter'd that Resolution, and he is come over to *England* also, where we resolve to spend the Remainder of our Years in sincere Penitence, for the wicked Lives we have lived" (*M*, 342-43). It will be a most comfortable penance. Moll at the end of the novel has turned herself into a wife and mother, luxuriating in the warmth of visits with her son and bowing to the wishes of her husband. With nothing given to her, Moll has made herself into the independent gentlewoman that she had described as a child. Defoe's next heroine, seemingly with everything in place at the beginning of the story, must follow the same path of insuring her own survival that Moll takes. At the end of the novel Roxana has accumulated even greater wealth than Moll and, like Moll, is respectably and happily married. The ending of *Roxana*, however, is considerably darker than that of *Moll Flanders*, for in Defoe's last, very complex novel, the character cannot quite escape the reach of her past. Defoe's characterization of Roxana is different from the essentially linear progress of Moll.[16] But while the psychological complexity of the eponymous character is greater in *Roxana* than in *Moll Flanders*, the focus on financial matters as the single most significant aspect of the character's life is the same.

Roxana is another woman who must struggle to survive, and like Moll she is put in situations where virtue and survival seem at odds. Money is survival to Roxana as it is to Moll, and her financial dealings take much of her time and energy, often clearly becoming her primary concern. In contrast to Moll, Roxana begins life in financial security. She marries well, that is, she marries a reasonably rich, good-looking young man. In the time it takes him to provide Roxana with five children, her husband through mismanagement and disregard for their affairs dissipates his entire fortune. Roxana watches him bleed their business of its cash while he otherwise neglects it:

> I foresaw the Consequence of this, and attempted several times to perswade him to apply himself to his Business; I put him in Mind how his Customers complain'd of his Neglect of his Servants on one hand, and how abundance Broke in his Debt, on the other hand, for want of the Clerk's Care to secure him, *and the like;* but he thrust me by, either with hard words, or fraudulently, with representing the Cases otherwise than they were. . . . [H]e began to find his Trade sunk, his Stock declin'd, and that, in short, he could not carry on his Business. . . . This allarm'd him, and he resolv'd to lay down his Trade; which, indeed, I was not sorry for; foreseeing that if he did not lay it down in Time, he would be forc'd to do it another Way, namely, as a Bankrupt. . . .
>
> I thought myself happy when he got another Man to take his Brewhouse clear off of his Hands; for paying down a large Sum of Money, my Husband found himself a clear Man, all his Debts paid, and with between Two and Three Thousand Pound in his Pocket; . . . and happy I thought myself, all things consider'd, that I was got off clear, upon so good Terms;

and had my handsome Fellow had but one Cap full of Wit, I had been still well enough.

I propos'd to him either to buy some Place with the Money, or with Part of it, and offer'd to join my Part to it, which was then in Being, and might have been secur'd; and so we might have liv'd tollerably, at least, during his Life. But [he] liv'd on as he did before . . . and nothing was done all this while; but the Money decreas'd apace, and I thought I saw my Ruin hastening on, without any possible Way to prevent it.[17]

When they are penniless, he leaves Roxana with the five children. Because of him, Roxana also has lost the money she should have inherited: her father, unwilling to entrust Roxana's inheritance to her husband, left it in care of her brother, who in turn lost the money in business reverses. Roxana knows all along that her husband is destroying their finances, and she tries to warn him into better methods. Clearly, if Roxana were in charge, the business would not fail. But Roxana has no say here, and "it was not above three Years that all the Ready-Money was thus spending off" (R, 43). These accounts set up the dynamics of the novel, focusing the reader's attention on Roxana's helplessness even in the face of her own good business sense. Later, when Roxana has control of her money, her first priority is maintaining that control.

Roxana has done just what society prescribed: as a dutiful daughter, she married at age fifteen the man of her father's choice. This brings her to absolute poverty and the responsibility for five children. There is no question of living carefully, for her resources unrenewed simply cannot support her large family. For a year she lives on her "little Stock" (R, 47); applications to her husband's well-off relatives bring only denials. It is impossible for her to earn enough money by needlework. She sells off her goods and ornaments until there is nothing left. Roxana's situation deteriorates at first slowly, and then with greater and greater urgency: "as Time run on a Week, two Weeks, a Month, two Months, and so on, I was dreadfully frighted at last, and the more when I look'd into my own Circumstances, and consider'd the Condition in which I was left; with five Children, and not one Farthing Subsistence for them, other than about seventy Pound in Money, and what few Things of Value I had about me. . . . What to do I knew not, nor to whom to have recourse. . . . I remain'd in this dejected Condition near a Twelve-month" (R, 45). When Roxana realizes that she has no way to feed her children, she resolves with her servant Amy that she should dump them either on the relatives or the parish. Roxana's argument recalls Moll's when she first turned to theft;

Moll reminds her reader "that a time of Distress is a time of dreadful Temptation, and all the Strength to resist is taken away; Poverty presses, the Soul is made Desperate by Distress, and what can be done?" (M, 191). Roxana, similarly, explains that "the Misery of my own Circumstances hardned my Heart against my own Flesh and Blood; and when I consider'd they must inevitably be Starv'd, and I too, if I continued to keep them about me, I began to be reconcil'd to parting with them all . . . that I might be freed from the dreadful Necessity of seeing them all perish, and perishing with them myself" (R, 52). The situation is desperate; Roxana and Amy have almost no food. When their landlord comes to dine, Amy must go out to the butcher for a joint of meat, and, Roxana notes, "poor Amy and I had drank nothing but Water for many Weeks" (R, 59). Roxana's landlord begins to show her many kindnesses, and both Roxana and Amy have their suspicions as to where these kindnesses may lead. In what justly has become one of the most discussed passages in the book, Roxana and Amy argue the merits of Roxana's going to bed with the landlord. Amy takes the affirmative side, and she seems to have the better of the argument. "Why, Madam, *says Amy*, I hope you won't deny him, if he should offer it" (R, 61). Roxana insists that she would "starve first" (R, 61).

> I hope not, Madam, I hope you would be wiser; I'm sure if he will set you up, as he talks of, you ought to deny him nothing; and you will starve if you do not consent, that's certain.
>
> What, consent to lye with him for bread? . . .
>
> Nay, Madam . . . I don't think you wou'd for any thing else; it would not be Lawful for any thing else, but for Bread, Madam; why nobody can starve, there's no bearing that, I'm sure.
>
> Ay . . . but if he would give me an Estate to live on, he should not lye with me. [R, 61-62]

Roxana's argument sounds virtuous; Amy's goes far toward making it ridiculous. For Amy says that she would gladly lie with the landlord to save Roxana and herself—and Roxana is shocked. But, says Amy, she would starve for Roxana, she would die for Roxana—and the reader must note at this point that Amy is right: of the three, whoring, starving, and dying, whoring does seem the most logical alternative. Thus when Roxana closes the argument, for this time at least, by insisting that "Hitherto I had not only preserv'd the Virtue itself, but the virtuous Inclination and Resolution; and had I kept myself there, I had been happy, tho' I had perish'd of meer Hunger; for, without question, a Woman ought rather to die, than to prostitute her Virtue and Honour, let the Temptation be what it will" (R, 62-63), Amy's view seems more sensible. Since the novel follows Amy's analysis of the situation rather than Roxana's, I think we must agree with critics like Katharine Rogers that Defoe is being ironic in Roxana's speech here.[18] Amy is very convincing: "Your Choice is fair and plain; here you may have a handsome, charming Gentleman, be rich, live pleasantly, and in Plenty; or refuse him, and want a Dinner, go in Rags, live in Tears; in short, beg and starve" (R, 74). The landlord is an honest, decent man who wishes that he could marry Roxana; unfortunately, he is legally married, although he has no contact with his wife. This of course is very similar to Roxana's situation. The landlord sets up Roxana so that she can make a living renting rooms, assuring her that she "will easily get a good comfortable subsistence" (R, 66) from the project. He treats her with gentleness and respect, explaining that he cannot marry her but insisting that otherwise "he wou'd be every thing else that a Woman cou'd ask in a Husband . . . he resolv'd to ask nothing of me but what it was fit for a Woman of Virtue and Modesty, for such he knew me to be, to yield" (R, 67).

The relationship between the landlord and Roxana is based on attraction and need, with the two melding into one another. Roxana says as much: "I confess, the terrible Pressure of my former Misery, the Memory of which lay heavy upon my Mind, and the surprizing Kindness with which he had deliver'd me, and withal, the Expectations of what he might still do for me, were powerful things" (R, 67). Roxana understands the mix of her emotions. "O let no Woman slight the Temptation that being generously deliver'd from Trouble, is to any Spirit furnish'd with Gratitude and just Principles: This Gentleman had freely and voluntarily deliver'd me from Misery, from Poverty, and Rags; he had made me what I was, and put me in a Way to be even more than I ever was, namely, to live happy and pleas'd, and on his Bounty I depended" (R, 69). If only I could marry him, Roxana repines to Amy, everything would be perfect, for "if I cou'd take him fairly, you may be sure I'd take him above all the Men in the World; it turn'd the very Heart within me, when I heard him say he lov'd me; how cou'd it do otherwise? when you know what a Condition I was in before; despis'd, and trampled on by all the World" (R, 71). Surely in any but legal terms Roxana's marriage to her husband was a degradation, while this illegal relationship, illegal not by the will of the people involved but because the laws of England do not allow for divorce in cases of desertion,[19] will provide emotional sustenance and material security. Roxana struggles with her conscience; the thought of where she just has been, and the ease with which she can fall back, tortures her. "But Poverty was my Snare; dreadful Poverty! the Misery I had been in, was great, such as wou'd make the Heart tremble at the Apprehensions of its Return. . . . Add to this, that if I had ventur'd to disoblige this Gentleman, I had no Friend in the World to have Recourse to; I had no Prospect, no, not of a Bit of Bread; I had nothing before me, but to fall back into the same Misery that I had been in before" (R, 73). Roxana accepts the landlord. He fulfills all his promises, in fact providing financial safeguards for her that are significantly better than those she might have had if they were legally married.[20] He has a contract drawn up in which, in addition to promising to live with Roxana as if she were his wife, he obliges himself to pay her £7,000 should he abandon her; there is also "a Bond for 500 *l.* to be paid to [her], or to [her] Assigns, within three Months after his Death" (R, 76). He draws up a new will, which he shows to Roxana and then gives her to keep. In it "he gave a thousand Pounds to a Person that we both knew very well, in Trust, to pay it, with the Interest from the Time of his Decease, to me, or my Assigns; then he Will'd the Payment of my Jointure, as he call'd it, *viz.* his Bond of a Hundred Pounds, after his Death; also he gave me all my Houshold-Stuff, Plate, &c." (R, 85). Thus begins Roxana's climb up the financial ladder; the improvement in her finances is paralleled by an improvement in the way she is treated by men, for all of Roxana's "irregular" attachments treat her far better than her legal husband did.

Roxana lives very happily with her lover; unfortunately, he is killed by robbers while he and Roxana are on a business trip to Paris. She mourns him honestly and sees to it that he is appropriately buried. But she also is careful to keep track of her affairs. After her first husband had run away, Roxana with disgust described his attitude: "To be out of all Business was his Delight; and he wou'd stand leaning against a Post for half an Hour together . . . with all the Tranquillity in the World, . . . and this even when his Family was, as it were starving, that little he had wasting, and that we were all bleeding to Death" (R, 47). Roxana has better business sense, and when she is not fettered by someone else's right to ruin her, she works efficiently. Immediately she takes stock of her assets, just as we have seen Moll do so many times in Defoe's earlier novel. In addition to what the jeweller had given her, Roxana finds among his effects "seven Hundred Pistoles in Gold" plus "Foreign-Bills accepted, for about 12000 Livres; so that, in a

Word, [she] found [her]self possess'd of almost ten Thousand Pounds Sterling, in a very few Days after the Disaster" (*R*, 90). She sends to Amy immediately, ordering her to liquidate the household so that the lawful wife cannot claim any of the goods. Roxana lets it be known that her "husband" was carrying valuable jewels when he was killed, and thus she keeps the supposedly stolen items without any inquiry. She deals with the head manager, who comes over to Paris from London, and he returns happy that he has been able to get anything at all to take back with him. "I got good Advice at *Paris*, from an eminent Lawyer . . . and laying my Case before him, he directed me to make a Process in Dower upon the Estate, for making good my new Fortune upon Matrimony, which accordingly I did; and, upon the whole, the Manager went back to *England*, well satisfied, that he had gotten the unaccepted Bills of Exchange, which . . . with some other things . . . amounted to 17000 Livres; and thus I got rid of him" (*R*, 92). Further, Roxana charms the prince for whom her "husband" had been working when he was murdered; Roxana carefully downplays her financial situation, and the prince grants her two thousand livres a year "as the Widow of Monsieur" (*R*, 95). Roxana casts her accounts; she dissolves her household; she explores her legal necessities; she furthers her contacts with the rich and powerful. Not bad for a mere woman, and certainly much better than she was ever allowed to do when her first, legal husband was managing her business affairs. Roxana repeatedly reminds us of the sordid source of her wealth, but although she feels guilt for her whoring, she never loses sight of the value of her financial independence. Whatever fluctuations befall her otherwise, her financial control never slips once she has that control in her own hands.

The prince becomes Roxana's lover, and he showers her with expensive gifts so often that she has no occasion ever to ask for anything. Roxana inventories his bounty:

> First of all, he sent me a Toilet, with all the Appurtenances of Silver, even so much as the Frame of the Table; and then, for the House, he gave me the Table, or Side-board of Plate I mentioned above, with all things belonging to it, of massy Silver; so that, in short, I could not, for my Life, study to ask him for any thing of Plate which I had not.
>
> He could then accommodate me in nothing more but Jewels and Cloaths, or Money for Cloaths; he sent his Gentleman to the Mercer's, and bought me a Suit, or whole Piece, of the finest Brocaded Silk, figur'd with Gold, and another with Silver, and another of Crimson; so that I had three Suits of Cloaths, such as the Queen of *France* would not have disdain'd to have worn at that time. . . .

I had no less than five several Morning Dresses besides these, so that I need never be seen twice in the same Dress; to these he added several Parcels of fine Linnen, and of Lace, so much, that I had no room to ask for more, or indeed, for so much. [*R*, 106]

Roxana has accrued quite a fortune; the modern reader will understand the value of the plate and other durable items but also should be aware of the great value represented by the suits of clothing that Roxana lingers over so lovingly. This accounting of the clothes is particularly interesting in the context of my next chapter, for a precisely parallel accounting scene takes place between Clarissa and Mrs. Harlowe, when Mrs. Harlowe explains to Clarissa just how rich she will be, and what suits of clothes (or their equivalent in cash) will be hers if she accepts Solmes. There is perhaps less love between Mrs. Harlowe and her daughter than between Roxana and her prince, but no less precise an accounting.[21]

When the prince needs to take an extended trip to Italy, Roxana is not unhappy to accompany him, except that she has one "terrible Difficulty . . . and that was, in what Manner to take Care of what I had to leave behind me; I was Rich . . . very Rich, and what to do with it, I knew not, nor who to leave in Trust, I knew not" (*R*, 137). Although she does not want to ask help from the prince—she prefers that he not realize how wealthy she is—he nonetheless recognizes her problem and provides means for her to keep her stock safe while she is traveling abroad. "The next Day he sent me in a great Iron Chest, so large, that it was as much as six lusty Fellows could get up the Steps, into the House; and in this I put, indeed, all my Wealth; and for my Safety, he order'd a good honest ancient Man and his Wife, to be in the House with [Amy] . . . and a Maid-Servant, and Boy, so that there was a good Family, and *Amy* was Madam" (*R*, 138).

Roxana and the prince are gone two years. Their relationship remains good, with the prince thanking Roxana—much to her surprise—for keeping him "honest." That is, he is with no other woman for all this time, and while Roxana occasionally remarks that the princess really should have been on this trip, learning and growing from these experiences, the relationship between the prince and Roxana is stable and decent. As with the landlord, while her tie here is not legal, it is far from a casual liaison. And just as she had matured in her relationship with the landlord, Roxana grows ever more competent and accomplished in her years with the prince. She mentions that she has learned "the *Turkish* Language" (*R*, 140) from a Turkish slave; "I need not say," she comments offhandedly, "I learnt *Italian* too, for I got pretty well mistress of that, before I had been there a Year; and as I had Leisure enough, and lov'd the Language, I read all the *Italian* Books I cou'd come at" (*R,* 140). Roxana is a bright woman. We will see her becoming involved in, and comprehending fully, all kinds of financial transactions. Her facility in picking up languages—so casually re-marked—is an additional aspect of Defoe's emphasis on the intel-ligence of his character. When Richardson talks about Clarissa's command of foreign languages, it is in the context of a special accom-plishment.[22] When Fielding talks about "learned ladies," it is always with some distaste. But Defoe, as so often wonderfully positive in his delineation of female potential, sees Roxana's acquisition of two lan-guages in such a short period as simply unremarkable—worthy of mention but not of acclaim.

The prince's business concluded, he returns with Roxana to France. She finds everything in good order when she gets back. Never unmindful of the past, Roxana sets out to safeguard her wealth further: "[i]n all this Affluence of my Good Fortune, I did not forget that I had been Rich and Poor once already, alternately." She realizes that bear-ing children—simply aging—she is likely to lose her beauty and with it the interest of her lover: "I might be dropt again . . . therefore, it was my Business to take Care that I shou'd fall as softly as I cou'd." She accordingly sets out "to make as good Provision for myself, as if I had had nothing to have subsisted on, but what I now gain'd; whereas I had not less than ten Thousand Pounds . . . which I had amass'd, or secur'd, rather out of the Ruins of my faithful Friend, the Jeweller. . . . My greatest Difficulty now, was, how to secure my Wealth, and to keep what I had got; for I had greatly added to this Wealth, by the generous Bounty of the Prince" (*R,* 143). After eight years, the prince does turn her away, not, as it happens, because he tires of Roxana, but because his dying wife reforms him before she expires. Roxana under-stands his change of heart, and she accepts her new situation matter of factly, actually, with some satisfaction. For she indeed has come out of this relationship very well. She is aware that she "was grown not only well supply'd, but Rich, and not only Rich, but . . . very Rich" (*R,* 148). Her problem is not losing the prince but figuring out what to do with all the money: "for the Truth of it was, that thinking of it sometimes, almost distracted me, for want of knowing how to dispose of it, and for fear of losing it all again by some Cheat or Trick, not knowing any-body that I could commit the Trust of it to" (*R,* 148). Roxana wants to go back to England, but is at a loss when faced with transporting her considerable wealth. She turns to "a *Dutch* Merchant" of whom she has heard good reports; through Amy she opens her negotiations.

> When I came to him myself, I presently saw such a plainness in his Dealing, and such Honesty in his Countenance, that I made no Scruple to tell him my whole story, *viz.* That I was a Widow; that I had some Jewels to dispose of, and also some Money, which I had a-mind to send to *England*, and to follow there myself; but being but a Woman, and having no Correspondence in *London*, or any-where else, I knew not what to do, or how to secure my Effects.
>
> He dealt very candidly with me, but advis'd me, when he knew my Case so particularly, to take Bills upon *Amsterdam*, and to go that Way to *England*; for that I might lodge my Teasure in the Bank there, in the most secure Manner in the World; and that there he cou'd recommend me to a Man who perfectly understood Jewels, and would deal faithfully with me in the disposing them.
>
> I thank'd him, but scrupled very much the travelling so far in a strange Country, and especially with such a Treasure about me; that whether known, or conceal'd, I did not know how to venture with it: Then he told me, he wou'd try to dispose of them there, that is, at *Paris*, and convert them into Money, and so get me Bills for the whole. [R, 149-50]

Roxana herself is quite aware that, as she comments, "Now I was become, from a Lady of Pleasure, a Woman of Business, and of great Business too, I assure you" (R, 169).[23] Efficiently and single-mindedly Roxana sees to her "business." She goes first to England, and from there, having employed a servant who speaks Dutch, she goes to Rotterdam.

> [I] soon found out the Merchant to whom I was recommended, who receiv'd me with extraordinary Respect; and first he acknowledg'd the accepted Bill for 4000 Pistoles, which he afterwards paid punctually; other Bills that I had also payable at *Amsterdam*, he procur'd to be receiv'd for me; and whereas one of the Bills for a Thousand two Hundred Crowns, was protested at *Amsterdam*, he paid it me himself, for the Honour of the Endorser, as he called it, which was my Friend, the Merchant at *Paris*.
>
> There I enter'd into a Negociation, by his Means, for my Jewels, and he brought me several Jewellers, to look on them, and particularly, one to Value them, and to tell me what every Particular was worth. . . .
>
> All this Work took me up near half a Year, and by managing my Business thus myself, and having large Sums to do with, I became as expert in it, as any She-Merchant of them all; I had Credit in the Bank for a large Sum of Money, and Bills and Notes for much more. [R, 169-70]

A large part of the action from the death of the jeweller to here has been financial, and financial matters will remain a primary focus of the novel until its conclusion. Roxana does not merely worry about keeping her money safe; she actively works at the investment of her fortune. Just as she made precise financial arrangements with the landlord/jeweller, so after his death she counts up her assets and takes care not to lose any more than she must to the legal heirs. After she parts from the prince she again takes stock; even richer, she has more to care for. Roxana needs the Dutch merchant to help her not because she is a woman but because she has such considerable assets; it would be unwise for anyone, male or female, to attempt to transport so much cash and jewels. She chooses her associates with care; realizing that she must trust someone to help her to transport her wealth, she inquires into the reputations of possible intermediaries, finally deciding on the Dutch merchant, who seems to have the best reputation. Having chosen the merchant, however, she does not merely put her affairs in his hands but remains involved in each step of the dealings. Between them they work out the details. She wants to convert her jewels into cash. She will take bills upon certain merchants in Rotterdam; other bills she takes on merchants in Amsterdam. Roxana never shrinks either from understanding what dealings are necessary or from carrying them out; that all of this work takes her half a year she reports as fact, with pride rather than complaint. From time to time in the novel Roxana shows weakness and indecision when she discusses her moral position; she never shows anything of the sort with regard to financial matters. Here she is fully in control. The moral implications of Roxana's financial capability are difficult to deal with within a traditional moral framework, for of course Roxana can have the freedom to exercise her capability only if she takes the license to live outside traditional patterns. Defoe makes a very good case in *Roxana* for the woman outside the traditional bounds. We have seen Roxana as a lawfully wedded wife; she does much better as a mistress or an unattached woman. There is a point, in fact, when Roxana considers going back to her legal husband and using her wealth to set them both up respectably. But Defoe shows that this course is not possible; having once married a fool, there is no possibility of turning him into a responsible partner.

During the period when she is the prince's mistress, Roxana accidentally finds her legal husband. She has Amy make inquiries about him, and Amy even goes to talk to him. Roxana learns that he is "a meer Sharper; one that would stick at nothing to get Money, and that there was no depending on any thing he said" (*R*, 129). He pretends to Amy that he needs money to buy a commission; Roxana, tempted thus to help him, learns that he has used the same scam with many people, never with the intention of buying a commission and always planning not to repay the loan. Roxana comments that

> had he been a Man of any Sence, and of any Principle of Honour, I had it in my Thoughts to retire to *England* again, send for him over, and have liv'd honestly with him: But as *a Fool* is the worst of Husbands to do a Woman Good, so *a Fool* is the worst Husband a Woman can do Good to: I wou'd willingly have done him Good, but he was not qualified to receive it, or make the best Use of it; had I sent him ten Thousand Crowns, instead of eight Thousand Livres, and sent it with express Condition that he should immediately have bought himself the Commission he talk'd of, with Part of the Money, and have sent some of it to relieve the Necessities of his poor miserable Wife at *London*, and to prevent his Children to be kept by the Parish, it was evident, he wou'd have been still but a private Trooper, and his Wife and Children should still have starv'd at *London*, or been kept of meer Charity, as, for ought he knew, they then were. [*R*, 130-31]

All that she can do, then, is to keep out of his sight and be careful that they do not accidentally meet. The only sure way Roxana has to avoid an accidental meeting is for her to know where her husband is at all times, and she therefore employs someone to watch him and report on all of his movements. Roxana thus is presented with a journal of her husband's days.

> By this Management I found an Opportunity to see what a most insignificant, unthinking Life, the poor indolent Wretch, who by his unactive Temper had at first been my Ruin, now liv'd; how he only rose in the Morning, to go to-Bed at Night; that saving the necessary Motion of the Troops, which he was oblig'd to attend, he was a meer motionless Animal, of no Consequence in the World; that he seem'd to be one, who, tho' he was indeed alive, had no manner of Business in Life, but to stay to be call'd out of it; he neither kept any Company, minded any Sport, play'd at any Game, or indeed, did any thing of moment; but, *in short*, saunter'd about, like one, that it was not two Livres Value whether he was dead or alive; that when he was gone, would leave no Remembrance behind him that ever he was here; that if ever he did any thing in the World to be talk'd of, it was, only to get five Beggers, and starve his Wife: The Journal of his Life, which I had constantly sent me every Week, was the least significant of any-thing of its Kind, that was ever seen. [*R*, 132]

Roxana is disgusted by the life her husband leads: "for whole Weeks together, he wou'd be ten Hours of the Day, half asleep on a Bench at the Tavern-Door where he quarter'd, or drunk within the House" (R, 133). She is repelled by the uselessness, the aimlessness of such a life—and she is angered that as his wife she must take care not to make herself known to him, for having once had the power to ruin her, all he would need is to find her in order to ruin her once more: "once I had nothing to hope for, but to see him again; now my only Felicity was, if possible, never to see him, and above all, to keep him from seeing me" (R, 133). Roxana's encounter with her husband is an important incident in the book. In contrast to the landlord, to the prince, and to Roxana herself, the husband leads a useless existence, taking no responsibility for his actions and no control of his life. It needs to be remarked that Defoe gives this role to a male character. The landlord and the prince are men of affairs, each functioning productively in his own sphere. The Dutch merchant from whom Roxana gets such good advice is another such person. And Roxana herself builds a fortune. In Defoe novels, gender in this context of human capability is essentially irrelevant as it will not be again in any eighteenth-century novel.

But in contemporary law, of course, gender and marital status determine a person's legal profile, for the fact of being a woman and married effectively eliminates the person's status as an individual under the law—legally, the married woman essentially is subsumed into her husband. Specifically, she virtually loses her right to own and control property. Having experienced marriage, Roxana has no desire to be married; in the face of all tradition, she prefers to be on her own. She argues that a wife has nothing of her own, but a mistress has what is hers as well as what is her lover's:

> I had no Inclination to be a Wife again, I had had such bad Luck with my first Husband, I hated the thoughts of it; I found that a Wife is treated with Indifference, a Mistress with a strong Passion; a Wife is look'd upon, as but an Upper-Servant, a Mistress is a Sovereign; a Wife must give up all she has; have every Reserve she makes for herself, be thought hard of, and be upbraided with her very *Pin-Money*; whereas a Mistress makes the Saying true, *that what a Man has,* is hers, and *what she has,* is her own; the Wife bears a thousand Insults, and is forc'd to sit still and bear it, or part and be undone; a Mistress insulted, helps herself immediately, and takes another. [R, 170-71]

Roxana's case for the other side—a wife "appears boldly and honourably with her Husband" and has the right to his house, servants, and children, while a "Whore sculks about in Lodgings" (*R*, 171)—is not nearly as convincing. The arguments on the side of marriage are those of social position and custom; the arguments for being a mistress are economic, and these Defoe presents as much the stronger set. Defoe draws a world in which lawful wedlock implies no degree of safety but financial accumulation does.

Roxana entirely breaks out of the traditional female role, sometimes to her own surprise and certainly to the surprise of her Dutch merchant. Roxana's lecture on the relative merits of being a mistress and a wife is followed by a situation in which Roxana must translate her principles into action. The Dutch merchant, her friend and adviser, wants her to marry him. Roxana does not wish to marry because she does not want to give up her freedom. Thinking that if he can get Roxana to have sexual intercourse with him, she then surely would marry him, the merchant manages with a sort of passive connivance of his victim to get Roxana into bed. They have what she refers to as three nights and three "very merry" (*R*, 182) days, and then he again asks her to marry him. Roxana says that nothing has changed.

This episode of the merchant's proposal goes on for twenty-four pages, and the entire passage is interlaced with financial comments. Sometimes Roxana's emphasis on money is comical, although given the original source of her relationship with the merchant, it is quite natural that when he hesitates and goes round and round whatever his point might be, Roxana expects him to talk of some financial reversal. He tells her that he wants something from her, but "declin'd making the Proposal, *as he call'd it* . . . I began to think he might have met with some Disaster in his Business" (*R*, 178). Several days later, they are talking again: "Now I expected it wou'd come out, but still he put it off . . . from whence I concluded, it cou'd not be a Matter *of Love*, for that those things are not usually delay'd in such a manner, and therefore it must be a Matter of Money" (*R*, 179). Roxana asks him if he has any business problems and if he needs money from her: "if he wanted Money, I wou'd let him have any Sum for his Occasion, as far as five or six Thousand Pistoles" (*R*, 180). Roxana's would-be lover thanks her very politely, refuses her kind offer, and then takes her in his arms and kisses her passionately.

The merchant tells Roxana he wants a wife; marriage is the one thing she cannot give him, Roxana answers. It does cross her mind that what he wants is her money, but more specifically, the problem is that whether or not that is his aim, the loss of her financial independence would be the result of marriage—a result that is unacceptable to

Roxana: "I knew that while I was a Mistress, it is customary for the Person kept, to receive from them that keep; but if I shou'd be a Wife, all I had then, was given up to the Husband, and I was thenceforth to be under his Authority only; and as I had Money enough, and needed not fear being what they call *a cast-off Mistress*, so I had no need to give him twenty Thousand Pound to marry me, which had been buying my Lodging too dear a great deal" (*R*, 183). Noting that Roxana has to be "the first Woman in the World that ever lay with a Man, and then refus'd to marry him," the merchant guesses at Roxana's reason: "I have an Offer to make to you, that shall take off all the Objection, *viz.* That I will not touch one Pistole of your Estate, more, than shall be with your own voluntary consent; neither now, or at any other time, but you shall settle it as you please, for your Life, and upon who you please after your Death" (*R*, 185-86).

Roxana and the merchant argue the marriage case at length, with Roxana reverting repeatedly to her basic argument: the unmarried woman with money has the most security of any woman. Roxana can find other good arguments against marriage, but the most urgent is that "the divesting myself of my Estate, and putting my Money out of my Hand . . . made me refuse to marry" (*R*, 187). The merchant, who is drawn by Defoe as a fair-minded and reasonable man, still argues to Roxana that although "he cou'd not say but I was right in the Main; that as to that Part relating to managing Estates . . . it was in some Sence, right, if the Women were able to carry it on so, but that in general, the Sex were not capable of it; their Heads were not turn'd for it, and they had better choose a Person capable, and honest, that knew how to do them Justice, as Women, as well as to love them; and that then the Trouble was all taken off of their Hands" (*R*, 192-93). This analysis from a character who is portrayed as among the most open-minded of men implies that such a perception of women is the customary one; even the merchant, who given his business dealings with Roxana might be expected to doubt the truth of such a position, cannot quite move away from it. Defoe implies that the majority of men cannot see beyond this perspective—a limitation that Defoe himself clearly transcends.[24] If the merchant finds that women must "let the Trouble" of managing their money be "taken off of their Hands," Roxana finds "it was a dear Way of purchasing their Ease; for very often when the Trouble was taken off of their Hands, so was their Money too; and that I thought it was far safer for the Sex not to be afraid of the Trouble, but to be really afraid of their Money; that if no-body was trusted, no-body wou'd be deceiv'd; and the Staff in their own Hands, was the best Security in the World" (*R*, 193).[25]

Defoe subverts the view of woman as child. Roxana sees herself as requiring a financial consultant, not a husband. She sees marriage as danger rather than protection. She knows that she is capable of managing her own financial affairs and feels far safer in actively pursuing financial goals than in leaving her business to anyone else. This viewpoint would be nothing surprising for a man, of course; Defoe knows full well how remarkable it seems in a woman. But, in the context of the book, especially within the context of Roxana's married life, Defoe leaves the reader no choice but to agree with Roxana that "the Staff in [her] own Hands, [is] the best Security in the World."

The merchant finally gives up and returns to Paris. Roxana regrets her decision somewhat but considers her loss of the merchant to be quite final. "[S]o I sat and cry'd intollerably, for some Days, nay, I may say, for some Weeks; but I say, it wore off gradually; and as I had a pretty deal of Business for managing my Effects, the Hurry of that particular Part, serv'd to divert my Thoughts, and in part to Wear out the Impressions which had been made upon my Mind" (*R*, 202). And Roxana goes about her business:

> I had sold my Jewels, all but the fine Diamond Ring, which my Gentleman, the Jeweller, us'd to wear; and this, at proper times, I wore myself; as also the Diamond Necklace, which the Prince had given me, and a Pair of extraordinary Ear-Rings, worth about 600 Pistoles; the other, which was a fine Casket, he left with me at his going to *Versailles*, and a Small Case with some Rubies and Emeralds, *&c.* I say, I sold them at the *Hague* for 7600 Pistoles; I had receiv'd all the Bills which the Merchant had help'd me to at *Paris*, and with the Money I brought with me, they made up 13900 Pistoles more; so that I had in Ready-Money, and in Account in the Bank at *Amsterdam*, above One and Twenty Thousand Pistoles, besides Jewels; and how to get this Treasure to *England*, was my next Care.
>
> The Business I had had now with a great many People, for receiving such large Sums, and selling Jewels of such considerable Value, gave me Opportunity to know and converse with several of the best Merchants of the Place; so that I wanted no Direction now, how to get my Money remitted to England; applying therefore, to several Merchants, that I might neither risque it all on the Credit of one Merchant, nor suffer any single Man to know the Quantity of Money I had; I say, applying myself to several Merchants, I got Bills of Exchange, payable in *London;* for all my Money; the first Bills I took with me; the second Bills I left in Trust,[26] (in case of any

Disaster at Sea) in the Hands of the first Merchant, him to whom I was recommended by my Friend from Paris. [*R*, 202-3]

Roxana has much to do, and she turns almost immediately to affairs. Note that, having been working with these merchants quite extensively, she no longer has any problem finding appropriate channels for her financial dealings; like any businessperson, she is now free to act because she has all the necessary contacts in place. And she needs to get things in good order, for she also must prepare for a lying-in: the merchant has left her a souvenir. Her attention to detail does not flag. Her care again extends beyond the amassing of fortune to the safeguarding of it—she apportions her money among several merchants so as not to entrust the entire sum to any one. When she and her money have safely arrived in England, she must "get all [the] Bills accepted" (*R*, 204), and she attends to that business. Nearing her term, she takes a house and makes arrangements for the birth, but this is not her major concern. "I had now all my Effects secur'd; but my Money being my great Concern at that time, I found it a Difficulty how to dispose of it, so as to bring me in annual Interest; however, in some time I got a substantial safe Mortgage for 14000 Pound, by the Assistance of the famous Sir *Robert Clayton*, for which, I had an estate of 1800 Pounds a Year bound to me; and had 700 Pounds *per Annum* Interest for it. This, with some other Securities, made me a very handsome Estate, of above a Thousand Pounds a Year" (*R*, 204). Roxana very briefly (one paragraph) discusses her lying in and her unsuccessful hints to the merchant to come back to her and the child. Almost immediately, she returns to financial matters. She repeats in precise detail the financial advice she enjoys and her procedures for following it. She feels a great deal of gratitude to Sir Robert Clayton, who

as he found I was not inclin'd to marry . . . frequently took Occasion to hint, how soon I might raise my Fortune to a prodigious Height, if I would but order my Family-Oeconomy so far within my Revenue, as to lay-up every Year something, to add to the Capital.

I was convinc'd of the Truth of what he said, and agreed to the advantages of it; you are to take it as you go, that Sir *Robert* suppos'd by my own Discourse, and especially, by my Woman, *Amy*, that I had 2000 *l*. a Year Income; he judg'd, as he said, by my way [of] Living, that I cou'd not spend above one Thousand; and so, he added, I might prudently lay-by 1000 *l*. every Year, to add to the Capital; and by adding every Year the additional Interest, or Income of the Money to the Capital, he prov'd to me, that in ten

Year I shou'd double the 1000 *l. per Annum,* that I laid by; and he drew me
out a Table, as he call'd it, of the Encrease, for me to judge by; and by which,
he said, if the Gentlemen of *England* wou'd but act so, every Family of them
wou'd encrease their Fortunes to a great Degree, just as Merchants do by
Trade; whereas now, *says* Sir *Robert,* by the Humour of living up to the
Extent of their Fortunes, and rather beyond, the Gentlemen, *says he,* ay, and
the Nobility too, are, almost all of them, Borrowers, and all in necessitous
Circumstances. [*R,* 207-8]

Roxana and Sir Robert, she reports, have many conversations. He
counsels that "I shou'd encrease my Estate, if I wou'd come into his
Method of contracting my Expenses; and by this Scheme of his, it
appear'd, that laying up a thousand Pounds a Year, and every Year
adding the Interest to it, I shou'd in twelve Years time have in Bank,
One and twenty Thousand, and Fifty eight Pounds; after which I
might lay-up two Thousand pounds a Year" (*R,* 208). Roxana cannot
bring herself to be quite as careful in her savings as her adviser
suggests, but she gives much thought to his proposals, accepting at
least some parts of the plan. As in these passages, Defoe often uses
Roxana to enunciate his own financial beliefs. That Defoe uses a female
character for such a purpose itself implies that he sees nothing incongruous in a woman being engaged in business. This is borne out by
Defoe's remarks in *The Complete English Tradesman.* As Katherine
Rogers notes, Defoe, "[b]elieving women capable of business . . .
thought a wife should understand and participate in her husband's
trade rather than passively consume his gains, and should be prepared
to fend for herself in case of widowhood. . . . [H]e insisted that a
tradesman's widow should understand his business and accounts, lest
she find herself at the mercy of lawyers and apprentices who might
defraud her of everything." [27]

Defoe chooses Sir Robert Clayton, a historical figure, as Roxana's
financial adviser; this choice lends seriousness to Roxana's financial
dealings. Michael Shinagel comments that "Defoe significantly mentions Sir Robert Clayton in his *Tour* . . . as a lively example of those
mighty merchants 'whose beginnings were small, or but small com-
par'd, and who have exceeded even the greatest part of the nobility of
England in wealth.' " [28] In the long conversations between Sir Robert
and Roxana, Defoe gives the reader precise investment advice while at
the same time extolling the virtues of trade and merchant industry.
When we accept Roxana's business dealings as an intrinsic part of the
novel, and her interest in financial matters as a legitimate concern
rather than merely a manifestation of avarice, these extended passages

with Sir Robert seem integral to the novel rather than an example of Defoe just getting "carried away with enthusiasm."[29] Certainly Sir Robert's advice to Roxana and her consideration of it is afforded careful attention by Defoe. For example, Roxana decides that she really can't discipline herself enough to save a thousand pounds a year, but she tells Sir Robert that

> as I had not come to him for my Interest half-yearly, as was usual, I was now come to let him know, that I had resolv'd to lay-up that seven Hundred Pound a Year, and never use a Penny of it; desiring him to help me to put it out to Advantage.
>
> Sir *Robert*, a Man thorowly vers'd in Arts of improving Money, but thorowly honest, *said to me*, Madam, I am glad you approve of the Method that I propos'd to you; but you have begun wrong; you shou'd have come for your Interest at the Half-Year, and then you had had the Money to put out; now you have lost half a Year's Interest of 350 *l*. which is 9 *l*. for I had but 5 *per Cent*. on the Mortgage.
>
> Well, well, Sir, says I, can you put this out for me now?
>
> Let it lie, Madam, *says he*, till the next Year, and then I'll put out your 1400 *l*. together, and in the mean time I'll pay you Interest for the 700 *l*. so he gave me his Bill for the Money, which he told me shou'd be no less than 6 *l. per Cent*. Sir *Robert Clayton*'s Bill was what no-body wou'd refuse; so I thank'd him, and let it lie; and next Year I did the same; and the third Year Sir *Robert* got me a good Mortgage for 2200 *l*. at 6 *per Cent*. Interest: So I had 132 *l*. a Year added to my Income; which was a very satisfying Article. [R, 209-10]

In addition to advising Roxana about finances, Sir Robert also discusses with her the merits of the merchant. Roxana recounts Sir Robert's enthusiastic description of the place and figure of the merchant; the same eulogistic terms Defoe uses will appear repeatedly in later eighteenth-century novels.

> Sir *Robert* and I agreed exactly in our Notions of a Merchant; Sir *Robert* said, and I found it to be true, that a true-bred Merchant is the best Gentleman in the Nation; that in Knowledge, in Manners, in Judgment of things, the Merchant out-did many of the Nobility; that having once master'd the World, and being above the Demand of Business, tho' no real Estate, they were then superior to most Gentlemen, even in Estate; that a Merchant in flush Business, and a capital Stock, is able to spend more Money than a Gentleman of 5000 *l*. a Year Estate; that while a Merchant spent, he only spent what he got, and not that; and that he laid up great Sums every Year.
>
> That an Estate is a Pond; but that a Trade was a Spring; that if the first is

once mortgag'd, it seldom gets clear, but embarrass'd the Person for ever; but the Merchant had his Estate continually flowing; and upon this, he nam'd me Merchants who liv'd in more real Splendor, and spent more Money than most of the Noblemen in *England* cou'd singly expend, and that they still grew immensly rich.

He went on to tell me, that even the Tradesmen in *London*, speaking of the better sort of Trades, cou'd spend more Money in their Families, and yet give better Fortunes to their Children, than, generally speaking, the Gentry of *England* from a 1000 *l.* a Year downward, cou'd do, and yet grow rich too. [*R*, 210-11][30]

Sir Robert is trying to convince Roxana that she should marry a merchant; she is not yet ready for matrimony, but, we should remember, she does indeed eventually marry her merchant friend. Meanwhile, Roxana's respect for the merchant class is totally in character. Defoe admires that class, and Roxana's attitude here indicates to the reader her good financial sense.

Roxana's wealth grows rapidly, and she becomes an extremely rich woman. Within seven years of coming to town, she notes with some pride, "I had laid-up an incredible Wealth [including] near 5000 Pounds in Money . . . besides abundance of Plate, and Jewels. . . . In a word, I had now five and thirty Thousand Pounds Estate; and as I found Ways to live without wasting either Principal or Interest, I laid-up 2000 *l.* every Year, at least, out of the meer Interest, adding it to the Principal; and thus I went on" (*R*, 223-24). This is Roxana at fifty: rich, well maintained, and feeling good. She is doing very well indeed; if we contrast the fifty-year-old whore to the starving young wife, it is hard to fault her whoring. Still a mistress, Roxana does not find it necessary to touch even a portion of her wealth. But Roxana's financial security does raise the question of why she continues in her whoring. Roxana's affair with the landlord had been a matter of necessity; later, her intense desire for money is understandable in view of her early poverty and her fear of slipping back. "But this was all over now; Avarice cou'd have no Pretence; I was out of the reach of all that Fate could be suppos'd to do to reduce me; now I was so far from Poor, or the Danger of it, that I had fifty Thousand Pounds in my Pocket at least; nay, I had the Income of fifty Thousand Pounds . . . and besides Jewels and Plate, and Goods, which were worth near 5600 *l.* more; these put together, when I ruminated on it all in my Thoughts . . . added Weight still to the Question, as above, and it sounded continually in my Head, what's next? *What am I a Whore for now*" (*R*, 245)? Although Roxana says that the question of why she continues "a Whore" sounds continually in her head, she makes no very careful attempt to explain her moral position, quite in contrast to the precise account she gives of her financial acts.

Thus it is fitting that after Roxana finally does marry the merchant, the two of them should put their financial cards on the table—at Roxana's request. The mutual accounting scenes, as in *Moll Flanders*, are among the most joyous in the book. Roxana's enumeration of her own and her husband's assets goes on for pages: Roxana gets a lovely surprise, for, contrary to her expectation, she finds that the merchant's estate has increased since she had last inquired.

> So we open'd the Box; there was in it indeed, what I did not expect, for I thought he had sunk his Estate, rather than rais'd it; but he produc'd me in Goldsmith's Bills, and Stock in the *English East-India Company*, about sixteen thousand Pounds Sterling; then he gave into my Hands, nine Assignments upon the Bank of *Lyons* in *France*, and two upon the Rents of the Town-House in *Paris*, amounting in the whole to 5800 Crowns *per Annum*, or annual Rent, *as 'tis call'd there*; and *lastly*, the Sum of 30000 *Rixdollars* in the Bank of *Amsterdam*; besides some Jewels and Gold in the Box, to the Value of about 15 or 1600 *l.* among which was a very good Necklace of Pearl, of about 200 *l.* Value; and that he pull'd out, and ty'd about my Neck; telling me, That shou'd not be reckon'd into the Account. [*R*, 302]

Roxana comments that "it was with an inexpressible Joy, that I saw him so rich" (*R*, 302). The Dutch merchant has still more, and Roxana counts it up in loving detail: "an eighth Share in an *East-India* ship then Abroad; an Account-Courant with a Merchant, at *Cadiz* in *Spain*; about 3000 *l.* lent upon *Bottomree*, upon Ships gone to the *Indies*; and a large Cargo of Goods in a Merchant's Hands, for Sale, at *Lisbon* in *Portugal*; so that in his Books there was about 12000 *l.* more; all which put together, made about 27000 *l.* Sterling, and 1320 *l.* a Year." And, Roxana goes on, her new husband tells her "this is not all neither; then he pull'd me out some old Seals, and small Parchment-Rolls, which I did not understand; *but he told me*, they were a Right of Reversion which he had to a Paternal Estate in his Family, and a Mortgage of 14000 *Rixdollars*, which he had upon it, in the Hands of the present Possessor; so that was about 3000 *l.* more." It is true that he also has some very large debts, "but after all this, upon the whole, he had still 17000 *l.* clear Stock in Money, and 1320 *l.* a-Year in Rent" (*R*, 303).

Then Roxana sets forth her stock:

> *First*, I pull'd out the Mortgage which good Sir *Robert* had procur'd for me, the annual Rent 700 *l. per annum*; the principal Money 14000 *l.*

*Secondly*, I pull'd out another Mortgage upon Land, procur'd by the same faithful Friend, which at three times, had advanced 12000 *l.*

*Thirdly*, I pull'd him out a Parcel of little Securities, procur'd by several Hands, by Fee-Farm Rents, and such Petty Mortgages as those Times afforded, amounting to 10800 *l.* principal Money, and paying six hundred and thirty six Pounds a-Year; so that in the whole, there was two thousand fifty six Pounds a-Year, Ready-Money, constantly coming in. [*R*, 303-4]

Again, as is the pattern in this book, a cheerful, extremely detailed analysis of finances is followed by Roxana's dramatic breast-beating about how she came to her wealth. Here she vows to keep her ill-gotten gains separate from her husband's honestly earned riches; in view of the earlier care Roxana had taken to keep her resources under her own control, perhaps she also has other reasons for keeping her share separate. The merchant agrees to this plan, and in return Roxana insists on making a very fair contribution to the family finances so that her husband will suffer no loss by having the estates kept separate. Note how carefully these financial details have been analyzed by Roxana:

*Well, says I*, seeing you will have it be kept apart, *it shall be so*, upon one Condition, which I have to propose, and no other; and what is the Condition, *says he?* why, *says I*, all the Pretence I can have for the making-over my own Estate to me, is, that in Case of your Mortallity, I may have it reserv'd for me, if I outlive you; well, *says he*, that is true: But then, *said I*, the Annual Income is always receiv'd by the Husband, during his Life, as 'tis suppos'd for the mutual Subsistance of the Family; now, *says I*, here is 2000 *l.* a Year, which I believe is as much as we shall spend, and I desire none of it may be sav'd; and all the Income of your own Estate, the Interest of the 17000 *l.* and the 1320 *l.* a Year may be constantly laid by for the Encrease of your Estate, and so, *added I*, by joining the Interest every Year to the Capital, you will perhaps grow as rich as you would do, if you were to Trade with it all, if you were oblig'd to keep House out of it too.

He lik'd the Proposal very well, *and said*, it should be so. [*R*, 305]

The discomfort Roxana feels in the midst of her prosperity parallels the happy scenes of domesticity. Roxana suffers her terrors and sees to her business, and the one never detracts from the other. A fine example of this kind of parallelism comes just after Roxana arranges for the separation of her own and her husband's estates. With all their affairs explored and found to be in the best order, Roxana immediately begins to feel that her good fortune must soon explode.

And let no-body conclude from the strange Success I met with in all my wicked Doings, and the vast Estate which I had rais'd by it, that therefore I either was happy or easie: No, no, there was a Dart struck into the Liver, there was a secret Hell within, even all the while, when our Joy was at the highest; but more especially now, after it was all over, and when according to all appearance, I was one of the happiest Women upon earth. . . .

In a word, it never Lightn'd or Thunder'd, but I expected the next Flash would penetrate my Vitals, and melt the Sword in this Scabbord of Flesh; it never blew a Storm of Wind, but I expected the Fall of some Stack of Chimneys, or some Part of the House wou'd bury me in its Ruins. . . .

But I shall perhaps, have Occasion to speak of all these things again by-and-by; the Case before us was in a manner settl'd; we had full four thousand Pounds *per Annum* for our future Subsistence, besides a vast Sum in Jewels and Plate; and besides this, I had about eight thousand Pounds reserv'd in Money. . . .

With this Estate, settl'd as you have heard, and with the best Husband in the World, I left *England* again. [R, 305-6]

We have to remark Roxana's psychological pain; she is not hypo-critically posturing. But we also must note her control of her practical reality: she is psychologically uncomfortable but at the same time also adds up her accounts (" four thousand Pounds *per Annum*"). The psychological reality of Defoe's portrait of Roxana at points like these is extraordinary, for this is precisely the way a strong person such as Roxana indeed would compartmentalize her experience. In what are perhaps her most trying moments—the incidents relating to the daughter who discovers that Roxana probably is her mother—this pattern of psychological distress hand in hand with practical action dominates. Having made some good guesses as to the true identity of the respectable merchant's wife, the daughter threatens Roxana's posi-tion; Amy finally proposes the girl's murder. Roxana won't hear of such a thing, of course—but we are left unclear as to whether Amy does actually do the deed and, if so, whether Roxana knows about it. With such frights around her, we might expect Roxana to become preoccupied with these matters and lose touch with her financial affairs. This never happens. In fact, Roxana finds that one major problem with having to break with Amy is that Amy had been con-ducting so much of her business: "I was, for want of *Amy*, destitute; I had lost my Right-Hand; she was my Steward, gather'd in my Rents, *I mean my Interest-Money*, and kept my Accompts, and, *in a word*, did all my Business" (R, 366). Roxana is very upset to think, as she seems to, that Amy had murdered her daughter, but after about a month, "finding *Amy* still come not near me, and that I must put my Affairs in a Posture that I might go to Holland" (*R*, 374-75), she makes other arrangements. She sets her friend the Quaker "in *Amy*'s stead" and "in the . . . Affairs of receiving Money, Interests, Rents, *and the like* . . . she was as faithful as *Amy* cou'd be, and as diligent" (*R*, 375). Finally, Roxana prepares detailed financial arrangements for her children. Of the last five pages of the novel, four discuss financial matters in one context or another.

The novel ends with Roxana going off in respectability and afflu-ence with her husband to Holland. They arrive "with all the Splendor and Equipage suitable to our new Prospect" (*R*, 379), as well they should, in the face of their careful and sensible plans. This ending makes perfect sense in terms of all that has gone before: we have seen Roxana build this base for her life. But Roxana as a person does not seem to deserve such a happy fate, and although this ending is logical enough, Defoe seems to have felt that he needed to leave some sop to the reader's sympathy. That sop becomes the one sentence in which Roxana alludes to her future Misery, a misery which, coming only as an allusion, carries little real weight in the ending of the novel. Several critics have accused Defoe of having not finished the novel, of having not been able to finish it, or of having not wanted to finish it, and have then explained the causes of this inability or lack of will in various ways.[31] But the novel is finished: we do not see any final calamity because things, we have been shown, are under control.

*Roxana* is not a neat novel. Roxana herself is clearly not a character in whose good fortune we can wholeheartedly rejoice, nor do we unreservedly wish for her downfall. At times, particularly in the incident in which she forces Amy into the landlord's bed, Roxana is quite vile.[32] Much of the time Roxana's moral visage is somewhat more ambiguous, though it is never very pretty. This ambiguity arises from Roxana's initial circumstances. The collapse of Roxana's life under the ruin of her husband's financial failure provides the motivation for all of her ensuing struggles. Roxana's fascination with money and the atten-dant dealings in financial matters must be considered part of the delineation of her character. *Roxana* is a more complex novel than *Moll Flanders*, and Roxana is a more psychologically complex character than Moll. At times she is quite awful (if she does not actually connive at the murder of her daughter, she certainly does not do much to stop Amy from killing the girl), but she also can be decent. In the last pages of the novel, for example, she makes careful arrangements to help several of her children—even sending one of them a wife! Further, she herself is aware of the complexity of her own emotions, caring quite normally for one child, and without any feeling at all for another.

> It is with a just Reproach to myself, that I must repeat it again, that I had not the same Concern for it, tho' it was the Child of my own Body; nor had I ever the hearty affectionate Love to the Child, that [its father] had; what the reason of it was, I cannot tell; and indeed, I had shown a general Neglect of the Child, thro' all the gay Years of my *London* Revels; except that I sent *Amy* to look upon it now and then, and to pay for its Nursing; as for me, I scarce saw it four times in the first four Years of its Life, and often wish'd it wou'd go quietly out of the World; whereas a Son which I had by the Jeweller, I took a different Care of, and shew'd a differing Concern for, tho' I did not let him know me; for I provided very well for him; had him put out very well to School; and when he came to Years fit for it, let him go over with a Person of Honesty and good Business, to the *Indies;* and after he had liv'd there some time, and began to act for himself, sent him over the Value of 2000 *l.* at several times,[33] with which he traded, and grew rich; and, *as 'tis to be hop'd,* may at last come over again with forty or fifty Thousand Pounds in his Pocket. . . . I also sent him over a Wife; a beautiful young Lady, well-bred, an exceeding good-natur'd pleasant Creature. [*R*, 308-9]

Defoe has not been remarked by critics as a psychological novelist, but in passages like these there is much to interest us. Roxana is not a monster; certainly she is not a saint. Defoe makes no effort to make everything within Roxana's character fit, but rather than suggesting authorial carelessness, it seems to me that the inconsistencies in Roxana's psychology reflect her humanity, and are thus a sign more of Defoe's genius as a writer than of his carelessness as a craftsman.[34] Roxana's very different feelings for various of her children may surprise, even shock the reader, but siblings often are treated quite differently by their parents. Roxana owns up to her feelings—perhaps that it what shocks us. This is yet another point at which Defoe's characterization so richly gets beyond the clichés of the feminine, here the maternal, to delineate the individual.

Defoe did not draw a morally admirable character, but he did draw a very capable person. These two qualities, moral imperfection and personal capability, exist side by side in Roxana, and Defoe never implies that the former detracts from the latter. Defoe is fascinated by Roxana's ability to become a woman of fortune after beginning from total destitution. Roxana's business sense is admirable, not unfeminine. That Roxana as a woman could be so enthralled by financial affairs is not surprising. Women and their relation to money is a frequent object of scrutiny in the eighteenth-century novel, but what is extraordinary is Defoe's obvious pleasure in this female character's financial dealings. When Defoe discusses Roxana's financial manipulations, it is irrelevant that the character is female. The salient fact is that she is so capable. In this, she is full sister to Moll.

# THREE

# Samuel Richardson:
## *Clarissa*

*Moll Flanders* and *Roxana* are chronicles of women moving through a wide range of experiences and places; Richardson's novels about women, *Clarissa* and the earlier *Pamela,* are domestic novels in which the world beyond the home impinges almost not at all on the heroines. Richardson's images of women are, arguably, the most limited of those of all the major eighteenth-century novelists; certainly the outside world is almost invisible in both *Pamela* and *Clarissa.* In *Pamela* the vision is limited to Pamela's circle at Mr. B's house; the extension of the circle merely enlarges the domestic group to include her parents. *Clarissa*'s world is narrower yet, its fifteen hundred pages devoted to virtually limitless exploration of the minds of two teenage girls. Defoe's female characters travel far afield both socially and geographically; Fielding's Sophia experiences the roads and the inns of England, and Fanny Burney's Evelina is educated into the ways of the world. Jane Austen's characters are aware that the world exists beyond the borders of their villages, if only in that the soldiers garrisoned nearby too soon move off. But the consciousness Richardson gives us is of small enclosed spaces. Within those spaces the themes of the novel, money, filial duty, and death, merge into and shape each other. Clarissa and Anna, for all their talk, never seem prepared to leave the parental shelter. Clarissa does physically leave home, but that departure essentially is accidental; she is tricked into running away, and literally to her death regrets her action. Richardson does not question the limited nature of Clarissa's world, or suggest that a wider scope for her would be appropriate. Pamela can marry or be a servant; Clarissa, even more narrowly, can die. Reading *Clarissa* as a Christian narrative[1] is perhaps the only way that its view of woman is not absolutely limiting, but this is to see it only as a Christian allegory.[2] Certainly the book read this way is of less universal interest than other important eighteenth-century novels; this limitation might explain why readers who do not see the book as Christian allegory often find the novel lacking, and in distinction to its critical defenders, see the elongated death scenes as simply morbid.

The entire novel is, in a real sense, a preparation for Clarissa's death. In her first letter Clarissa already mentions her own death, admitting to Anna that she has "sometimes wished that it had pleased God to have taken me in my last fever, when I had everybody's love and good opinion."[3] But Clarissa has lost that love and good opinion forever, or at least until she dies,[4] because her inheritance from her grandfather has made her a rival to her brother James for the fortunes of yet other relatives. Thus Clarissa splits the family wealth just by living, and, in the minds of her father and brother at least, she prevents the family from gaining social preferment. Clarissa cannot undo her "crime"; her attempt to give back her inheritance, to leave control of her fortune in her father's hands, does not limit the damage.[5] The pretensions of her family doom Clarissa. Clarissa cannot live without the approval of her family—and so she dies.

Richardson does not allow wealth to free his heroines as Defoe does. Defoe's images are of women outside the domestic circle. Free to wander and function not only in their own initial environments, but through England, Europe, and even America, Defoe's women increasingly develop their capabilities as their adventures continue. Money frees them on many levels, and as they become wealthier, their horizons continue to expand. They learn from their dealings with the world, and much of what they learn pertains to money. Learning how to manage—accrue, save, invest—their financial resources, they increasingly control how society treats them. Richardson's images of women are altogether different from Defoe's. Moll and Roxana see the world; Richardson's women see the insides of houses—Mr. B's, the Harlowe's, the Howe's, "Mrs. Sinclair's."[6] Richardson is as fascinated with money as Defoe, but he does not see it as giving women power.[7] Having or not having money seems largely irrelevant for women in terms of broadening either their social or psychological base. Richardson's women don't learn much about any but their own domestic worlds; of all the important eighteenth-century female characters, they act in the narrowest range. Richardson does not countenance the concept of forced marriage; he does not say that for the sake of family peace and prosperity Clarissa should marry Solmes. But he also does not take the position that Clarissa should rebel against the clear injustice of her family's ruling. As Terry Eagleton notes, "Richardson writes at a transitional point . . . where a growing regard for the subject deadlocks with a still vigorous patriarchal tyranny. . . . [I]ndividual sensibility . . . is tragically at odds with a grimly impersonal power structure."[8] Clarissa can only escape from her family situation—and remain a paragon—by dying. Richardson never suggests, as novelists later in the century do, that a woman should have some other alternative to a repugnant marriage than staying in her parents' house or dying. Part of what makes Clarissa so attractive to her creator, in fact, is that her only way to "live" is to die and "live" in heaven— surely a very restricting view of woman.[9]

Richardson is explicit about the subject of his novel. *Clarissa* is "The History of A Young Lady: Comprehending the Most Important Concerns of Private Life and particularly showing The Distresses That May Attend The Misconduct Both of Parents And Children, In Relation To Marriage." Richardson emphasizes here "particularly" the relationship between parents and children; there is misconduct on both sides. The beginning of the novel, with the references in the first lines of Anna's opening letter to "the disturbances that have happened in your family" (39) and Clarissa's very early comment that "our family has indeed been strangely discomposed—*Discomposed!*—It has been in *tumults*" (41), points us immediately to Richardson's subject. The relationship between Clarissa and Lovelace is perhaps more interesting to most modern readers than the relationship between Clarissa and her family; feminist readers find justified interest in Richardson's depiction of the female friendship between Clarissa and Anna.[10] But Clarissa's relationship with her family is the heart of the book, providing not merely plot machinery but the basic structure of the psychological scaffolding of the novel.[11] The primary conflict in the novel is not between Clarissa and Lovelace but between Clarissa and her father. She must die not because Lovelace cannot be a husband to her, but because she cannot be reconciled with her father unless she marries Solmes—and that she cannot do. When at the end of the novel Clarissa repeatedly laments that her primary desire is to be reconciled with her family, she means just that. It is not only Clarissa whose letters describe in detail the goings-on in her family; Anna's letters are full of the opinions, actions, thoughts, and preferences of *her* mother. And

Lovelace's family too enters largely and often into the novel, not only in his letters but in references by Clarissa and Anna.

Although Richardson in *Clarissa* argues against the concept of forced marriage, he does not argue that parental authority is inappropriate; he would like Clarissa's father to act more reasonably, but he never argues that Mr. Harlowe is not entitled to the familial authority he exerts. Clarissa cannot rationally assess her situation, decide that her father is behaving inappropriately, and arrange her life accordingly. She has the financial means to be independent—as a single, not yet betrothed woman she can control property[12]—but she does not have the psychological strength to exert that economic independence. Richardson sees this lack of strength as one of her virtues. When Clarissa repeatedly asserts that she could not possibly litigate with her papa, we are to understand that she is good; when in the face of her mistreatment she never wavers in her respect for her father and mother, Richardson presents her unflinching devotion as evidence of Clarissa's virtue. Filial obedience and family finances are intimately connected in the Harlowe family. Money plays an extraordinarily large role in *Clarissa*. One of the most interesting aspects of the development of Clarissa's and Anna's characters is that Richardson gives each woman a strong interest in money and a good understanding of financial matters. These very young women, whom we might expect to be only marginally interested in money, discuss every aspect of the financial tangles of the Harlowes. Tell me the details of your grandfather's will, Anna asks in one of her very earliest letters, and Clarissa obliges at length.

The Preamble that Anna asks about gives us much information about women in eighteenth-century English society. Clarissa's grandfather explains that he feels justified in leaving his fortune to Clarissa because everybody in the family already has a great deal of money, with the expectation, in just about every case, of even more to come. The sources of these fortunes are varied, but two of them are specifically female in origin, suggesting that it is not unusual for very large sums of money either to be controlled by a woman or to come with her as her marriage portion. The middle son is "very rich . . . by what has as unexpectedly fallen in to him on the deaths of several relations of his present wife . . . over and above the very large portion which he received with her in marriage" (53). And "my grandson James will be sufficiently provided for by his godmother Lovell's kindness to him, who having no near relations assures me that she has, as well by deed of gift as by will, left him both her Scottish and English estates" (53). Thus when the grandfather wills his estate to Clarissa, even within the family there is precedent for fortunes to be controlled by women. He appeals directly to his sons and grandchildren not to "impugn or contest the . . . bequests and dispositions in favour of my said grand-daughter Clarissa, although they should not be strictly conformable to law or the forms thereof; nor suffer them to be controverted or disputed on any pretence whatsoever" (53-54). Clarissa also writes a will, a very detailed one; as a single woman, she legally can direct her monies. In fact, as Erna Reiss explains, "The property rights of a single woman— in legal language, of a *feme sole*—were at Common Law identical with those of a man; she could dispose of it either during her lifetime or by will. But if she was betrothed to be married her rights were immediately curtailed. The property of a married woman [was] vested in her husband."[13]

Everything in the Harlowe family revolves around money, and while Clarissa does not act from the same motives as the rest of her family, she too is interested in monetary issues. Clarissa seems very much aware, for example, that she has made a real sacrifice in giving up her grandfather's fortune to her father's control. "I dare not ask to go to my dairy-house, as my good grandfather would call it; for I am now afraid of being thought to have a wish to enjoy that independence to which his will has entitled me. . . . And, indeed, could I be as easy and happy here as I used to be, I would defy that man [Lovelace], and all his sex, and never repent that I have given the power of my fortune into my papa's hands" (56). In the same letter Clarissa continues, "You know, my dear, that there is a great deal of solemnity among us. But never was there a family more united in its different branches than ours. Our uncles consider us as their own children, and declare that it is for our sakes that they live single. So that they are advised with upon every article relating to, or that may affect, us" (56). The "living single" clearly relates to the unmarried uncles' fortunes being reserved to the Harlowe children, and Clarissa obviously views this arrangement with approbation. The fact that the fortunes will stay in the family for Clarissa signals family closeness. When Clarissa complains about the "family fault" (61)—avarice—she complains of a fault in degree, not kind. Clarissa is not disrespectful of money, only of the loss of perspective that a misplaced emphasis on the accumulation of wealth implies. To skip over fourteen hundred pages or so, she herself is very careful in her own will to dispose properly of *her* personal wealth. So that here at the beginning of the book, when she disparages the family's fascination with Solmes's wealth, it is only the lack of perspective (Solmes, no matter how rich, cannot be attractive as a mate) that she deplores.

Letter 13, seven closely printed pages long, shows that Clarissa fully understands that the source of her problem is economic. As she points out, "Were ours a Roman Catholic family, how much happier for me, that they thought a nunnery would answer all their views!" (83). The tone perhaps is ironic, but given Clarissa's own repeated assertion that she would be perfectly happy to stay unmarried if only she were left in peace, the idea of a convent would not be very unpleasant to her. And in Catholic countries the religious retreat historically often has been the outlet for a surplus of economically unproductive women. I will return later to the theme of Clarissa's own distaste for marriage. But in terms of the economics of her family, Clarissa's remark is quite perceptive. Surely what they want most of all is for her to be out of the running for greater accumulation in contest with James. Letter 13 has been seen as Clarissa's statement of her lack of interest in money, but in fact she has a keen interest in finances—as the detail in this extremely long letter suggests. To gain some perspective on Clarissa's financial awareness before we discuss the extraordinary detail of this letter, it is instructive to take a quick look at an exchange that takes place between Clarissa and her sister Arabella a little later in the novel.

Richardson is very much the middle-class author writing for the middle-class audience; it comes as no surprise by now that all the talk in *Clarissa* of financial alliances and growth into titles reflects the strong pressures in society as the rising middle class sought to consolidate its position with regard to the older power structure, the aristocracy.[14] Part of, and extending from this context, something else is at play too: the hint, here and there, of the importance of the proper management of resources. The angelic Clarissa, in an argument with her diabolic sister Arabella, sounds much like Roxana in one of Roxana's "good business" speeches:

[Arabella] "What then have you done with the sums given you from infancy to squander?—Let me ask you . . . has, has, has, Lovelace, has your rake put it out at interest for you?"

[Clarissa] "Oh that my sister would not make me blush for her! It *is*, however, out at interest!—And I hope it will bring me interest upon interest!—Better than to lie rusting in my cabinet, as yours does." [195]

Clarissa not only discusses her investments but actually asserts her superior morality to Arabella in that her own money is not "rusting" like Arabella's! With this dialogue in mind, Clarissa's analysis of her family's financial manipulations can be seen to be perhaps more astute—less an innocent's recitation—than we might expect from a young girl.

Letter 13 is a remarkable document. In it, Clarissa explores the source of the family's displeasure with her, the financial manipulations, possible or fantastic, that motivate them, and the character flaws of each family member. It is a masterful exposition not only of contemporary attitudes toward wealth and social advancement but of family dynamics. Clarissa notes that the hatred for Lovelace manifested by her brother and sister grows not from the causes publicly given—a "college-begun antipathy on his side, or . . . slighted love on hers" (77)—but "an apprehension" that the uncles intend to follow the grandfather's example and leave significant portions of their estates to Clarissa. Clarissa reminds Anna of the Harlowe obsession with *"raising a family,"* that is, with attaining "rank and title" to go with their prosperity.

> My uncles had once extended this view to each of us three children, urging that as they themselves intended not to marry, we each of us might be so portioned, and so advantageously matched, as that our posterity if not ourselves might make a first figure in our country—While my brother, as the only son, thought the two girls might be very well provided for by ten or fifteen thousand pounds apiece; and that all the real estates in the family, to wit, my grandfather's, father's, and two uncles', and the remainder of their respective personal estates, together with what he had an expectancy of from his godmother, would make such a noble fortune and give him such an interest as might entitle him to hope for a peerage. Nothing less would satisfy his ambition. [77]

James has always considered his grandfather's and his uncles' estates as his own—grandfather and uncles are "his stewards" (77). When the grandfather's will "lop[s] off one branch of [James's] expectation" (77), James is very unhappy with Clarissa. Clarissa finds herself in trouble with everyone, not just James. "Nobody indeed was pleased: for although everyone loved me, yet being the youngest child, father, uncles, brother, sister, all thought themselves postponed as to matter of right and power; . . . and my father himself could not bear that I should be made sole, as I may call it, and independent, for such the will as to that estate and the powers it gave (unaccountably, as they all said), made me" (77-78). Clarissa tries to propitiate her family: "I gave up to my father's management . . . not only the estate, but the money bequeathed to me . . . contenting myself to take, as from his bounty, what he was pleased to allow me, without the least addition to my annual stipend. And then I hoped I had laid all envy asleep" (78).

But giving the management of her estate to her father does not solve the real problem, which is that her uncles, now that she has her grandfather's fortune, see her as the likely recipient of their wealth too. This is the thread that snags on Lovelace's pursuit of Clarissa—for the uncles see Lovelace as a good prospect, and in fact encourage his courtship of their niece. Lovelace is not so bad, they find several ways to prove, and he is, most to be amired, very rich indeed. Lovelace thus presents a serious threat to James's and Arabella's financial pretensions. All this is laid out in elaborate detail. James and Arabella

> were bitterly inveighing against [Lovelace] in their usual way, strengthening their invectives with some new stories in his disfavour, when my uncle Antony having given them a patient hearing declared: 'That he thought the gentleman behaved like a gentleman, his niece Clary with prudence, and that a more honourable alliance for the family, *as he had often told them*, could not be wished for; since Mr Lovelace had a very good paternal estate, and that, by the evidence of an enemy, all clear. Nor did it appear that he was so bad a man as had been represented; wild indeed, but it was at a gay time of life. He was a man of sense, and he was sure that his niece would not have him if she had not good reason to think him reformed, or by her own example likely to be so.' [78]

Uncle Antony emphasizes that he sees Lovelace as a man of principle and of good financial sense, recounting with approbation Lovelace's philosophy of management: " 'that his tenants paid their rents well; that it was a maxim with his family, from which he would by no means depart, never to rack-rent old tenants or their descendants, and that it was a pleasure to him, to see all his tenants look fat, sleek and contented' " (79). Lovelace has the potential to bring Clarissa a title. Uncle Antony notes that

> 'besides his paternal estate, [Lovelace] was the immediate heir to very splendid fortunes; that when he was in treaty for his niece Arabella, Lord M. told him what great things he and his two half-sisters intended to do for him, in order to qualify him for the title (which would be extinct at his Lordship's death) and which they hoped to procure for him, or a still

higher, that of those ladies' father, which had been for some time extinct on
failure of heirs male; that his view made his relations so earnest for his
marrying; that as he saw not where Mr Lovelace could better himself, so,
truly, he thought there was wealth enough in their own family to build up
three considerable ones; that therefore he must needs say he was the more
desirous of this alliance as there was a great probability, not only from Mr
Lovelace's descent, but from his fortunes, that his niece Clarissa might one
day be a peeress of Great Britain—and upon that prospect . . . he should,
for his own part, think it not wrong to make such dispositions as should
contribute to the better support of the dignity.' [79]

Clarissa is well aware (*"here was the mortifying stroke"* [79]) that Lovelace
can represent a very serious threat to her brother's inheritance. This is
the real reason that her parents are against him. Her other uncle
seconds Antony. Clarissa precisely understands the threat to her
implicit in her uncles' leanings; had she known about all this earlier,
she says, she would have been more on her guard. Her brother, she
adds wryly, could not "but be very uneasy to hear *two of his stewards*
talk at this rate to his face" (80). Clarissa describes James's reaction:
" 'See, sister Bella,' said he, in an indecent passion before my uncles
. . . 'See how it is!—You and I ought to look about us!—This little siren
is in a fair way to *out-uncle* as well as *out-grandfather* us both!' " (80).
Lovelace's fault is the financial threat he poses to James, and James has
his father's ear. No matter how Clarissa might feel, she would be in
contest with her father if she were to marry Lovelace. Lovelace's
character flaws, although they facilitate Richardson's plot, are essentially less relevant to the novel's structure than his financial portfolio.
      Richardson emphasizes this truth repeatedly. "The family union
was broken" (80) after these declarations by the uncles—the family
union is destroyed, then, by the uncles' potential financial reshuffling.
Clarissa underscores her awareness of the situation when she tells
Anna about the family's attempt to coerce her into approving Solmes.
If she gives in she will have presents, jewels, she "cannot tell what,
from every one of the family!" (80). "[B]ut I am afraid that my brother's
and sister's design is to ruin me with them at any rate. Were it
otherwise, would they not on my return from you have rather sought
to court than frighten me into measures their hearts are so much bent
to carry?" (81). Clarissa's intuition is right: there is no reason to suspect
that her siblings' campaign to estrange Clarissa from her parents will
end or that it will become less successful. Otherwise, as she notes, the
strategy would be one of persuasion rather than intimidation. The
situation always balances on the same point: the grandfather's legacy.

As Clarissa explains, Solmes has promised to shut out all of his relatives in her favor. If she herself dies without an heir, the entire estate can revert to her family—not only Solmes's estate but Clarissa's, including her grandfather's property, will revert to the Harlowes: "now a *possibility* is discovered (which such a grasping mind as my brother's can easily turn into a *probability*) that my grandfather's estate will revert to it, with a much more considerable one of the man's own. Instances of estates falling in, in cases far more unlikely than this, are insisted on; and my sister says, in the words of an old saw, *it is good to be related to an estate*" (81). This far-fetched possibility, then, is what makes Solmes preferable to Lovelace in James's and Arabella's view. Clarissa can only lament "the family fault which gives those inducements such a force as it will be difficult to resist" (81). Clarissa cannot expect help from any of her relatives. Her comments are sharply critical: her mother never opposes her father's will; her uncles "have as high notions of a child's duty as of a wife's obedience" (82). Clarissa finds a way out of the situation, but unfortunately it is not a solution open to her. "Were ours a Roman Catholic family" (83), she laments, but it is not. And so this extremely long letter, in which family and finance are so intertwined as to become one, ends with a solution that does not apply to Clarissa. There will be no solution but death.

Although Letter 13 is the longest and most detailed exposition of the financial basis of the novel, financial detail threads through the book. Clarissa's mother on several occasions attempts to communicate with her "dearest daughter" on the subject of settlements and booty. Arabella argues with Clarissa that she has no right to the estate; Anna begs Clarissa to take control of the estate that is hers and thus show some independence from those who torture her. Clarissa herself, as the novel goes on, talks not only about the estate in general but about financial particulars, especially regarding her most ready-to-hand assets, her clothes. Finally, there is her own will, an involved and detailed document. The conversations between Clarissa and Mrs. Harlowe that relate to money are very blunt. Mrs. Harlowe makes no pretense, for example, that there is any but a financial motive in marrying Clarissa to Solmes.

But what shall we do about the *terms* Mr Solmes offers. Those are the inducements with everybody. He has even given hopes to your brother that he will make exchanges of estates, or at least that he will purchase the northern one; for, you know, it must be entirely consistent with the family views that we increase our interest in this county. Your brother, in short, has given in a plan that captivates us all; and a family so rich in all its branches that has its views to honour must be pleased to see a very great probability of being on a footing with the principal in the kingdom. [101]

When Clarissa continues to refuse the match, Mrs. Harlowe gets tough. "Take notice that there are flaws in your grandfather's will; not a shilling of that estate will be yours, if you do not yield" (107). And if the family loses Solmes's wealth through Clarissa's opposition, then she will be "destitute" and "unable to support [her]self" (107). When the stick does not seem to be working, Mrs. Harlowe, acting on Mr. Harlowe's orders, tries the carrot. The terms of the bribery are direct: Clarissa can have goods or their equivalent in cash, as she chooses. Mrs. Harlowe's letter to Clarissa (most communication between Clarissa and her parents takes place by letter even though they live in the same house)[15] is businesslike. "Patterns of the richest silks" (188) had been ordered and now have arrived. They are sent up to Clarissa at the command of her father, accompanied by the letter from her mother: "These are the newest, as well as richest, that we could procure" (188). Then comes the accounting.

> Your papa intends you six suits (three of them dressed) at his own expense. You have an entire new suit; and one besides, which I think you never wore but twice. As the new suit is rich, if you choose to make that one of the six, your papa will present you with a hundred guineas in lieu.
>
> Mr. Solmes intends to present you with a set of jewels. As you have your grandmother's and your own, if you choose to have the former new-set and to make them serve, his present will be made in money; a very round sum—which will be given in full property to yourself; besides a fine annual allowance for pin-money, as it is called. [188]

Mrs. Harlowe bluntly sums up: as a wife, Clarissa will be financially independent. She reminds Clarissa that although she herself had brought a larger fortune to Mr. Harlowe than Clarissa will bring Mr. Solmes, she "had not a provision made [her] near this that we have made for you" (188). Well aware of Clarissa's "dislike" for Mr. Solmes, "Yet should I be sorry if you cannot to oblige us all, overcome a dislike" (188). The other relatives, Cousin Antony, for example, are equally forthright about the mercenary nature of the marriage transaction. Clarissa should remember that her estate is theirs, she is told. The corollary to this proposition, of course, is "we [ought] to have a choice who shall have it in marriage" (155). The large amount of wealth in the family is concomitant with a constant awareness of resources. When

Clarissa has no ready cash at hand and borrows a few guineas from Mrs. Lovick, it is only on the condition that Mrs. Lovick take a diamond ring until Clarissa can repay her (1081). The value of Clarissa's clothes and effects is mentioned in several contexts by Clarissa herself and by others.[16] And in her will Clarissa very carefully arranges for the distribution of her wealth upon her death—even asking that the monies her father had given her since she assumed her grandfather's legacy be repaid him out of that estate.

Clarissa's will is an extraordinary document in which the major themes of the novel—money, filial duty, and death—come together seamlessly. The barely nineteen-year-old Clarissa explains in a "Preamble" to the will itself that she has been preparing the document "for some time past" (1412). She wants it understood that her will has been thought out carefully, over a long period: "I . . . employed myself in penning down heads of such a disposition; which, as reasons offered, I have altered and added to; so that I never was absolutely destitute of a *will*, had I been taken off ever so suddenly" (1412). Richardson does not suggest that this preparation, that a young girl so carefully ready for death, is anything but normal. The will itself comprises eight densely printed pages of endless detail. The girl who so meticulously budgets the minutes of her day surely as carefully apportions her belongings.

The document consists of the preamble and a text of seven pages. Clarissa's sainthood, within Richardson's terms, is reinforced once again at the outset of the document in Clarissa's parallel themes: she values above all things the forgiveness of her father; she wants only female hands to touch her corpse. Clarissa's filial credentials thus are reemphasized, as are her virginal ones. After all her experiences, Richardson shows us that Clarissa is just the same good girl she was at the outset of the novel. The sentimentalism and sanctimonious undertone of the novel are nowhere more apparent than in Clarissa's will. Clarissa's first bequest is her corpse, and this she gives, not surprisingly, to her father: "In the first place, I desire that my body may lie unburied three days after my decease, or till the pleasure of my father be known concerning it" (1413). She orders that the corpse itself "not on any account . . . be opened; and it is my desire that it shall not be touched but by those of my own sex" (1413). These two sentences form the first paragraph of Clarissa's instructions, and the juxtaposition of her remarks about her father and about "being opened" and not being "touched but by those of my own sex" are fascinating. I am not the first to note an undercurrent of morbid prurience in the novel, an undercurrent that seems particularly obvious here.[17] Clarissa continues at length with her plans for disposing of her corpse. She would like to be buried in the family vault at the feet of her dear grandfather, but if that is not allowed, then she wants to be interred in the churchyard, "between the hours of eleven and twelve at night; attended only by Mrs Lovick and Mr and Mrs Smith, and their maidservant" (1413). The sense here is that she would be violated even by being seen dead, and so she wants to be put in her coffin as soon as possible—unless any of her relations wants to see her.

Having in effect held her breath until she turned blue—willed herself to die—Clarissa gets what revenge she can out of her demise. Her "dear relations" she smothers in a dripping sweetness of piety and devotion. Lovelace she tortures another way. While the others can see her if they wish, Lovelace is not to be allowed the sight of her corpse. But should he insist on seeing her—and she throws in her dagger: he has once before seen her "in a manner dead" (1413)—then

> let his gay curiosity be gratified. Let him behold and triumph over the wretched remains of one who has been made a victim to his barbarous perfidy: but let some good person, as by my desire, give him a paper whilst he is viewing the ghastly spectacle, containing those few words only: 'Gay, cruel heart! behold here the remains of the once ruined, yet now happy, Clarissa Harlowe!—See what thou thyself must quickly be—and REPENT!—'
>
> Yet to show that I die in perfect charity with *all the world*, I do most sincerely forgive Mr Lovelace the wrongs he has done me. [1413]

If Clarissa "sincerely forgive[s]" Lovelace, she has a delightful way of showing it.[18] And then she comes back to her father. She's fairly nasty in her comments about Lovelace, but returns to the stance of the wounded daughter seeking forgiveness when she gives still further instructions about disposing of her body. "If my father can pardon the error of his unworthy child so far as to suffer her corpse to be deposited at the feet of her grandfather . . . I could wish (my misfortunes being so notorious) that a short discourse might be pronounced over my remains before they be interred. The subject of the discourse I shall determine before I conclude this writing" (1413). This discourse, provided near the end of the will, has been seen as a sign of Richardson's "feminism," but it seems to me that Clarissa makes merely a reasonable choice of pronoun rather than a political statement. The discourse she wants delivered at the funeral is from Job; Clarissa changes the pronouns to feminine gender: " 'Let not *her* that is deceived trust in vanity; for vanity shall be *her* recompense. *She* shall be accomplished before *her* time; and *her* branch shall not be green. *She* shall shake off *her* unripe grape as the vine and shall cast off *her* flower as the blighted olive'" (1419). The will is replete with reminders that she has been wronged, and that she has been hoping to the last for forgiveness from her "friends." Her summing up must then include: "I am now at this time very weak and ill; having put off the finishing hand a little too long, in hopes of obtaining the last forgiveness of my honoured friends" (1419). Finally, she gives herself to heaven: "And now, oh my blessed REDEEMER, do I, with a lively faith, humbly lay hold of Thy meritorious death and sufferings; hoping to be washed clean in Thy precious blood from all my sins: in the bare hope of the happy consequences of which, how light do those sufferings seem (grievous as they were at the time) which I confidently trust will be a means, by Thy grace, to work out for me a more exceeding and eternal weight of glory!" (1420). The tone of the will, from beginning to end, is that of the suffering martyr, her eyes fixed backward in longing for the forgiveness of her "friends," and forward in glad contemplation of her date with her Redeemer. This is, after all, the ethereal Clarissa writing a will. But the level of financial detail in the will could not be more down-to-earth. She gives fully six pages of exact instructions "with regard to the worldly matters [goods or inheritances]" (1413) she will dispose of. I avoid the full litany and indicate here only a sampling of Clarissa's concerns.

She gives all her estates "to my ever-honoured father James Har-lowe, Esq., and that rather than to my brother and sister, to whom I had once thoughts of devising them, because if they survive my father, those estates will assuredly vest in them, or one of them, by virtue of his favour and indulgence, as the circumstances of things with regard to marriage settlements or otherwise may require; or as they may respectively merit by the continuance of their duty" (1413-14). The remark about the continuance of James's and Arabela's duty is wonderful in its irony. She bequeaths to her father "the house late my grandfather's, called *The Grove*" and *"my dairy-house*, and the furniture thereof as it now stands (the pictures and large iron chest of old plate excepted)" (1414), asking only that Mrs. Norton be allowed to live there until her death—"her prudent management will be as beneficial to my father as his favour can be convenient to her" (1414). This note of charity mixed with practicality runs throughout the document. Remarkable for a young girl is Clarissa's use of legal language—or perhaps Richardson loses track of the age and status of his heroine:

But with regard to what has accrued from that estate since my grandfather's death, and to the sum of nine hundred and seventy pounds which proved to be the moiety of the money that my said grandfather had by him at his death, and which moiety he bequeathed to me for my sole and separate use (as he did the other moiety, in like manner, to my sister) and which sum (that I might convince my brother and sister that I wished not for an independence upon my father's pleasure) I gave into my father's hands, together with the management and produce of the whole estate devised to me—These sums, however considerable when put together, I hope I may be allowed to dispose of absolutely, as my love and my gratitude (not confined wholly to my own family, which is very wealthy in all its branches) may warrant: and which therefore I shall dispose of in the manner hereafter mentioned. But it is my will and express direction that my father's account of the above-mentioned produce may be taken and established absolutely (and without contravention or question) as he shall be pleased to give it to my cousin Morden, or to whom else he shall choose to give it; so as that the said account be not subject to litigation, or to the control of my executor or any other person. [1414]

Note that she explicitly attempts to forestall any challenge to her father's account of the wealth she is distributing; his word is to be taken as binding by her executor.

Clarissa next allows that her father should pay himself back from the estate for the "quarterly sums" he has given her as a clothing and trinket allowance. Clarissa's instructions come with repeated interjections of her own unworthiness and of the goodness of her father. She must be either unutterably naive or extremely adept at reinforcing the guilt of her persecutors in the name of love and respect; both of course are true. Clarissa again is the self-deprecating victim:

My father of his love and bounty was pleased to allow me the same quarterly sums that he allowed my sister for apparel and other requisites; and (pleased with me then) used to say that those sums should not be deducted from the estate and effects bequeathed to me by my grandfather: but having *mortally* offended him (as I fear it may be said) by one unhappy step, it may be expected that he will reimburse himself those sums—It is therefore my will and direction that he shall be allowed to pay and satisfy himself for all such quarterly or other sums which he was so good as to advance me from the time of my grandfather's death; and that his account of such sums shall likewise be taken without questioning: the money, however, which I left behind me in my escritoire being to be taken in part of those disbursements. [1414]

She gives the family pictures to Uncle John Harlowe, who had complained that they were not bequeathed to him in the first place; the "old family plate" (1414) goes to Uncle Antony. Mrs. Norton gets six hundred pounds, plus "thirty guineas mourning money" (1415), and "To Mrs Dorothy Hervey, the only sister of my honoured mother, I bequeath the sum of fifty guineas for a ring; and I beg of her to accept of my thankful acknowledgements for all her goodness to me from my infancy; and particularly for her patience with me in the several altercations that happened between my brother and sister, and me, before my unhappy departure from Harlowe Place" (1415). Clarissa bequeaths her watch, and her "best Mechlin and Brussels head-dresses and ruffles" (1415); she gives away a gown and petticoat, "which having been made up but a few days before I was confined to my chamber, I never wore" (1415). Her harpsichord, her books, "twenty-five guineas for a ring to be worn in remembrance" (1415), a little miniature "set in gold" by a "famous Italian master," a "rose diamond ring," a "ring of twenty-five guineas price" (1415)—the list of Clarissa's bequests, large and small, goes on and on. Each gift comes with a sentimental explanation of why that particular bequest is being made. There is "a best diamond ring" to Anna, fifty pounds to "my late maidservant" (1416), "ten pounds each" to "the coachman, groom and two footmen, and five maids at Harlowe Place" (1417), her wearing apparel, "all my linen, and all my unsold laces" (1417); Clarissa even remembers to give away "the few books I have at my present lodgings" (1417), and, of course, her collected letters (not surprisingly) to Anna. And then there is Clarissa's "Poor's Fund," to be supplied from whatever is left after her other bequests have been taken out, and to include the money from the sale of Clarissa's quite considerable collection of jewels: the set of jewels that once belonged to her grandmother and the "diamond necklace, solitaire and buckles, which were properly my own" (1419). If someone in her family wishes to have any of these, Clarissa wants the jewels to be "purchased" and the money to go into her Poor's Fund— unless her father wants to use the jewels to repay himself for the money he had advanced her since the death of her grandfather.

The section of the will that deals with the Poor's Fund is Clarissa's philosophical and practical guide to the philanthropic duties of the rich to the poor. Richardson's young heroine has a clearly articulated system of benevolence and in her wisdom knows exactly who is worthy of aid and who is not. She also concerns herself with the conservation of resources, remarking that while under normal circumstances she expects the awards to be paid from interest, in cases of dire need funds can be taken from principal as well. The comments are worth quoting in full.

[I]t may be proper to mention in this last solemn act, that my intention is that this fund be entirely set apart and appropriated to relieve temporarily, from the interest thereof (as I dare say it will be put out to the best advantage) or even from the principal, if need be, the honest, industrious, labouring poor only; when sickness, lameness, unforeseen losses, or other accidents disable them from following their lawful callings; or to assist such honest people of large families as shall have a child of good inclinations to put out to service, trade or husbandry.

It has always been a rule with me in my little donations, to endeavour to aid and set forward the sober and industrious poor. Small helps, if seasonably afforded, will do for such; and so the fund may be of more extensive benefit: an ocean of wealth will not be sufficient for the idle and dissolute: whom, therefore, since they will be always in want, it will be no charity to relieve, if worthier creatures shall by that means be deprived of such assistance as may set the wheels of their industry going, and put them in a sphere of useful action.

But it is my express will and direction that let this fund come out to be ever so considerable, it shall be applied only in support of the *temporary exigencies* of the persons I have described; and that no one family or person receive from it, at one time, or in one year, more than the sum of twenty pounds. [1419]

The sanctimonious self-assurance of Clarissa's instruction is typically eighteenth-century. Clarissa wants to help "the honest, industrious, labouing poor only," and only under such circumstances—"sickness, lameness," and so on—as "disable them from following their lawful callings." Her "rule" in her "little donations [has always been] to endeavour to aid and set forward the sober and industrious poor"; it is important to give these people "such assistance as may set the wheels of their industry going." In other words, Clarissa sees her charity as a means to keep the poor working. We may smile at the plan this dying girl has for the improvement of the productivity of the nation, but the thoroughly mercantile cast of Clarissa's benevolence must be noted. The question of class, specifically the place of the newly rich middle class in society, drives the plots of many eighteenth-century novels in addition to *Clarissa*,[19] and while the smugness of these remarks coming from a girl whose "work" consists basically of writing letters to her friends does indeed put the reader off, the ideas expressed here are central to the thought of the period. Compare Clarissa's remarks with this description of the results of a good dinner and "a crown in silver" given to the heads of deserving families in a slightly later, very widely read novel by Henry Brooke:

> By the means of this weekly bounty, these reviving families were soon enabled to clear their little debts to the chandlers, which had compelled them to take up every thing at the dearest hand. They were also further enabled to purchase wheels and other implements, with the materials of flax and wool, for employing the late idle hands of their houshold. They now appeared decently clad, and with happy countenances; their wealth increased with their industry; and the product of the employment of so many late useless members became a real accession of wealth to the public. So true it is that the prosperity of this world, and of every nation and society therein, depends solely on the industry or manufactures of the individuals.[20]

The thrust is precisely Clarissa's: the poor must be given only enough to keep them working; Clarissa, remember, says that no person or family is to receive more than twenty pounds in a given year.

Clarissa's will shows us the perfect woman in her final, thoughtful statement. She is solicitous of her family and friends. She remembers each person with some bequest, even the lower servants at Harlowe House. She forgives, indeed asks the forgiveness of, everyone. She claims no rancor toward Lovelace: her note to him is for the good of his soul. She has social responsibility, allowing not just for a Poor's Fund but for the proper allocation of its resources. The pretentiousness the modern reader sees, the revenge against family and Lovelace who have hurt her, these Richardson seems not at all aware of; as so often in this book, Richardson's images of virtue—Clarissa's famous ordering of her day comes to mind—to the modern reader are petty trivializations of experience. What is not trivial is the wealth Clarissa possesses. The list seems to go on endlessly—sets of jewels from one source or another; this diamond ring to one friend, another diamond ring to the next. Pictures, plate, clothes, lace . . . all made even more impressive when we remember the relatively great cost of such items in the eighteenth century.[21] As I noted earlier, an unmarried woman could control her own property, and Clarissa has a great deal of property indeed. And at least in death she exerts an extraordinary care in disposing of every last trinket.

But although Clarissa in death can dispose of her wealth as she wishes, while she lives her property gives her very little power. Richardson, as we have seen, shows that even the merely potential shift of resources to Clarissa victimizes her. The social context in which Clarissa lives mandates that filial obedience is the highest moral virtue, and filial obedience, like all aspects of family life, is to be directed toward the aggrandizement of the family, as defined by the father and eldest son. Clarissa is trapped in this grid. And Clarissa, although sometimes able to see that her parents are acting improperly, cannot free herself from her dependence on their approval.

Richardson finds it appropriate that wealth does not give Clarissa independence. Anna is wrong, in Richardson's context, when she encourages Clarissa to litigate with her father for her estate; no matter what the parents do, a child should not set herself against them. Richardson shows not only that money does not give women power, but that it should not: Clarissa could enter litigation and be free, but good girls die first. And this brings us to another of Richardson's assumptions: while the author is allowed to be critical of the way Clarissa's parents treat her, Clarissa herself may not be. In order for Clarissa to be a paragon, she must never waver from her belief in her parents' goodness and in her own guilt. Reality must not enter into the victim's perception of the authority figure. This perspective is also Fielding's, as we will see in the next chapter; in Fielding's novels, as in *Clarissa*, fathers and husbands enjoy freedom from accountability to their victims. Fielding's voice can comment on the many imperfections of Squire Western in *Tom Jones* and of Booth in *Amelia*, but Sophia and Amelia never are allowed a critical perspective. This double vision exists quite late into the eighteenth-century novel. In *Evelina*, for example, the father who had abandoned Evelina in her infancy nonetheless draws unconditional fealty from his daughter when Evelina learns who he is just before her marriage; suddenly, Evelina's marriage plans become dependent on his will.

The reader of *Clarissa* sees the Harlowes as rigid, cruel, and tragically obsessed with their own agenda of family aggrandizement; the father is the deciding player, and the mother, although she seems to want to be more responsive to Clarissa's needs, offers not even passive resistance to the torture of her daughter. Richardson's portrayal of the Harlowe family is unambiguous. Anna Howe is allowed straightforwardly negative comments on the Harlowes, Lovelace makes a number of very accurate remarks, and the reader himself, drawing somewhat on these sources and even more on his own observations from Clarissa's letters, adds to the negative sum. But Clarissa, no matter what actions she is forced to take in her desperation, is not allowed to resent her parents or to allow others to comment negatively on them. It is part of Clarissa's virtue that her filial regard for her parents is absolutely unshakable.

Although Clarissa's love and respect for her mother never waver, she realizes that more firmness from her mother might have prevented some of the problems. But Clarissa does not blame her mother for passivity, pitying Mrs. Harlowe instead for the ill effects the family contests have on her soft nature. "Neither nights nor mornings have been my own. My mamma has been very ill and would have no other nurse but me. I have not stirred from her bedside, for she kept her bed, and two nights I had the honour of sharing it with her" (54), she tells Anna. And why was mother so ill? "The contentions of these fierce, these masculine spirits, and the apprehension of mischiefs that may arise from the increasing animosity which all *here* have against Mr Lovelace, and his too-well-known resentful and intrepid character, she cannot bear" (54). Clarissa believes that "would [Mrs. Harlowe] but exert that authority which the superiority of her fine talents gives her, all these family-feuds might perhaps be crushed in their . . . beginnings" (54), but she goes no further than that. Clarissa would like her mother to be able to do more, but she does not blame her for what she is. Ever hopeful that her mother will intercede on her behalf, Clarissa repeatedly is disappointed. Whatever Mr. Harlowe says, mama echoes "Very true" (60).

Richardson's portrait of Mrs. Harlowe is not one-dimensional. Torn between what she perceives as her duty to her husband and her feelings of tenderness and pity for Clarissa, she tries to reconcile her loyalties by attempting to convince Clarissa to accept Solmes. "My mamma was all kindness and condescension" (88), Clarissa tells Anna. Mother and daughter both cry: "And drawing her chair still nearer to mine, she put her arms around my neck and my glowing cheek, wet with my tears, close to her own. Let me talk to you, my child, since silence is your choice; hearken to me, and *be* silent" (89). But the assumption, even from the relatively sympathetic mother, is that Clarissa has no choice but to obey her parents.

> Still on my knees, I had thrown my face cross the chair she had sat in.
> Look up to me, my Clary Harlowe. No sullenness, I hope!
> No, indeed, my ever-to-be-revered mamma—and I arose. I bent my
> knee.
> She raised me. No kneeling to me, but with knees of duty and com-

pliance—Your heart, not your knees, must bend—It is absolutely determined—Prepare yourself therefore to receive your *papa* when he visits you
by and by, as he would wish to receive *you*. But on this one quarter of an
hour depends the peace of my future life, the satisfaction of all the family,
and your own security from a man of violence. And I charge you *besides*, on
my blessing, that you think of being Mrs Solmes. [89]

Mrs. Harlowe is sympathetic to Clarissa's distaste for Solmes, but she
still tries to convince Clarissa to accept him. There is no doubting her
position: "I am tired out with your obstinacy—The most unper-*suade-
able* girl!—You forget that I must separate myself from you, if you will
not comply" (112). Clarissa's parents turn everyone against her, including Mrs. Howe, from whom Clarissa might have sought help. The
matter becomes one of simple obedience for the elder Harlowes. Mrs.
Harlowe complains to Mrs. Norton that Clarissa is "capable of so determined an opposition to her" (177).[22]

   Clarissa, pushed and punished by her parents, forbidden to talk or
even write to them directly, never allows herself to be anything but the
adoring daughter. Both before and after she leaves home, she extravagantly defends and praises her parents.

   There is not a worthier person in England than my mamma. Nor is my
   papa that man you sometimes make him. Excepting in one point, I know
   not any family which lives up more to their duty, than the principals of ours.
   [249]
   I desire that you will not think I stoop too low [in a conciliatory letter to
   her sister]; since there can be no such thing as that, in a child, to parents
   whom she has unhappily offended. [1140]
   What, alas! has not my mother, in particular, suffered by my rashness!
   [1337]

   It is relatively unusual for an eighteenth-century novel to have
more mothers than fathers in residence; in novels where the education
of children is stressed, men generally are depicted as the significant
preceptors, and most eighteenth-centuy novels that center on young
people do deal in some major context with their development.
Richardson, unlike most of his contemporaries, presents two female
parents—and neither of them is particularly admirable. Mrs. Harlowe
is passive and lacks character; Mrs. Howe does nothing to earn our
respect either, with her championing of Hickman, her belief that
Clarissa should marry Lovelace, and her negative summation of the
mother-daughter relationship: "None but parents know the trouble

that children give: they are happiest, I have often thought, who have none. And these women-grown girls, bless my heart! how ungovernable!" (1112).

What of the male parent? Mr. Harlowe simply expects to be obeyed and has trained his son to exact similar obedience.[23] Without softness and without compassion, the father is a tyrant without redeeming features. And it is Clarissa's duty to obey him. Richardson sees Clarissa as virtuous, not stupid, when she wishes to the very last for a reconciliation with her father. Papa is always telling people things "sternly" (58); Clarissa kneels to him and receives only coldness and anger: "My *papa*, with vehemence both of action and voice (my father has, you know, a terrible voice, when he is angry!), told me that I had met with too much indulgence in being allowed to refuse *this* gentleman and the *other* gentleman, and it was now *his* turn to be obeyed" (60). Even near the end, Clarissa's main concern is having her father revoke "the heavy curse [he] had laid upon her" (1101). Belford comments that Clarissa "talked in such a dutiful manner of her parents, as must doubly condemn them . . . for their inhuman treatment of such a daughter" (1101). But that is Belford's comment, not Clarissa's. Toward her father, in fact, Clarissa is even less critical than toward her mother. If she can occasionally wish that her mother were a little different, she cannot bring herself to find any fault with her father. Quite the opposite: any men that she can allow to get near her, the doctor and Mr. Goddard, for example, she regards as fatherly figures—she "looked upon [the doctor] and Mr Goddard, from their kind and tender treatment of her, with a regard next to filial" (109); "I have an excellent physician, Dr H., and as worthy an apothecary, Mr Goddard—Their treatment of me, my dear, is perfectly *paternal*!" (1088).

Clarissa relates to men only in a filial manner.[24] Neither Clarissa nor Anna has any desire to marry, or even to be in the company of men. Words like "beloved" (1455) and "flaming love" (1087) are used for the relationship between them, while all references to suitors are coldly derogatory. And men, unless specifically labeled "paternal," are to be feared and avoided. Both girls have been courted assiduously by seemingly appropriate suitors; Clarissa has turned down each and every comer, while Anna accepted Hickman—she explains at length—only under duress, and then essentially by a sort of accident. Clarissa has been courted not just by Solmes and Lovelace but by a Mr. Symmes, a Mr. Mullins, and a Mr. Wyerley (56). She has rejected these men earlier, and when Lovelace comes courting she essentially considers it none of her business—it is her father's decision whether or not she should accept Lovelace's visits, and she doesn't seem to care one way or the other. It is her brother who "shall never be easy or satisfied till I am married, and finding neither Mr Symmes nor Mr Mullins will be accepted, has proposed Mr Wyerley once more. . . . This I have again rejected, and but yesterday he mentioned one who has applied to him by letter, making high offers. This is Mr Solmes; *rich* Solmes, you know they call him" (56). Clarissa wonders to Anna why she must "be pushed into a state which, although I reverence, I have no wish to enter into?" (67). Anna, as usual, is even more forthright:

> Upon my word, I most heartily despise that sex! I wish they would let our fathers and mothers alone; teasing *them* to tease *us* with their golden promises, and protestations, and settlements, and the rest of their ostentatious nonsense. How charmingly might you and I live together and despise them all!—But to be cajoled, wire-drawn, and ensnared, like silly birds, into a state of bondage or vile subordination: to be courted as princesses for a few weeks, in order to be treated as slaves for the rest of our lives—[133]

Clarissa and Anna discuss marriage and its pitfalls (never its good points) in several lengthy exchanges. Clarissa notes

> *Marry first and love will come after*, was said by one of my dearest friends! But 'tis a shocking assertion! A thousand things may happen to make that state but barely tolerable, where it is entered into with mutual affection: what must it then be, where the husband can have no confidence in the love of his wife, but has reason rather to question it from the preference he *himself* believes she would have given to somebody else, had she been at her own option? What doubt, what jealousies, what want of tenderness, what unfavourable prepossessions will there be in a matrimony thus circumstanced? How will every look, every action, even the most innocent, be liable to misconstruction?—While, on the other hand, an indifference, a carelessness to oblige may take place; and fear *only* can constrain even an *appearance* of what ought to be the real effect of undisguised love? [149]

And then she continues, not surprisingly, that she would just as well not marry at all: "I have offered to engage not to marry at all, if that condition may be accepted" (149) or, again, "I could with great sincerity declare for a single life, which had always been my choice" (166).

The problem, as Clarissa points out, is that marriage is "for life" (179), and no man in Clarissa's or Anna's prospect is someone to whom either girl would want to be tied. In her "entirely whimsical" (210) letter on the subject of men and marriage, having described in detail Solmes, Hickman, and Lovelace, Anna concludes to Clarissa "that all men are monkeys more or less, or else that you and I should have such baboons as these to choose out of is a mortifying thing" (210). Anna's letter is mostly about Hickman, and her discussion of him is cruelly derogatory. She describes Hickman's dress: "in general, he cannot, indeed, be called a sloven, but sometimes he is too gaudy, at other times too plain, to be uniformly elegant" (208). She is not satisfied with his face: "Then I have a quarrel against his face, though in his person, for a well-thriven man, tolerably genteel—not to his features so much neither—for what, as you have often observed, are features in a man!—But Hickman, with strong lines, and big cheek and chin bones, has not the manliness in his aspect, which Lovelace has with the most regular and agreeable features" (208). His mien and character do not please either: "as for honest Hickman, the good man is so *generally* meek, as I imagine, that I know not whether I have any *preference* paid me in his obsequiousness. And then, when I rate him, he seems to be so naturally fitted for rebuke, and so much expects it, that I know not how to disappoint him, whether he just then deserve it, or not" (209). Her contempt for this man she will marry is quite entire. "Hickman is a sort of fiddling, busy . . . *un*-busy man: has a great deal to do and seems to me to dispatch nothing" (208). Clarissa, although she generally dislikes men, does find something good to say for Hickman—as a choice for Anna: "If Mr Hickman has not that assurance which some men have, he has that humanity and gentleness which many want: and which, with the infinite value he has for you, will make him one of the properest husbands in the world for a person of your vivacity and spirit" (234).

Anna, who never shows the smallest interest herself in marrying, "would not that [Clarissa], who [is] so admirably qualified to adorn the matrimonial state, should always be single" (240). Although obviously angered by Lovelace's treatment of Clarissa, Anna nonetheless is convinced that Clarissa should marry him, and in this she shares and echoes Mrs. Howe's opinion. Lovelace's relations try to use Anna as a go-between, and Anna in her turn is convinced that the sincere good will of Lovelace's family will make up for Lovelace's character defects: she tells Clarissa "the wretch [Lovelace] has bound himself to [his family], in the solemnest manner, to wed you in their presence if they can prevail upon you to give him your hand" (1042). Anna sounds not unlike the Harlowes themselves in recounting the inducements proposed for Clarissa to marry Lovelace:

He promises by them to make the best of husbands; and my lord and his two sisters are both to be guarantees that he will be so. Noble settlements, noble presents, they talked of: they say they left Lord M. and his two sisters talking of nothing else but of those presents and settlements, how most to do you honour, the greater in proportion for the indignities you have suffered; and of changing of names by Act of Parliament, preparative to the interest they will all join to make to get the titles to go where the bulk of the estate must go at my lord's death, which they apprehend to be nearer than they wish. [1042]

While Anna notes that "I made a great many objections for you—all, I believe that you could have made yourself, had you been present" (1042-43), she goes on, "I have no doubt to advise you, my dear (and so does my mother), instantly to put yourself into Lady Betty's protection, with a resolution to take the wretch for your husband" (1043). Even more, "You *must* oblige them: the alliance is splendid and honourable" (1043).

Anna waits impatiently for an answer. But Clarissa has been arrested falsely for debt, and the imprisonment cycle plays out, with its attendant intensification of feeling against Lovelace, before Clarissa can respond to Anna. Anna is shocked when she hears about the imprisonment—"what, my dearest creature, have been your sufferings!" (1086)—but she immediately gets back to prodding Clarissa to accept Lovelace. Anna reiterates that

His relations are persons of *so much* honour—They are so *very* earnest to rank you among them—The wretch is so *very* penitent: *every one* of *his* family says he is—*Your own* are so implacable—Your last distress, though the consequence of his former villainy, yet neither brought on by his direction, nor with his knowledge; and so much resented by him—that my mamma is absolutely of opinion that *you should be his*—especially if, yielding to my wishes as in my letter and those of all his friends, you *would* have complied had it not been for this horrid arrest. [1086-87]

(Anna, incidentally, quite rightly assumes that Lovelace is innocent of instigating the arrest; his letter to Belford [Letter 330] clearly expresses his horror at the news.) Clarissa, finally answering Anna, says simply "my dear, I will *not* have that man" (1087). Anna's argument "that marriage is now the only means left to make your future life tolerably easy" (1087) makes no impression on Clarissa, who has chosen for herself another way to escape her plight.

Clarissa, however, to the end of the novel encourages Anna to wed

Hickman. Since Clarissa is clearly saintlike, her viewpoint must be valid. Richardson's paradigm after all is that Hickman—chosen by Anna's mother—is a reasonable husband; Lovelace—disavowed by Clarissa's family—cannot be a good or a moral choice. Clarissa is firm in her advocacy of Hickman. The already fading Clarissa tells Hickman he is her brother (perhaps an unfortunate metaphor in this particular novel) and blesses his union with Anna: "you are my brother, and my friend. . . . And tell [Anna] . . . that in this posture [kneeling down on one knee], you see me, in the last moment of our parting, begging a blessing upon you both, and that you may be the delight and comfort of each other for many, very many, happy years!" (1131). Anna, on the other hand, contemptuously describes Hickman as he accompanies Mrs. Howe, "who had him by his leading-strings—by his sleeve, I should say" (1136).

Most of the discussion of marriage in the last several hundred pages of the novel comes from Anna, and all her comments are negative. Although it is certain at the end of the novel that she indeed will marry Hickman, marriage clearly is not her preference. She explains passionately

> If I lose you, my more than sister, and lose my mamma, I shall distrust my own conduct, and will not marry. And why should I?—Creeping, cringing in courtship:—Oh my dear, these men are a vile race of *reptiles* in *our day*, and mere *bears* in *their own*. See in Lovelace all that was desirable in figure, in birth, and in fortune: but in his heart a devil!—See in Hickman— Indeed, my dear, I cannot tell what anybody can see in Hickman, to be always preaching in his favour. And is it to be expected that I, who could hardly bear control from a mother, should take it from a husband?—from one too, who has neither more wit, nor more understanding, than myself? Yet he to be my instructor?—So he will, I suppose; but more by the insolence of his will than by the merit of his counsel. It is in vain to think of it—I cannot be a wife to any man breathing whom I at present know. [1312]

Belford, who in the last few hundred pages of the novel provides a reflection for all the main characters, is asked rhetorically by Anna, "Do you think I ought not to resolve upon a single life?" And she goes on in amazing detail to attack the concept of marriage—and the worth of the male sex. Anna's arguments, like those quoted above, are surely perceptive but, at the same time, strike the reader as remarkably bitter.

> When I look round upon all the married people of my acquaintance, and see how *they* live, and what *they* bear, who live *best*, I am confirmed in my

dislike to the state. Well do your sex contrive to bring us up fools and idiots in order to make us bear the yoke you lay upon our shoulders; and that we may not despise you from our hearts (as we certainly should if we were brought up as you are) for your ignorance, as much as you often make us do (as it is) for your insolence. . . . Mr Hickman was proposed to me. I refused him again and again. He persisted: my mother his advocate. My mother made my beloved friend his advocate too. I told him my aversion to all men: to him: to matrimony—Still he persisted. I used him with tyranny: led indeed partly by my temper, partly by design; hoping thereby to get rid of him; till the poor man (his character unexceptionally uniform) still persisting, made himself a merit with me by his patience. This brought down my pride . . . and gave me, at one time, an inferiority in my own opinion to him; which lasted just long enough for my friends to prevail upon me to promise him encouragement; and to receive his addresses.

Having so done . . . I found I had gone too far to recede. [1456-57]

So Anna will marry Hickman as it were in accident, and marriage itself is a deadly state for a woman. Richardson's female protagonists are both doomed. From the male chauvinism of Uncle Antony ("He is your brother . . . and a *man*" [157]),[25] to the Harlowes, father and son, from Lovelace to Hickman, Richardson shows little that is admirable in men. Understandably, in the context of the book, it is female friendship that provides sustenance for Clarissa and Anna.

While good male-female relationships and good parent-child relationships are shown to be difficult if not impossible in *Clarissa,* the female friendship of peers is held up as the most successful, and arguably the most intense, of human bonds. Anna and Clarissa are very conscious of the depth and quality of their relationship, and they talk about the fact and ideal of friendship a great deal. While filial piety is celebrated in the abstract—Clarissa wishes she could be a more perfect daughter—female friendship is shown as functioning and supportive. The relationship between Anna and Clarissa is the primary tie in both their lives; toward the end of the novel, as Clarissa slips towards death, Anna laments in terms we normally associate not with girlfriends but with lovers.

The first line of the book makes reference to Anna's concern for "my dearest friend" (39). She gives Clarissa advice freely, reminding her that "a friendship like ours admits of no reserves" (67), and assuring her that "you may trust my impartiality" (67), for "have you not taught me that friendship should never give a bias against justice?" (68). One of the more interesting technical aspects of the novel is that although Clarissa is portrayed as the wiser and more prudent of the two girls, much of her wisdom is reflected in Anna's letters, as here in the lesson about friendship. At the end of the book, when Anna gives us Richardson's ideal of womanhood in her protracted description of Clarissa's daily schedules, this device becomes most active. Anna talks often of her feelings for Clarissa. "I love and admire you" (76), she says; "never was there a heart that more glowed with friendly love" (76). Repeatedly she uses the endearment "child" (128). But her affection does not cloud her perspective—as she often points out to Clarissa. On the matter of filial obedience, for example, she clearly feels that Clarissa goes much too far in her submissiveness:

Your insolent brother, what has *he* to do to control you?—Were it me (I wish it were for one month, and no more), I'd show him the difference. I'd be in my own mansion, pursuing my charming schemes and making all around me happy. I'd set up my own chariot. I'd visit them when they deserved it. But when my brother and sister gave themselves airs, I'd let them know that I was their sister, and not their servant; and if that did not do, I would shut my gates against them; and bid them be company for each other. [129]

And as for Solmes, "What a dreadful thing must even the love of such a husband be!" (129). All Anna's advice-giving brings her to think more about the relationship between Clarissa and herself.

I never wrote to please myself but I pleased you. A very good reason why—we have but one mind between us—only, that sometimes you are a little too grave, methinks; I, no doubt, a little too flippant in your opinion.

This difference in our tempers, however, is probably the reason that we love one another *so* well, that . . . no *third love* can come in between: since each in the other's eye having something amiss, and each loving the other well enough to bear being told of it; and the rather, perhaps, as neither wishes to mend it; this takes off a good deal from that rivalry which might encourage a little, if not a great deal, of that latent spleen which in time might rise into envy, and that into ill-will. So, my dear, if this be the case, let each keep her fault, and much good may do her with it, say I: for there is constitution in both to plead for it: and what a hero or heroine must he or she be, who can conquer a constitutional fault? Let it be *avarice*, as in some I *dare not* name: let it be *gravity*, as in my *best friend:* or let it be *flippancy*, as in—I need not say whom. [131]

These observations lead Anna to think about other relationships. "I most heartily despise that [male] sex!" (133), Anna cries; "[h]ow charmingly might you and I live together and despite them all!" (133).

She closes, "Who indeed, as you say, would marry, that can live single?" (134). This combination of passion for Clarissa and against men is the pattern of the interplay between Anna and Clarissa. Certainly the gentleness between the girls is remarkable. Clarissa answers this long, thoughtful, somewhat teasing letter of Anna's with her usual seriousness.

> You very ingeniously account for the love we bear to one another, from the *difference* in our tempers. I own, I should not have thought of that. There may possibly be something in it: but whether there be, or not, whenever I am cool, and give myself time to reflect, I will love you the better for the correction you give me, be as severe as you will upon me. . . . One of the first conditions of our mutual friendship was that each should say or write to the other whatever was upon her mind, without any offence to be taken; a condition that is indeed an indispensable in all friendship. [135]

The gentleness between the girls becomes undisguised passion toward the end of the book as Clarissa's situation worsens. "You know not how I love her!" (1045), Anna writes to Charlotte Montague.

> She was my earthly saviour, as I may say!—My own soul is not dearer to me than my Clarissa Harlowe!—Nay, she *is* my soul!—for I now have none!—only a miserable one, however!—for she was the joy, the stay, the prop of my life! Never woman loved woman as we love one another! It is impossible to tell you half her excellencies. It was my glory and my pride that I was capable of so fervent a love of so pure and matchless a creature! [1045]

"Never woman loved woman as we love one another"? Even in full awareness of the seriousness of Clarissa's situation, this is inflated rhetoric. Clarissa herself is a bit overwhelmed by Anna's passion: "You oppress me, my dearest Miss Howe, by your flaming, yet steady love" (1087), Clarissa responds at one point, although she soon goes on to speak in much the same way: "Love me still, however. But let it be with a weaning love. I am not what I was when we were *inseparable* lovers" (1088). And then Clarissa deeds Anna to a male partner: "Resolve, my dear, to make a worthy man happy, because a worthy man must make *you* so—And so, my dearest love, for the present adieu!—Adieu, my dearest love!" (1088). A little later, she insists again to her "dear and *only* love" (1117), Anna, that she will not marry Lovelace, "and if not *this, any* man" (1117). Repeatedly in the book, as in these examples, the love expressed by Anna or Clarissa is paired with a statement regarding the necessity, or more often the lack of necessity, for marrying a male. The constant and the good is female love; male/female union is at most a social necessity.[26] Female friendship can extend in some ways to the older generation; although Anna often makes fun of Mrs. Howe's attitudes, she does respect her opinions in many matters, and she often quotes her. Anna especially joins her mother in Mrs. Howe's admiration of Clarissa:

> You are . . . employed in writing. I hope it is in penning down the particulars of your tragical story. And my mother has put me in mind to press you to it, with a view that one day, if it might be published under feigned names, it would be of as much use as honour to the sex. My mother says she cannot help admiring you for the propriety of your resentment in your refusal of the wretch; and she would be extremely glad to have her advice of penning your sad story complied with. And then, she says, your noble conduct throughout your trials and calamities will afford not only a shining example to your sex; but, at the same time (those calamities befalling SUCH a person), a fearful warning to the inconsiderate young creatures of it. [1152]

Anna's admiration for Clarissa is limitless; perhaps the fullest expression of their friendship comes in Anna's long letter to Belford after Clarissa's death explaining to him just what it was that made Clarissa so special. In this letter, Anna details not only Clarissa's philosophy and general lifestyle, but the disposition of virtually each hour of her life. This is the letter that has made the most stalwart admirers of the novel cringe. But those who find mere cause for embarrassment here miss much, for the letter gives the modern reader an incredibly detailed account of how a very, very good eighteenth-century girl should behave. There is nothing in this letter that has not been implicit in Clarissa's character all along. Woman for Richardson is a creature created to look pretty and to spend her days at busy work. Clarissa's "complexion [was] so lovely, and her whole person and manner was so distinguishedly charming, that she could not move without being admired and followed by the eyes of everyone. . . . In her dress she was elegant beyond imitation" (1466). Affability was never "more eminent in any person, man or woman, than in her," and "It has been observed, that what was said of Henry IV of France might be said of her manner of refusing a request; that she generally sent from her presence the person refused nearly as well satisfied as if she had granted it" (1466-67). Her actions and thought were always impec-

cable, and even if she somehow were found to be wrong, even in her
error she was better than those superficially wiser.

> Severe as she always was in her reprehensions of a wilful and studied
> vileness; yet no one accused her judgement, or thought her severe in a
> wrong place: for her charity was so great that she always chose to defend or
> acquit, where the fault was not so flagrant that it became a piece of justice to
> condemn it. . . . [B]eing upbraided by a severe censurer, upon a person's
> proving base, whom she had frequently defended: 'You had more penetra-
> tion, madam, than such a young creature as I can pretend to have. But
> although human depravity may, I doubt, oftener justify the person who
> judges harshly, than them who judge favourably, yet will I not part with my
> charity. [1467]

Clarissa's moral penetration extended to her daily pursuits. Richardson's ideal is defined by the female "accomplishments" and educa-
tional limitations against which women throughout the eighteenth
century bitterly inveighed; such arguments culminate in Mary Wollstonecraft's laments but are expressed by many women, and by men as
well—Robert Bage and Thomas Holcroft, for example. Clarissa could
not understand why females

> are generally so averse as they are to writing; since the pen, next to the
> needle, of all employments is the most proper and best adapted to their
> geniuses; and this as well for improvement as amusement: 'Who sees not,
> would she say, that those women who take delight in writing excel the men
> in all the graces of the familiar style? The gentleness of their minds, the
> delicacy of their sentiments (impoved by the manner of their education) and
> the liveliness of their imaginations, qualify them to a high degree of prefer-
> ence for this employment.' [1467-68]

Writing and sewing—Clarissa considers these the ideal female accomplishments ("if you please," women should spell accurately and not
stop merely "at *sound*" [1468]).

Clarissa of course had an "admirable facility" in that accomplishment of the upwardly mobile young lady, "learning languages" (1468).
In addition to these

> acquirements, she was an excellent ECONOMIST and HOUSEWIFE. And these
> qualifications, you must take notice, she was particularly fond of inculcat-
> ing upon all her reading and writing companions of the sex: for it was a
> maxim with her, "That a woman who neglects the *useful* and the *elegant*,
> which distinguish *her own sex*, for the sake of obtaining the learning which is

supposed more peculiar to the *other*, incurs more *contempt* by what she *foregoes* than she gains *credit* by what she *acquires*.

'Let our sex therefore (she used to say) seek to make themselves mistresses of all that is excellent and not incongruous to their sex in the *other*; but without losing anything commendable in *their own*. ' [1468]

Anna's proof of all these accomplishments is that Clarissa was "the most elegant dairymaid that ever was seen" (1468). These descriptions reflect a severely limited and limiting view of women. Clarissa was wonderful, Anna says, because she lived by the maxim that women must do women's things and not cross over into the territory of men's learning. We should note the familiar eighteenth-century concept that there indeed are separate territories of men's and women's learning, and note as well that Richardson heartily endorses the distinction. Defoe's liberation of the minds of his female characters seems all the more remarkable when we compare his perspective with Richardson's.

The good Clarissa remains within her proper sphere of learning, and teaches all young ladies who come in contact with her the proper precepts:

> no young lady could be in her company half an hour, and not carry away instruction with her, whatever was the topic. Yet all sweetly insinuated; nothing given with the air of prescription; so that while she seemed to ask a question for information-sake, she dropped in the needful instruction, and left the instructed unable to decide whether the thought . . . came primarily from herself, or from the sweet instructress. [1468]

Clarissa is always giving lessons in her delicate way; readers have enough to be embarrassed by in Richardson's smugness long before we get to the hourly accounting of the saintly heroine's day. And indeed Richardson's praise, and his prose, gets worse and worse. Clarissa's needlework is so wonderful, we are told, that one of her relatives wanted to carry it to Italy, "to show the curious of *other* countries . . . for the honour of *his own*, that the cloistered confinement was not necessary to make English women excel in any of those fine arts, which nuns and recluses value themselves upon" (1468-69). Clarissa is musical; she has a lovely voice (required for every heroine). She enjoys being charitable—even in her reading! But charitable reading stops at the sight of moral imperfection: "In all her readings, and in her conversations upon them, she was fonder of finding beauties than blemishes: yet she used to lament that certain writers of the first class, who were capable of exalting virtue and of putting vice out of countenance, too generally employed themselves in works of imagination only, upon subjects merely speculative, disinteresting, and unedifying; from which no good moral or example could be drawn" (1469). After all this, naturally, Anna assumes Belford wants to know how Clarissa could manage so many accomplishments, and she sets before him "the particular distribution of [Clarissa's] time." These are the passages that have elicited so much rueful critical comment; it would be hard indeed to find anything more sanctimonious in English literature. Anna quotes Clarissa—"She used to say, 'It was incredible to think what might be done by rising early, and by long days well filled up' "—and goes on to enumerate precisely the hours of Clarissa's "well filled up" day. Richardson, supposedly showing us a purposeful use of time, actually details a pathetic round of busy work.[27]

She slept only six hours; three hours in the morning served for "closet duties" and "epistolary amusements;" two hours "to domestic management," including taking care of the housekeeper's bills—"for she was a perfect mistress of the four principal rules of arithmetic." Five hours she passed in sewing, drawing, music and so on, three hours to meals, including "conversation" —and if sudden guests or whatever social duty required more time, she "would *borrow*, as she called it, from other distributions." And then there is the one hour "to the neighbouring poor," her benevolence essentially consisting of her good advice: "to a select number of [the poor], and to their children, she used to give brief instructions and good books: and as this happened not every day, and seldom above twice a week, she had two or three hours at a time to bestow in this benevolent employment" (1471). Finally, the last four hours "she called *her fund*, upon which she used to draw to satisfy her other debits: and in this she included visits received and returned, shows, spectacles, etc. which, in a country-life not occurring every day, she used to think a great allowance, no less than *two* artificial days in *six*, for amusements only: and she was wont to say that it was hard if she could not steal time out of such a fund as this for an excursion of even two or three days in a month" (1471). Poor Clarissa: with all this work, she barely can steal a few days a month for fun. The seventh day, "she kept, as it ought to be kept."

Richardson really seems to account this a work week, for Anna remarks that when Clarissa visited the Howes, Clarissa's "account book" notes " 'from *such a day*, to *such a day*, all holidays, at my dear Miss Howe's.' At her return: 'Account resumed *such a day*, ' naming it;

and then she proceeded regularly as before" (1471). Clarissa "reckon[s] with herself" once a week—to the hour: "if within the 144 hours contained in the six days she had made her account even, she noted it accordingly: if otherwise, she carried the debit to the next week's account; as thus: *Debtor to the article of benevolent visits* so many hours" (1471). But, graciously, no one except Clarissa ever knew that her time was being impinged on. She would give of herself to all callers, and only she—Anna suggests—suffered at the upset to her accounting: "But it was always an especial part of her care that, whether visiting or visited, she showed in all companies an entire ease, satisfaction, and cheerfulness, as if she kept no such particular account, and as if she did not make herself answerable to herself for her occasional exceedings" (1471).

This letter is Anna's tribute to her great friend: it shows us a woman whose life has little purpose. Except for her paying of the household accounts, Clarissa's well-ordered days are filled with busy work of all descriptions. Conversation with the neighbors, letters to her friends, a little sewing—these are major aspects of her work. Even her benevolence is empty, consisting of pieties rather than practical aid. I began this chapter by pointing to the extremely limited view of women that Richardson gives us in *Clarissa*; nowhere are those limitations more apparent than in Anna's summation here. Clarissa's job is being virtuous. The point of her regimen is to impart virtue even to such mundane pursuits as conversation with neighbors. The limits on such an existence are inelastic; if Clarissa cannot function within these parameters that she and her parents have set, she cannot function at all. And as I discussed earlier in this chapter, the attitudes and intransigency of her family make it impossible for Clarissa to continue to be the good girl. As she seems to sense from the earliest letters (I wish I had died when everybody loved me), death is her only way to continue virtuous. And so she dies.

Clarissa's death has elicited a great deal of critical comment, much of it centering on the issue of whether she dies by some tragic wasting illness or whether she wills herself to die.[28] Although Clarissa claims not to forward her own death ("I will eat and drink what is sufficient to support nature. A very little, you know, will do for that" [1117-18]), there are enough comments from the doctor and the apothecary to suggest that Clarissa's illness is, if not absolutely self-induced, at least worsened by her own attraction to martyrdom. "You must, in a great measure, be your own doctress. Come, *dear* madam . . . cheer up your spirits. Resolve to do all in your power to be well; and you'll soon grow better" (1082), they tell her over and over again.[29] Lovelace is right when he complains that he cannot understand how a healthy young girl can just sicken and die. But Clarissa herself sees no way out of her difficulties but to die; Richardson's message is that this is a fitting, if tragic, ending to the train of events that began when Clarissa left home.[30] Further, only in dying can she remain noble and virtuous; presumably, to live would be to become ordinary, less than perfect in having to deal with the grubby details of everyday life.

Clarissa joyfully welcomes not just the release of death but all of its advance trappings. She plans her demise exquisitely. I spoke earlier about her will; Clarissa's other preparations are every bit as thorough. She pays the undertaker (1306); she orders her coffin and has it delivered to her room—where she in the meantime uses it as furniture (1316). She decorates the coffin with her own designs (1305-06). Repeatedly she compares her two options, marriage to Lovelace and death, and she clearly prefers death. Lovelace finds it strange that she would rather die than marry (1107); Richardson does not. She explains that she must die, because the rest of her life could only be spent brooding over her fall (1117). The connection between marriage and death, and her clear preference for the latter, is explicit: "As for me, never bride was so ready as I am. My wedding garments are bought—and though not fine or gaudy to the sight, though not adorned with jewels and set off with gold and silver (for I have no beholders' eyes to wish to glitter in), yet will they be the easiest, the *happiest* suit, that ever bridal maiden wore—for they are such as carry with them a security against all those anxieties, pains, and perturbations, which sometimes succeed to the most promising outsettings" (1339). Clarissa has no complaint about her *"Death from grief"* except that it is *"the slowest of deaths"* (1341). Finally, "happy as I am," she blesses everyone at her deathbed and welcomes the "blessed Lord—JESUS!" (1362). She had told Mrs. Norton that she was "upon a better preparation than for an earthly husband" (1121), and she has found him. And so come the readings of the book as Christian allegory, with Clarissa as a most satisfactory saint. But in terms of the earthly woman, Richardson gives us a very narrowly proscribed set of possibilities. As the many linked references to marriage and death suggest, a woman can either marry or die. Anna will do the first; Clarissa, of course, succumbs to the second. The third option, living single, the one they both clearly prefer, is not allowed them.

As we turn to Fielding's images, the world seems to enlarge for women. Fielding's female characters represent a wide spectrum of social classes and character types; they encounter a splendid variety of situations and cope with those situations in all sorts of ways. The range of Fielding's female characters reaches from Mrs. Partridge to Sophia, from Miss Mathews to Amelia. And yet Fielding, like Richardson, can acknowledge only one type of the "good" woman. For him, as for Richardson, the ideal is narrowly defined, and like Richardson's, Fielding's homage is very restrictive of the woman it honors.

# FOUR

# Henry Fielding:
## *Tom Jones* and *Amelia*

Fielding's attitude toward women is inconsistent. On some issues, he is perceptive and generous. When he writes about marriage, for example, he understands fully the potentially disastrous consequences even a socially acceptable marriage can have for the woman; women are portrayed by Fielding as the victims in marriage far more often than men. Fielding's heroines, Sophia Western in *Tom Jones* and Amelia in his last novel, are both obviously dear to his heart, and each is idealized in her way as the most perfect of women. As Martin Battestin says of Amelia, "we had best take her for what she was so plainly meant to be—the finest compliment Fielding could pay to the woman whose memory he cherished."[1]

But Fielding often shows a good deal of hostility to women as well, characterizing them negatively as a sex and dealing in generalizations about the sex that by the eighteenth century had long been clichés, and that in fact go back to classical satire. Each of the mature novels has descriptions of grotesque physical female forms; parallel descriptions of males do not appear. The physical grotesques have behavioral counterparts; women as a sex are often pointed to as dangerous to each other and, still more important, to men. Fielding's ambivalence about women juts sharply from his discussions and often shows itself most obviously in asides to panegyrics on his idealized heroines. Sophia and Amelia are so special, Fieldng explains time and again, precisely because they act differently from other women.

Fielding is entirely comfortable with women only when they stay within traditional limits of discourse and behavior.[2] Thus one of

Sophia's greatest charms, as defined by Allworthy, is that she will not have an opinion in the company of men. Women who move or act beyond traditional limits—women with a fair amount of "learning," for example—make him uneasy. Fielding's descriptions of Amelia racing up the stairs to see her children, or of her cooking Booth's favorite dinner, are wholeheartedly approving; descriptions of women who have some learning and want to show it, from Jenny Jones to Mrs. Atkinson, are always denigrating. Mrs. Allworthy and Sophia's mother, Mrs. Western, are saints like Amelia, good wives all. But women who do not fit the nurturing role for the male are looked on with enormously less approval by Fielding. And into this last group, unfortunately, very often fall the generality of women against which paragons like Sophia and Amelia are to be measured.

All of the women we meet in the early pages of *Tom Jones* are negatively portrayed. The first woman in the book is Mrs. Deborah Wilkins, the servant of Bridget Allworthy. Squire Allworthy summons her to his room the night he discovers the infant Tom Jones. She reacts with "horror" and enormous vehemence against the unknown "Hussy its Mother."[3] She hopes Allworthy will send out a warrant for the miscreant, and, she goes on,

> I should be glad to see her committed to *Bridewel*, and whipt at the Cart's Tail. Indeed such wicked Sluts cannot be too severely punished. . . . [W]hy should your Worship provide for what the Parish is obliged to maintain? For my own Part, if it was an honest Man's Child indeed; but for my own part, it goes against me to touch these misbegotten Wretches, whom I don't look upon as my Fellow Creatures. Faugh, how it stinks! It doth not smell like a Christian. If I might be so bold to give my Advice, I would have it put in a Basket, and sent out and laid at the Church-Warden's Door. It is a good Night, only a little rainy and windy; and if it was well wrapt up, and put in a warm Basket, it is two to one but it lives till it is found in the Morning. [*TJ*, I, 40-41]

Mrs. Wilkins's meanness is underlined for the reader some few pages later when Fielding comments that "it is the Nature of such Persons as Mrs. **Wilkins,** to insult and tyrannize" (*TJ*, I, 47) any one over whom they have power.

The second female we meet is Bridget Allworthy. Her most socially redeeming feature, of course, is that she is Tom's mother. Otherwise, she is an unpleasant and hypocritical woman. We can understand her reluctance to tell the truth to Allworthy at the time the infant Tom appears, but Fielding lets us know that even in other, less immediate situations, she is not always to be trusted: "When her Master was departed, Mrs. **Deborah** stood silent, expecting her Cue from Miss **Bridget**; for as to what had past before her Master, the prudent Housekeeper by no means relied upon it, as she had often known the Sentiments of the Lady in her Brother's Absence to differ greatly from those which she had expressed in his Presence" (*TJ*, I, 45).

The series of negatively characterized women that comes at the beginning of *Tom Jones* is perhaps capped by Fielding's portrait of Mrs. Partridge, a shrewish woman who browbeats her husband unmercifully. Having chosen the servant Jenny Jones because she is unlikely to catch the eye of Mr. Partridge, Mrs. Partridge becomes jealous of her anyway. At dinner one day, Jenny blushes at an exchange with Partridge. "Mrs. **Partridge,** upon this, immediately fell into a Fury, and discharged the Trencher on which she was eating, at the Head of poor **Jenny,** crying out, 'You impudent Whore, do you play Tricks with my Husband before my Face?' and, at the same Instant, rose from her Chair, with a Knife in her Hand" (*TJ*, I, 84); fortunately, Jenny, nearer the door than her mistress, escapes. "[A]s to the poor Husband . . . he sat staring and trembling in his Chair" (*TJ*, I, 84). This scene is hardly violent at all in comparison to when Mrs. Partridge gets the idea that Jenny's rumored babies were in fact fathered by Partridge:

> with . . . Fury did Mrs. **Partridge** fly on the poor Pedagogue. Her Tongue, Teeth, and Hands, fell all upon him at once. His Wig was in an Instant torn from his Head, his Shirt from his Back, and from his Face descended five Streams of Blood, denoting the Number of Claws with which Nature had unhappily armed the Enemy.
>
> Mr. **Partridge** acted for some Time on the defensive only . . . but as he found that his Antagonist abated nothing of her Rage, he thought he might, at least, endeavour to disarm her, or rather to confine her Arms; in doing which, her Cap fell off in the Struggle, and her Hair being too short to reach her Shoulders, erected itself on her Head; her Stays likewise, which were laced through one single Hole at the Bottom, burst open, and her Breasts, which were much more redundant than her Hair, hung down below her Middle; her Face was likewise marked with the Blood of her Husband; her Teeth gnashed with Rage; and Fire, such as sparkles from a Smith's Forge, darted from her Eyes. So that, altogether, this Amazonian Heroine might have been an Object of Terror to a much bolder Man than Mr. **Partridge.** [*TJ*, I, 89]

Mrs. Partridge is the Amazonian nightmare[4]—she is huge and wild and, of course, out of control. She tears the flesh of poor Partridge with her "claws," while her hair stands on end and her enormous breasts hang "down below her middle." Having done her worst, Mrs. Partridge "dissolv[es] in tears," and falls into a fit. The neighborhood seems to be peopled with many Mrs. Partridges, for when Partridge calls for the neighbors to help his wife, the neighbors turn on Partridge—the very blood which Mrs. Partridge had drawn from her husband is pointed to as proof that he had brutalized her. The female neighbors, of course, immediately join in the wish that the blood in question had come "from his Heart, instead of his Face;" further, they promise that if their husbands should "lift their Hands against them, they would have their Heart's Bloods out of their Bodies" (*TJ*, I, 90).

The physical ugliness of Mrs. Partridge is more than equaled in the description of Blear-Eyed Moll in *Amelia*, and finds its echoes in female portraits in *Joseph Andrews* as well. Blear-Eyed Moll is the first woman in *Amelia* that Fielding talks about in detail. The description goes on for a full page, and is remarkable for its hideousness:

> The first Person who accosted [Booth] was called *Blear-Eyed Moll*; a Woman of no very comely Appearance. Her eye (for she had but one) whence she derived her Nick-name was such, as that Nick-name bespoke; besides which it had two remarkable Qualities; for first, as if Nature had been careful to provide for her own Defect, it constantly looked towards her blind Side; and secondly, the Ball consisted almost entirely of white, or rather yellow, with a little grey Spot in the Corner, so small that it was scarce discernible. Nose she had none; for *Venus*, envious perhaps at her former Charms, had carried off the gristly Part; and some earthly Damsel, perhaps from the same Envy, had levelled the Bone with the rest of her Face: Indeed it was far beneath the Bones of her Cheeks, which rose proportionally higher than is usual. About half a dozen ebeny Teeth fortified that large and long Canal, which Nature had cut from Ear to Ear, at the Bottom of which was a Chin, preposterously short, Nature having turned up the Bottom, instead of suffering it to grow to its due Length.
>
> Her Body was well adapted to her Face; she measured full as much round the middle as from Head to Foot; for besides the extreme Breadth of her Back, her vast Breasts had long since forsaken their native Home, and had settled themselves a little below the Girdle.
>
> I wish certain Actresses on the Stage, when they are to perform Characters of no amiable Cast, would study to dress themselves with the Propriety, with which *Blear-Eyed Moll* was now arrayed. For the Sake of our squeamish Reader, we shall not descend to Particulars. Let it suffice to say,

nothing more ragged, or more dirty, was ever emptied out of the Round-house at St. *Giles's*. [*A*, 27-28]

There is no other description so long, nor even remotely so grotesque, in all the list of people Booth meets as he explores the prison.[5] The more usual description in these scenes is that of Robinson, "This Person was not himself of the most inviting Aspect. He was long visaged, and pale, with a red Beard of above a Fortnight's Growth. He was attired in a brownish black Coat, which would have shewed more Holes than it did, had not the Linen which appeared through it, been entirely of the same Colour with the Cloth" (*A*, 29), or the old soldier: "This was a Wretch almost naked, and who bore in his Countenance, joined to an Appearance of Honesty, the Marks of Poverty, Hunger, and Disease. He had, moreover, a wooden Leg, and two or three Scars on his Forehead" (*A*, 35).

For images of ugliness similar to the portraits of Mrs. Partridge and Blear-Eyed Moll we can go back to *Joseph Andrews*. Mrs. Slipslop is described as

a Maiden Gentlewoman of about Forty-five Years of Age, who having made a small slip in her Youth had continued a good Maid ever since. She was not at this time remarkably handsome; being very short, and rather too corpulent in Body, and somewhat red, with the Addition of Pimples in the Face. Her Nose was likewise rather too large, and her Eyes too little; nor did she resemble a Cow so much in her Breath, as in two brown Globes which she carried before her; one of her Legs was also a little shorter than the other, which occasioned her to limp as she walked.[6]

Similarly, Fielding tells us of Mrs. Tow-wouse that

Nature had taken such Pains in her Countenance, that *Hogarth* himself never gave more Expression to a Picture.

Her Person was short, thin, and crooked. Her Forehead projected in the middle, and thence descended in a Declivity to the Top of her Nose, which was sharp and red, and would have hung over her Lips, had not Nature turned up the end of it. Her Lips were two Bits of Skin, which, whenever she spoke, she drew together in a Purse. Her Chin was peeked, and at the upper end of that Skin, which composed her Cheeks, stood two Bones, that almost hid a Pair of small red Eyes. Add to this, a Voice most wonderfully adapted to the Sentiments it was to convey, being both loud and hoarse. [*JA*, 61-62]

All of these portraits emphasize specifically female ugliness; each of the first three, one in each novel, makes reference to hideously long and deformed breasts; the portrait of Mrs. Tow-wouse is that of a witch.

The nightmare that these women in their physical description present is repeated throughout the novels in the series of contextless negative remarks about women as a sex. Women in these remarks are always described as mean, catty, ungenerous, and destructive. These attacks are different from Fielding's negative remarks about male characters, which attack individual human beings, their faults not tied specifically to their sex (just as physical descriptions of men make no allusion to their specifically male organs); women are most often attacked as women. Within this context it becomes easier to see, if not to account for, the rather large number of gratuitous negative female stereotypes Fielding presents; in *Tom Jones* alone there are perhaps a dozen fairly obvious ones in the shape of assorted asides and remarks. Quite often, the attack is clothed in the garb of a compliment to one particular woman who is unlike the others. Thus, early in *Tom Jones* we are told that

> Women who, like Mrs. **Western,** know the World, and have applied themselves to Philosophy and Politics, would have immediately availed themselves of the present Disposition of Mr. **Western's** Mind; by throwing in a few artful Compliments to his Understanding at the Expence of his absent Adversary; but poor **Sophia** was all Simplicity. By which Word we do not intend to insinuate to the Reader, that she was silly, which is generally understood as a synonimous Term with simple: For she was indeed a most sensible Girl, and her Understanding was of the first Rate; but she wanted all that useful Art which Females convert to so many good Purposes in Life, and which, as it rather arises from the Heart, than from the Head, is often the Property of the silliest of Women. [*TJ*, I, 337-38]

This putative compliment to Sophia is barbed against women at a number of points. Sophia, who unlike the Learned Lady is a good female, is not too simple to play up to the unsuspecting male caught in an off-guard moment (indeed, she has a first-rate understanding), but she would not. Why not? Sophia does not have all that "useful art" — falseness—that "Females convert to so many good Purposes in Life." This "art" is natural to such females.

Similarly, in the scene in which Mrs. Waters is awakened in the inn by the sound of Tom and Mr. Fitzpatrick fighting in her bedroom, Mrs.

Waters begins "to scream in the most violent Manner, crying out
Murder! Robbery! and more frequently Rape! which last, some, perhaps, may wonder she should mention, who do not consider that
these Words of Exclamation are used by Ladies in a Fright, as Fa, la, la,
ra, da, &c. are in Music, only as the Vehicles of Sound, and without
any fixed Ideas" (*TJ*, II, 530). "Ladies," then, are to be seen as a group,
and the group is at best ridiculous. Thoughtlessly women cry rape at
any occasion; their cries are no more meaningful than nonsense sylla-
bles used to hum a tune. Later in the same scene Fielding brings a
broader and more serious accusation against women: they have the
appearance of virtue but are not necessarily virtuous. Tom comes to
apologize to Mrs. Waters for having appeared before her in his night-
shirt.

> The Reader may inform himself of her Answer, and, indeed, of her whole
> Behaviour to the End of the Scene, by considering the Situation which she
> affected, it being that of a modest Lady, who was awakened out of her Sleep
> by three strange Men in her Chamber. This was the Part which she under-
> took to perform; and, indeed, she executed it so well, that none of our
> Theatrical Actresses could exceed her, in any of their Performances, either
> on or off the Stage.
>
> And hence, I think, we may very fairly draw an Argument, to prove
> how extremely natural Virtue is to the Fair Sex: For tho' there is not,
> perhaps, one in ten thousand who is capable of making a good Actress; and
> even among these we rarely see two who are equally able to personate the
> same Character; yet this of Virtue they can all admirably well put on; and as
> well those Individuals who have it not, as those who possess it, can all act it
> to the utmost Degree of Perfection. [*TJ*, II, 532]

This pattern persists throughout the book. When Fielding gives
Sophia credit for bravery, he also takes several shots at "Ladies," who
manipulate and frighten and even murder, not to mention drive men
to suicide. All this from a compliment to his heroine:

> Notwithstanding the many pretty Arts, which Ladies sometimes practise,
> to display their Fears on every little Occasion, (almost as many as the other
> Sex uses to conceal theirs) certainly there is a Degree of Courage, which not
> only becomes a Woman, but is often necessary to enable her to discharge
> her Duty. It is, indeed, the Idea of Fierceness, and not of Bravery, which
> destroys the Female Character: For who can read the Story of the justly
> celebrated **Arria,** without conceiving as high an Opinion of her Gentleness
> and Tenderness, as of her Fortitude? At the same Time, perhaps, many a

Woman who shreiks at a Mouse, or a Rat, may be capable of poisoning a Husband; or, what is worse, of driving him to poison himself. [*TJ*, II, 559]

Ladies "display" their fears—Fielding implies that women are merely pretending to be fearful—but while he can fault them for being fearful, he can also fault them for too much courage. There is indeed some degree of courage in a woman that is not only allowable but perhaps even necessary if she is to do her duty. But we have to be very careful to keep this degree in mind, and to stay safely away from the threatening Amazon: "it is the Idea of Fierceness, and not of Bravery, which destroys the Female Character." Where has the idea of fierceness come from in this passage? Fielding was talking about Sophia; surely no one could think of her as fierce. The idea comes from an underlying stereotype of the Amazon: "Female character" is "destroy[ed]" by showing a bravery that is threatening. And women are threatening, even sinister, it seems, even the ones who seem most stereotypically timid. Women are nasty and hateful in whole categories of behavior, especially to each other. Fielding tells his readers

> to look carefully into human Nature, Page almost the last, and there he will find, in scarce legible Characters, that Women, notwithstanding the pre-posterous Behaviour of Mothers, Aunts, &c. in matrimonial Matters, do in Reality think it so great a Misfortune to have their Inclinations in Love thwarted, that they imagine they ought never to carry Enmity higher than upon these Disappointments; again he will find it written much about the same Place, that a Woman who hath once been pleased with the Possession of a Man, will go above half way to the Devil, to prevent any other Woman from enjoying the same. [*TJ*, II, 866]

Women are vain: "There are some fine Women (for I dare not here speak in too general Terms) with whom Self is so predominant, that they never detach it from any Subject; and as Vanity is with them a ruling Principle, they are apt to lay hold of whatever Praise they meet with; and, though the Property of others, convey it to their own Use" (*TJ*, II, 869); women are catty: Sophia's extreme unhappiness is described as such that "a good-natured Woman would hardly wish more Uneasiness to a Rival, than what she must at present be supposed to feel" (*TJ*, II, 875). And of course, women are not loyal. While Tom's servant Partridge has stayed with him through all his adventures, Lady Bellaston has "ingratiated herself" into the favor of Sophia's Honour and "the violent Affection which the good Waiting-woman had formerly borne to **Sophia,** was entirely obliterated by that great Attachment which she had to her new Mistress" (*TJ*, II, 904).[7]

Similar views of women, again including remarks that very often have little contextual point, are woven throughout *Amelia*. Early in the novel, as Miss Mathews begins to recount to Booth the story of how she came to be in the prison, Fielding interrupts her account to volunteer "a Word or two to the Critics" (*A*, 44) about the kind of language Miss Mathews uses: "Sentiments," he tells the reader, "becoming the Lips of a *Dalila, Jezebel, Medea, Semiramus, Parysatis, Tanaquil, Livilla, Messalina, Agrippina, Brunichilde, Elfrida,* Lady *Macbeth, Joan* of *Naples, Christina* of *Sweden, Katharine Hays, Sarah Malcolm, Con. Philips,* or any other Heroine of the tender Sex, which History sacred or prophane, antient or modern, false or true, hath recorded" (*A*, 44-45). Fielding's only purpose in providing such a list can be to suggest that perfidy like Miss Mathews's is a female tradition of long standing.[8]

Negative remarks about women come in Fielding's own voice, as in this passage, or are made by the characters themselves; whether the speaker is a trustworthy witness, like Booth or Amelia, or a bad character, like Miss Mathews, the remark is, so to speak, on the record. Thus when Miss Mathews acquaints Booth with the history of her infatuation with Hebbers, she recounts how he pretended to give his attention to Mrs. Cary, a visiting widow, instead of to her. He could act this part because " 'this faithless Woman [was not] wanting in her Part of the Deceit. She carried herself to me all the while with a Shew of Affection, and pretended to have the utmost Friendship for me. But such are the Friendships of Women' " (*A*, 52). Most women are cruel to each other. Miss Mathews, deceived by Hebbers into living with him as his mistress because she believes he is already married, learns after a year of their cohabitation that he has in fact just married his old friend, the widow Cary. Miss Mathews tells Booth, " 'I know not what Answer I made . . . I presently fell dead on the Floor, and it was with great Difficulty I was brought back to Life by the poor Girl [her landlady's daughter]; for neither the Mother, nor the Maid of the House, would lend me any Assistance, both seeming to regard me rather as a Monster than a Woman' " (*A*, 59).

Miss Mathews, it might be argued, is not herself a very reliable witness. But Booth, recounting Amelia's experience after the accident to her nose, makes precisely the same points about the falsity of female friendship and the cruelty of women. The most awful part of Amelia's ordeal after her mishap is not the undergoing of " 'the most painful and dreadful Operations of Surgery' " nor even " 'the Loss of exquisite

Beauty.' " The " 'Circumstance which outweighed all the other Ingre-dients . . . was the cruel Insults [Amelia] received from some of her most intimate Acquaintance, several of whom, after many Distortions and Grimaces, have turned their Heads aside, unable to support their secret Triumph, and burst into a loud Laugh in her hearing' " (A, 67). Booth describes being

> 'one Day in Company with several young Ladies, or rather young Devils, where poor *Amelia's* Accident was the Subject of much Mirth and Pleasan-try. One of these said, *She hoped Miss would not hold her Head so high for the future.* Another answered, *I don't know, Madam, what she may do with her Head, but I am convinced she will never more turn up her Nose at her Betters.* Another cry'd, *What a very proper Match might now be made between* Amelia *and a certain Captain,* who had unfortunately received an Injury in the same Part, though from no shameful Cause. Many other Sarcasms were thrown out, very unworthy to be repeated. I was hurt with perceiving so much Malice in human Shape.' [A, 67-68]

As in many of the passages I noted in *Tom Jones*, the malice portrayed here is specifically and especially female. Fielding reverts to the same theme once more in the context of Booth's courtship of Amelia, when Amelia herself recounts the scene between her best friend and herself at Amelia's supposed death bed: " 'Indeed when I reflect how much I loved the Woman who hath treated me so cruelly, I own it gives me Pain—When I lay, as I then imagined, and as all about me believed, on my Death-bed, in all the Agonies of Pain and Misery, to become the Object of Laughter to my dearest Friend.—O Mr. *Booth,* it is a cruel Re-flection!' " (A, 72). The cruel reflections can come from all sorts of wit-nesses, but the images of women are consonant. And as in *Tom Jones,* purely gratuitous negative characterizations of woman underscore the relatively more integrated remarks. Thus when Miss Mathews acci-dentally meets Amelia some time after her seduction of Booth, Miss Mathews "expected from [Amelia] some of those Insults, of which virtuous Women are generally so liberal to a frail Sister; but she was mistaken, Amelia was not one, *Who thought the Nation ne'er would thrive, Till all the Whores were burnt alive.* Her Virtue could support itself with its own intrinsic Worth, without borrowing any Assistance from the Vices of other Women; and she considered their natural Infirmities as the Objects of Pity, not of Contempt or Abhorrence" (A, 159-60). Amelia's virtue is not in question in this situation; the passage serves instead to bring in a negative generalization about good women:

"virtuous Women" are mean to their less virtuous sisters. Fielding turns a positive comment about a specific woman into a negative point about the generality of women. Here it seems that a woman is either meanly virtuous or fallen—or she is a rare exception to this rule, like Amelia. Interesting, too, is Fielding's characterization of women of vice as having "natural infirmities."

One of these natural infirmities for Fielding seems to be a woman's response to a husband who, without notice, has stayed out all night. Amelia waits vainly for Booth to come home during one of those long evenings that he spends gambling. Fielding describes the scene in long and sympathetic detail—the supper cooked but not shared, the passing hours, and Amelia's going to bed at midnight, "leaving the Maid to sit up for her Master. She would indeed have much more willingly sat up herself; but the Delicacy of her own Mind assured her that *Booth* would not thank her for the Compliment. This is indeed a Method which some Wives take of upbraiding their Husbands for staying abroad till too late an Hour, and of engaging them, thro' Tenderness and Good-nature, never to enjoy the Company of their Friends too long, when they must do this at the Expence of their Wives Rest" (*A*, 434). Typically, the complaint is lodged in terms of what "some Wives" do to their men. In the context of this scene, where all the wrong is so clearly on Booth's side, the insertion of the backhanded complaint against women has no inherent place. The doubleness of Fielding's view of women is very apparent in this scene, where despite the fact that his sympathy is very clearly with Amelia, he nonetheless makes this remark about "some Wives." Many of his misogynistic comments are about wives, and imply that in many marriages the husband's life is made miserable indeed by the horror of a nagging or shrewish mate.

References to the stereotypical situation of the unhappy husband almost seem to be like figures of speech for Fielding, unconsidered formulations that can arise in any context: in the preface that he contributed to his sister Sarah's *David Simple,* talking about the literary works of dubious merit that have been ascribed to him and which he disclaims, Fielding says, "There is not, I believe, (and it is bold to affirm) a single **Free Britain** in this Kingdom, who hates his Wife more heartily than I detest the Muses."[9] Many of Fielding's comments about women reflect this kind of clichéd reaction. The remarks about women as a sex, as opposed to what we see in his more developed characterizations, give us Fielding's most misogynistic formulations; the remarks are so strong precisely because they are untouched by the qualifications that define more developed characterizations: evil in a particular character can be seen as part of that character, whereas contextless remarks point to failings in the whole sex of women. This perhaps accounts for the fact that even the most evil of his developed female characters rarely approaches the nastiness of the images in the general remarks on women as a sex.

Fielding is relatively kind, for example, to sexually promiscuous women, making a distinction between sexual permissiveness and evil, between such characters as Molly Seagrim and Mrs. Waters on one hand and Lady Bellaston and Miss Mathews on the other. It is clear, for example, that Nancy, Mrs. Miller's daughter, is a "good" girl even though she had sex with Nightingale. But truly virtuous women, Sophia and Amelia, are sexually virtuous first of all, and relatively kind does not imply entirely approving, for even the good fun with a character like Molly is qualified by numerous complaints.

Molly Seagrim and her family begin the series of "loose women" Fielding gives us in *Tom Jones*. Molly's beauty and mind are masculine; not that she is not a fine girl, Fielding assures us—"Now though **Molly** was, as we have said, generally thought a very fine Girl, and in reality she was so, yet her Beauty was not of the most amiable Kind. It had indeed very little of Feminine in it, and would have become a Man at least as well as a Woman; for, to say the Truth, Youth and florid Health had a very considerable Share in the Composition" (*TJ*, I, 174). Fielding takes away from Molly the pretension to beauty, ascribing her attractiveness simply to youth and good health. And his remark about the masculine nature of her looks prepares us for the more serious indictment: not only does she look masculine, she acts in a masculine fashion. For Molly takes upon herself the male prerogative: she does the seducing.

> Nor was her Mind more effeminate than her Person. As this was tall and robust, so was that bold and forward. So little had she of Modesty, that **Jones** had more Regard for her Virtue than she herself. And as most probably she liked **Tom** as well as he liked her; so when she perceived his Backwardness, she herself grew proportionably forward; and when she saw he had entirely deserted the House, she found Means of throwing herself in his Way, and behaved in such a Manner, that the Youth must have had very much, or very little of the Heroe, if her Endeavours had proved unsuccessful. In a Word, she soon triumphed over all the virtuous Resolutions of **Jones**: For though she behaved at last with all decent Reluctance, yet I rather chuse to attribute the Triumph to her: Since, in Fact, it was her Design which succeeded.
>
> In the Conduct of this Matter, I say, **Molly** so well played her Part, that

**Jones** attributed the Conquest entirely to himself, and considered the young Woman as one who had yielded to the violent Attacks of his Passion. [*TJ*, I, 175]

In addition to seducing Tom, Molly leaves him convinced that she had been the one seduced. Later we find out that she has had a number of lovers, among whom Tom is not the first nor even the latest. Eventually, we find Square in her bedchamber. Since Molly was not in fact seduced, Tom's morality is not compromised. Similarly, Tom's supposed impregnation of Molly carries little onus for him; we learn that Molly has had so many lovers, and some within the relevant period, that it is impossible to determine who had fathered her child. Tom, who seems culpable and careless in the Molly episode, is exonerated of responsibility because of the kind of girl Molly turns out to be. While Molly is seen as rather thoroughly corrupt, Tom is seen as only a little thoughtless, and, in fact, quite admirable in his care for her. Tom's adventure with Molly shows him only in a good light: he is virtuous because he thinks about the ruin to which he would condemn Molly if he were to leave her. The fact that he does so soon think about leaving her is not commented on, and certainly not condemned. "The Ruin, therefore, of the poor Girl must, he foresaw, unavoidably attend his deserting her; and this Thought stung him to the Soul" (*TJ*, I, 222). Tom's own humanity, Fielding tells us, prevents Tom from dropping her: "His own good Heart pleaded her Cause" (*TJ*, I, 222). Fielding portrays Tom, who at this point not only considers himself the father of Molly's baby but the original seducer of Molly as well, as an especially fine person because of the conflict he feels between what he thinks he owes Molly and his attraction to Sophia. But Tom only momentarily is torn; he soon gives in to the blandishments of Sophia's muff.

Fielding lets his hero off the hook by letting us know that Molly really is not worthy of any sympathy. When Tom goes to her to say that he can't marry her, she bursts into "a Flood of Tears" (*TJ*, I, 228) and proceeds to a series of accusations that form the stock speech of the seduced and abandoned woman. Tom is like all other men, she tells him; men have their "wicked Wills" (*TJ*, I, 228) of women and then forsake them. He promised that this would not happen. How can he suggest that she might find happiness with another man—sometime during this speech the rug hiding Square gives way, and Tom and the reader discover the philosopher in a most unphilosophical position.

The irony here is that Molly's legitimate accusations thus become the hypocritical ranting of a lying and unfaithful woman; when we discover that Tom and Square are but two in a list of Molly's lovers, she seems very close to a whore. Tom is not to be faulted for being willing to abandon Molly but, on the contrary, is to be congratulated both for his decency and for his lucky escape. And Molly, she of the masculine looks and masculine mind, is to be thought very little of indeed. She transfers all her supposed affection for Tom to Square; soon we learn that she loves one Will Barnes and in all probability he has fathered her child.

But in case Molly's behavior is not enough of an indictment of woman, in the course of recounting these happenings between Molly and Tom, Fielding includes three other, separate examples of less than moral women. While Tom is engaged in his soul-searching about the degradation to which he would condemn Molly if he were to abandon her, part of his consideration is the fury of other women to which she would be subjected: "for he well knew the Hatred which all her Neighbours, and even her own Sisters, bore her, and how ready they would all be to tear her to Pieces." The passage goes on, "Indeed he had exposed her to more Envy than Shame, or rather to the latter by Means of the former: For many Women abused her for being a Whore, while they envied her her Lover and her Finery, and would have been themselves glad to have purchased these at the same Rate" (*TJ*, I, 222). Molly is not to be anyone's model: Fielding sees her not as a free spirit like Tom, but as a conniving, manipulative woman of loose morals. To conclude, then, that many women would act as she does if they could get the same "rewards," while they hypocritically condemn Molly for being Tom's lover, is a very negative judgment. And the individual women Fielding discusses here in addition to Molly reinforce this negative perspective. Molly's mother is quite happy to share in her daughter's earnings, and Molly's sister Betty is so vicious that she exposes Molly's infidelity to Tom just to satisfy her "implacable Hatred" (*TJ*, I, 235) of her sister. Molly herself is described as "yet but a Novice in her Business" (*TJ*, I, 232)—"novice" implying that she will go on in her development and has not yet "that Perfection of Assurance which helps off a Town Lady in any Extremity; and either prompts her with an Excuse, or else inspires her to brazen out the Matter with her Husband; who from Love of Quiet, or out of Fear of his Reputation . . . is glad to shut his Eyes, and contented to put his Horns in his Pocket" (*TJ*, I, 232).

Molly is one of a line of women, in the country and in the town, who brazenly cuckold their men. Lady Bellaston, later in the book, is much worse than Molly. She uses Tom as a plaything with no regard whatever to affection or sentiment. Lady Bellaston calculates only her pleasure, and that pleasure extends not only to sexual fun but to the malicious manufacturing of problems between Tom and Sophia. In contrast to the good women in the book, Lady Bellaston hates the very idea of marriage, talking of "that monstrous Animal a Husband and Wife" (*TJ*, II, 820). She is so vehemently against marriage that Nightingale offers Tom a foolproof way to escape his involvement with her: Tom must offer to marry her. Lady Bellaston, horrified by Tom's proposal, cuts off all further meetings: "I see you are a Villain; and I despise you from my Soul. If you come here, I shall not be at Home" (*TJ*, II, 821). Mrs. Waters, the other of Tom's more mature lovers, is quite unlike Lady Bellaston. Lady Bellaston uses people, whereas Mrs. Waters good-humoredly and rather generously loves them. From her early encounter with Tom, when she deliberately leaves her breasts uncovered, to the marvelous meal they share when she makes Tom even more aware of her desires, Mrs. Waters's sensuality is always full of life and lust—it is unlike the corrupt, manipulative sexuality of Lady Bellaston. Mrs. Waters is a more positive figure than either Molly or Lady Bellaston. She does not dishonestly try to use Tom, as both Molly and Lady Bellaston do. It is between Tom and Mrs. Waters, rather than Tom and either of these other two women, that we see a purely and delightedly sexual relationship. There are two points to be made here. One is that Fielding finds sensuality attractive and positive. The other, somewhat less obvious, I think, is that Fielding shows us quite a lot of female use of sexuality for control of the male. After Nightingale tells Tom about the long list of his predecessors, and about their place in Lady Bellaston's life, Tom "look[s] on all the Favours he had received, rather as Wages than Benefits, which depreciated not only her, but himself too in his own Conceit" (*TJ*, II, 819).

Another woman who uses sex to manipulate men is Miss Mathews in *Amelia*, and Booth's final feeling about her is close to Tom's about Lady Bellaston. Like Lady Bellaston, Miss Mathews has no redeeming or mitigating features, and, like her again, Miss Mathews does not respect the institution of marriage. It is not so much her sexual promiscuity as her willingness to spoil the Booth marriage that marks her as evil. Miss Mathews seduces Booth, and most of the fault is on her side; Booth, through it all, is constant in all but deed to his Amelia. Fielding "desires" that the reader

> will be pleased to weigh attentively the several unlucky Circumstances which concurred so critically, that Fortune seemed to have used her utmost

Endeavours to ensnare poor *Booth's* Constancy. Let the Reader set before his Eyes a fine young Woman, in a manner a first Love, conferring Obligations, and using every Art to soften, to allure, to win, and to enflame; let him consider the Time and Place; let him remember that Mr. *Booth* was a young Fellow, in the highest Vigour of Life; and lastly, let him add one single Circumstance, that the Parties were alone together; and then if he will not acquit the Defendant, he must be convicted; for I have nothing more to say in his Defence. . . . A Whole Week did our Lady and Gentleman live in this criminal Conversation, in which the Happiness of the former was much more perfect than that of the latter; for tho' the Charms of Miss *Mathews,* and her excessive Endearments, sometimes lulled every Thought in the sweet Lethargy of Pleasure; yet in the Intervals of his Fits, his Virtue alarmed and roused him, and brought the Image of poor injured *Amelia* to haunt and torment him. [*A,* 154-55]

Booth, like Tom, is seduced and, being seduced, suffers bouts of conscience even amidst the pleasures of the affair. Miss Mathews, like Molly and Lady Bellaston with Tom, uses her powers of seduction to "ensnare" her prey, and, again like the bad seductresses in *Tom Jones,* Miss Mathews feels no qualms of conscience. In *Tom Jones* Fielding's ironic tone undercuts the seriousness of the charge—Tom is not going to be hurt by either Molly or Lady Bellaston. But there is much less irony in this description of Booth's fall into the affair with Miss Mathews, where so much is at stake. Miss Mathews's seduction of Booth matters because he is a married man.

All the negative remarks about women notwithstanding, Fielding believes earnestly in the institution of marriage. I began by saying that Fielding's attitudes toward women are inconsistent: he can be extremely negative in remarks about women, and he can also be quite sensitive in his perceptions of women in personal and societal relationships. When he talks about marriage itself, in *Tom Jones* and in *Amelia,* Fielding presents the case for a warm, loving, genuinely shared relationship between the partners—the case for what Lawrence Stone terms the companionate marriage. Believing in this model, Fielding emphasizes all the necessary aspects of such a marriage: choice of a compatible mate by the man and woman involved, mutual respect in the relationship, and the unselfconscious show of caring and softness by the man as well as the woman. Fielding's positive female characters are almost always respectable women of essentially (or potentially) domestic nature.

*Tom Jones,* which is largely plotted around the courtship of Tom and Sophia, talks a great deal about how matchmaking should be done and about potential outcomes of various paradigms. Fielding recognizes the importance of the marital choice, and gives a great deal of attention, in what is after all a comic novel, to serious discussion of the need for the decision to marry to be the mutual choice of the couple involved. Because much of this discussion is worked into the actual plotting of the novel—Squire Western's mistaken choice of Blifil for Sophia sets off much of the journey and chase machinery—we may not notice how thoroughly Fielding examines the subject of choice in the marriage decision and how carefully he analyzes the results of various models of marriage. We think of *Amelia* as Fielding's novel about marriage, but even in *Tom Jones* he looks very closely, and sometimes quite perceptively, at what marriage entails.

Fielding defines a good marriage in terms of the domestic happiness of the couple, and that happiness is further defined in terms of the companionship between the spouses. In *Tom Jones* the best and worst possibilities of marriage are quickly sketched in the descriptions of the marriages of the older generation. The Allworthy marriage was happy. Mrs. Allworthy was "a very worthy and beautiful Woman, of whom [her husband] had been extremely fond" (*TJ*, I, 35). Except that she had had three children, and that she had died five years before the period of the novel, we know no more about her; she is defined simply by her characterization as a good wife. Mrs. Western, Sophia's mother, also is a good woman. Sophia's mother, like Mrs. Allworthy, is defined by her role in the household, and her marriage presents a clear contrast to Mrs. Allworthy's. Without the luck to be married to a man like Allworthy, Mrs. Western leads a miserable life:

> The Squire, to whom that poor Woman had been a faithful upper Servant all the Time of their Marriage, had returned that Behaviour, by making what the World calls a good Husband. He very seldom swore at her (perhaps not above once a Week) and never beat her: She had not the least Occasion for Jealousy, and was perfect Mistress of her Time: for she was never interrupted by her Husband, who was engaged all the Morning in his Field Exercises, and all the Evening with Bottle Companions. She scarce indeed ever saw him but at Meals; where she had the Pleasure of carving those Dishes which she had before attended at the Dressing. From these Meals she retired about five Minutes after the other Servants, having only stayed to drink the King over the Water. Such were, it seems, Mr. **Western's** orders: For it was a Maxim with him, that Women should come in with the first Dish, and go out after the first Glass. [*TJ*, I, 338]

Fielding goes on to note that she was "rather a good Servant than a good Wife" (*TJ*, I, 339), although she sometimes did meddle in things that did not concern her, such as when she attempted to interfere in the "violent Drinking of her Husband" (*TJ*, I, 339). Her misfortune comes not from her character but from her marriage. Squire Western's mistreatment of his wife is a good example of what Fielding sees as the likely result of a forced marriage. Although Fielding is in favor of marriage being contracted by the couple involved, he is aware that such marriages also may be disastrous, especially for women. His example is the marriage of Mrs. Fitzpatrick, who chose her husband herself against a good deal of advice to the contrary. In company he had seemed charming and lively; at home, "far from clearing up the Gloom of Solitude, [he] soon convinced [her], that [she] must have been wretched with him in any Place, and in any Condition" (*TJ*, II, 589). She makes a very interesting point: a man acts differently to his wife, sister, daughter from the way he does in the world, so that she may be quite badly treated at home while outside he has a reputation for charm and gallantry. She tells Sophia that

'he was a surly Fellow, a Character you have perhaps never seen: For indeed no Woman ever sees it exemplified, but in a Father, a Brother, or a Husband. [He] had formerly appeared to me the very Reverse, and so he did still to every other Person. [At home, men] make themselves Amends for the uneasy Restraint which they put on their Tempers in the World; for I have observed the more merry and gay, and good-humoured my Husband hath at any Time been in Company, the more sullen and morose he was sure to become at our next private meeting.' [*TJ*, II, 589-90]

Mrs. Fitzpatrick has a "Superiority of Understanding" (*TJ*, II, 595) as compared with her husband; he hates her for it, and she cautions Sophia against the mistake of marrying someone of meaner understanding than her own. In one of the most generous remarks about women in the book, Mrs. Fitzpatrick says that she might give up any thing, "'but never this. Nature would not have allotted this Superiority to the Wife in so many Instances, if she had intended we should all of us have surrendered it to the Husband. This indeed Men of Sense never expect of us'" (*TJ*, II, 595). It should be noted that "sense" here is quite different from "learning;" I will discuss a little later Fielding's discomfort with the Learned Lady. But "ladies" of course are allowed to be intelligent, as long as they do not try to use their knowledge.

Thus, poor Mrs. Fitzgerald, alone and miserable, turns to books for her comfort and reads "almost all Day long" (*TJ*, II, 596). Meanwhile, ignoring his wife completely, Mr. Fitzpatrick devotes himself to her money, and within a short time has spent as much of it as he can. She refuses to give up the remaining bit, and vowing to take it from her, he imprisons her for several weeks. Fielding is well aware of the helplessness and unfairness to which women may be subjected by men in his society, remarking on "the savage Authority too often exercised by Husbands and Fathers" (*TJ*, II, 607). He goes on, "I have often suspected that those very Enchanters with which Romance every where abounds, were in Reality no other than the Husbands of those Days; and Matrimony itself was perhaps the enchanted Castle in which the Nymphs were said to be confined" (*TJ*, II, 607). These are remarkably perceptive remarks, and quite different from the totally superficial pronouncements I have pointed to earlier.

The example of Mrs. Fitzpatrick notwithstanding, Fielding argues repeatedly against marriages that are contracted by parents for their children. Squire Western is ready to do anything to make his daughter happy as long as she does not go against his wishes. When Blifil comes for his first visit as suitor, the squire has no idea that Sophia is not in agreement with the plan for the match. As Blifil emerges from the interview, he is kissed and embraced by the squire, who then goes to look for Sophia in order to congratulate her. He "pour[s] forth the most extravagant Raptures, bidding her chuse what Clothes and Jewels she pleased; and declaring that he had no other Use for Fortune but to make her happy" (*TJ*, I, 296). Although Squire Western was an indifferent, uncaring husband, he is a genuinely caring father. But as soon as Sophia says that she does not want to marry Blifil, she forfeits all of her father's love. Responding to her father's "Fit of Affection" (*TJ*, I, 296) by confessing that she can't stand Blifil and does not want to marry him, Sophia, "after many warm and passionate Declarations of Affection and Duty," begs the squire "'not to make her the most miserable Creature on Earth, by forcing her to marry a Man whom she detest[s].'" Further, she tells him, "'To force me into this Marriage, would be killing me.'" Her father angrily responds, "'You can't live with Mr. **Blifil**! . . . Then die and be d—ned'" (*TJ*, II, 296). The squire finds Sophia's qualms ridiculous—and a threat to his authority. When he visits Allworthy to discuss his daughter's match, and Allworthy commiserates with him on his unhappiness at Sophia's choice, Squire Western rebuffs Allworthy's attempt at solace: "'I am resolved I will

turn her out o'Doors, she shall beg and starve and rot in the Streets'"
(*TJ*, I, 305).

Fielding's comments against parentally planned marriage are repeated in many contexts. The tone, most often, is wry wonder at the
madness of human beings. Squire Western's estate "was all to be
settled on his Daughter and her Issue; for so extravagant was the
Affection of that fond Parent, that provided his Child would but
consent to be miserable with the Husband he chose, he cared not at
what Price he purchased him" (*TJ*, I, 346). The financial nature of the
transaction is made explicit in Squire Western's comment on the marriage as a marriage of his and Allworthy's properties: " 'nothing can lie
so handy together as our two Estates. . . . [T]he two Estates are in a
Manner joined together in Matrimony already, and it would be a
thousand Pities to part them'" (*TJ*, I, 276-77). Western cannot even
imagine a match between Sophia and Tom because of the inequality of
their wealth: "He did indeed consider a Parity of Fortune and Circumstances, to be physically as necessary an Ingredient in Marriage, as
Difference of Sexes, or any other Essential; and had no more Apprehension of his Daughter's falling in Love with a poor Man, than with
any Animal of a different Species" (*TJ*, I, 300). Squire Western's belief
in his own authority goes so far that he feels no compunction at all in
locking up this daughter who won't obey him; his sister's only objection to this treatment of Sophia is that it is ineffective.

Fielding's arguments for the companionate marriage are essentially those of common sense: as Honour so elegantly puts it, the
people who have to go to bed together should make the choice, or, as
Tom tells the Quaker, the tragedy of a daughter choosing against her
father's wishes is no tragedy unless the father makes it one. If Sophia,
drawn by Fielding as an ideal, presents so convincing a case against the
parent's right to choose a mate for his child, then the case is unargu-
able. But for all that, Fielding is not being very radical. Stone finds that
by 1749 it was quite usual for the young person herself to choose her
mate.[10] And Sophia demands only the right of refusal rather than the
right of choice, making Fielding's statement in *Tom Jones* less than
revolutionary. Nevertheless, Fielding's insistence that the woman
must have a say in the choice of her mate, his suggestion in the
Allworthy marriage of what a good marriage can be, and his depiction
in the Fitzpatrick and Western marriages of the horrors of a bad union,
all are very strongly supportive of the woman and her needs in marriage. In *Amelia*, Fielding looks even more closely at marriage forms.

Much of the novel depicts the Booth marriage—in Fielding's eyes apparently a model relationship. Fielding's discussion of Amelia's marriage is so tightly woven into his characterization of Amelia herself that she really only can be talked about within its context. Fielding's portrait of Amelia is meant to be completely positive. Martin Battestin finds that "Amelia is the idealized portrait of [Fielding's] first wife [Charlotte Cradock] (*A*, xix). As I noted earlier Battestin reminds us that "As for Amelia, that amiable and long-suffering heroine, we had best take her for what she was so plainly meant to be—the finest compliment Fielding could pay to the woman whose memory he cherished." This is the Amelia critics traditionally have seen. And yet the novel also often has been described as what Robert Alter calls "Fielding's problem novel,"[11] at least in part because of its heroine. We may wonder a little at Fielding's version of the ideal. Amelia's measure of things is her Billy. She is loyal, unselfish, hard-working, and decidedly unintellectual—a very important plus for a Fielding woman. Her Billy can do no wrong, and she only can do right in terms of how her actions are reflected in her husband's eyes. She is a good mother. And although she is quite fit and healthy, she faints at every stress. She is, then, the sentimental heroine in her purest form.

Fielding's perspective and, certainly, his sense of humor desert him entirely whenever he describes Amelia. Booth, describing Amelia's reaction to having "'her lovely Nose . . . beat all to pieces'" (*A*, 66), exclaims on the "'Magnanimity of Mind'" she shows. "'If the World have extolled the Firmness of Soul in a Man who can support the Loss of Fortune; of a General, who can be composed after the Loss of a Victory; or of a King, who can be contented with the Loss of a Crown; with what Astonishment ought we to behold, with what Praises to honour a young Lady, who can with Patience and Resignation submit to the Loss of exquisite Beauty, in other Words, to the Loss of Fortune, Power, Glory; every Thing which human Nature is apt to court and rejoice in!'" (*A*, 67). Although Amelia's bravery is exaggerated, there is no suggestion that we are to take this passage with less than full seriousness. Similarly, when Booth recounts how wonderful Amelia was when he fooled her into thinking he loved someone else, no irony is intended: "'Poor *Amelia* presently swallowed this Bait, and, as she hath told me since, absolutely believed me to be in earnest. Poor dear Love! how should the sincerest of Hearts have any Idea of Deceit? for with all her Simplicity I assure you she is the most sensible Woman in the World. . . . [My] Angel was now, if possible, more confused than before. She looked so silly, you can hardly believe it—'" (*A*,

70-71). It is fine for Amelia to look "silly" in the name of love—or, more accurately, in the course of believing Booth.

It can be argued that both of these examples are images of Amelia seen through Booth's eyes and that Booth is not the most trustworthy observer. But everything Amelia does and says fits the mold of the worshipful, unquestioning female. Amelia is capable when she is "supposed" to be capable, as in cooking Booth's dinner or watching over their children. But she is never capable to the point of being what Fielding would consider unfeminine. The sign of her femininity is her proclivity to faint. Amelia comes near to fainting, or does faint, on at least nine occasions in the book. Some of these faints are caused by actual threats to Amelia herself, but a fainting fit can be brought on even by a frightening story—a story, say, of a seduction. Amelia faints when Booth confesses that he loves her (A, 73); she passes out when Booth is about to leave for military service (A, 104). She faints when she gets to the prison where Booth is being held (A, 159); on another occasion she is "scarce able to support her tottering limbs" (A, 181) when her little boy is threatened. During Mrs. Bennet's story of her mother's death, Amelia takes a glass of water with some "Hartshorn Drops infused into it" (A, 270) and manages to stay conscious, but later in the same story, when Mrs. Bennet meets "the vile Betrayer," Amelia indeed faints and requires "proper Applications" to bring "her back to Life" (A, 296). A letter from the Colonel brings her near fainting (A, 443), and, of course, the news of the restoration of her fortune, no matter how gently put, makes her "a little faint" (A, 529). Amelia's propensity for fainting is one of the characteristics that marks her as a good woman. Miss Mathews, for example, does not faint at moments of stress or great emotion; Mrs. James fakes faints but certainly never actually is overcome. Amelia's sensibility is manifested in her propensity to succumb to her strong feelings. Her fainting does not show physical or emotional weakness—Fielding emphasizes Amelia's strength on both levels. Fielding draws Amelia as the most feminine of women, defining femininity in specific terms: the extraordinary courage needed to survive the impairment of beauty, the tendency to faint, the complete subjection to a husband's will, and, of course, the epitomizing of motherhood.

Amelia never argues with a male authority figure like Booth (whose judgment is so often questionable) or Dr. Harrison. She will take a position opposite to Booth's when either her honor or his safety is at stake, but even at these times she must explain her opposition fully or be thought unreasonable. Booth is never questioned. When

Booth's supposed friend Bagillard attempts to seduce Amelia, she wants to avoid the seduction without letting her husband know about the attempt because she is afraid that he will insist on avenging the insult. Booth humors her when she asks him to see less of his friend: "if that excellent Woman could ever be though unreasonable, I thought she was so on this Occasion" (A, 126). When the Bagillard incident is over, and Booth has learned the truth, Amelia tells him how difficult it was for her to know that he must think her " 'a little unreasonable' " (A, 133) and to know that she " 'was daily lessening [her]self in [Booth's] Esteem' " (A, 134). The good woman, for Fielding, reduced to subterfuge to prevent her hotheaded husband from fighting, at the same time worries that he will think the less of her because she cannot explain her motivation to him. Although Booth does not hesitate to consider Amelia somewhat unreasonable, Amelia never can think of Booth in that way. When Booth forbids Amelia to go to Ranelagh—proffering no reasons for his demand—Amelia merely says, "with great gravity, 'I shall never desire to go to any Place contrary to *Mr. Booth's* Inclinations' " (A, 247). Mrs. Ellison ironically asks " 'is a Woman to be governed then by her Husband's Inclinations, tho' they are never so unreasonable?' " But Amelia firmly corrects her: " 'Pardon me, Madam . . . I will not suppose Mr. *Booth's* Inclinations ever can be unreasonable' " (A, 248). Not only does Booth expect her to accede to his demand, he also " 'had rather [she] would not ask' " (A, 249) why he makes it.

While Amelia does not have the right to decide whether or not to go to a masquerade, she does have the right repeatedly to attempt to repair the damage Booth does to their family by his misjudgments. When, for example, Booth borrows fifty pounds from Trent at the gambling table—fifty pounds that he himself has absolutely no way of repaying—he realizes that the only way he can repay the money is "by stripping his Wife not only of every Farthing, but almost of every Rag she had in the World; a Thought so dreadful, that it chilled his very Soul with Horrour; and yet Pride at last seemed to represent this as the lesser Evil" (A, 473) to not paying. He decides to ask Amelia not for money but for advice, thus putting her in the position of having to volunteer to give up everything she has. Amelia, of course, makes no complaint. When Booth marvels that she does " 'not once upbraid [him] for bringing this Ruin on [her]' " (A, 473), she answers " 'Upbraid you, my Dear! . . . Would to Heaven I could prevent your upbraiding yourself. But do not despair. I will endeavour by some Means or other to get you the Money' " (A, 473). What more could a man want? She's just sorry that he's upset. Off she goes to pawn everything she can; back she comes with enough money to pay the debt. With "good Humour" (*A*, 475) in her countenance, Amelia hands over the money, and Booth leaves to repay Trent. But Trent, unfortunately, is not at home. As he is returning from his unsuccessful mission, Booth meets an acquaintance who tries to convince him that he would do better to place a bribe in a "Great Man's" hands than to repay his debt; the more Booth drinks, the better the scheme sounds. "In the Morning *Booth* communicated the Matter to *Amelia*, who told him she would not presume to advise him in an Affair, of which he was so much the better Judge" (*A*, 476). While Fielding makes it clear that Booth's judgment is questionable, he does not suggest that Amelia's stance is anything but commendable.

Amelia's domesticity is at the center of Fielding's characterization of her. "I question whether it be possible to view this fine Creature in a more amiable Light," Fielding enthuses, "than while she was dressing her Husband's Supper with her little Children playing round her" (*A*, 488). To save money, she has eaten nothing all day but a slice of bread and butter, but she buys her husband the foods that he most loves. "As soon as the Clock struck seven, the good Creature went down into the Kitchin [sic], and began to exercise her Talents of Cookery, of which she was a great Mistress, as she was of every OEconomical Office, from the highest to the lowest; and as no Woman could outshine her in a Drawing-Room, so none could make the Drawing-Room itself shine brighter than *Amelia* (*A*, 488). When he does come home, Booth says he must go out again and won't be eating with her. She merely says, "'I say no more. I am convinced you would not willingly sup from me. I own it is a very particular Disappointment to me to Night, when I had proposed unusual Pleasure; but the same Reason which is sufficient to you, ought to be so to me'" (*A*, 489). Booth is on his way to a date with Miss Mathews, during which he hopes to break off their relationship. Amelia, having pawned the only thing of any value she had left to pay for the dinner, and having spent all day looking forward to preparing it, merely sits "down to supper with her Children; with whose Company she was forced to console herself for the Absence of her Husband" (*A*, 489). Significantly, whatever comfort Amelia can find for her disappointment is found in her children. Amelia is a good mother. She can be "highly delighted all the Morning" (*A*, 230) with the pleasures of her children; it is her habit to check on them as soon as she comes back from an outing (*A*, 419) and to look in on them as she passes from one chore to another (*A*, 501). But while she pays a good deal of attention to her children, it is still Booth who gets the greatest share of her concern. Battestin reminds us that "as summarized in *The Covent-Garden Journal* (1 August 1752) . . . Fielding's ideal conception of women does not emphasize their intellectual, but their moral and domestic attributes . . . 'the two principal Female Characters, [being] that of Wife, and that of Mother'" (*A*, note, p. 255). Amelia's role as mother is not exceptional, but her deportment as a wife, to which Fielding devotes a great deal of attention, surely must mark her as one of the most pliable and agreeable of eighteenth-century spouses.

It is not so much that Amelia ignores Booth's infirmities as a husband, as that she is not aware of them. Amelia is completely satisfied with her Billy and with her marriage; furthermore, a good marriage seems to her to be the height of female felicity. Having a good husband, she says, "'is the greatest Blessing a Woman can be possessed of'" (*A*, 220); she cannot "'wonder . . . at any Woman's surviving'" (*A*, 204) the loss of a loved husband. Certainly, if a woman has lost a husband, for that woman to marry again seems unthinkable to Amelia (*A*, 254ff). Amelia looks on herself "'as the happiest Woman in the World.'" Rhetorically, she asks "'what Fortune can be put in the Balance with such a Husband as mine?'" (*A*, 238).

What makes Amelia so content? In a fairly typical scene in the novel, Fielding describes what Amelia is doing while Booth is at the gambling table.

> It was about seven when *Booth* left her to walk in the Park: From this Time till past Eight she was employ'd with her Children, in playing with them, in giving them their Supper, and in putting them to Bed.
>
> When these Offices were performed, she employ'd herself another Hour in cooking up a little Supper for her Husband, this being . . . his favourite Meal, as indeed it was hers; and in a most pleasant and delightful Manner they generally passed their Time at this Season. . . .
>
> It now grew dark, and her hashed Mutton was ready for the Table, but no *Booth* appear'd. Having waited therefore for him a full Hour, she gave him over for that Evening; nor was she much alarmed at his Absence, as she knew he was in a Night or two to be at the Tavern with some Brother Officers. She concluded therefore that they had met in the Park, and had agreed to spend this Evening together.
>
> At Ten then she sat down to Supper by herself. . . . Having sat some Time alone reflecting on their distress'd Situation, her Spirits grew very low; and she was once or twice going to ring the Bell to send her Maid for half a Pint of White-wine, but check'd her Inclination in order to save the little Sum of Sixpence; which she did the more resolutely as she had before

refused to gratify her Children with Tarts for their Supper from the same Motive. And this Self-denial she was very probably practicing, to save Sixpence, while her Husband was paying a Debt of several Guineas incurred by the Ace of Trumps being in the Hands of his Adversary. . . .

To Bed then she went, but not to sleep. Thrice indeed she told the dismal Clock, and as often heard the more dismal Watchman, till her miserable Husband found his Way home, and stole silently, like a Thief, to Bed to her; at which Time pretending then first to awake she threw her snowy Arms around him. [*A*, 433-34]

In the first part of the scene Amelia's domesticity is emphasized. She plays with her children; she gives them supper and puts them to bed. For another hour, she cooks "a little Supper for her Husband;" a full hour after the food is ready, she is still waiting for her Booth. There is no indication that Amelia resents having prepared a dinner and waited for a husband who simply finds something else to do than arrive home. When she finally sits down to eat by herself, her spirits grow low—not because she feels that Booth has ill served her but because she thinks about their "distressing" situation. It is true that Fielding contrasts her action with Booth's (while she is saving the sixpence for the wine, he is gambling away large sums of money), but, significantly, the complaint is Fielding's, not Amelia's. Fielding's ambivalence toward women is very clear in this passage. Amelia is a jewel of a woman; she allows Booth to exploit her and to destroy their family finances—and all in the absence of even an implicit complaint. The "snowy Arms" welcoming Booth define Amelia's purity and virtue as surely as the standard epithets describe fleet-footed Achilles or white-armed Hera in Greek epic. But, on the other hand, as so often in Fielding, the wondrous heroine is defined by a gratuitous thrust at other women. And, as so often, the complaint is lodged in terms of what women do to men. Amelia doesn't sit up so that Booth will feel guilty, but "some Wives" use that method of "upbraiding their Husbands for staying abroad till too late an Hour" (*A*, 434).

Further, the next chapter of *Amelia*, titled "*Read, Gamester, and observe*," presents Booth and Amelia's conversation the next morning. Booth not surprisingly is perturbed, and Amelia asks what is bothering him.

'I am indeed afflicted, and I will not, nay I cannot conceal the Truth from you. I have undone myself, *Amelia.*'

'What have you done, Child?' said she, in some Consternation, 'pray tell me.'

'I have lost my Money at Play,' answered he.

'Pugh!' said she, recovering herself,—'what signifies the Trifle you had in your Pocket? Resolve never to play again, and let it give you no further Vexation. I warrant you we will contrive some Method to repair such a Loss.' [A, 435]

The angelic Amelia offers Booth the eleven guineas she has in her purse; he begins to count up what her "Diamond Ring" (A, 435) and the children's watches would bring at the pawnbroker's; Amelia says she's already computed how much money they could raise in an emergency—and promises that they will manage even on this tiny sum, for "'though the Sum which is now in our Power is very small; yet we may possibly contrive with it to put ourselves into some mean Way of Livelihood. I have a Heart, my Billy, which is capable of undergoing any Thing for your Sake; and I hope my Hands are as able to work, as those which have been more inured to it'" (A, 436). Booth already has gambled away a sum equal to all they have. From the title of the chapter it seems clear that Fielding intends to show here the pathetic destructiveness of Booth's weakness. But he also is presenting an image of how a loving and good wife should act in such circumstances.

What does Fielding's characterization of Amelia tell us about his view of women? The good woman is absolutely reliable and will always be there to comfort and support her mate. She is intelligent—it is no accident that when Booth begins to add up all their resources, Amelia already had done the accounting; remember, too, that she can converse with Dr. Harrison, the most intellectual character in the book, on an intelligent, but not learned, level. She is sexually virtuous, and she is immune to the desire occasionally to flirt. The main interest in her life is her husband, followed, but not followed closely, by her children. She takes real pleasure in domestic attainments, and views marriage—to her husband of all men—as the state of highest human felicity. Most important, none of these characteristics is subject to change, so that no matter what the man does, she never questions or judges him. A marriage like Booth and Amelia's represents for Fielding a very positive human relationship. For Amelia, and for Fielding, the inequality of the match—all Booth's obvious failings as a man and as a husband—does not make the match less perfect. The last sentence of the book is Fielding's affirmation of the quality of the relationship: "*Amelia* declared to me the other Day, that she did not remember to have seen her Husband out of Humour these ten Years; and upon my insinuating to her, that he had the best of Wives, she answered with a Smile, that she ought to be so, for that he had made her the happiest of Women" (*A*, 533). While Fielding allows Booth many serious imperfections, he is careful to emphasize that Booth is openly and unashamedly loving toward his wife. He attends Amelia at the birth of one of their children, for example. As Booth tells Miss Mathews, " 'in Defiance of your Laughter, I lay behind her Bolster, and supported her in my Arms, and upon my Soul, I believe I felt more Pain in my Mind than she underwent in her Body. And now answer me as honestly: Do you really think it a proper Time of Mirth, when the Creature one loves to Distraction is undergoing the most racking Torments, as well as in the most imminent Danger? And—but I need not express any more tender Circumstances' " (*A*, 128). To Miss Mathews's comment that he is "an Angel of a Man," Booth insists that "there are many such Husbands" (*A*, 128). Booth's affection is underscored in an argument he has with Colonel James, when, in opposition to James's point that variety, or at least discord, is necessary to keep up interest in relationships, Booth insists "with regard to Love, I declare I never found any thing cloying in it. I have lived almost alone with my Wife near three Years together, was never tired with her Company, nor ever wished for any other" (*A*, 226). The love that Booth and Amelia have for each other helps them through all their misfortunes. But not all marriages are based on love, Fielding knows, and those marriages entered into for considerations such as wealth and position, or in which the early affection of the partners has died, are at best unpleasant and at worst degrading. Not surprisingly, in Fielding novels the degraded marriages are shown as most frequent in the upper class, where position and wealth might be likely considerations in the choice of partner.

Colonel and Mrs. James barely tolerate each other. Although they present the picture of "the fondest Couple in the Universe" (*A*, 456) to company, in private they share only insults and acrimony. When the Colonel has had enough of his wife, he threatens to send her to the country. She, as part of her bargaining repertoire, agrees to help him to seduce another woman. The Trents have a similar marriage; whatever moderate affection once existed has long been replaced by indifference, if not dislike. But lack of affection does not preclude the Trents from having a productive marriage, for Trent sells his wife's charms to a high bidder, thereby "turning her Beauty itself into a Fortune" (*A*, 469), and he and his wife quite contentedly join the ranks of society: "*Trent* now immediately took a House at the polite End of the Town, furnished it elegantly, and set up his Equipage, rigged out both himself and his Wife with very handsome Cloaths, frequented all publick Places where he could get Admission, pushed himself into Acquaintance, and his Wife soon afterwards began to keep an Assembly, or in the fashionable Phrase, to be at home once a Week; when, by my Lord's Assistance, she was presently visited by most Men of the first Rank, and by all such Women of Fashion as are not very nice in their Company" (A, 471). When his Lordship's interest in Mrs. Trent is over, Trent and his wife maintain their position by being "useful to my Lord in a Capacity, which, though very often exerted in the polite World, hath not, as yet . . . acquired any polite Name" (A, 471). With the Jameses and the Trents, Fielding is showing the marriage that is a marriage in name only. The partners in each of these marriages, having given up on their respective relationships as the source of all the human satisfactions that Booth and Amelia would expect, use their marriages instead as the means to extramarital sexual satisfaction in one case and monetary and social betterment in the other.[12]

The marriage of Sergeant and Mrs. Atkinson presents a third category of relationship. The Atkinsons, like the Booths, are moral and caring people for whom money would never replace affection. Like the Booths, the Sergeant and his wife have no social pretensions and are not subject to the temptations by which the Jameses and Trents allow themselves to be degraded. But the Atkinson marriage, unlike the Booth marriage, is not a model relationship, for while Amelia sees Booth as the ideal man and mate, Mrs. Atkinson feels superior to her husband because of her learning. The Atkinson marriage, then, while generally a good relationship, is imperfect—and the imperfection is entirely on Mrs. Atkinson's side. Fielding does not fault the Booth marriage because of Billy's shortcomings, but the Atkinson marriage is treated satirically at various times in the novel because of Mrs. Atkinson's pride in her learning.[13] Fielding dissects the Learned Lady largely by showing how a woman's learning affects her relationship with her husband. Fielding's argument is put by Dr. Harrison, who asks, quite rhetorically, " 'if a learned Lady should meet with an unlearned Husband, might she not be apt to despise him?' " (A, 408). Mrs. Atkinson, taking the bait, responds " 'I think I have shewn myself that Women who have Learning themselves, can be contented without that Qualification in a Man' " (A, 408). But Dr. Harrison's point is that the learned lady will be ready to contend with her husband one for one in arguments, and by drawing Mrs. Atkinson into argument, Dr. Harrison proves that point. When Mrs. Atkinson tries to bring Amelia into the discussion, Amelia—the perfect Amelia—demurely refuses to participate; she tells Mrs. Atkinson, " 'I have the Advantage of you . . . for I don't understand [the doctor's argument]' " (*A*, 409). Fielding's moral is clear: intellectual argument between the sexes produces discord between them. The conversation is closed when Booth's arrival puts an "end to that learned Discourse, in which neither of the Parties had greatly recommended themselves to each other, the Doctor's Opinion of the Lady being not at all heightened by her Progress in the *Classics*; and she on the other hand, having conceived a great Dislike in her Heart towards the Doctor, which would have raged, perhaps, with no less Fury from the Consideration that he had been her Husband" (*A*, 410). Fielding emphasizes this perspective again in his last glance at the Atkinson marriage: "Mr. *Atkinson* upon the whole hath led a very happy Life with his Wife, though he hath been sometimes obliged to pay proper Homage to her superior Understanding and Knowledge. This, however, he chearfully submits to, and she makes him proper Returns of Fondness" (*A*, 532). A man, and his spouse, is better off if the woman does not have too much learning; learning in a woman produces contentiousness and an inflated sense of the value of her own opinions. Amelia, forever deferring to the opinions of her husband and Dr. Atkinson, is more to Fielding's liking. For Fielding, learning is not feminine; even in his compliments to his sister Sarah in the preface he wrote to *David Simple*, Fielding carefully distinguishes between learning and understanding. Fielding emphasizes that Sarah is not learned. He has corrected "some Grammatical and other Errors in Style," he tells us, and, later, "the Imperfections of this little Book . . . arise . . . not from want of Genius, but of Learning [and] lie open to the Eyes of every Fool, who has had a little Latin inoculated into his Tail."[14] The beauties of Sarah's book lie in its "Penetration into human Nature,"[15] a penetration that is, we are assured, untutored. This intuition is quite unlike the learning he disparages in the novels in characters like Mrs. Atkinson in *Amelia* and Mrs. Western and Jenny Jones in *Tom Jones*, for Sarah's intuition is neither the result of study nor the source of prideful display.

But learning in a woman is quite different. Jenny Jones, although "no very comely Girl" (*TJ*, I, 48), has "a very uncommon Share of Understanding" and "an extraordinary Desire of learning" (*TJ*, I, 48). Living as servant to the schoolmaster Partridge, she has picked up a good deal of Latin. Fielding notes that "it is not to be wondered at, that a young Woman so well accomplished should have little Relish for the Society of those whom Fortune had made her Equals, but whom Education had rendered so much her Inferiors" (*TJ*, I, 48). She is a better scholar than her male mentor, Fielding notes, but her learning makes her prideful and thus, he implies, spoils her. The description of the learning of Squire Western's sister—not even real learning since it consists not of Latin but of modern literature and politics—is even more clearly negative: "She had considerably improved her Mind by Study; she had not only read all the modern Plays, Operas, Oratorios, Poems and Romances; in all which she was a Critic; but had gone thro' **Rapin's** History of *England,* **Eachard's Roman History,** and many **French Memoires pour servir a l'Histoire;** to these she had added most of the political Pamphlets and Journals, published within the last twenty Years. From which she had attained a very competent Skill in Politics, and could discourse very learnedly on the Affairs of **Europe"** (*TJ,* II, 272-73). Fielding is not impressed. This lady is an unnatural creature, a "masculine" woman, and has never had any "Affairs of her own" either because no man has ever been interested in her or because she has had no interest in men, "which last is indeed very probable: For her masculine Person, which was near six Foot high, added to her Manner and Learning, possibly prevented the other Sex from regarding her, notwithstanding her Petticoats, in the Light of a Woman" (*TJ,* I, 273-74).[16]

One of the good things about understanding in a woman, as opposed to learning, is that understanding is so comfortable and comforting for the man. Because understanding is essentially subjective, when the male disagrees with the female's assessment, he can simply dismiss her view. This dismissal is all the easier since Fielding delimits a category—women and children—that precludes much authority for the woman. Dr. Harrison's behavior is defined in one instance by the fact that he bore toward Amelia "all that Love which Esteem can create in a good Mind, without the Assistance of those selfish Considerations, from which the Love of Wives and Children may be ordinarily deduced" (*A,* 422). Amelia herself is often treated as a woman-child in discussions with both her husband and Dr. Harrison, both of whom respect her understanding, but only up to a point; beyond that point, neither attempts to convince her by argument—he just changes the subject. Presumably, Amelia's attention, like a child's, thus easily can be drawn to another object. In one conversation, for example, Amelia is discussing with Booth her doubts about the religious principles of Dr. Harrison. She feels that he is little better than an atheist, "A Consideration which did not diminish her Affection for him; but gave her great Uneasiness." Booth's reaction to her apparently is habitual: "On all such Occasions *Booth* immediately turned the

Discourse to some other Subject; for tho' he had in other Points a great Opinion of his Wife's Capacity; yet as a Divine or a Philosopher he did not hold her in a very respectable Light, nor did he lay any great Stress on her Sentiments in such Matters. He now therefore gave a speedy Turn to the Conversation, and began to talk of Affairs below the Dignity of this History" (A, 451). Similarly, in the conversation between Dr. Atkinson and Amelia about the Colonel's seduction attempts and Amelia's problems in holding him off, the Doctor repeatedly answers Amelia's earnest comments with teasing, condescending remarks. Amelia is "a little Flatterer" (A, 376), he says; later he tells her that he could challenge her faith in his wisdom merely by telling her that he does not think she is beautiful. Female conversation in *Amelia* is almost always lightweight, with Fielding reserving the long and philosophical discussions to the men. Except to satirize the conversation of a Learned Lady, Fielding does not often give us women engaged in discussion of issues not related to domestic concerns. And when he shows us men debating hot and heavy, the entrance of the ladies puts an end to all interesting conversation: "Tea-table Conversation," as Fielding puts it, "tho' extremely delightful to those who are engaged in it, may probably appear somewhat dull to the Reader" (A, 368).

Fielding's ideal woman is pretty, charming, and able to make her male consort moral and worthy by the force of the intense sweetness of her personality. Sophia, like Amelia, satisfies these requirements; in fact, Sophia is so perfect that Fielding finds it necessary to comment on the extravagance of his own descriptions in mock heroic introductions to those descriptions, thus detaching himself a bit from the perfection of the creature he presents.[17] Fielding's good women, the young Sophia and the somewhat more matronly Amelia, are always seen as the moral, stable half of the male. This stability is emphasized in *Amelia*, where in the face of Booth's repeated financial and even moral failures Amelia struggles selflessly and without complaint to keep the household together, and it is the underlying support of the relationship between Sophia and Tom as well.

Sophia does not grow morally because she is already perfect,[18] while the whole of *Tom Jones* chronicles Tom's moral development: he must improve himself until he is worthy of Sophia. The ideal of woman springs fully formed from, merely, her self as woman. In a novel that shows us the growing up into adulthood of the children Sophia and Tom, it is strange that Sophia never needs to learn and mature as Tom does. Fielding emphasizes the humanity of Tom—and the femaleness of Sophia. Fielding's portrait of Sophia, while flattering in idealizing womanhood, dehumanizes the individual woman.

Fielding emphasizes Sophia's perfection repeatedly, and critics traditionally have taken him at his word.[19] Sophia does indeed represent prudence, and sweetness and light, but Fielding has a great deal of trouble with major female characters, and his heroines, Sophia and Amelia, are exaggerations of the good female just as his bad women are caricatures of female weakness.[20] Amelia is good beyond the point of admiration: in her uncomplaining support of her bumbling husband, at some point in the story she slips over the line from virtuous helpmate to willing victim. Similarly, Sophia's goodness too begins to cloy. At the end of the novel, Sophia's perspective on the circumstances of her near betrothal to Blifil is perhaps too forgiving, especially of her father. Having been threatened by her father, locked up by him, made to flee her home because he insisted on forcing her into a marriage that horrified her, she still primarily is concerned with being a dutiful daughter to this man. After all the mysteries have been cleared up, Allworthy comes to Sophia to set things right. He apologizes that "had I at first known how disagreeable the Proposals had been, I should not have suffered you to have been so long persecuted" (*TJ*, 737).

> 'Sir,' said *Sophia*, with a little modest Hesitation, 'this Behaviour is most kind and generous, and such as I could expect only from Mr. *Allworthy*: But as you have been so kind to mention this Matter, you will pardon me for saying it hath indeed given me great Uneasiness, and hath been the occasion of my suffering much cruel Treatment from a Father, who was, 'till that unhappy Affair, the tenderest and fondest of all Parents. . . . I assure you, Sir, nothing less than the certain Prospect of future Misery could have made me resist the Commands of my Father.' [*TJ*, II, 952-53]

Squire Allworthy teases Sophia a little, telling her that he has another near relation he would like her to meet; she responds, "My only Desire is to be restor'd to the Affection of my Father, and to be again the Mistress of his Family. This, Sir, I hope to owe to your good Offices" (*TJ*, II, 953). Sophia might seem to be taking this stance in an attempt to avoid fresh entanglements because she is still in love with Tom—but when Allworthy tells her about Tom's new position in his family, Sophia reverts again to her feelings for and obligations to her father.

> 'I have told you my Resolution. I wonder not at what my Father hath told you; but whatever his Apprehensions or Fears have been, if I know my

Heart, I have given no Occasion for them; since it hath always been a fixed Principle with me, never to have marry'd without his Consent. This is, I think, the Duty of a Child to a Parent; and this, I hope, nothing could ever have prevailed with me to swerve from. I do not conceive, that the Authority of any Parent can oblige us to marry, in direct Opposition to our Inclinations. To avoid a Force of this Kind, which I had Reason to suspect, I left my Father's House, and sought Protection elsewhere. This is the Truth of my Story; and if the World, or my Father, carry my Intentions any farther, my own Conscience will acquit me.' [TJ, II, 955]

Part of Sophia's female perfection is that she shows no resentment at the way she has been treated by her father, and, further, that even in light of the events that lead up to this point, she reaffirms his authority.

A generally ignored section of the book epitomizes what makes Sophia so special for Fielding. The passage comes in the discussion among Squire Allworthy, Squire Western, and Blifil about whether Sophia should be forced to marry Blifil. Allworthy is flatly against the marriage being forced on the young woman, and in most decided terms refuses even to consider the idea of the match—however much he personally would have liked to welcome Sophia to his family. His remarks in praise of Sophia herself, remarks that precede this marriage discussion, are presented straightforwardly and without irony.

'with Regard to the young Lady, not only the concurrent Opinion of all who knew her, but my own Observation assured me that she would be an inestimable Treasure to a good Husband. I shall say nothing of her personal Qualifications, which certainly are admirable; her Good-nature, her charitable Disposition, her Modesty are too well known to need any Panegyric: but she hath one Quality which existed in a high Degree in that best of Women, who is now one of the first of Angels [his wife], which as it is not of a glaring Kind, more commonly escapes Observation; so little indeed is it remarked, that I want a Word to express it. I must use Negatives on this Occasion. I never heard any thing of Pertness, or what is called Repartee out of her Mouth; no Pretence to Wit, much less to that Kind of Wisdom, which is the Result only of great Learning and Experience; the Affectation of which, in a young Woman, is as absurd as any of the Affectations of an Ape. No dictatorial Sentiments, no judicial Opinions, no profound Criticisms. Whenever I have seen her in the Company of Men, she hath been all Attention, with the Modesty of a Learner, not the Forwardness of a Teacher. You'll pardon me for it, but I once, to try her only, desired her Opinion on a Point which was controverted between Mr. **Thwackum** and Mr. **Square,** To which she answered with much Sweetness, "You will pardon me, good Mr. **Allworthy,** I am sure you cannot in Earnest think me capable of deciding any Point in which two such Gentlemen disagree." **Thwackum** and **Square,** who both alike thought themselves sure of a favourable Decision, seconded my Request. She answered with the same good Humour, "I must absolutely be excused; for I will affront neither so much, as to give my Judgment on his Side." Indeed, she always shewed the highest Deference to the Understandings of Men; a Quality absolutely essential to the making a good Wife. I shall only add, that as she is most apparently void of all Affectation, this Deference must be certainly real.' [*TJ*, II, 882-83]

At the end of this panegyric Squire Western's eyes "were full of Tears at the Praise of Sophia" (*TJ*, II, 883). Allworthy goes on that "I have dwelt so long on the Merit of this young Lady, partly as I really am in Love with her Character" (*TJ*, II, 883).[21] What Allworthy finds so sterling in Sophia's character apparently is that she honestly believes (as opposed to merely conforming to the idea) that women are inferior to men in their understandings: "'Indeed, she always shewed the highest Deference to the Understandings of Men . . . [and] this Deference must be certainly real.'" Sophia, Allworthy repeats twice, will be a treasure of a wife. She already has proven herself, we have seen, to be a loyal and most respectful daughter. If Tom should continue getting into scrapes after he is married, perhaps into debt, Sophia will stand by him loyally, as she does by her father. Sophia, in short, from what we see of her in the novel, will grow up to be a woman not unlike Amelia.

In any discussion of images of women in *Tom Jones*, Sophia must be seen as the measure of womanhood. She shows us, not surprisingly, that Fielding's ideal woman is a reflection of male values.[22] That she is chaste is assumed; that she be deferential to the opinions of males is almost as desirable. Sophia's first role is daughter, her second, wife. In support of this view, we might briefly look again at Sophia's relationships to the two primary male figures in her life, Squire Western and Tom. The only time she argues with Squire Western is when he maligns her mother; in fact, the argument is not so much a spirited defense as a refusal to join in the vilification. She resists her father's attempts to marry her to Blifil, but she does not go so far as to demand the right to choose her own mate—in both cases, then, she can veto her father's idea, but she does not insist (as Tom would) on the right to her own. She allows Tom an enormous moral latitude while remaining within rigid moral limits herself. It is quite true that Sophia's setting off on her own is itself a courageous act, but she is after all accompanied by her maid and is on her way to the haven of a female relative. And a bit of spunk, it might be noted, is an element in most portraits of an ideal woman. Of course, Sophia's spunk is always regulated by her very "feminine" propensity conveniently to faint when she is under stress, as in the scene when she hears her father's voice after her first argument with him about Blifil (*TJ*, 230).

When we look at the ideal of Sophia herself, Fielding's other "ideals" —of whore, of learned lady, of Amazon—take on sharper focus. Very few female characters in Fielding escape stereotyping. In *Amelia*, I think, none do; in *Tom Jones*, of all the female characters, Mrs. Miller and her daughter are perhaps the least typed of the women. Mrs. Miller and her daughter are, along with Mrs. Waters, rather special characters just for this reason. There is no ready-to-hand capitalized category for them: the Whore, the Ideal, the Suffering Wife, the Shifty Servant—no standard characterization comes to mind. But Fielding generally does categorize female characters, and his categories basically divide women into those who, in Janet Todd's phrase,[23] are "female monster[s]" like Miss Mathews, and those who, like Sophia and Amelia, provide what Patricia Spacks calls "the still point in a turning world."[24] Fielding's attitude toward women is inconsistent in that the monster and the angel cannot be brought together, but exist side by side in the novels; as Claude Rawson puts it: "the phenomenon of Blear-eyed Moll and that of Amelia simply cannot connect."[25] But we can make sense of the two together. Fielding's perspective in all the novels is the same: women of domestic or potentially domestic nature are positively characterized, and women who do not fit the domestic mold are portrayed as frightening and, often, quite evil. Fielding is relatively perceptive and sensitive when he talks about good—that is, domestic—women. He sympathizes with the woman who finds herself in a bad marriage, and he is very aware of the vulnerability of any married woman, even when she is part of a loving marriage. This awareness of the importance of marriage to the woman explains what might otherwise seem to be an inordinate amount of discussion in *Tom Jones* of the need for the involvement of the man and woman themselves in their marriage plans as opposed to the model of the parentally planned marriage. Fielding is comfortable with the idea of the domestic woman. But he is markedly uncomfortable with other kinds of women, and the misogynistic remarks that I analyzed at the beginning of this chapter pertain to all but the women who order the domestic world. Felicity Nussbaum's excellent discussion of the eighteenth-century's ideal of woman perfectly defines this quality in Fielding. Nussbaum notes "the formula for the ideal woman of the period:

she was to be a chaste companion who cheerfully created order and fostered domestic serenity. Such a woman should be even-tempered, patient, modest, and prudent."[26] She goes on, "It is a woman's natural function to bring stability to the larger society by ordering the domestic world. . . . In the fiction of satire, men on the one hand describe women as inherently giddy and unstable, while on the other they create an ideal woman, the mirror of their highest expectations, who is to establish order in the domestic sphere."[27]

Each of Fielding's four major novels ends with a markedly domestic description. We might expect that the hero and heroine live happily ever after, but Fielding emphasizes as well that the hero and heroine have children, and that the family circle is happy and loving. Even *Jonathan Wild* ends this way:

> His Wife and he are now grown old in the purest Love and Friendship; but never had another Child. *Friendly* married his elder Daughter at the Age of nineteen, and became his Partner in Trade. As to the younger, she never would listen to the Addresses of any Lover, not even of a young Nobleman, who offered to take her with two thousand Pounds, which her Father would have willingly produced, and indeed did his utmost to persuade her to the Match: but she refused absolutely, nor would give any other Reason, when *Heartfree* pressed her, than that she had dedicated her Days to his Service, and was resolved, no other Duty should interfere with that which she owed the best of Fathers, nor prevent her from [being the] Nurse of his old Age.
>
> Thus *Heartfree*, his Wife, his two Daughters, his Son-in-Law, and his Grandchildren, of which he hath several, live all together in one House; and that with such Amity and Affection towards each other, that they are in the Neighborhood called *the Family of Love*."[28]

*Joseph Andrews* ends with a similar, if less complete, scene: "Mr. Booby hath with unprecedented generosity given *Fanny* a Fortune of two thousand Pound, which *Joseph* hath laid out in a little Estate in the same Parish with his Father, which he now occupies, (his Father having stock'd it for him;) and *Fanny* presides, with most excellent Management in his Dairy; where, however, she is not at present very able to bustle much, being . . . extremely big with her first Child" (*JA*, 344). *Tom Jones* ends not with Tom and Sophia as a couple but with them as the parents of two charming children—and with Squire Western as the adoring grandfather playing with his granddaughter in the nursery! "*Sophia* hath already produced [Tom] two fine Children, a Boy and a Girl, of whom the old Gentleman is so fond, that he spends much of his

Time in the Nursery, where he declares the tattling of his little Grand-Daughter, who is above a Year and half old, is sweeter Music than the finest Cry of Dogs in *England"* (*TJ*, II, 981). As in the other novels, the domestic circle is multigenerational; Squire Western lives with Tom and Sophia as a welcome and loved member of the household, and Squire Allworthy is loved by both Tom and his wife "as a Father" (*TJ*, 761). The emphasis on domestic detail in Fielding's final novel, then, stands as part of his usual pattern:

> [Booth] hath two Boys and four Girls; the eldest of the Boys, he, who hath made his Appearance in this History, is just come from the University, and is one of the finest Gentlemen, and best Scholars of his Age. The second is just going from School, and is intended for the Church, that being his own Choice. His eldest Daughter is a Woman grown, but we must not mention her Age. A Marriage was proposed to her the other Day with a young Fellow of a good Estate, but she never would see him more than once; 'for Dr. *Harrison*,' says she, 'told me he was illiterate, and I am sure he is ill natured.' The second Girl is three Years younger than her Sister, and the others are yet Children.
>
> *Amelia* is still the finest Woman in *England* of her Age. *Booth* himself often avers she is as handsome as ever. Nothing can equal the Serenity of their Lives. [*A*, 532-33]

In keeping with the pattern of the other novels' endings, Dr. Harrison completes the Booth's family circle, dividing "his Time between his Parish, his old Town, and *Booth's*" (*A*, 532).

In these passages Fielding manifests no ambivalence. These women are gentle, sustaining, and emphatically maternal. Not only do wives take care of husbands, but, ideally, daughters do the same for fathers and for father-figures; the ending of *Jonathan Wild* talks about a daughter's plan to be the nurse of her father's old age, and Fielding tells us at the end of *Amelia* that Amelia is Dr. Harrison's nurse during a fit of gout and that "her two oldest Daughters sat up alternately with him for a whole Week" (*A*, 532). It is other kinds of women who are disturbing, even dangerous—women who are not pliant and giving, who do not provide a stable center. Fielding divides women into the categories I have discussed throughout this chapter and, in the dividing, exaggerates their characteristics. There are angels and monsters enough in Fielding's characterizations of women; it is the merely mortal woman who is a rarity in his gallery of images.

# FIVE

# The Male Radical Novelists

## Thomas Holcroft: *Anna St. Ives*
## William Godwin: *Caleb Williams*
## Robert Bage: *Hermsprong*

Neither delight in the domestic woman nor fear of the Other is an issue in the radical novels of the nineties. While woman herself is not to be feared, however, the often actively hostile social structure that surrounds her provokes angry comment, as in Wollstonecraft's *Maria or the Wrongs of Woman*. But even in that novel, and most obviously in the novels of the male radicals—Holcroft, Godwin, and Bage—female intellect draws the central interest of the novel. Woman's mind, and the equality of male and female intelligence, is celebrated in the radical novel. This emphasis largely precludes categorizing men and women by social roles, as Fielding and Richardson so often do. In the novels of the nineties "woman's place" becomes an irrelevant concept, for woman and man, as intellectual equals, share social responsibility.

The formula that shapes Thomas Holcroft's *Anna St. Ives* is typical of these books: women are the equals of men in intellectual capacity, in moral depth, and in physical courage. Holcroft's Anna is a Thinking Woman who is seen as a heroine, not, as in Fielding, an object of derision. Anna is the daughter of a baronet, the silly, self-indulgent, self-impoverished Sir Arthur St. Ives. She loves Frank Henley, or would love him if she thought her duty to society allowed it. She fears that if she marries Frank, the son of her father's steward, people will assume that she was moved by passion rather than reason, and she therefore could lose her ability to influence society by herself being seen as a model of rational behavior. In the course of the novel Frank convinces her that together the two of them would be of even greater use to society than each could be alone, i.e., that their marriage would be a rational act. Anna, who had decided to marry the villainous Coke Clifton so that she could reform him, finally abandons this plan when Coke kidnaps and attempts to rape her. Coke finally reforms, and Anna and Frank with good conscience can marry each other.[1]

The outstanding significance of *Anna St. Ives* is that Holcroft created in Anna and Frank a pair of absolutely equal protagonists. Anna is Frank's match in intellect, in moral stature, and in physical courage. Coke Clifton kidnaps Frank as well as Anna and imprisons them in separate houses; it is Anna who manages to escape by climbing a wall that, she had been told, "no woman could climb."[2] And in their philosophical discussions, Anna and Frank alternately contribute insight and direction. Anna is no Clarissa: it is her duty not merely to moralize but to act.[3] Anna and Frank believe that society is changed for the better through the action of the individual. The already enlightened human being has the responsibility to reform those in error, just as people with money have the duty to relieve others in distress. Further, the financially able must provide the means for the enlightened but poor man to aid his fellows. This philosophy translates into direct action: both Frank and Anna are on the lookout for people in need of moral reform or financial aid. Anna repeatedly insists that Frank accept money from her so that he will have the means to do good should an opportunity present itself. Thus when Frank comes upon the pathetic scene of a decent young man about to be arrested by the bailiffs for a small debt, he can save the man from jail because he has the twenty pounds Anna had forced on him. When Anna learns that Frank has expended all his money "in acts of benevolence" (*A*, 41), she insists that he accept another twenty pounds: "It is as much my duty, at present, to afford you the means which you want, as it was yours . . . [to] aid the distressed Peggy. You ought to suffer me to perform my duties, both for my sake and your own" (*A*, 45). In a similar vein, Anna notes that Frank "has no common part to act" in society, and that he needs to broaden his education by travel so that he can "act it well" (*A*, 45). It is her duty to help him; she wants him to go to France with her, and if Frank will not accept money from her for the expenses, he must take it as a loan. They debate, and finally she overcomes his hesitation:

> I again refer to your duties. However, since you are so tenacious on the subject, I will become a usurer to satisfy your feelings, and you shall pay for risk. Fifty pounds, unless you meet with more Peggies, I dare say will bear you free. . . . You shall give me eighty whenever you have a thousand pounds of your own.

Madam!—

Well, well! You shall give me a hundred. . . . It almost vexes me, Frank, to be refused so very slight a favour; for I can read refusal and opposition in your eye. But, if you persist, you will give me great pain; for you will convince me that, where your own passions are concerned, you are not superior to the paltry prejudices by which the rest of the world are governed.

I own, madam, my mind has had many struggles on the subject; and I am afraid, as you say, it has been too willing to indulge its prejudices, and its pride. But if you seriously think, from your heart, it is my duty to act in this case as you direct—

I do, seriously, solemnly, and from my heart, think it is your duty.

Then, madam, I submit. [*A*, 45-46]

The rational argument convinces Frank. Anna carefully has examined the possibilities for benevolent action that are open to her as a woman, to him as a man, and to the two of them as a couple. Aware that her direct field of action is limited because she is a woman, "Few opportunities present themselves to a woman, educated and restrained as women unfortunately are, of performing any thing eminently good" (*A*, 37), Anna has decided that the most important task available is "restoring a great mind, misled by error, to its proper rank" (*A*, 37). Thus she determines to take on Clifton's reformation. As we have seen, she also uses others as her agents: Frank, supplied with Anna's money, can help the unfortunate in ways that Anna herself cannot. Anna worries a great deal about "the question, not of love, but of duty. Love must not be permitted, till duty shall be known" (*A*, 50). She fears that if she marries Frank people will assume that she was attracted by qualities other than his superior mind.

Who ever saw those treated with esteem who are themselves supposed to be the slaves of passion? And could the world possibly be persuaded that a marriage between me and the son of my father's steward could ever originate, on my part, in honourable motives?

Ought I to forget the influence of example? Where is the young lady, being desirous to marry an adventurer, or one whose mind might be as mean as his origin, who would not suppose her favourite more than the equal of Frank? For is not the power of discrimination lost, when the passions are indulged? And ought my name to be cited? Ought they to be encouraged by any act of mine? [*A*, 50]

On the other hand, she confesses that "I cannot sometimes help asking myself whether the good that might result from the union of two strong minds, mutually determined to exert their powers for the welfare of society, be not a reason superior even to all those I have enumerated" (*A*, 51). Eventually she becomes convinced not that passion should be indulged but that the most rational course indeed is to marry the worthiest man—clearly Frank. In Holcroft's novel, the demands of romance are satisfied by the same criteria as those of reason. After Anna's doubts about marrying Frank have been resolved, the lovers rhapsodize together about the good they will do in society. Anna is almost unique among eighteenth-century heroines in her focus beyond the self and beyond the domestic circle of family and friends. Moll and Roxana function as part of the larger society, working, investing, and so on, but they work and invest with themselves as center. Anna looks to her place in the wider society, and she actually changes that society. She does not merely talk about reforming villains; she reforms her abductor Coke Clifton. She does not merely counsel courage; she escapes from her jailor. Even her casual comments to Louisa focus largely on nondomestic matters.

Louisa is a fit friend for Anna. Highly intelligent, with a rationality equal to Anna's, Louisa's character reaffirms in the novel the intellectual capability of women. Louisa's mother, too, is a person of marked ability—we are told that she had rescued the family from financial ruin. Not only are women's minds entirely the equal of men's, Holcroft insists, women's relationships are as important as men's. One of the most significant aspects of the book is that Anna has much the same kind of friendship with Frank that she has with Louisa. Excluding the sexual aspect of Anna's attraction to Frank, her relationship with both friends is based on a shared intellectual and moral vision. And in both cases, intense concern for the well-being of the friend illuminates the friendship. Anna describes her feelings about Louisa in the first letter of the novel. Planning to meet Louisa's brother Coke in Paris, Anna expects to fall in love with him because

> He cannot but resemble his sister. He cannot but be all generosity, love, expansion, mind, soul! I am determined to have a very sincere friendship for him; nay I am in danger of falling in love with him at first sight! Louisa knows what I mean by falling in love. Ah, my dear friend, if he be but half equal to you, he is indeed a matchless youth! Our souls are too intimately related to need any nearer kindred; and yet, since marry I must . . . I could almost wish . . . that it might be to the brother of my friend.[4]
>
> Do not call me romantic: if romance it be, it originates in the supreme satisfaction I have taken in contemplating the powers and beauties of my

Louisa's mind. Our acquaintance has been but short, yet our friendship
appears as if it had been eternal. [A, 2-3]

Louisa's mind, her compassion, generosity, and intellect attract Anna.
Louisa in her turn admires Anna's intellect and character, just as she
recognizes similar strengths in her mother. Affection for a female
parent we have seen before in these novels—Clarissa loves her mother—but respect for the elder woman's qualities of mind and character
is rare. Holcroft portrays female friendship not only within but across
generations, and always the friendship is based on qualities of mind:
"Do not her virtues and her wisdom communicate themselves to all
around her? Are not her resignation, her fortitude, and her cheerfulness in pain, lessons which I might traverse kingdoms and not find
an opportunity like this of learning? (A, 4), Louisa remarks about her
mother.

Rational attachment rather than the family tie determines the
depth of a relationship. Louisa cannot be loyal to her brother at the
expense of her friend; Mrs. Clifton, too, agrees that Louisa should
point out Coke's flaws of character to Anna. A family loyalty based not
on rational attachment but mere blood tie Louisa describes as "prejudice." Repeatedly Louisa begs Anna carefully to consider the young
man and to make no allowance because he is the brother of her friend.
"Forget his sister," Louisa enjoins Anna, "be true to yourself and your
own judgment" (A, 5). Later Louisa cautions, "With respect to my
brother . . . it is my earnest advice that you should be careful to put no
deception on yourself, but to see him as he is. His being the brother of
your friend cannot give him dignity of mind, if he have it not already"
(A, 31). Louisa adds that, although her mother would like to see Anna
and Coke married, she "approves" what Louisa has written to Anna.
"Her affection for me," Louisa comments, "makes her delight in every
effort of my mind to rise superior to the prejudices that bring misery
into the world" (A, 31-32). Louisa tries to educate Coke, but his mind is
closed. While Louisa, Anna, and Mrs. Clifton can share intelligent
discourse, Louisa finds only frustration in her attempts to reach her
brother. Proving just how unenlightened he is, Coke dismisses all her
arguments merely because she is a woman; underscoring the limits of
his own intelligence, Coke has no great respect for his mother's understanding. Louisa knows that Coke objects to her moralizing, but what,
she asks, should she talk about—"Shall I describe to him the fashion of
a new cap; or the charms of a dress that has lately travelled from Persia
to Paris, from Paris to London, and from London to Rose-Bank?" (A,

58-59). She would much rather discuss the qualities she finds important in a human being: "well-digested principles, an ardent desire of
truth, incessant struggles to shake off prejudices, . . . emanations of
soul, bursts of thought, and flashes of genius" (A, 59). Coke dismisses
Louisa's careful comments. "These girls, tied to their mother's apron-
strings, pretend to advise a man who has seen the world" (A, 65), he
laughs to his friend Guy. And to Louisa herself he writes "Prithee, my
good girl, jingle the keys of your harpsichord, and be quiet. Pore over
your fine folio receipt book, and appease your thirst after knowledge.
Satisfy your longing desire to do good, by making jellies, conserves,
and caraway cakes. Pot pippins, brew raspberry wine, and candy
orange chips. Study burns, bruises, and balsams. Distil surfeit, colic,
and wormwood water. . . . Spin, sew and knit. Collect your lamentable rabble around you, dole out your charities, listen to a full chorus of
blessings, and take your seat among the saints" (A, 85). Coke cannot
see beyond his image of woman as maker of jellies, but in Holcroft's
novel only the stupid or the villainous take such a view of woman. As
Coke is educated by Anna and Frank, he learns to appreciate the force
of the female mind. He begins by chafing at Anna's moral lessons as
well as Louisa's; only after he reforms can he accept moral instruction
from a woman. Thus one proof of a man's enlightenment in *Anna St.
Ives* is his ability to see men and women as equals. Coke should know
better than to dismiss female reason, for he has seen his mother
reinvigorating the family finances that had been left "in absolute
distress" (A, 213) at his father's death. Louisa notes that Mrs. Clifton
had saved the family "by her economy and good sense. . . . Her plans
have been severe; and of long continuance; deeply thought on, and
perseveringly executed" (A, 213). Although Coke is respectful to his
mother, there is no evidence that he is aware of her as a particularly
competent manager. Louisa, on the other hand, appreciates her mother's financial aptitude and herself has a good grasp of money matters.

Anna's father is being bled of his fortune by his corrupt steward
Abimelech Henley, who urges Sir Arthur continually to make "improvements" on his estates. Anna and Louisa discuss this matter at
length; not only are they aware of the danger Abimelech poses (a
danger to which Anna's father is oblivious), but Louisa sternly argues
that Anna should be more forceful in trying to convince her father of
his folly. Thus Louisa writes to Anna

I like Sir Arthur's favourite, Abimelech Henley, still less than you do. My
fears are rather strong. When once a taste for improvement . . . becomes a

passion, gaming itself is scarcely more ruinous. I have no doubt that Sir
Arthur's fortune has suffered, and is suffering severely; and that while that
miserly wretch, Abimelech, is destroying the fabric, he is purloining and
carrying off the best of the materials. I doubt whether there be an acre of
land in the occupation of Sir Arthur, which has not cost ten times its
intrinsic value to make it better. It is astonishing how Sir Arthur can be
[pardon the expression, my dear] such a dupe! I have before blamed, and
must again blame you, for not exerting yourself sufficiently to shew him his
folly. It concerns the family, it concerns yourself, nearly. [A, 5-6]

A little later Anna complains to Louisa about "this wretch, this *honest
Aby*, as my father calls him, [who] would not willingly suffer a guinea
to be spent, except in improvements: that is, not a guinea which
should not pass through his hands" (A, 21). Anna repeatedly remon-
strates with her father, but to no avail. Anna has very specific ideas
about the uses of fortune. As she tells her father, money should be
employed to advance the welfare of mankind. Those who have wealth
are responsible for enhancing the lives of others, and if the owner of
property is limited in how the money can be used, then the money
must be put in the hands of those who can use it better; thus Anna,
whose sex, age, and social position all limit her active involvement in
society, must help Frank, capable but poor, to aid others. Anna judi-
ciously distributes her wealth; very much aware of the value of money,
she is careful in her benevolence and admires monetary prudence in
others. With admiration, she notes of Frank that

> there is no propensity in [him] to waste [a] guinea. Without the least love of
> money, Frank is a rigid economist. The father indulges no false wants
> because it would be expensive; the son has none to indulge. Habits which in
> the one are the fruits of avarice, in the other are the offspring of wisdom.
> . . . He is anxiously studious to discover how he may apply the wealth that
> may revert to him most to benefit that society from which it first sprang. The
> best application of riches is one of our frequent themes; because it will be
> one of our first duties. The diffusion of knowledge, or more properly of
> truth, is the one great good to which wealth, genius, and existence ought all
> to be applied. This noble purpose gives birth to felicity which is in itself
> grand, inexhaustible, and eternal. [A, 381-82]

The careful dissemination of wealth in the service of their scheme of
social improvement is Anna and Frank's goal throughout the book.
They attempt to reform a young highwayman, for example. It turns
out that he is the nephew of the family's housekeeper, a woman Anna

"almost revere[s] as [a] mother, because of the excellence of her heart and the soundness of her understanding" (*A*, 39). This woman, Mrs. Clarke, refuses to take money from Anna for the relief of her nephew, and Anna does not try to force the money on her. "I do not wish to encourage the most distant approaches to a spirit of avarice" (*A*, 48), she explains. Anna's responsibility is not simply to distribute largesse but to be sure that the funds are used wisely.

It is not only money that must be used wisely and well but moral direction. Anna works very hard to reform Coke Clifton, resulting in some of the most preaching lover's speeches in literature. She writes to Louisa about Coke that she must "weed out those few errors, for few I hope they are, which impoverish a mind in itself apparently fertile and of high rank. . . . The attempt must be made—With what obstinate warfare do men encounter peril when money, base money is the proposed reward! And shall we do less for mind, eternal omnipotent mind?" (*A*, 83). She discusses with Coke "the grand distinction between general and individual happiness" (*A*, 170). She lectures him on the philosophy she requires in a husband: "I hope to see my husband forgetting himself, or rather placing self-gratification in the pursuit of universal good, deaf to the calls of passion, willing to encounter adversity, reproof, nay death, the champion of truth, and the determined, the unrelenting enemy of error" (*A*, 171).[5] Even after consenting to marry Coke, she notes that "I was still more determined to exert myself; that the due influence which reason ought always to have, over passion, might not be lost, and sink into habitual and timid concession" (*A*, 192). Still later, another very long dialogue of moral improvement ends with Coke planning to go home to make notes on their conversation and Anna promising, "I will spare you the trouble of writing, if you think proper, and send you a tolerably correct transcript of my thoughts tomorrow morning. I can easily repeat them, assisted by some memorandums that I have already made, and by the strength of my recollection and my feelings, which I think are in no danger of a sudden decay!" (*A*, 265-66).

Inflated as Anna's comments may seem to a modern reader, Holcroft's intent in giving Anna these speeches of moral philosophy is to show the value and the depth of a female mind. Anna intellectually and morally outshines Coke; she must be a force in his improvement. The duty of all enlightened human beings is to spread their enlightenment. As Frank ecstatically notes, it is "an age when light begins to appear even in regions that have hitherto been thick darkness; . . . I myself am so highly fortunate as to be able to contribute to the great the universal cause; the progress of truth, the extirpation of error, and the general perfection of mind! I and those dear friends I have named; who are indeed dear because of their ardent and uniform love of virtue!" (A, 383). The duty to promulgate enlightenment extends to every relationship, untrammeled by the limits of social convention. The effort must be made to correct any perceived error. And so Anna must attempt to educate not only her peers, but her parent.

Sir Arthur does not take kindly to Anna's lessons. "Do you hear, Anna? I am too old to be schooled. I don't like it! Mind me! I don't like it!" (A, 25) he fumes. But although Anna is capable of lecturing her father about his improvement mania, she is not able to challenge him on the level of her filial duty: because she thinks Sir Arthur would not approve of her marriage to the son of his steward, she insists to Frank that she cannot marry him. She explains her position; the man she marries must be "a person of whom no prejudice, no mistake of any kind, should induce the world, that is, the persons nearest and most connected with me in the world, to think meanly—Shall I be cited by the thoughtless, the simple, the perverse, in justification of their own improper conduct? . . . Nor is this the most alarming fear—My friends!—My relations!—My father!" (A, 132). Anna goes on that "To incur a father's reproach for having dishonoured his family were fearful: but to meet, to merit, to live under his curse!—God of heaven forbid!" (A, 132). But Anna is wrong; rationally and romantically, she should marry Frank, and the novel makes her error quite clear. Yet this particular error, bowing to the prejudices of a man of so mean an understanding as Sir Arthur's simply because he is her father, for Holcroft seems to make Anna all the more admirable. Anna not only is intelligent, brave, and unselfish, she is deeply moved by filial piety. Holcroft has it both ways: he can show in Frank's comments that Anna is wrong and still have her virtuous even on this level of filial behavior. Not surprisingly, as the plot develops, Sir Arthur positively comes to pant after Frank as his daughter's mate; we will see that Bage too, for all the radical ideas in Hermsprong, brings his plot around so that his lovers gain parental approval.[6] Anna's relationship with her father is not the only issue on which Holcroft fudges his revolutionary principles. In a long discussion about marriage in the ideal society, Frank explains that once men and women stop behaving selfishly, there will be no possessive relationships. All will act for the good of the whole. There will be no servants. Children will be "children of the state." And the sense in which we understand marriage and the affirmation—*This is my wife*—neither the institution nor the claim can in such a state, or indeed in justice exist. Of all the regulations which were ever suggested to the mistaken tyranny of selfishness, none perhaps to this day have surpassed the despotism of those which undertake to bind not only body to body but soul to soul, to all futurity, in despite of every possible change which our vices and our virtues might effect, or however numerous the secret corporal or mental imperfections might prove which a more intimate acquaintance should bring to light! [*A*, 279]

But for now, since society has not yet reached this goal of enlightened mutual interest, marriage still is needed to protect women. The radical view of marriage as an often inhuman yoking of unlike individuals—Wollstonecraft's precise image in *Maria*—is softened by an insistence that in the imperfect state of things as they are, marriage still provides a necessary social safeguard.

Holcroft's radicalism is tempered too by the essentially traditional nature of his plot, which after all centers on the romantic pairing off of the hero and heroine. But the emphasis that Holcroft places on the quality of his heroine's mind is not diminished by the eventual romantic outcome of the novel. Anna will marry Frank because their minds are equal; the repeated references to the good they will be able to do together, their discussions of themes for the betterment of society, Anna's vision of "the good that might result from the union of two strong minds, mutually determined to exert their powers for the welfare of society" (*A*, 51) all emphasize this aspect of the relationship. Holcroft does bow to romantic convention—Anna is so beautiful that her fame has reached Italy. But it is also true that he gives her these words: "I know not, but I begin to fear that no permanent good can be effected at present, without peril. If so, shall I listen only to my fears; shrink into self; and shun that which duty bids me encounter? No. Though the prejudices of mankind were to overwhelm me with sorrows, for seeking to do good, I will still go on: I will persevere, will accomplish or die" (*A*, 146). Holcroft has imagined an intelligent and brave human being, thoughts directed beyond the self, who is a woman; in the eighteenth century this image of woman is almost unique. The novel is talky at times, the characters sometimes inflated and often pedantic; Holcroft is not a good enough novelist to prevent his philosophies from occasionally overwhelming his characterizations.[7] But he contributed a characterization of woman that frees her from the limits of domestic boundaries without taking her beyond the pale of social acceptability. Anna St. Ives is intellectually connected to the world and still part of normal, decent society. Defoe, when he freed Moll and Roxana, had to loose them from the bounds of respectable society; Holcroft's vision is that a woman can be intellectually active, socially concerned, and positively engaged with both the domestic and the larger society, and still remain part of that society. Near the end of the novel the imprisoned Anna tells her jailor that "there is no such mighty difference [between men and women] as prejudice supposes. Courage has neither sex nor form: it is an energy of mind" (A, 423). Anna is not limited by the social conventions that tell her she cannot climb a wall—or that she cannot think. The equal of any, she is equally the friend of her female friend Louisa and her male friend Frank, and such a portrait of friendship too is almost unique to Holcroft. One outstanding characteristic of *Anna St. Ives* is the normality of its heroine. Anna is brave and bright; she is not a saint. She is not too good for this world, and this is perhaps one of the most positive aspects of Holcroft's image of woman.

Godwin's women, in contrast, are saintly victims. Incarnations of perfection themselves, they are destroyed by the badly damaged men around them. Holcroft emphasizes the capability of women to influence the people around them and even to change the outcomes of events; Godwin like Holcroft gives his women mind and courage, but he sees them crushed by their inability to control their lives: women in Godwin novels are always secondary characters. In all his novels Godwin emphasizes the disastrous effects of society's misshaping of the individual, and this is true for men as well as for women. Falkland, Tyrrel, and finally Caleb in *Caleb Williams*, and St. Leon in *St. Leon*, all are warped by a society that damages the individual by substituting the distortions of rank and pride, and social vanity, for human trust, love, and compassion. These players are all men, as are the protagonists in each of Godwin's later novels.[8] Women in these novels are not active in the larger society but are destroyed by the men closest to them. Emily in *Caleb Williams* and Marguerite in *St. Leon* are remarkable in their goodness. And they are very vulnerable.

In *Caleb Williams* the story of Emily and her persecution by Tyrrel is the prelude to Falkland's tyrannizing of Caleb. The evil Tyrrel uses his power to crush Emily; the virtuous Falkland, himself perverted by a society that destroys the normal ties between human beings, does the same thing to Caleb. In the state of "Things As They Are," the subtitle of Godwin's novel, those with power destroy the powerless; the horror is that it matters very little whether the particular man begins as evil or as good: he ends a tyrant. Godwin sees many opportunities for the misuse of power in his society; between master and servant, land owner and tenant, rich relative and female dependent, the potential exists for the tyranny of the strong over the weak. Godwin takes this last category as the simplest case, and the story of Emily's destruction by Tyrrel serves in the book as a model of the danger of arbitrary power sanctioned by law.

Emily is a child when she comes under the protection of her cousin Tyrrel. Her mother, in marrying against the family's wishes, had forfeited her claim to a share of its fortune. The orphaned Emily comes to live with Tyrrel and his mother in an ambiguous position, not quite relative and not yet servant: "Mrs. Tyrrel conceived that she performed an act of the most exalted benevolence in admitting miss Emily into a sort of equivocal situation, which was neither precisely that of a domestic, nor yet marked with the treatment that might seem due to one of the family."[9] Emily is raised with young Tyrrel; when her aunt dies, she is left entirely under her cousin's care. Although

> in equity perhaps [Emily] was entitled to that portion of fortune which her mother had forfeited by her imprudence, and which had gone to swell the property of the male representative . . . this idea had never entered into the conceptions of either mother or son. . . . The death of her aunt made very little change in her situation. This prudent lady, who would have thought it little less than sacrilege to have considered miss Melvile as a branch of the stock of the Tyrrels, took no more notice of her in her will, than barely putting her down for one hundred pounds in a catalogue of legacies to her servants. [*Caleb*, 38-39]

Emily's well-being, her life itself as Godwin shows, depends on the good will of her protector. But Emily antagonizes Tyrrel when she innocently allows him to see her growing admiration for his perceived rival Falkland. Tyrrel is furious, and because he is rich and powerful society puts no limits on the venting of his anger. Maliciously, he decides to force Emily to marry a local farmer's son, an "uncouth and half-civilised animal" (*Caleb*, 47). Tyrrel's first thought had been "to thrust her from his doors, and leave her to seek her bread as she could. But he was conscious that this proceeding would involve him in considerable obloquy" (*C*, 47); he chooses, instead, to torture her in a socially acceptable manner. Godwin comments that Emily at the age of seventeen "had not reflected on the insuperable distance that custom has placed between the opulent and the poorer classes of the community" (C, 41). As Emily's story unfolds, it is clear that this distance is largely measured in access to the law. Emily takes quite some time to realize her danger. Up to this point, Emily had largely been "exempted from the oppression of despotism. Her happy insignificance had served her as a protection" (C, 48). When Tyrrel tells her she will marry Grimes, Emily simply responds "No, sir, I do not want a husband" (C, 48), pointing out that they are totally unfit to be a pair. She appeals to her cousin's sense of family propriety, only to be rebuffed with "Our family? Have you the impudence to think yourself one of our family?" (C, 48). Emily mistakenly thinks that family has something to do with relations; Tyrrel points out that the question is one of respective amounts of cash:

> Why, sir! was not your grandpapa my grandpapa? How then can we be of a different family?
> From the strongest reason in the world. You are the daughter of a rascally Scotchman, who spent every shilling of my aunt Lucy's fortune, and left you a beggar. You have got a hundred pounds, and Grimes's father promises to give him as much. How dare you look down upon your equals? [C, 48]

Tyrrel never thinks that Emily has any say in the matter of her marriage. To anyone who questions his right to marry her to Grimes, he hints that he acts for her own good and for the family honor. Without guidance and forceful regulation, she is likely to "be a whore, and at last no better than a common trull . . . if I were not at all these pains to save her from destruction. I would make her an honest farmer's wife, and my pretty miss cannot bear the thoughts of it!" (C, 50). Tyrrel's accusations are totally without basis, but Emily's innocence is irrelevant. Tyrrel uses the fact of her femaleness to justify his action in getting her married. The circumstance of being female, like being poor, makes Emily vulnerable. Repeatedly Tyrrel uses his pretended fears for Emily's own good to rebuff any pleas. She begs him not to yoke "two people for a whim, who are neither of them fit for one another in any respect in the world," and his answer is "that it is necessary to put you out of harm's way" (C, 53).

Tyrrel finally imprisons Emily in her own room; at the same time he continues to do "every thing in his power to blast the young lady's reputation, and represented to his attendants these precautions as necessary, to prevent her from eloping to his neighbour, and plunging herself in total ruin" (C, 56). By these means Tyrrel keeps Emily from contact with the outside world. Emily steadfastly refuses to bow to her cousin's pressure. Finally, he presents the bare face of his tyranny.

> So you want to know by what right you are here, do you? By the right of possession. This house is mine, and you are in my power. There is no Mrs. Jakeman now to spirit you away; no, nor no Falkland to bully for you. I have countermined you, damn me! and blown up your schemes. Do you think I will be contradicted and opposed for nothing? When did you ever know any body resist my will without being made to repent? And shall I now see myself brow-beaten by a chitty-faced girl? I have not given you a fortune? Damn you, who brought you up? I will make you a bill for clothing and lodging. Do not you know that every creditor has a right to stop his runaway debtor? You may think as you please: but here you are till you marry Grimes. Heaven and earth shall not prevent, but I will get the better of your obstinacy! [C, 57]

This grotesque analysis of the situation—that Emily owes him the costs of her subsistence—earns Tyrral the domination he wants. The law supports Tyrrel, and through legal persecution he kills Emily.

Threatened with marriage by force if not by consent, Emily in desperation arranges with Grimes that he will help her to escape. She runs away from Tyrrel's house with Grimes's help, but Grimes turns on her. With great courage and presence of mind Emily manages to elude him and finally is saved by Falkland, who conducts her to a safe and respectable shelter. Exhausted with the shock of her escape, Emily falls ill. Tyrrel has her taken from her sick bed to the county jail, and this further shock kills her. No one can help Emily; no one can prevent Tyrrel from committing this outrage. Even Tyrrel's hard-hearted aide tries to make him hold off: "I have heard as how that miss Emily is sick a-bed. You are determined, you say, to put her in jail. You do not mean to kill her, I take it" (C, 82). But Tyrrel, free to act on his whim, is not to be stopped: "Let her die! I will not spare her for an hour. I will not always be insulted. She had no consideration for me, and I have no mercy for her. I am in for it! They have provoked me past all bearing, and they shall feel me! Tell Swineard, in bed or up, day or night, I will not have him hear of an instant's delay" (C, 82).

*Caleb Williams* explores the effects on human relationships of unbridled and arbitrary power. The story of Emily is only one of Godwin's examples of the destruction that rank and wealth can wreak, and although Emily's history provides some of the most tragic moments in the novel, her story is only a minor part of the whole. Godwin in all his novels, including *Caleb Williams*, is much more interested in analyzing

the minds of male than of female characters. Nevertheless, this episode is clearly meant specifically to be Godwin's exploration of the
vulnerability of women in his society, and he alludes in this brief
section of the novel to a broad range of issues. Emily is vulnerable to
attack not because of any failures of intellect or nerve on her part but
because she is a woman and dependent. She is an adept student we are
told; the tutors hired to teach Tyrrel give instruction to the willing little
girl instead. But her mind and her courage are irrelevant in the face of
her social position. Custom and law support Tyrrel in his torture of the
young woman; had he managed to get her married to Grimes, society
would have seen him fulfilling his duty as Emily's guardian in protect-
ing her from the pitfalls attendant on being female and single. It is this
social support that he counts on. When his plan does not work, the law
supports the lowest levels of spiteful behavior and allows him to crush
Emily.

Godwin does not otherwise in his novels pay much attention
specifically to the interface between women and society. There is little
direct discussion of the issues his contemporaries Holcroft and Bage
consider—Godwin does not theorize in the novels about women's
education or women's potential for social action, for example. He
does, like both Holcroft and Bage, celebrate the female mind. This
appreciation of the female intellect to some degree sets apart these
male radical novelists of the end of the century from their predecessors. Defoe alone in the novel tradition paid attention to women's
intellect, but, as with his male characters, he was more interested in
practical capabilities than a broader intellectual reach. Clarissa's
thoughts, as we have seen, revolve in the very limited tracks of her
domestic world. Amelia isn't much of a thinker, either. But Godwin,
like Holcroft and Bage, is fascinated by the range not just of a man's but
of a woman's mind, and the character of Marguerite in *St. Leon*,
Godwin's homage to Mary Wollstonecraft, is a woman not only of
emotional but of intellectual depth and grace.

The plot of *St. Leon* is convoluted, as befits a gothic novel dealing
with a philosopher's stone and the elixir of life. It is not nearly as good a
novel as *Caleb Williams*, but of Godwin's later novels, it is the most
worthy of attention. The book is of particular interest in a discussion of
images of women, for *St. Leon* is the anarchist Godwin's hymn to
domesticity.[10] Generations of critics have been amused by Godwin's
about-face in *St. Leon* from his attitudes on marriage in *Political Justice*,
but I think they are missing something in the texture of *St. Leon*'s
domestic scene that makes this turnaround less drastic than we might

assume. Godwin's domesticity has a fairly radical edge to it. Marguerite, the wife of St. Leon, is not very different in spirit from Anna St. Ives. Like Holcroft's character, she is smart, capable, and brave. Like Anna, too, she is intellectually the match of any man. Marguerite is a more than equal partner in her marriage. Godwin's novel celebrates the joys of domesticity, but it is a rather different domesticity he celebrates from the traditional images we saw in Fielding, for example. The marriage between St. Leon and Marguerite is first of all a union of minds. Repeatedly St. Leon describes their conversations about books; they discuss philosophies of education for their children and philosophies of life for themselves and for society. Little attention is paid to Marguerite's cooking, but a great deal to her reading. Fielding's Amelia spends hours preparing Booth's favorite dinner; Godwin's Marguerite shares her ideas with St. Leon.

> We were both of us well acquainted with the most eminent poets and fine writers of modern times. But when we came to read them together, they presented themselves in a point of view in which they had never been seen by us before. It is, perhaps, more important that poetry, and every thing that excites the imagination or appeals to the heart, should be read in solitude, than in society. But the true way to understand our author in these cases, is to employ each of these modes in succession. The terrible, the majestic, the voluptuous and the melting, are all of them, in a considerable degree, affairs of sympathy; and we never judge of them so infallibly, or with so much satisfaction, as when in the presence of each other, the emotion is kindled in either bosom at the same instant, the eye-beams, pregnant with sentiment and meaning, involuntarily meet and mingle; the voice of the reader becomes modulated by the ideas of his author, and that of the hearer, by an accidental interjection of momentary comment or applause, confesses its accord. It was in this manner that we read together the admirable sonnets of Petrarch, and passed in review the sublime effusions of Dante. The letters of Eloisa to Abelard afforded us singular delight. We searched into the effusions of the Troubadours, and, among all their absurdities and inequality, we found a wildness, a daring pouring forth of the soul, an unpruned richness of imagination, and, from time to time, a grandeur of conception and audacious eccentricity of thought, that filled us with unlooked for transport. At other times, when not regularly engaged in this species of reading, we would repeat passages to each other, communicate the discoveries of this sort that either had made in solitude, and point out unobserved beauties, that perhaps neither of us would have remarked, but for the suggestions of the other. It is impossible for two persons to be constituted so much alike, but that one of them should have a more genuine and instantaneous relish for one sort of excellence, and another for another.

Thus we added to each other's stores, and acquired a largeness of conception and liberality of judgment that neither of us would have arrived at if separate.[11]

The intellectual aggrandizement is truly mutual. Marguerite's knowledge of literature predates her marriage to St. Leon, so there is no suggestion that one of the marriage partners guides the other; her understanding and appreciation of literature is equal to his. Note the length of the passage. Godwin emphasizes the importance of this intellectual aspect of married life by his very detailed description. None of this might seem worth commenting on if we did not have other images of Learned Ladies to compare with Godwin's celebration of Marguerite and of the joy of intellectual intercourse between man and wife. St. Leon applauds the quality of his wife's mind: "She derived her happiness from the tone of her own mind, and stood in no need of the gaping admiration and stupid wonder of others to make her feel herself happy" (SL, 42). Certainly she is an equal preceptor with St. Leon himself in the education of their children.

When St. Leon first meets Marguerite he has begun to live a profligate life; the promise of winning this woman of "singular . . . intellectual accomplishments" and "uncommon prudence of . . . judgments" (SL, 34) convinces St. Leon to reform, and the two of them marry and live together very happily for some time. She bears five children in ten years, and the children bring them even closer. St. Leon's description of the feelings they share after the birth of their first child, Charles, glows with gentleness and love:

Never shall I forget the interview between us immediately subsequent to her first parturition, the effusion of soul with which we met each other after all danger seemed to have subsided, the kindness which animated us, increased as it was by ideas of peril and suffering, the sacred sensation with which the mother presented her infant to her husband, or the complacency with which we read in each other's eyes a common sentiment of melting tenderness and inviolable attachment!

This, she seemed to say, is the joint result of our common affection. It partakes equally of both, and is the shrine in which our sympathies and our life have been poured together, never to be separated. Let other lovers testify their engagements by presents and tokens; we record and stamp our attachment in this precious creature, a creature of that species which is more admirable than any thing else the world has to boast, a creature susceptible of pleasure and pain, of affection and love, of sentiment and fancy, of wisdom and virtue. [SL, 43-44]

Having babies is obviously women's work, although St. Leon seems to share in the experience as much as he can. But this is the only area of stereotypically separated behavior that Godwin talks about. Just as with intellectual affairs, he makes no distinction between St. Leon's and Marguerite's interests and talents in the conduct of the practical matters of day to day living. Marguerite is never the mere helpmate. At several crucial moments, in fact, she takes charge of financial arrangements, determines moves, and buys and sells property.

After many years of domestic contentment, St. Leon succumbs once more to his weakness for gambling. He loses a great sum, then collapses in guilt and shock into a nervous breakdown. Marguerite takes over.[12] She manages to pay St. Leon's debts by selling off all the family property and most of their effects. Marguerite, St. Leon marvels, "only borrowed vigour from her situation, and rose in proportion to the pressure of the calamity" (SL, 73). St. Leon himself sinks into "a period of frenzy" (SL, 73) and

> It was in this condition that Marguerite conducted me and my children to an obscure retreat in the canton of Soleure, in the republic of Switzerland. Cheapness was the first object; for the most miserable pittance was all she had saved from the wreck of our fortune. . . . Hither, then, it was that she led me, our son, and three daughters. Immediately upon our arrival she purchased a small and obscure, but neat, cottage. . . . My paternal estates, as well as those which had fallen to me by marriage, had all been swallowed up in the gulf, which my accursed conduct had prepared. Marguerite made a general sale of our movables, our ornaments, and even our clothes. A few books, guided by the attachment to literature which had always attended me, were all that she saved from the wreck. A considerable part of the sum thus produced was appropriated by my creditors. Marguerite had the prudence and skill to satisfy them all, and was contented to retain that only which remained when their demands were discharged. [SL, 73-74]

Later, after they have partially recovered from the shock of their loss of fortune and St. Leon's illness, calamity once more strikes them. Their little house and the garden and livestock from which they take their subsistence are destroyed by a storm. Marguerite once again determines their next "place of residence. . . . She had heard much of the beauty and richness of the country bordering on the Lake of Constance, and she thought that, while we denied ourselves expensive pleasures, or rather while they were placed out of our reach, there would be a propriety in our procuring for ourselves a stock of those pleasures which would cost us nothing. This was a refinement beyond me, and serves to evince the superiority which Marguerite's virtue and force of mind still retained over mine" (SL, 99).

Marguerite adjusts with no complaint to the poverty and simplicity of their life in Switzerland; in good radical/romantic fashion she goes so far as to wonder if St. Leon in losing all their money has "done . . . a mischief, or . . . conferred a benefit?" (SL, 85). She is the moral tutor of her children and also of her husband, teaching all of them to respect simplicity and to be happy in their poverty. Godwin draws a woman with enormous reserves of character. The portrait of Marguerite is sentimental, to be sure. But it nonetheless presents a remarkable image of a woman capable not alone of moral strength and philosophical vision but of practicality as well. Godwin's ideal woman, like Holcroft's, is able to shape those around her by the force not just of her moral but of her practical sense. Godwin in his novels does not normally draw his women carefully—most of his female characters, like St. Leon's mother, are significant for their effect in shaping the character of the male protagonist. But the heroic and capable Marguerite is his admirable, and amiable, exception.

The women in Robert Bage's *Hermsprong* are both admirable and amiable. *Hermsprong* is one of the most delightful of all eighteenth-century novels, and its heroines are two of the smartest women in these novels. *Hermsprong*'s tone is wry, its images sunny yet always just abutting shadow. Bage presents a world where reason and good do triumph, but they win out by very narrow margins over the ubiquitous insanities of eighteenth-century England's laws, social customs, and patterns of male-female relationships. Bage's view of women is one of the most positive in the eighteenth-century novel; his images of women are marvelously mixed, ranging from the witty, intelligent, brave and charming Maria Fluart to the idiotic ladies of the Sumelin family, mother and daughter. His heroine, Caroline Campinet, is not quite the paragon of rationality that Maria is, but, intelligent and charming at the outset of the novel, Caroline learns to trust to her good sense rather than to custom as the novel goes on. By the end of the action she overcomes her earlier prejudices and limitations, thus exemplifying in the novel the fulfillment of human potential that rational persuasion applied to a receptive intelligence can bring about. Bage makes fun of fretful damsels, and he respects rational women— he gibes a bit at "fair readers" and the "dangers" women face in any and all sorties beyond the hearth, but these gibes emphasize his real regard for the capable, sensible woman like Maria Fluart or Caroline Campinet.

The central action of the novel is intellectual, moving Caroline from her belief that filial duty requires submission to a father's irrational demands to the understanding that every human being must choose a course of action based on rational motivation; duty must be based on mutual respect, not merely filial devotion. Caroline, the critic must sadly admit, is not a quick study, and it takes Hermsprong virtually the entire novel to bring her around. It is not that Caroline lacks a model of rational behavior: her best friend, Maria Fluart, questions all formulas, including that of filial obedience, and presents a marvelously reasonable pattern of action for Caroline to follow. Maria is one of the most extraordinary female characters in the eighteenth-century English novel. Maria's intelligence, her wit, and her scepticism are emphasized as aspects not of an ideal but of a normal human being. Reinforcing Bage's insistence on the normality of Maria's character is his portrait of Mrs. Garnet, an older—and an eminently respectable—type of Maria. Mrs. Merrick, Caroline's guardian, is a third example in the novel of such a woman.

We first get to know Maria in the letter she writes to Caroline about the elopement of Miss Sumelin. Miss Sumelin and her mother are empty-headed women who seem incapable of rational thought, although this defect does not prevent them from being highly opinionated. Miss Sumelin has run off with a Mr. Fillygrove, "a young man with a sweet pretty face, and two well enough shaped legs."[13] Maria wryly notes that "These are considered as great accomplishments by young ladies. . . . [and] Miss Harriet Sumelin could not resist such weighty attractions" (H, 26). Maria, like Mr. Sumelin, Harriet's father, is not unduly perturbed by what Mrs. Sumelin insists is a disaster, and as Maria recounts the weighty conversation about Harriet's elopement, Bage points up the ridiculousness of the conventions that govern much of society's view of women—conventions represented here by Mrs. Sumelin. Maria reports that "Mr. Sumelin, who had eaten his breakfast with perfect composure, said, 'Well, and for what is all this noise and pother, Mrs. Sumelin? Your daughter is gone to be married, that's all. I suppose you intended she should marry one day' " (H, 27). But Mrs. Sumelin is horrified: her daughter is marrying " 'so much beneath her,' " she laments.

> 'No, Mr. Sumelin! So rich you as you are, and a young lady with your daughter's accomplishments!'

'As to riches, Mrs. Sumelin, they are my own, and at my own disposal. I may give Mrs. Fillygrove a large fortune, and I may not. It is true I do not much like masses of money in the hands of fools; but she is my daughter;— I shall not let her want; and her puppy husband may one day be weaned of his folly, and may make as respectable a man as his poverty of understanding will permit.'

'And so you really mean to forgive them without any ado?'

'Forgive them! yes. Why, I am hardly offended.' [H, 27]

Maria comments, "In truth, if the old gentleman had spoke the whole truth, I believe he was rather pleased than offended" (H, 27). He refuses to send after the young couple to prevent them from marrying.

Maria finds Mrs. Sumelin ridiculous, but Mrs. Sumelin's reactions are the societally expected ones. Her daughter is marrying beneath her; her daughter should be made to smart. Mr. Sumelin's response is Bage's; the entire crisis is farce: nothing has happened that calls for tears and hysteria. In this short dialogue Bage punctures the assumptions that govern marriage in the polite classes. Bage considers worth defined by a parent's wealth and accomplishment defined as a lack of repellent characteristics insufficient grounds for pride. And a woman's actions, silly though they may be, do not imply instantaneous doom just because they are performed without parental consent. Mrs. Sumelin will be unhappy if her daughter has married and she will be unhappy if Harriet returns single, Hermsprong points out. "'Dear madam,'" he tells her, "''you puzzle me! If your daughter is married, you disown her because she is married. This is the first case. The second is, if she is not married, you disown her because—because she is not married'" (H, 30).[14] The emphases of the account are Maria's. She agrees with Hermsprong and Mr. Sumelin that Harriet's unfinished elopement is merely comical. Clearly impressed by Hermsprong, Maria tells Caroline, "He is not an Adonis, like Mr. Fillygrove" (H, 28); siding with Mr. Sumelin, she remarks that "Mrs. Sumelin continuing much upon the fret, Mr. Sumelin went to the counting-house, and we saw no more of him (a thing that happens often) till the next morning. Indeed, we scarce saw him for several days after this; for Mrs. Sumelin was always at him, with all the agreeable garrulousness of a fretful woman, and the candour of a wife, who is perfectly convinced that her husband is always wrong" (H, 28).

Maria's rationality shapes her every encounter. Thus when Mrs. Stone, Lord Grondale's housekeeper and companion, attempts to assume Caroline's rightful place in the household, Maria ironically greets her as if she were mistress of the house. Reprimanded by Lord

Grondale for affronting Mrs. Stone, Maria "regrets" her mistake: " 'She was so kind as to welcome me just as a lady Grondale would have done: so, though I had not heard of it, I concluded your lordship had taken a wife: accordingly I paid my respects. It surprised me, to be sure, to see her bounce off as if she was affronted: but, my dear lord, you must make it up for me' " (*H*, 81). Bage notes that "Miss Fluart did fib a little, for she knew Mrs. Stone very well; but the whim of mortifying the poor woman came into her head, who indeed did outstep propriety in her officious welcome; and whom Miss Fluart could not forgive for taking her friend's place at Lord Grondale's table" (*H*, 81). At the next meal, Caroline "took her accustomed place" and Maria, pretending to assume that she was being called upon to "do the honours of the table" took Mrs. Stone's chair. Caroline corrects Maria—" 'That is Mrs. Stone's chair' " —and Maria responds, " 'I wish Mrs. Stone was either Lady Grondale or not; one shall always be making mistakes' " (*H*, 82). The small battle over Mrs. Stone is instructive. Maria upsets the Grondale household because her actions are not congruent with social pretence. Bage insists that interactions between people must be based on reality, not on social formulas. Maria has the strength of character to refuse to participate in the farce that Lord Grondale has set up with Mrs. Stone. Caroline must develop this strength; for most of the novel she yields to social pressure, as here, when she asks Maria to cede precedence to Mrs. Stone. Under the tutelage of Maria and Hermsprong, Caroline grows out of her adherence to convention.

One of the social conventions that most damages women is the assumption that a girl owes unconditional allegiance to her parent without regard to the appropriateness of his demands. This obedience is no trivial matter, since parents involve themselves in the matrimonial future of the female child, and thus easily can blight not only her youth but her entire life. Maria's attempt to make Caroline understand that Lord Grondale does not have unlimited rights over her begins before there is a question of courtship. Part of Maria's campaign against Mrs. Stone's usurpation of Caroline's place in the household is to make Caroline understand her rights—opposed to Caroline's perception of her duty, which is, Maria scornfully tells Lord Grondale, " 'to bear all you choose to inflict' " (*H*, 80). As Caroline remarks to Maria, " 'All I have to do is to submit, and comfort myself with the reflection, that I have not incurred [Lord Grondale's displeasure] by any indecorums, or any contumacy of my own' " (*H*, 81). Maria ironically agrees that " 'there is great consolation in being whipped for having been good,'" and talks of "'unnatural fathers'" (*H*, 82). Caroline's position is that "'Lord Grondale is my father; he may have his failings, but is it fit for a daughter to see them? In short, he is my father; I say everything in that'" (*H*, 85). Caroline returns again and again to her duty: "'I refer to the duty I owe; a duty which forbids my giving him offence.'" Maria argues that fatherhood hardly "'sanctifies'" Lord Grondale, and that in relationships there is such a word as "'reciprocity,'" but Caroline responds that she cannot "'bargain'" (*H*, 85) with her father. The father who draws such dutifulness from Caroline treats her very badly.[15] He arranges his household to his own whim, holding months-long assemblies of carousing men, and essentially making Caroline, when she is in residence at her home, an isolated prisoner. After the early death of her mother, Caroline had been raised by her aunt, Mrs. Merrick, to whom Lord Grondale gave a very modest allowance for the upkeep of his daughter. Caroline, as Maria ironically points out, has been "'debarred from society, and the common pleasures of life, by pure paternal affection'" (*H*, 85).

The first crack in Caroline's dutifulness is made not by appeals to her own mistreatment but by the suggestion that her strict adherence to one perceived duty is at the expence of an equally demanding concern. Hermsprong and Maria convince Caroline that obeying her father's command to avoid her aunt Garnet means wounding a kind and deserving woman. Caroline's own feelings and good sense tip the balance against filial obedience, but even this small rebellion is achieved only after much argument. Caroline and Maria meet Hermsprong, Mrs. Garnet, and Mr. Glen at Lippen Crag.[16] Caroline and Maria greet the gentlemen and move quickly on, only to be stopped by Hermsprong. He tells Caroline the sad history of Mrs. Garnet, who has been denied her place in the family—without cause, of course. Caroline, torn between her father's command and her humane instinct, does not know what to do: "'indeed, Mr. Hermsprong, I wish to pay my duty to my venerable relation,—to pay it this instant, but, situated as I am, is it proper?'" (*H*, 101). Hermsprong merely says "'You are ever amiable . . . even in your errors,'" leaving Caroline to wonder that "'filial obedience [can] ever be error?'" (*H*, 101). Hermsprong bases his argument on "'the truth of things only'" (*H*, 101); Caroline argues from social convention. "'An illegal act you must not do, even by the command of a father; and ought you to to a wrong one?'" (*H*, 101), asks Hermsprong. Caroline cannot yet free herself from a restrictive sense of what she owes her father merely because he is a father: "'But surely it may be wrong to do a right thing, when prohibited by a father,'" she answers. At last, however, Caroline decides that "'Whatever be the consequence, I will obey the impulse of my heart,'" and she asks to be introduced to her "'revered aunt'" (*H*, 101). Still markedly uncomfortable with her rebellion, she turns to Maria for support: "'Do you condemn me'" (*H*, 101), she wonders, and Maria seconds Caroline's decision.

The questions raised in Caroline's discussion with Hermsprong are not trivial ones. "'[C]an filial obedience ever be in error?'" Caroline wonders, and "'ought a child to erect herself into a judge of her father's motives?'" (*H*, 101). As soon as the answer to these questions becomes "yes," the structure of society has undergone a radical change. To understand how radical, we need only try to imagine Clarissa answering in the affirmative here. Woman in the eighteenth century is limited by the closely linked commandments that she be dutiful to her parents and be sexually pure. Bage underscores this tie in the discussion of Harriet Sumelin's elopement, where the elopement does not become a tragedy because Mr. Sumelin simply refuses to make it into one. When we realize the impossibility of Mr. Harlowe reacting the same way to Clarissa's disobedience and her departure from his house, we see how far Bage takes his novel from what even in the nineties still would have been a prevalent view of woman. Bage assumes that filial obedience can be an error, and that a child indeed ought to judge a parent's motives. This perspective frees woman from one of the areas of greatest despotism: the demand for unquestioning acceptance of any decision about how she will live her life. One of the most serious areas of parental despotism, as we saw in *Clarissa*, is parental interference in the woman's marriage decisions. But as Bage very astutely suggests, this limitation is part of a larger despotism that reaches into many important areas of a woman's life and is strongly supported by her internalized perception of her duty to the despot. Hermsprong and Maria must first help Caroline to question the basic premises of her perception of duty before they can persuade her to act rationally. Her decision to talk to Mrs. Garnet, based on the assessment of the situation to which Hermsprong incites her, is a crucial first step in Caroline's emancipation. Maria Fluart, who manages both to enjoy a liberated perspective and at the same time to live respectably involved in her society, from the beginning of the story presents a model for Caroline.

Maria is intensely alive and really quite happy. It is the obedient and traditionally dutiful Caroline who repeatedly bursts into tears. In the dinner scene at Grondale Hall that immediately follows Caroline's meeting with her aunt, Lord Grondale drives Caroline from the table. Maria, however, gives better than she gets. Lord Grondale abuses Caroline for what he sees as her suspicious intimacy with Hermsprong and his friends, ignoring or reproving Caroline for all the explanations that she makes about how and why she has been in company with Hermsprong. Caroline never effectively counters any of Lord Grondale's accusations, crumbling with " 'How cruel this is!' " and "bursting into tears" (H, 103). Maria carries on the argument. In response to Lord Grondale's silly tale of Caroline's duplicity and collusion with Hermsprong, Maria tells him that his suppositions form " 'the completest triumph of pride and prejudice over common sense, that has ever fallen under my notice' " (H, 103). When Lord Grondale insists that " 'Such may be my suspicions . . . without any impeachment of my understanding,' " Maria retorts, " 'I allow [the accusation] to be very cunning and very characteristic . . . I only deny its truth' " (H, 103). These are not the polite responses that a young lady might be expected to make. When Lord Grondale blurts out that " 'What I expect from my daughter is obedience; and I dare say I shall have it,' " Maria pushes him—" 'What my lord, implicit obedience and unconditional submission?' " (H, 105). He agrees that, yes, this is exactly what he wants, and Maria reminds him that " 'That never sits well upon men's stomachs, and hardly upon women's' " (H, 105). Part of the background to these remarks of course is the contemporary political debate about The Rights of Man, but even as the title of Paine's pamphlet suggests, discussion of the rights of man did not automatically lead to discussion of the rights of woman. Bage here, wonderfully, points precisely to the woman as equal in her entitlement to freedom. It is not Maria but the dutifully sniffling Caroline who is wrong.

When Maria goes to Caroline, she finds her friend "still in tears" (H, 106). Maria argues that the quality of Lord Grondale's affection is not very good and that Caroline must deal with reality. Caroline can expect fortune from Lord Grondale, but not affection, Maria suggests, and if Caroline is willing to risk losing her inheritance, she can free herself from Lord Grondale's tyranny. Caroline fears that even if she could " 'buy peace with the loss of fortune,' " her peace would be " 'as much wounded by my own breach of filial obligation, as by my father's unkindness' " (H, 107). Caroline is wrong. There is no filial obligation to bow to tyranny. Caroline tells Maria that " 'It is a sight of every day . . . that women, wives at least, continue to love the tyrants, when the tyranny has become almost insupportable,' " but Maria finds that response " 'nothing but a habit of fondness the silly things have acquired, and not had time to get rid of'" (H, 107). She simply dismisses Caroline's rationalizations about her father. Caroline has no reason to honor Lord Grondale, still less to defend him, yet she insists on doing both. Hers is the societally approved mode: honor your father without pausing to ask if he deserves respect. Society has given the same good bargain to husbands; Maria extends her attack on filial blindness to include the marital relationship. All tyrants are first of all to be recognized as such and then to be denied their power. Bage emphasizes the two aspects of response equally; that is, before Caroline can refuse Lord Grondale his tyranny over her, she must recognize his behavior for the tyranny it is. As Caroline's long conversion suggests, even for the intelligent woman it can be very difficult to recognize as inappropriate behavior that is reinforced both by social and family ties. Maria tells Caroline to "'keep the fifth commandment, and honour your father—if you can. No doubt it is a very pretty duty when it is possible to be performed. Where it is not, children must do as well as they can'" (H, 118).

Caroline slowly realizes that she cannot honor Lord Grondale's arbitrary commands. Her duty as a daughter does not demand that she ignore her moral responsibility as a human being, nor, for that matter, her feelings. Slowly she edges away from complete obedience in the matter of Mrs. Garnet; by the end of the novel she has become convinced that her responsibility to herself is an important responsibility as well, and she refuses to relinqish her happiness to her father's whim. Her letter to Mrs. Garnet, written after Lord Grondale's fit of temper, marks a first timid step towards emancipation.

> My father forbids my attentions, and never could he have more severely taxed my obedience. Whether I owe implicit submission to a command I cannot help thinking as unjust as cruel, I am in doubt. Condescend, dear madam, to instruct, to guide me. If you say, Come,—although I should not choose openly, and as it were in defiance against his direct commands, yet I would endeavour to find some more concealed mode of indulgence. . . . Whatsoever may have been the prejudices which have produced a prohibition, to me so painful, I know them not. If I am acquainted with my own heart, it feels for you only the sincerest esteem and affection. [H, 114-15]

Caroline cannot yet take the responsibility for her own actions; on the other hand, she might disobey her father if she were given moral encouragement by Mrs. Garnet. This is a small but significant step away from her former blind obedience to Lord Grondale.

Caroline's relationship with her father is the most obvious example in *Hermsprong* of the miseducation of women by society. Women
are not taught to explore ideas, to question premises; rather, they have
"minds imprisoned" (*H*, 135). A long passage about the education of
women sets out the novel's view of woman and her potential. Hermsprong insists that there is " 'no subject improper for ladies, which
ladies are qualified to discuss; nor any subject they would not be
qualified to discuss, if their fathers first, and then themselves, so
pleased' " (*H*, 135). Women's minds have been limited, he says, first by
custom and then, in a self-fulfilling dynamic, by women themselves,
whose minds " 'instead of ranging the worlds of physics and metaphysics, are confined to the ideas of . . . routs and Ranelaghs' " (*H*,
135). Referring by name to Mrs. Wollstonecraft, he agrees with her that
" 'the mode of [women's] education turns the energies of their minds
on trifles' " (*H*, 136). Rather than developing their intellectual capabilities, women " 'submit to [an] inferiority of character' " in return for
" 'the homage that men pay to youth and beauty' " (*H*, 136). Women
must be " 'better taught,' " Hermsprong explains, and the " 'change, if
change there can be, must begin with men. Lovers must mix a little
more wisdom with their adorations. Parents, in their mode of education, must make less distinction of sex!' " (*H*, 136-37).

Bage shows throughout *Hermsprong* that women's minds are as
good as men's; certainly Maria is a match for Hermsprong. And just as
there are silly women—Mrs. Sumelin and her daughter—there are
silly men: it would be hard to find a better example of inanity than Sir
Philip Chestrum. Mrs. Garnet and Mrs. Merrick are admirable, reasonable human beings. By peopling his novel with such a relatively large
proportion of admirable women, Bage underscores his point that
women's minds are inherently as good as men's. By showing us the
reeducation of his heroine Caroline, whose rational faculties early in
the novel often are circumscribed by social proscriptions, he gives the
reader a kind of test case. Caroline, it must be said, is already kind,
charming, and intelligent when we meet her. Hermsprong and Maria,
freeing Caroline from the prejudices of her education, bring her to the
same level of rationality they have attained.

Bage presents Hermsprong as the very type of the rational man.
His view of any matter defines that subject for the reader; Hermsprong's discourses on morality, on politics, and on human relationships are clearly to be taken as Bage's. That Maria Fluart holds her own
in every exchange with Hermsprong is perhaps Bage's greatest proof
of male-female equality. The many conversations between Herm-

sprong and Maria in which they match wits do more than add grace to the novel, they show that men and women can be intellectual equals. Hermsprong and Maria agree that Caroline must be weaned from her misplaced filial idealism, and as in the scene following Hermsprong's run-in with Sir Philip Chestrum, they lend each other support as they attempt to reeducate her. The incident begins when Sir Philip accosts the two women and Hermsprong, pestering Caroline and insulting Hermsprong himself. Hermsprong less than ceremoniously dumps Sir Philip over the rails at the side of the road. As he rejoins the ladies, having done his work with Sir Philip, he finds "Miss Fluart laughing—Miss Campinet in terror" (*H*, 153). Caroline is terrified of the "consequences." What consequences? " 'May not all this go misrepresented and aggravated to Lord Grondale?' " (*H*, 153).

The difference in the girls' reactions is significant. Maria reacts to the reality: Sir Philip is an idiot and a pest, and appropriately he has been rebuffed by Hermsprong. Caroline fears the social consequences: her father will be angry. She cannot understand why Hermsprong, who claims to "entertain an affection" (*H*, 154) for her, does not care what her father thinks. Hermsprong merely asks, " 'Of what consequence is [Lord Grondale's reaction] to me?' " (*H*, 154). Caroline is upset. Although he seeks to gain her affection, she tells him, " 'upon no occasion [do] you take the trouble to conceal your contempt of my father.' " Hermsprong retorts that " 'I think not of your father; it is you, not him, that I love; from you I expect my happiness, not him' " (*H*, 154). Maria seconds Hermsprong: Lord Grondale has no hold over Caroline except that which Caroline herself gives him. Maria brings the conversation around to money, which she sees as the true, if not the acknowledged, source of parental influence; she already had made the same point to Caroline during a discussion about Caroline's perception of filial duty. Here Maria plays devil's advocate:

> 'In this country,' said Miss Fluart, 'fathers, of rank and fortune especially, have great powers over their children.'
> 'They have indeed, if they have the power to direct or control their affections,' said Hermsprong.
> 'Perhaps,' Miss Fluart replied, 'they do not reach that point quite; but pray is not Love a much more lively and lovely gentleman when he has golden wings?'
> 'I have not the honour to know Love with golden wings.'
> 'Let us descend:—Lord Grondale has great efficient powers in his strong box; such as Love, airy as he is, may need.'

'I cannot condescend to mix the idea of strong boxes with felicity and Caroline Campinet.'

'You are a sublime mortal; but do you know a lady called Prudence?'

'I hope I do.'

'And will she allow Miss Campinet to give up a splendid fortune for love and Mr. Hermsprong?'

'If that is a necessary consequence, I hope she will.'

'On the part of Miss Campinet, I presume this requires a tolerable portion of humility.'

'Not more, I hope, than Miss Campinet possesses.'

'To ladies who have been brought up in affluence and splendour, they are said to become necessaries of life.'

'Affluence may be Miss Campinet's, as high, if she pleases, as she herself can wish; but if grandeur in its usual glittering forms be to her a necessary of life, I fear it is not mine to supply it. Millions of revenue would not make me exchange the comforts of life for its parade.' [H, 154]

The implication that filial obedience rests on pecuniary rather than moral grounds discomforts Caroline. Not yet capable of seriously challenging the net of moral and social values in which she is caught, she responds to Hermsprong that she cannot disregard her duties. Hermsprong insists that the question is not one of duty but of "'prejudice'" and repeats his hope that "'Miss Campinet will not require of me the sacrifice of my integrity to pride, or, meaner still, to money'" (H, 155).

If, as Bage suggests, filial duty for women may have monetary rather than moral roots, a woman can free herself from parental tyranny by renouncing her father's fortune. Bage implies that truth in the advertising of motives would go far in making the woman's duty to the unreasonable parent less oppressive. Even Caroline herself is not unaware of the mercenary element in her relationship with her father; she notes "with a faint smile" that if "'the heartache [of her problem with her father] must be borne, one may as well have the girandoles along with it'" (H, 107). And Lord Grondale, like so many fathers in eighteenth-century fiction, immediately responds to any "liberty" of his daughter with the threat that he will withhold his "property" (H, 106) from her. As in most eighteenth-century novels, money plays a very important role in defining a woman's options. Caroline understands these limitations: "'I wish for happiness, and shall not choose to risk it by imprudence'" (H, 156), she admits. To which Maria retorts, "'Especially the imprudence of losing a duchess's revenue?'" (H, 156).

But money is not Caroline's only tie to her father. Her perception of her duty lingers even as the urgings of her friends, in tune with her own good sense, suggest that she should break away from Lord Grondale's tyranny. When the ridiculous Sir Philip writes to Lord Grondale proposing marriage to Caroline, and Lord Grondale accepts, Caroline realizes that she cannot allow this courtship to continue. But to say no is to defy her father. "The English language did not supply words to express what she meant, without conveying at the same time a sort of intention to have a will of her own" (H, 157). Caroline comes close at this point, but does not quite defy her father; later, when Lord Grondale actually invites Sir Philip to their house, "there was a something in his daughter . . . which militated against one of his most firm opinions that unconditional submission was the duty of a child, and especially of a daughter" (H, 179). Caroline begins the process of disengaging herself; Caroline's eventual enfranchisement is the last in a series of painful steps, each of which Lord Grondale counters by threatening to withhold his fortune. When Caroline continues to avoid Sir Philip, Lord Grondale asks Maria if it is " 'of any consequence to Miss Campinet to know, that if she marries Hermsprong she loses all my fortune' " (H, 181). Maria asks him to choose anybody but Sir Philip—" 'a man a little lame, or blind, or humpbacked' " (H, 181); Lord Grondale tells her that she is not a " 'prudent' " friend to Caroline, and Maria makes his implication explicit: " 'If, as I suppose, by prudence, your lordship means money, you are probably right' " (H, 181). Caroline tells Sir Philip that she will never marry him—thus finally openly defying her father. Calling Caroline to him, Lord Grondale subjects her to a verbal assault that impugns her filial decency and attacks her general good sense. Caroline insists that she can be dutiful and still have the right not to be made miserable; Lord Grondale reverts again and again to the subject of his money. Caroline finds that filial obedience is limited " 'by reason alone' " (H, 184). Lord Grondale is furious at Caroline's partiality to Hermsprong and her refusal to " 'obey' " his " 'command' " (H, 185) to marry Sir Philip, finally leading Caroline to ask him " 'Is it not right, my lord, that I, whom marriage is to make happy or miserable, should be allowed a judgment and a will?' " (H, 185). Lord Grondale finds such an argument in itself insulting.

> 'Obey me, you have a father. If otherwise, I have not a daughter.'
> 'My lord, I humbly conceive I know my duty, and am disposed to fulfil it; but I hope it is no part of my duty to make myself miserable for life.'
> 'You reason, Miss Campinet; I also reason. It is my duty to give you sustenance, because I have the honour to be your father; but I know of no

law which binds me to bestow immense fortune upon a daughter, as a reward for disobedience.'

'It is, sir, and it ought to be, your pleasure which determines as to fortune, whether I shall have little or much. To your pleasure, in that respect, I cheerfully submit; and humbly request you will permit me the choice of that condition which is for ever to constitute my happiness or misery.'

'From what pretty playbook have you learned these fine words? . . . And you really, Miss Campinet, prefer poverty and Hermsprong, to affluence and Sir Philip Chestrum?'

'I speak not of Mr. Hermsprong, my lord; but I prefer any condition to that of being Sir Philip Chestrum's wife.'

'That being the case, Miss Campinet, and since it has cost you no more trouble to decide, I suppose all connection between you and me is at an end. No tragedy, Miss Campinet. You will, no doubt, consider yourself in future as a free independent person, mistress of the superb fortune left you by your foolish aunt. It will procure you food and raiment; and so philosophical a lady, and so much in love, what else can she want?' [H, 185-86]

When Caroline refuses to pay homage to her father's fortune, Lord Grondale's hold over her is enormously reduced. Their debate here centers on whether Lord Grondale can force Caroline into a marriage that is repugnant to her: simple logic dictates that he does not have the right "to make [her] miserable for life," but Caroline has come to this posture only with a great effort of will and at the urging of her most trusted friends. And even with this support, Lord Grondale's response to her refusal still leaves her "pierced with grief" (H, 186).

These discussions about the respective rights of father and daughter are central to Bage's depiction of women in society. Lord Grondale assumes that he arbitrarily can direct Caroline's life; in large part, she makes the same assumption. Bage suggests not only that parents do not have the prerogatives that Lord Grondale takes as his due but that children themselves should reevaluate the scheme of behaviors that they see as filial duty. At every step, Caroline must be prodded by Maria and Hermsprong to act sensibly, as opposed to dutifully. When Caroline says, "'he is my father; I say every thing in that'" (H, 85), Bage insists that she says very little—parental rights are human rights, and do not extend beyond what we grant others. Women, if they are not to be tyrannized, must make this distinction. Lord Grondale confines Caroline to her room, where she must await the departure of his drinking companions. Maria joins her in the confinement, and by the end of three days has "almost persuaded Miss Campinet that fathers may be wrong" (*H*, 190). In the meantime, Lord Grondale threatens to marry Caroline to Sir Philip by force and even to make her consummate the marriage if that is necessary. He continues to harass her, finally striking and knocking her to the ground. He orders Caroline to her room to "prepare for marriage on the next morning" (*H*, 206). Only then does she actually defy him, escaping the paternal home by disguising herself as Maria. From the very proper refuge of her Aunt Garnet's house, Caroline pleads forgiveness—a forgiveness which she does not find. Hermsprong tries to reason with her.

> 'I had a father, whom I always obeyed, whom I always thought it my duty to obey; because his commands seldom wounded my feelings, and never insulted my understanding. I loved him. Could I have loved a tyrant? In vain would the reasoners of this polished country say, every thing is due to the authors of our existence. Merely for existence, I should have answered, I owe nothing. It is for rendering that existence a blessing, my filial gratitude is due. If I am made miserable, ought I to pay for happiness? Suppose me the child of an ancient Grecian parent, who, not choosing to support me, had, according to the existing laws of his country, exposed me to perish;—suppose me preserved and educated by a stranger, whose compassion would not permit me to perish;—is it to the author of my existence, or of the happiness of that existence, to whom I am in debt? For a moment, lovely Miss Campinet, lay aside your preconceived notions of duty, and tell me, In what part of Lord Grondale's conduct to you, can you recognise the care and tenderness of a father?' [*H*, 217-18]

But Hermsprong reasons in vain. His arguments cannot overcome Caroline's perception of her duty. And things get worse when she realizes that Hermsprong is the rightful heir to her father's property.[17] She returns to Lord Grondale, forsaking all those who truly love her— Maria, Mrs. Garnet, and Hermsprong. It requires still another round of mistreatment by her father and entreaty by her friends for Caroline finally, at very long last, to see where her loyalties should be. Conveniently, Lord Grondale, fearing his own disenfranchisement by the rightful heir, makes Caroline's position easier by himself seeking a reconciliation with Hermsprong. Caroline really never does have to choose, although it is clear by the end of the novel that if she had to make a choice, she would choose Hermsprong.

Caroline is intelligent, witty, and kind. She is capable of effective action, as when she helps the villagers the morning after a great storm. But she also is caught up in a pattern of irrational responses that she has internalized as her filial duty. Her father's unkindness is not easily answered with indifference because Caroline feels that she owes him unconditional regard. Hermsprong and Maria believe that no authority is valid solely because of rank or relationship. Caroline's father is incensed by Hermsprong's disregard for his rank even before he hates him for his courtship of Caroline. Bage's psychological portrait of Caroline is perceptive: her attachment to Lord Grondale endures despite, or perhaps in some ways because of, his mistreatment of her. Separating her from her father is a slow, painful process because Caroline has a great deal of difficulty distinguishing between her feelings and her common sense when her parent is the object of scrutiny. Caroline's intelligence guides her well in other aspects of her life, but the parental tie, supported both by emotional attachment and social custom, is difficult to analyze rationally. Bage's depiction of Caroline's struggle with herself as well as with her father as she breaks away is one of the subtler characterizations in the novel of this period.

Maria Fluart's rationalist perspective stands in sharp contrast to Caroline's ambivalence. In Maria, Bage has given us a wonderful model for what a woman can be. Maria is intelligent, charming, witty, and morally and physically unafraid; she is true to her friends and an excellent judge of who those friends should be. She is complete as a person and content as a woman; we must reflect for a moment to realize how significant this contentment is. Maria throughout the novel is never shy, backward, or fawning in anyone's company, and she always has something sensible to add to any subject under consideration. In social situations she conducts herself as any man's equal, and she is, indeed, up to any conversation and equal to any occasion. She faces down Lord Grondale (once with a pistol); she goes point for point with Hermsprong. And of course she debates endlessly with the very slow-to-change Caroline. Bage presents Maria's wit and intelligence as part of her charm; far from being pretentious or precious, she quite often even is flirtatious. Bage gives us a woman, then, who can be a functioning, thinking person and who is still very much female. It is true that Bage backs away from making Maria his heroine and awarding her the prize of Hermsprong; that would be another novel, and not nearly as good as the one he wrote. One structural problem with making Maria and Hermsprong the lovers would be that the tension of Caroline's emancipation from Lord Grondale would be irrelevant. But there would be an even more unfortunate consequence: the novel would become an *Anna St. Ives*, with two paragons spouting wisdom at each other. Rather than marry Maria to Hermsprong, Bage chooses to make her happy as a still single woman, suggesting, almost alone in the eighteenth-century novel, that such a being as a happy, unmarried woman is possible.

The supporting cast of female characters comprises a variety of types, from Mrs. Sumelin and her equally silly daughter to the wise Mrs. Garnet—each of them deftly drawn. In Mrs. Stone, Bage eschews the stereotype of the grubbing mistress to present instead a relatively complex character who does her best to secure her position in Lord Grondale's household but avoids doing harm to Caroline when she can. Finally, there is Hermsprong's mother, whom we meet when Hermsprong fills in his own history; she is noteworthy mostly because she marries Hermsprong's father against the express commands of her own tyrannical father, who though "extravagantly fond of his only child, [was] also extravagantly fond of his money" (H, 163). Hermsprong's father, without a fortune of his own, obviously "was not a proper match" (H, 163). Hermsprong's mother frees herself from a parental tyranny—a tyranny defined largely in terms of the denial of fortune—very similar to that which ensnares Caroline. Lord Grondale, then, is a type of the parental tyrant, not a unique case.

Bage's two female protagonists are almost entirely admirable; the more mixed group of secondary female characters completes his gallery of images of women, and provides the perspective against which we measure Maria and Caroline. There are plenty of silly women like the Sumelins, Bage implies, and there are many of a wiser stamp, like Mrs. Garnet. And some, like Hermsprong's mother, incorporate in their characters several aspects: the wisdom to defy her parent and marry the worthy young man is combined with the misplaced sense of purpose that leads to her attempts to convert her Indian hosts to Christianity. Bage believes in the equality of men and women, and just as he gives his reader examples of different types of men, he provides also varied images of women.

Toward the end of the novel Hermsprong says that " 'I consider a woman as equal to a man; but . . . I consider a man also as equal to a woman' " (H, 236). This is Bage's premise throughout the novel. " 'My recommendation to the ladies would be,' " Hermsprong says, " 'to acquire minds to reason, understandings to judge; for when they will take the trouble to reason a little, and judge for themselves, they do it so well, that propriety of action must follow of necessity, and then they are . . . women . . . heavenly women; such as a man might take to his bosom with a possibility of an increase to his happiness' " (H, 170). Bage makes fun of the things "all ladies know" (H, 122), and encourages women to act on the basis of their reason rather than society's models of feminine behavior. A woman who thinks is a fully developed human being, just as a man who thinks is her worthy consort. Neither the man nor the woman should be subservient to the other. Just about midway in the novel Bage sends his heroines from Lord Grondale's to Mr. Sumelin's house. Bage jokes that "All ladies know— for all ladies read novels—how extremely dangerous the roads of England are for female travellers who happen to be young and handsome." He continues, inflating the dangers to heroic proportions:

> The banditti who infest these roads are of the higher order of mortal men, such as seldom arrive at the gallows, whatsoever may be the pains they take to do it; lords, knights, and gentle squires. It is their cruel practice to seize and carry away *vi et armis*, that is, in chaises drawn by flying horses, that distinguished part of the fair sex called heroines, and confine them in very elegant prisons, where they sometimes cut off their heads; though, more generally, the sweet creatures are, as in days of yore, under the protection of some magician, by whose potent aid they escape without much injury. Surely, I did not consider these things, when I turned my two lovely girls into this wide world of danger, with no other guide but their own discretion; a quality indeed inherent in, and inseparable from, the dear sex; but deprived of a little of its original elasticity, by having passed through the hands of that great grandmother of us all, the too credulous Eve." [*H*, 122]

And then he gets the girls to their destination: "For this time, however, they escaped all danger, and were set down at the house of Mr. Sumelin" (*H*, 122). The dangers that lurk in the world for women, and that are used to restrict them, are largely chimeras, Bage suggests. Society tells women that they should not travel; bandits wait to cut off their heads. Society tells women that they should not defy their parents even when the parents are wrong. And society tells women that they should not think, that the realms of politics or of metaphysics do not belong to them. *Hermsprong* argues, emphatically and delightfully, for common sense and its inevitable consequence, equality.

# SIX

# The Female Radical Novelists

Elizabeth Inchbald: *Nature and Art*
Mary Wollstonecraft: *Maria or*
*the Wrongs of Woman*

Elizabeth Inchbald in *Nature and Art* writes the same kind of novel as Bage, bringing wit and skepticism to her depictions of life up and down the social scale. The focus of her book is the inanity and hypocrisy that she sees at the core of English society, a moral emptiness that can be ludicrous but at its most serious has devastating results. Of central interest within our context, Inchbald sees class rather than gender as the determinant of victimization: rich women are as obnoxious as rich men. Wollstonecraft has a very different perspective: for her, to be born female is to be born a victim. Inchbald, like the male radical novelists, sees woman's potential as the equal of man's. This is an important point since it means that, in the radical circle of the nineties, the view of woman as victim of society does not depend on the gender of the novelist.[1]

*Nature and Art* is the story of two brothers, William and Henry, who begin life with few resources and no friends except each other. Henry, the younger brother, plays the fiddle, and this unpretentious talent allows him to support himself and William and even to send William to university. William studies to be a clergyman; his hypocrisy and lack of scruples carry him to the top of his profession. His ascension results in what he perceives as a tremendous social gulf between himself and his brother the fiddler. The relationship becomes totally impossible after the two men marry. Henry's wife is a charming, simple woman; William, an avid social climber, marries "a woman of family, . . . Lady Clementina, the daughter of a poor Scotch earl, whom he had chosen, merely that he might be proud of her family;

and, in return, suffer that family to be ashamed of *his.*" [2] Lady Clementina is Inchbald's central female portrait in *Nature and Art.* She is a perfect wife for William, vain, pretentious, and absolutely without social responsibility. William is not an admirable character, but the wife is in every aspect a degree less admirable than the husband. Were Inchbald a male author, we might be tempted to see the portrayal of Lady Clementina and her equally abhorrent friends as misogynistic, but this would be an error. In these characterizations, Inchbald explores social problems that have nothing to do with gender and everything to do with class. The fact of Lady Clementina's own femaleness never victimizes her; the social position that she and William enjoy gives her the means to victimize others.

There is nothing admirable about Lady Clementina, although she lives in the service of her vanity. "If she complained she was ill, it was with the certainty that her languor would be admired; if she boasted she was well, it was that the spectator might admire her glowing health; if she laughed, it was because she thought it made her look pretty; if she cried, it was because she thought it made her look prettier still. . . . Forward, and impertinent in the company of her equals from the vanity of supposing herself above them, she was bashful even to shamefacedness in the presence of her superiors, because her vanity told her she engrossed all their observation" (*N*, 1, 34). Inchbald concludes that "THAT, which in a weak woman is called vanity, in a man of sense is termed pride—make one a degree stronger, or the other a degree weaker, and the dean and his wife were infected with the self-same folly" (*N*, 1, 36). This well-matched couple produce a child who "gratified the father's darling passion, pride; as well as the mother's vanity" (*N*, I, 43). Young William, brought up by such parents, grows into a man for whom truth and decency can never rival ambition and position.

William's brother Henry, meanwhile, leaves England after the death of his wife, taking with him his infant son. Years later the child, also Henry, appears at William's house. The young Henry is a worthy son to his parents: unpretentious, inherently kind, and partial to the truth. Lady Clementina, immediately discerning the innate superiority of young Henry to her own son, hypocritically remarks to her husband that "the arrival of this child will give you a still higher sense of the happiness we enjoy in our own" (*N*, I, 66). She takes in the boy because her vanity "represented to her how amiable her conduct would appear in the eye of the world, should she condescend to treat this destitute nephew as her own son—what envy such heroic virtue would excite in the hearts of her particular friends, and what grief in the bosoms of all those who did not like her" (N, I, 70). Her husband William, who is not quite so cold as his wife, encourages Lady Clementina's attention to the child by playing on her image of herself.

The marriage of Dean William and his wife is a practical affair, devoid of affection or personal regard. Each of Inchbald's couples is well matched, and the differences among the couples depend on the personalities of the people involved; these personalities, in turn, are determined by class-related assumptions. Unlike many other eighteenth-century writers, most obviously Wollstonecraft, Inchbald does not portray marriage as a relationship that militates against women. Rather, in a bad marriage the partners, having initially made the wrong assumptions, gnaw at each other's well-being. Conversely, in a good marriage—in Inchbald's scheme most often found in the lower classes—the marriage is a meeting of mind, interest, and morality. The elder Henry, for example, chose a woman who would be "a kind companion and friend, who would bear with his failings, and know how to esteem his few qualifications; therefore, he had chosen one of his own rank in life . . . who [had] a taste for music, and, as well as himself, an obligation to the art" (N, I, 25). She is a public singer and socially "as good as myself," Henry says. "I did not wish her to be better, for fear she should despise me" (N, I, 26). William married for social position. The result is an emptiness in which both partners exist together but do not join.

> If the dean had loved his wife but moderately, seeing all her faults clearly as he did, he must frequently have quarrelled with her: if he had loved her with tenderness, he must have treated her with a degree of violence in the hope of amending her failings: but having neither personal nor mental affection towards her sufficiently interesting to give himself the trouble to contradict her will in any thing, he passed for one of the best husbands in the world. Lady Clementina went out when she liked, stayed at home when she liked, dressed as she liked, and talked as she liked without a word of disapprobation from her husband, and all—because he cared nothing about her. [N, I, 85-86]

Lady Clementina's life is as empty as her marriage—incapable of introspection or reflection, she seems satisfied with both. "The dean's wife being a fine lady . . . she ran from house to house, from public amusement to public amusement; but much less for the pleasure of *seeing* than for that of being *seen*. Nor was it material to her enjoyment whether she were observed, or welcome, where she went, as she never entertained the smallest doubt of either; but rested assured that her presence roused curiosity and dispensed gladness all around" (*N*, I, 89-90). Inchbald obviously finds nothing of value in such a life. The target of Inchbald's satire throughout the book is the lack of social responsibility in the upper classes: those who have the means, both monetary and political, to make life better for the less fortunate ignore their responsibilities and instead devote all their energies to posturing for their peers. Inchbald directs her anger at both sexes: she is careful throughout the novel to show couples in which both partners play out the same social parts. Dean William seems to be engaged with social issues as he writes and rewrites his pamphlets on the state of the nation, but his documents are directed at earning political advancement from his superiors rather than at any amelioration, or even truthful description, of the state of England. And to emphasize that Dean William and Lady Clementina are representative of their class, Inchbald also develops the portraits of other members of their circle, particularly Lord and Lady Bendham.

These worthies are the country neighbors of the Dean, and, like William and Lady Clementina, they are hypocritical arbiters of morality. And, like the Dean and his wife, they are identical in their faults. Lord Bendham "possessed the office of a lord of the bed-chamber to his majesty" (*N*, I, 119); Inchbald with some asperity remarks that "a lord of the bed-chamber must necessarily be . . . one, wholly made up of observance, of obedience, of dependence, and of imitation—a borrowed character—a character formed by reflection" (*N*, I, 120). Lord Bendham's wife is just like him: "The wife of this illustrious peer, as well as himself, took her hue, like the chameleon, from surrounding objects; her manners were not governed by her mind, but were solely directed by external circumstances. At court, humble, resigned, patient, attentive—At balls, masquerades, gaming-tables, and routs, gay, sprightly, and flippant—At her country seat, reserved, austere, arrogant, and gloomy" (*N*, I, 120-121). It might be merely laughable, or sad, to imagine such a life if it were not for the very real harm such a person has the power to inflict in her community. "Whether in town or country, it is but justice to acknowledge, that in her own person she was strictly chaste; but in the country she extended that chastity even to the persons of others; and the young woman who lost her virtue in the village of Anfield, had better have lost her life. Some few were now and then found hanging or drowned, while no other cause could be assigned for their despair, than an imputation on their character, and dread of the harsh purity of Lady Bendham" (*N*, I, 122). But the harshness with which she treats those beneath her never extends to her social equals. She maintains, as Inchbald gently puts it, a "distinction of classes in female errors" that is indeed a fine one: "the adulterous concubine of an elder brother was her most intimate acquaintance, whilst the less guilty unmarried mistress of the younger, she would not sully her lips to exchange a word with" (*N*, I, 123). And of course, "like other ladies of virtue," in town she "visited and received into her house the acknowledged mistresses of a man in elevated life." So that, Inchbald concludes, it was not "the crime, but the rank which the criminal held in society, that drew down Lady Bendham's vengeance" (*N*, I, 123). This is precisely the measure of William and Lady Clementina, a double standard that allows young William to escape entirely from the consequences of his own actions while Hannah, discovered as the mother of William's child, is driven to crime and finally condemned to death, ironically enough by William himself as the trial judge.

The sexual double standard of rich to poor is only a part of the complaint that Inchbald has against the upper classes, whose general lack of responsibility to those less fortunate has such tragic consequences. Here again the husband and wife are in full harmony: an awareness by one might inform the other, but no such awareness manifests itself. The rich, Inchbald finds, are particulary obtuse when it comes to money matters. "With an ample fortune both by inheritance and their sovereign's favor" (*N*, I, 125), the Bendhams cannot manage their budget, and in fact are always in debt. But they cannot understand why the laboring poor have any financial problems. Lady Bendham is sure that the "wages of a labouring man with a wife and half a dozen small children" should be adequate ıf they would only learn a little oeconomy" (*N*, I, 125). After all, she explains to her husband, they really don't need to dress up, and so some basic clothes, a fire, and food are all they need. Lady and Lord Bendham believe that the poor should feel themselves "much obliged" (*N*, I, 127) for the small charities that enable them to avoid destitution. Inchbald is incensèd at the inequity in society that puts some people in the position of begging for the "Health, strength, and the will to earn a moderate subsistence [that] ought to be every man's security from obligation" (*N*, I, 128). Even worse is that fact that if people like the Bendhams wanted to help the poor rather than simply play to their own vanity, "my lord [could] speak a few words for the poor as a senator" (*N*, I, 129)—an act that far more effectively would address the problems of the poor than the intermittent charities for which they must beg.

The relationships of the younger generation, especially the destruction of Hannah Primrose, must be seen within the larger social context that Inchbald builds. The younger William encourages Hannah to fall in love with him and then tells her that he cannot marry her. William is not willing to forego social status for love; he marries a woman whom he dislikes and who dislikes him but who brings him social advancement. With this decision he earns for himself a lifetime of domestic emptiness, but like his father he seems not dissatisfied with his bargain. The tragedy falls on Hannah, whose life essentially stops when William deserts her. Inchbald gives Hannah's situation all the stuff of melodrama: a pregnancy, an attempt to kill her child, parents who die of grief because of her, neighbors who turn from her, and finally a fall into crime and a death sentence. Society refuses Hannah decent employment and makes her feel the shame of her situation as a seduced and abandoned woman. But Inchbald emphasizes as well that Hannah suffers not simply because she is a woman, but because she is a feeling human being. That is, she truly loves William. In fact, because William is so cold to her some months into their affair, Hannah does not even tell him about her pregnancy. Alone and destitute, she goes to live in London because she knows William is there; she just wants to be near him. Thus Inchbald partially plays on the clichéd themes of the seduced and abandoned woman, but the portrait goes beyond that. If Hannah were as unfeeling—as manipulative—as William, she might well not have been destroyed by him. In this case surely Hannah's gender leaves her vulnerable to the brutal indifference of society, but it is the psychological blow that destroys her. Inchbald implies that a man, too, can be emotionally vulnerable: the portrait of William is counterbalanced by that of Henry. William behaves in accordance with the art, and artifice, that governed his upbringing, Henry, with the nature that is the model by which he was formed. Henry truly loves his Rebecca and finds sustenance in the reciprocity of their feelings. As with the elder couples, here too Inchbald insists on the identical response of both members of the relationship. She describes a reunion between Henry and Rebecca: "Henry's sensations on his return . . . were the self-same as Rebecca's were: sympathy in thought, sympathy in affection, sympathy in virtue made them so" (N, I, 176). The paralleling of the two younger couples, and the examples of their elders, suggest that for Inchbald, as for many of her male peers, woman is not born victim but has, whatever her class, essentially the same social profile, for good or bad, as her male consort. Surely if a lower-class woman is unfortunate in her personal relationships society is quite ready to destroy her, but the discussion of female "virtue" with regard to Lady Bendham and her standards shows clearly that this vulnerability is as much a question of class as of gender. To emphasize this point, we are told that the younger William's wife "made a mistake, and went to another man's bed—and so her husband and she were parted" (N, II, 178). Mrs. Norwynne's adultery does not cost her anything: "she has married the other man. . . . [I]f it had been my wife or yours, the bishop would have made her do penance in a white sheet—but as it was a lady, why, it was all very well" (N, II, 178).

Further, Inchbald shows that even women without much money, if they are emotionally intact, can manage by themselves. Henry goes away to learn a trade and to find his long lost father. It takes him a little longer, presumably, than he had planned, and when he comes home nineteen years later, he finds Rebecca and her sisters living simply but decently in a cottage in the same village where he had left them so many years before. The women knit and spin for their living; they have managed to take care of themselves all these years. In fact, Rebecca's life does not significantly change after she marries Henry; her new household, with her husband and his father, is just about as simple as her former arrangement with her sisters. Inchbald's women function, then, much as her men do. The vicissitudes of social class and of temperament delineate their lives in virtually identical ways. Even at the last, women's experience parallels men's: Lady Clementina dies from a cold she contracts because she wears a gown cut ridiculously low; her friend Lord Bendham dies "from a mass of blood infected by high seasoned dishes, mixed with copious draughts of wine" (N, II, 191-92). Inchbald, very much like Bage, is both amused and angered by the callousness and irresponsibility of the rich. Both Inchbald and Bage see a great deal that is wrong in contemporary England, but they express their anger at social inequities with irony and amusement. It is when we get to Mary Wollstonecraft that the anger stands unmediated.

Wollstonecraft's *Maria or the Wrongs of Woman* is the most impassioned, and the most despairing, of all the novels I have discussed in this book. A tone of unrelieved despair is very unusual for an eighteenth-century novel; only William Godwin's *Caleb Williams* is equally insistent in its note of futile struggle against insurmountable social odds. Godwin's novel sees society grinding down the individuals subject to its persistent misshaping—men and women, Falkland, Caleb, and the young Emily are all victims. Wollstonecraft focuses on a more specific concern: the destruction of woman by a social system that gives her no power to act to save herself. Godwin in *Caleb Williams* is concerned with the destructiveness of arbitrary power, as exemplified by Tyrrel, by Falkland, and by the legal and penal systems themselves. Wollstonecraft's argument is that woman, just because of her sex, is doomed to be crushed by tyrannies not only social, legal, and political but—even more damaging because they are ubiquitous—domestic. The society she chronicles allows no possibility of a happy ending for most women because law and custom combine to make each woman an easy victim. The novel was not finished, left only partially written and edited at the time of its author's death in 1797. Polemical, with character and even plot left quite rudimentary, the book is a series of tales of woman's victimization. The tone is so angry, the repetition of worst-case examples is so overpowering, that it is uncertain the novel would have reached the level of good craft even had Wollstonecraft had the opportunity to revise it. But that lack of craft is almost irrelevant, for the book, even in its unfinished state, is overwhelming in its depiction of the pain Wollstonecraft saw as a woman's virtually inevitable portion in the eighteenth century.

In Austen's *Emma*, is it clear that being female is positive:

> Mrs. Weston's friends were all made happy by her safety; and if the satisfaction of her well-doing could be increased to Emma, it was by knowing her to be the mother of a little girl. She had been decided in wishing for a Miss Weston. She would not acknowledge that it was with any view of making a match for her, hereafter, with either of Isabella's sons; but she was convinced that a daughter would suit both father and mother best. It would be a great comfort to Mr. Weston as he grew older—and even Mr. Weston might be growing older ten years hence—to have his fireside enlivened by the sports and the nonsense, the freaks and the fancies of a child never banished from home; and Mrs. Weston—no one could doubt that a daughter would be most to her; and it would be quite a pity that any one who so well knew how to teach, should not have their powers in exercise again.[3]

This passage comes almost at the end of the book, and so serves as part of the summing up. Compare it with Wollstonecraft's comment on the birth of a girl-child: "[Maria] mourned for her child, lamented she was a daughter, and anticipated the aggravated ills of life that her sex rendered almost inevitable."[4] Wollstonecraft's novel catalogues those "aggravated ills of life."

The plot may be summarized briefly. Maria, the wife of a tyrannical and profligate husband, remains with him for years. Not only

does he treat her badly, he also uses her to get money from her kindly
uncle, and then he loses that money too. While he has many women,
Maria remains faithful to him, attempting to work at their relationship
as well as to mitigate his destruction of their resources. Slovenly,
irrational, and wasteful, he never appreciates any of her efforts and
regards Maria herself merely as another part of his property, to be used
or bartered as he wishes. When he actually tries to pander her to one of
his creditors, Maria finally rebels and announces that she is leaving
him. She runs away, and he hounds her from refuge to refuge until,
after the birth of her child, she attempts to leave the country.[5] She is
drugged, the child is stolen from her, and she wakes up in a private
madhouse where she has been imprisoned, essentially, for the crime
of being a woman.[6] Her husband had been marginally considerate
over the years in the hope of getting more and more money from
Maria's uncle; the uncle dead, and the money no longer a lure, he has
no reason to treat Maria with even minimal humanity.

The social and legal barriers that prevent a woman from earning
and holding money keep her vulnerable. The rest of the novel is a
series of tales introduced to give the reader glimpses into the lives of
other unfortunate women, all of them lower on the social scale than
Maria, and all of them equally victimized by the financial plight of the
female. Wollstonecraft makes some attempt to develop relationships
between Maria and Darnsford, a man imprisoned in the same madhouse, and between Maria and Jemima, her female keeper, but these
are subordinate to her main plan of setting out as intensively as
possible "The Wrongs of Woman." The first "wrong" is the legal
bondage of a woman to her husband. Maria is not mad, yet her
husband has no problem whatever keeping her in a madhouse. The
madhouse is real—that is, such institutions did exist, and a husband
legally could incarcerate his recalcitrant wife there.[7] But it is also a
metaphor, as Maria herself realizes: "to what purpose did she rally all
her energy?—Was not the world a vast prison, and women born
slaves?" (M, 27). The slaves are found in all classes, and Wollstonecraft
shows that women are easy victims because society takes away from
them virtually all means of dignified and sufficient maintenance as
well as, and as important, legal recourse. This last is a point Godwin
makes repeatedly in Caleb Williams: human beings, male or female,
cannot function properly in a society that does not provide equal
access to the law.

Jemima, even more than Maria, is the archetypal victim. Perhaps
the only positive note in her portrayal—and the same holds true for

Maria herself—is that in the face of brutal treatment her own humanity
stays alive. In Jemima's case, this humanity is all the more remarkable
because even as a child she had had no place in society. Maria recognizes that Jemima has "strength of mind" even though her mind has
been "clouded by the misanthropy of despair" (M, 31). Jemima is

> An insulated being, from the misfortune of her birth, she despised and
> preyed on the society by which she had been oppressed, and loved not her
> fellow-creatures, because she had never been beloved. No mother had ever
> fondled her, no father or brother had protected her from outrage; and the
> man who had plunged her into infamy, and deserted her when she stood in
> greatest need of support, deigned not to smooth with kindness the road to
> ruin. Thus degraded, was she let loose on the world; and virtue, never
> nurtured by affection, assumed the stern aspect of selfish independence.
> [M, 31]

In one of the novel's subtler strokes of characterization, Jemima gingerly lets herself join in the human atmosphere that Maria and Darnford create together in Maria's cell; allowing her reserve to diminish,
Jemima tells her remarkable and tragic story. The tale catalogues a
great many wrongs. Jemima herself is the daughter of a victim. Her
mother, seduced by a fellow servant, becomes pregnant. He refuses to
marry her and begins to "despise" (M, 52) the child even before she is
born. Jemima's mother works throughout her pregnancy, trying all the
while to disguise her condition, and finally, exhausted, she dies in
childbirth. Wollstonecraft's complaints are several here. In addition to
the obvious unfairness of disgrace and death coming to the woman but
not to the man, she comments also on the callousness with which
women often act toward each other: the mistress of the house, "the
mother of six children . . . scarcely permitting a footstep to be heard,
during her month's indulgence, felt no sympathy for the poor wretch,
denied every comfort required by her situation" (M, 52). This woman
forces the poor girl to suffer her labor in a "wretched garret," while the
father, "after a slight reproof, was allowed to remain in his place" (M,
52). No one is going to be interested in caring for young Jemima. Her
mother dies nine days after her birth, and her father places her with
"the cheapest nurse" (M, 53) he can find, a woman who is suckling her
own child in addition to "as many more as she could get." The nurse's
poverty, Jemima tells Maria, and the "habit of seeing children die off
her hands," harden her until she has no feelings at all for the children
she watches over, and Jemima laments that no "feminine caresses,

which seem a part of the rearing of a child, [were] ever bestowed on me." Not surprisingly, she became a "weak and rickety babe" (*M*, 53). Her father, meanwhile, married another "fellow-servant, who loved him less, and knew better how to manage his passion," than Jemima's mother. When the wife becomes pregnant, they decide "to keep a shop . . . [the wife] having obtained a sum of a rich relative for that purpose" (*M*, 53). Jemima, who already had been tending the children even younger than herself at her nurse's, is brought to the "house"—she is careful to make the distinction that the dwelling is not made her "home"—of her father and his new family to help care for her father's new child. This arrangement also saves her father the money for her maintenance. The young child is everyone's darling and learns that she can torment Jemima with impunity. Jemima, ill treated at every step, is forced to bear physical and emotional burdens beyond her abilities. She comes to hate her sibling because she is always ignored while the other is enveloped in caresses: "I perfectly remember," the adult Jemima tells Maria, "that it was the caresses, and kind expressions of my step-mother [to the other child], which first excited my jealous discontent" (*M*, 54).

Always left out of the emotional circle, fed literally with the leavings of her half-sister, Jemima learns to steal food and to try to cover up her transgressions when found out. She is punished by both father and stepmother, and then must watch her father play with the other child to "solac[e] himself" (*M*, 54) after Jemima's punishment. The circle going round and round, Jemima is accused of a "natural propensity to vice" (*M*, 55), and to get rid of her she is bound as apprentice to a woman who runs a slop-shop; the woman is a friend of the stepmother, and, warned of Jemima's "true colours," she vows "that she should break [her] spirit or heart" (*M*, 55). Having never in her life enjoyed a moment's warmth, Jemima sees her situation deteriorate still farther:

> Not only under the lash of my task-mistress, but the drudge of the maid, apprentices and children, I never had a taste of human kindness to soften the rigour of perpetual labour. I had been introduced as an object of abhorrence into the family; as a creature of whom my step-mother, though she had been kind enough to let me live in the house with her own child, could make nothing. I was described as a wretch, whose nose must be kept to the grinding stone—and it was held there with an iron grasp. . . . Often has my mistress, for some instance of forgetfulness, thrown me from one side of the kitchen to the other, knocked my head against the wall, spit in

my face, with various refinements on barbarity that I forbear to enumerate. [*M*, 55]

The various cruelties continue until she is sixteen. No one defends her. "I had no one to love me; or to make me respected, to enable me to acquire respect. . . . I had not even the chance of being considered as a fellow-creature" (*M*, 56). As she matures, her situation can only become worse. When she reaches an age at which she can be abused sexually, sexual exploitation is added to all the others. "My master had once or twice caught hold of me in the passage; but I instinctively avoided his disgusting caresses. One day, however . . . he contrived to be alone in the house with me, and by blows—yes; blows and menaces, compelled me to submit to his ferocious desire; and, to avoid my mistress's fury, I was obliged in future to comply, and skulk to my loft at his command, in spite of increasing loathing" (*M*, 56-57). She becomes pregnant, and even during her pregnancy he assaults her. When they are discovered, the wife attacks not her husband but Jemima. Jemima is beaten and expelled.

She swallows a potion to end her pregnancy and is very sick for some time, during which she begs in the streets; when she recovers, she turns to prostitution. "Fate dragged me through the very kennels of society: I was still a slave, a bastard, a common property" (*M*, 59). Jemima finds this life abhorrent, yet there is one aspect of it that she appreciates: "Detesting my nightly occupation, though valuing, if I may so use the word, my independence, which only consisted in choosing the street in which I should wander, or the roof, when I had money, in which I should hide my head, it was some time before I could prevail on myself to accept of a place in a house of ill fame" (*M*, 59-60). Wollstonecraft returns to this ideal of independence often in the novel; significantly, one of the very few ways she can visualize a woman who is independent is as an independent whore. But the legally constituted tyrants finally make even this life impossible: the watchmen "extort a tithe of prostitution, and harrass with threats the poor creatures whose occupation affords not the means to silence the growl of avarice" (*M*, 60). Jemima is forced into a brothel where she experiences—so horrible has been her past—an amelioration both of health and manner. From here she "accept[s] the offer of a gentleman, rather in the decline of years, to keep his house" (*M*, 60). The old man, Jemima hints, has strange erotic tastes, to which Jemima submits with natural repugnance. She does, however, have the opportunity to read, "and [thus] to gratify an inquisitive, active mind" (*M*, 61). She has, too, the opportunity to listen to good conversation between her master and his literary friends—conversation which is all the richer for not being censored down to what is believed to be appropriate for women. Since she is not a respectable woman, her presence does not change the tenor of the talk: "still I had the advantage of hearing discussions, from which, in the common course of life, women are excluded" (*M*, 61). Jemima's intellectual and moral horizons expand; she even becomes the audience for her master's writings. She begins "to have the ambition of returning to the respectable part of society," and, she comments bitterly, "was weak enough to suppose it possible" (*M*, 62).

Jemima has the capacity for remarkable intellectual and moral growth. Although no one has ever stopped to teach her, she is quick to soak up new ideas, and her moral faculty is also ready to flower. These traits should be contrasted with the characters of several women Wollstonecraft introduces whose infinitely more privileged social positions do not mean that they are kind to those less fortunate. Wollstonecraft seems to be saying that although women might be expected to show solidarity among themselves, with the better-off helping those lower down, that often is not the case; as a sort of corollary, the poor, mistreated woman may well have an innate value that her better-off sister lacks. The wife of her master's heir, for example, is a cold woman whose lack of compassion extends to every detail of their encounter. After Jemima's "protector" dies suddenly, Jemima tells Maria, "his heir, a man of rigid morals, brought his wife with him to take possession of the house and effects, before I was even informed of his death,—'to prevent,' as she took care indirectly to tell me, 'such a creature as she supposed me to be, from purloining any of them, had I been apprized of the event in time'" (*M*, 62). Jemima's first reaction to the death is grief, "which at first had nothing selfish in it" (*M*, 62). But the humanity of Jemima's reaction is quite different from that of the heir and his wife. They meet her grief with contempt, throwing her out in very short order; even the "trinkets and books" her master had given her are contested. She has trouble getting her wages, and finds herself flatly rebuffed when she asks for a character reference. The woman merely says "that it would go against her conscience to recommend a kept mistress" (*M*, 63). Jemima, whose feelings are never dulled by her misfortunes, reacts with "burning tears[,] for there are situations in which a wretch is humbled by the contempt they are conscious they do not deserve" (*M*, 63).

In a sense a new layer has now been added to Jemima's burden, for having experienced social and intellectual intercourse on a level hitherto unknown to her, she finds that "the solitude of a poor lodging was inconceivably dreary . . . after the society I had enjoyed. To be cut off from human converse, now I had been taught to relish it, was to wander a ghost among the living" (M, 63). Jemima misses not only the financial security but the humanizing atmosphere of her lover's house. For "five years" she "had lived with a literary man, occasionally conversing with men of the first abilities of the age; and now to descend to the lowest vulgarity, was a degree of wretchedness not to be imagined unfelt. I had not, it is true, tasted the charms of affection, but I had been familiar with the graces of humanity" (M, 63). Untaught and uncultivated as she has been, Jemima responds warmly to the finer aspects of culture. The gentle life of the rich, on the other hand, is no guarantor of humanity, compassion, or understanding. The pages that follow Jemima's expulsion from the rich man's house are central to Wollstonecraft's exploration of a number of the important social issues of her time. As we have seen, one of the most frequent complaints in novels that protest against social conditions is that the rich do not feel real compassion for the poor, and when they do make some gesture towards them, it is always insufficient and selfishly motivated. Generally, however, the rich treat the poor to a philosophy of self-betterment. The little bit of money that Jemima managed to get together soon runs out. She is willing to work, but there are no options for her: she has not been trained to do needlework and is not good enough to get a position sewing; even though the "servitude" would be difficult for her, she would be quite willing to take "a place," but without a "character" that is not possible. In these straits she happens to meet "one of the gentlemen, whom [she] had frequently dined in company with" (M, 63) at her master's house; she attempts to tell him her problem—he is in a hurry to get to a dinner party. "[H]e impatiently put a guinea into [her] hand, saying, 'It was a pity such a sensible woman should be in distress—he wished [her] well from his soul'" (M, 63). She writes to another of these gentlemen she knows from her days as a companion: "He was an advocate for unequivocal sincerity; and had often, in [her] presence, descanted on the evils which arise in society from the despotism of rank and riches" (M, 63). But he has no intention of helping her: "I received a long essay on the energy of the human mind, with continual allusions to his own force of character. He added, 'That the woman who could write such a letter as I had sent him, could never be in want of resources, were she to look into herself, and exert her powers; misery was the consequence of indolence, and, as to my being shut out from society, it was the lot of man to submit to certain privations' " (M, 64).

Beyond the lack of compassion lies an even more impassable barrier for the poor, the lack of employment possibilities. "How often have I heard," Jemima says, "and read in books, that every person willing to work may find employment? It is the vague assertion, I believe, of insensible indolence, when it relates to men; but, with respect to women, I am sure of its fallacy, unless they will submit to the most menial bodily labour; and even to be employed at hard labour is out of the reach of many, whose reputation misfortune or folly has tainted" (M, 64). Inchbald makes a similar complaint: "To obtain a permanent livelihood, is the good fortune but of a part of those who are in want of it"(N, 11).[8] The scarcity of employment possibilities makes dire poverty, poverty even to starvation, unavoidable for that portion of society that cannot find work. An absurd response to this sad state of affairs is to assert that poverty itself is not evil. Jemima, with some asperity, wonders "How writers, professing to be friends to freedom, and the improvement of morals, can assert that poverty is no evil" (M, 64). This response is made seriously even by Inchbald. At the end of Nature and Art, having denounced repeatedly the callousness and selfishness of the rich with regard to the poor, Inchbald suddenly loses all social perspective (not to mention common sense) and ends her book with a panegyric on poverty itself: "I remember, when I first came . . . to England, the poor excited my compassion; but now that my judgment is matured, I pity the rich. I know that in this opulent kingdom, there are nearly as many persons perishing through intemperance as starving with hunger—there are as many miserable in the lassitude of having nothing to do, as there are bowed down to the earth with hard labour. . . . Add to this, that the rich are so much afraid of dying, they have no comfort in living" (N, 190-91). Inchbald undoubtedly is influenced here by Soame Jenyns, whose A Free Inquiry into the Nature and Origin of Evil explains in some detail that it is really no worse to be poor than to be rich.[9] Wollstonecraft, unlike Inchbald, is not seduced by her pity for the poor into praising their poverty. Maria answers Jemima that she, too, cannot imagine where this supposed good of poverty can reside. There is no time for "thought or information" (M, 64), for reasoning or reflection. As Darnford says, "though riches may fail to produce proportionate happiness, poverty most commonly excludes it" (M, 65).

As if to prove the brutalizing effect of dire poverty and overwork, even Jemima, whose sensibility we by now have come to respect, confesses to behaving in a very ugly manner in an attempt to escape from her impossible situation. Able to find work only as a washer woman, Jemima works nineteen hours a day for eighteen or twenty pence. She meets a tradesman who offers to take her into his house. Jemima convinces him to turn away the girl already living with him, even though she is pregnant; the girl commits suicide. Passing by accident just at the moment the dead girl is discovered, the horrified Jemima resolves "not to live with the wretch. But he did not try me; he left the neighborhood. I once more returned to the wash-tub" (M, 66). Even this is not the nadir of Jemima's life. She drops a tub against her shin, and, unable to work, tries to get into a hospital. She is too poor to be admitted; finally, through the charity of her employer and her landlord, she raises the small sum necessary to get in but must leave before she is healed because she cannot afford the charges for having her linen cleaned: "I cannot give you an adequate idea of the wretched-ness of an hospital," she tells Maria and Darnford, "every thing is left to the care of people intent on gain" (M, 67).[10] Jemima becomes a thief "from principle," is "taken, tried, and condemned to six months' imprisonment" (M, 68), and ends up in a workhouse. The keeper of the workhouse "farmed the poor of different parishes, and out of the bowels of poverty . . . wrung the money with which he purchased this dwelling, as a private receptacle for madness" (M, 69). He offers to take Jemima with him to help care for the inmates, and she accepts: "The offer of forty pounds a year, and to quit a workhouse, was not to be despised, though the condition of shutting my eyes and hardening my heart was annexed to it" (M, 69).[11] The combination of being poor and being female makes life virtually impossible for Jemima. Woll-stonecraft does not ignore the problems in being male and poor, but she says that a poor man who works as hard as Jemima would be able to make a living, whereas Jemima cannot manage even a subsistence. The channels of employment open to women are simply not those that pay a living wage. As Moira Ferguson notes, much of this is based on Wollstonecraft's own observation: "At [Wollstonecraft's] mother's death, she took up residence with the family of her close friend, Fanny Blood and observed at first-hand the pitiful lack of occupations avail-able for women. They eked out a meager living: Fanny painted and Mary sewed until her eyes strained and she became ill. (Mrs. Blood had sewn daily for years to the point of blindness)."[12] Obviously women are vulnerable to seduction and pregnancy, and they do not have the same physical strength as men. But these impediments are not the center of the chapter that details Jemima's life; the most urgent problem is the financial one. Almost all of Jemima's movements are dictated by her need to find money: she becomes a whore, a mistress, a laundress, a thief, a keeper in a madhouse because she has no other means of keeping herself alive. Society essentially forces her to act in antisocial ways—much the point that Defoe had made in *Moll Flanders*.

What of the woman who does not live in dire poverty? Does she fare any better? Maria is Wollstonecraft's example of a middle-class woman, and certainly she is victimized as much as, although differently from, Jemima. The victimization, as with Jemima, begins in earliest childhood, even though she is born into and raised in a respectable family. Maria's father is a tyrant; the eldest male child copies his behavior. Between them, they destroy the happiness of everyone else in the family. The chain of nasty males in *The Wrongs of Woman* is virtually unbroken; the only positive male figure, with the exception of the shadowy Darnford, is Maria's uncle—who interestingly enough is not drawn as part of any domestic relationship.

Maria's father marries because he does not know what else he wants to do: "[He] had been a captain of a man of war; but, disgusted with the service, on account of the preferment of men whose chief merit was their family connections or borough interest, he retired into the country; and, not knowing what to do with himself—married" (*M*, 75). He married Maria's mother for love—that is, not for money—and he reminds her of that "benevolence" whenever she questions his authority. He is to be obeyed absolutely and instantaneously, as if he were still commanding a war ship. The eldest son is encouraged to emulate the father, and as the father tyrannizes over the family, the son rules the younger children. Maria remembers that "My eldest brother . . . became in due form the deputy-tyrant of the house. The representative of my father, a being privileged by nature—a boy, and the darling of my mother, he did not fail to act like an heir apparent" (*M*, 75). The mother, who nursed only the firstborn male, is so partial to him that "in comparison with her affection of him, she might be said not to love the rest of her children" (*M*, 75). Even as a child, Maria finds her situation "unreasonable." She and the younger children must accept "unconditional submission to orders" (*M*, 75), while the eldest son can do virtually anything he wants: "what was called spirit and wit in him, was cruelly repressed as forwardness in [the other children]" (*M*, 76). The mother, rather than interposing, "had an indolence of character, which prevented her from paying much attention to [the children's] education" (*M*, 76). Maria's uncle, her father's brother, however, also influences her. Betrayed by the woman he loved and his best friend, he "declar[es] an intention never to marry" (M, 77). His large fortune makes this decision most interesting to the family: "his relations were ever clustering about him, paying the grossest adulation to a man, who, disgusted with mankind, received them with scorn, or bitter sarcasms" (M, 77). Maria becomes his favorite, and their relationship molds all her perceptions. This uncle, rather than her parents, provides her moral education: "He inculcated, with great warmth, self-respect, and a lofty consciousness of acting right; independent of the censure or aplause of the world; nay, he almost taught me to brave, and even despise its censure, when convinced of the rectitude of my own intentions" (M, 78). The heroic points in Maria's character, her scepticism, her courage, her attitude of questioning the world's values, come from her uncle. Wollstonecraft suggests that heroism is neither male nor female. So, too, with mental capability: Maria repeatedly behaves with quick intelligence. We remember that even Jemima, downtrodden and lacking all education, enjoys—even needs—intellectual companionship. As desirable as these traits of character and intellect are, in both cases Wollstonecraft makes them the product of anyone but a parent's influence.[13]

Unfortunately for Maria, while her uncle's moral and intellectual influence on her is wide-ranging, he is limited in the practical ways he can help her; although he visits her often, "he did not remain long in the country to soften domestic tyranny" (M, 78). Significantly, "he brought [her] books, for which [she] had a passion, and they conspired with his conversation, to make [her] form an ideal picture of life" (M, 78)—not, to be noted, idealized but ideal: the life to strive for. Maria's father and mother represent no such ideals. Maria says, "I shall pass over the tyranny of my father, much as I suffered from it; but it is necessary to notice, that it undermined my mother's health; and that her temper, continually irritated by domestic bickering, became intolerably peevish" (M, 78). Although Jemima laments that all her misfortunes were caused by "the misfortune of having been thrown into the world without the grand support of life—a mother's affection" (M, 56), and although Maria often worries about how her daughter will manage without her, Wollstonecraft shows that the mere fact of shared femaleness, even the bond of maternity, does not assure sympathy. The mere circumstance of being male, however, especially of being the senior male, assures dominance and, generally, the ability to suppress the female. Thus Maria's eldest brother "gradually assumed a right of directing the whole family, not excepting [her] father" (M, 78). Father and mother support their son in his torture of their daughter: Maria remembers, "He seemed to take a peculiar pleasure in tormenting and humbling me; and if I ever ventured to complain of this treatment to either my father or mother, I was rudely rebuffed for presuming to judge of the conduct of my eldest brother" (*M*, 78-79). Thus, Wollstonecraft suggests, even within the family the female has no recourse from tyranny. And there is no recourse either from the favoritism that even a mother shows her son; though son Robert neglects her, and Maria shows "unceasing solicitude" (*M*, 86), the mother gives him whatever "little hoard . . . she had been some years accumulating" (*M*, 87). Maria's wry comment is that girls "but too frequently waste their health and spirits attending a dying parent, who leaves them in comparative poverty. After closing, with filial piety, a father's eyes, they are chased from the paternal roof, to make room for the first-born, the son, who is to carry the empty family-name down to posterity" (*M*, 86).

Maria assumes the responsibility for her younger sisters. Home becomes even gloomier. She is forced to watch her father's mistress, a mistress acquired during the illness of Maria's mother, take over: "my liberty was unnecessarily abridged, and my books, on the pretext that they made me idle, taken from me. My father's mistress was with child, and he, doating on her, allowed or overlooked her vulgar manner of tyrannizing over us" (*M*, 88). The woman even tries to seduce Maria's younger brother. Maria insists that such depravity is society's fault: "By allowing women but one way of rising in the world, the fostering the libertinism of men, society makes monsters of them" (*M*, 88). This submission to vice is then "brought forward as a proof of inferiority of intellect" (*M*, 88). Society misshapes women,[14] and women, twisted into perverted creatures, turn against each other in the attempt to court male favor.

Maria's uncle wants to help her escape this domestic situation. Still believing that "a marriage of mutual inclination" (*M*, 88) is the most promising road to happiness, he tries to arrange a match between Maria and George Venables, a local young man who seems to be relatively pleasant and industrious. Maria's uncle is wrong about George, however; what appears to be good nature and quiet maturity is in fact a combination of intellectual vacuity and sullen conceit. Maria, thinking "more of obtaining [her] freedom, than of [her] lover" (*M*, 89), agrees to the match. She does not know that her uncle "had promised [George] five thousand pounds" (*M*, 89). Later she truly regrets this circumstance, for had she known about the money, she says, she would have demanded that much of it be given to her sisters;

George surely would have been furious, and she would have understood his character in time to avoid marrying him. Maria's marriage,
like her family life, is disastrous, and for exactly the same reason:
society gives no power to the female. This lack of power destroys a
woman's chances not only for happiness but for social usefulness as
well, and Maria's inability to fulfill any of her "schemes of usefulness"
(M, 89) contributes in no small measure to her frustration. "Why was I
not born a man," Maria demands, "or why was I born at all?" (M, 90).
Wollstonecraft devotes two chapters to Maria's marriage. Like the
home life that she has escaped, her marriage is oppressively empty of
personal satisfaction and social meaning. Although she does not immediately understand her husband's "whole character," he very soon
becomes "sunk in [her] esteem" (M, 92). One early cause of disen-
chantment comes when he thwarts Maria's plan to aid her younger
sisters. This desire to help had, in fact, been part of her reason for
marrying: "a strong motive for marrying, was the desire of having a
home at which I could receive [my sisters], now their own grew so
uncomfortable" (M, 91). When her new husband vetoes the plan,
Maria begins to understand his true character. Wollstonecraft emphasizes that the signs were there all along, and that Maria makes the error
of not looking closely enough at this man into whose care she is
committing her life. Maria says that "I could not sometimes help
regretting my early marriage; . . . in my haste to escape from a temporary dependence, and expand my newly fledged wings, . . . I had been
caught in a trap, and caged for life" (M, 92-93).[15] Within the limits of
the cage, Maria does what she can to be useful to her sisters and also,
when and as she can, to her husband. She convinces her uncle "to
settle a thousand pounds on each [sister] . . . and to place them in a
school near town, where [she can] frequently visit, as well as have
them at home with [her]" (M, 93). She tries to help her husband also.
She suggests that he curb his spending; she repeatedly bails him out of
financial difficulty with her uncle's money. But Maria's efforts for her
husband are to no avail—he merely sinks further into financial difficulty while ever more shamelessly exploiting her. Finally, in a kind of
culmination of this exploitation, he attempts to sell her to a business
acquaintance of his in order to escape some of his debt. This is the point
at which Maria decides to run away.[16]

At the beginning Maria has the hope that she might make something worthwhile of the marriage. The first several months "glide
away" relatively pleasantly; "the novelty of London, and the attentive
fondness" (M, 93) of her husband lend some charm to Maria's situa-

tion. But there is no place for the relationship to grow: "we had few subjects in common; indeed he soon appeared to have little relish for my society, unless he was hinting to me the use he could make of my uncle's wealth" (M, 93). Maria tries to find some common ground, even if only by sharing the memory of an amusing or stirring experience, but he does not respond to these overtures: "With all my attention and affectionate interest, I perceived that I could not become the friend or confident of my husband. Every thing I learned relative to his affairs I gathered up by accident; and I vainly endeavoured to establish, at our fire-side, that social converse, which often renders people of different characters dear to each other. Returning from the theatre, or any amusing party, I frequently began to relate what I had seen and highly relished; but with sullen taciturnity he soon silenced me" (M, 93). After some time in his company she begins to feel that something is wrong with her, that she is "the most stupid creature in the world" (M, 93). All of this continues for five years, and during the entire time Maria is "extort[ing]" (M, 93) money from her uncle to pay her husband's debts. When she finally refuses to perform this service any longer, "indifference on his part was changed into rudeness, or something worse" (M, 94). Her husband does not dine at home; he comes back late, and drunk, and goes directly to bed. Maria no longer shares a room with him—and she is glad, since she finds "personal intimacy without affection . . . the most degrading, as well as the most painful state in which a woman of any taste . . . could be placed" (M, 94). Wollstonecraft delineates in Maria's marriage much of what she sees as wrong in contemporary relationships between men and women. She finds, not surprisingly, that the relationship is unequal, and that the inequality itself breeds contempt for the woman. Society countenances actions and lifestyles in men for which women would be ostracized. Thus Maria's husband not only has sexual relationships with other women but "his indulgences of this sort [were] entirely promiscuous, and of the most brutal nature" (M, 94). He tells Maria, when he is drunk, that "his favourites were wantons of the lowest class, who could by their vulgar, indecent mirth, which he called nature, rouse his sluggish spirits" (M, 94). Maria goes on that "the charms of youth and beauty had not the slightest effect on his senses, unless the possessors were initiated in vice" (M, 94). And yet society demands that Maria still be his sexual partner as well as his faithful wife. It is in this context that Maria asks the often quoted, eloquent question: "could I then have returned to his sullied arms, but as a victim to the prejudices of mankind, who have made women the property of their husbands?" (M, 94).

The socially accepted standard—a man may be as promiscuous as he wishes and his wife must nevertheless not only be faithful but accommodating—dehumanizes the woman, strips her at the same time of selfhood and dignity. And the male, himself having created this situation, then to satisfy his own ego looks on women as inferior creatures: "His intimacy with profligate women, and his habits of thinking, gave him a contempt for female endowments; and he would repeat, when wine had loosed his tongue, most of the common-place sarcasms levelled at them, by men who do not allow them to have minds, because mind would be an impediment to gross enjoyment. Men who are inferior to their fellow men, are always most anxious to establish their superiority over women" (M, 94-95). Wollstonecraft emphasizes the intellectual and moral capacity of women. We recall in the early chapters Maria's reading, and her thorough appreciation of the margin notations she finds in Darnford's books; similarly, throughout the novel Maria makes moral and social judgments that Wollstonecraft clearly intends to be astute, since they as clearly represent Wollstonecraft's own pronouncements. And other women in the book also exhibit these qualities— even Jemima, without any advantages of education, has remarkable perception. Maria's intellectual superiority to her husband is clear; her moral superiority is greater still. *Maria or the Wrongs of Woman* shows the world through female eyes, not the pretty, public world of dinner parties shining with social varnish but the real world of the unwashed, hung-over man in his soiled linen. Just as women are expected to ignore the sexual exploits of their husbands, they are supposed not to demand any standards of physical cleanliness and order. Maria complains:

Women who have lost their husband's affection, are justly reproved for neglecting their persons, and not taking the same pains to keep, as to gain a heart; but who thinks of giving the same advice to men. . . . It is not easy to be pleased, because, after promising to love, in different circumstances, we are told that it is our duty. I cannot, I am sure (though when attending the sick, I never felt disgust) forget my own sensations, when rising with health and spirit, and after scenting the sweet morning, I have met my husband at the breakfast table. . . . The squeamishness of stomach alone, produced by the last night's intemperance, which he took no pains to conceal, destroyed my appetite. I think I now see him lolling in an arm-chair, in a dirty powdering gown, soiled linen, ungartered stockings, and tangled hair, yawning and stretching himself. [M, 95][17]

Maria goes away for a time to try to sort out the financial affairs of her father and to prevent him from entirely destroying the inheritance of the whole family. In support of these ends, she gets her uncle to accompany her. When she returns to her husband, he is, unaccountably, reformed. "He became . . . tender and attentive; and attacking my weak side, made a confession of his follies, and lamented the embarrassments in which I, who merited a far different fate, might be involved. He besought me to aid him with my counsel, praised my understanding, and appealed to the tenderness of my heart" (*M*, 100). Wollstonecraft's analysis of Maria's response to this change is perceptive. Maria feels compassion, she says, but not love. And she is faced with a dilemma, for, repulsed by her husband's physical overtures, she nevertheless considers that she must accept them. "My husband's renewed caresses then became hateful to me; his brutality was tolerable, compared to his distasteful fondness. Still, compassion, and the fear of insulting his supposed feelings, by a want of sympathy, made me dissemble, and do violence to my delicacy. What a task!" (*M*, 101). Reflecting on her acceptance of her wifely duty, Maria finds no redeeming aspect to this betrayal of her principles. There had been "something of delicacy in my husband's bridal attentions; but now his tainted breath, pimpled face, and blood-shot eyes, were not more repugnant to my senses, than his gross manners, and loveless familiarity to my taste" (*M*, 102). Wollstonecraft uses the specifically detailed incident—tainted breath, a pimpled face—as a springboard for an analysis of the moral and social hypocrisy of the rules that govern the relations between men and women.

> Those who support a system of what I term false refinement, and will not allow great part of love in the female, as well as male breast, to spring in some respects involuntarily, may not admit that charms are as necessary to feed the passion, as virtues to convert the mellowing spirit into friendship. To such observers I have nothing to say, any more than to the moralists, who insist that women ought to, and can love their husbands, because it is their duty. . . . When novelists or moralists praise as a virtue, a woman's coldness of constitution, and want of passion; and make her yield to the ardour of her lover out of sheer compassion, or to promote a frigid plan of future comfort, I am disgusted. They may be good women, in the ordinary acceptation of the phrase, and do no harm; but they appear to me not to have those 'finely fashioned nerves,' which render the senses exquisite. They may possess tenderness; but they want that fire of the imagination, which produces *active* sensibility, and *positive* virtue. How does the woman deserve to be characterized, who marries one man, with a heart and imag-

ination devoted to another? Is she not an object of pity or contempt, when thus sacrilegiously violating the purity of her own feelings? Nay, it is as indelicate, when she is indifferent, unless she be constitutionally insensible; then indeed it is a mere affair of barter; and I have nothing to do with the secrets of trade. Yes; eagerly as I wish you [her daughter] to possess true rectitude of mind, and purity of affection, I must insist that a heartless conduct is the contrary of virtuous. Truth is the only basis of virtue; and we cannot, without depraving our minds, endeavour to please a lover or husband, but in proportion as he pleases us. [M, 101-2]

Wollstonecraft insists that between husband and wife there ought to be truth, and therefore equality, rather than dutiful submission, but she shows Maria submitting. Thus she underlines for the reader how very difficult it is for even a strong woman to resist social decree. Wollstonecraft's ideal woman is a being of passion and sexuality. Women who have sexual relations merely because it is expected of them as wives she finds to be "bartering" their persons for the comforts of domesticity. Wollstonecraft challenges the traditional view of marriage and sexuality: women have a right to their own sexuality, and this passion is not only acceptable but virtuous; cold submission is not virtuous.

Further, she presents man and woman as equal in the demands that they should be entitled to make upon each other. "A man would only be expected to maintain; yes, barely grant a subsistence, to a woman rendered odious by habitual intoxication; but who would expect him, or think it possible to love her?" (M, 102). He surely could not be expected to insist that, under forfeit of losing everything, he should never love another. But this is exactly what society demands of a woman; Maria ironically comments that "woman, weak in reason, impotent in will, is required to moralize, sentimentalize herself to stone, and pine her life away, labouring to reform her embruted mate" (M, 102). Even beyond being expected to live with such a husband, and to try to reform him, a woman must allow her husband to dissipate not only his own resources but hers as well—she has no right to attempt to control the waste. Meanwhile, she does not have the money even to try to find some comfort in society, for while he recklessly spends their money on dissipation, she is kept on a tight and often totally insufficient budget: Maria remembers that when "I demanded money for the house expences, which I put off till the last moment, his customary reply, often prefaced with an oath, was, 'Do you think me, madam, made of money?'—The butcher, the baker, must wait; and, what was worse, I was often obliged to witness his surly dismission of tradesmen, who were in want of their money" (M, 95-96). Wollstonecraft's emphasis is the same as Defoe's so much earlier in the century. We remember that Roxana's husband loses all their money, and Roxana, understanding just what is going wrong, is helpless to stop the steady erosion of their financial well-being. Wollstonecraft makes the same point: Maria says, "I endeavoured to prevail on him to retrench his expences; but he had always some plausible excuse to give, to justify his not following my advice.Humanity, compassion, and the interest produced by a habit of living together, made me try to relieve, and sympathize with him" (M, 103), but to no avail.

Maria's marriage provides her with no companionship, no physical pleasure, and no financial security. Yet she is expected to remain faithful to her mate. Wollstonecraft's analysis of marriage is bitter:

> for, only to lay a stress on the dependent state of a woman in the grand question of the comforts arising from the possession of property, she is . . . much more injured by the loss of the husband's affection, than he by that of his wife; yet where is she, condemned to the solitude of a deserted home, to look for a compensation from the woman, who seduces him from her? She cannot drive an unfaithful husband from his house, nor separate, or tear, his children from him, however culpable he may be; and he, still the master of his own fate, enjoys the smiles of a world, that would brand her with infamy, did she, seeking consolation, venture to retaliate. . . . The marriage state is certainly that in which women, generally speaking, can be most useful; but I am far from thinking that a woman, once married, ought to consider the engagement as indissoluble. . . . The magnitude of a sacrifice ought always to bear some proportion to the utility in view; and for a woman to live with a man, for whom she can cherish neither affection nor esteem, or even be of any use to him, excepting in the light of a housekeeper, is an abjectness of condition, the enduring of which no concurrence of circumstances can ever make a duty in the sight of God or just men. . . . The situation of a woman separated from her husband, is undoubtedly very different from that of a man who has left his wife. He, with lordly dignity, has shaken off a clog; and the allowing her food and raiment, is thought sufficient to secure his reputation from taint. And, should she have been inconsiderate, he will be celebrated for his generosity and forbearance. Such is the respect paid to the master-key of property! A woman, on the contrary, resigning what is termed her natural protector (though he never was so, but in name) is despised and shunned, for asserting the independence of mind distinctive of a rational being, and spurning at slavery. [M, 104-6]

Maria's husband actually does see her as property. But his attempt to trade her sexual favors in payment of his business debts is only the culmination of years of shamelessly using her, years of forcing her to wring money from her uncle. When Mr. Venables finds out about her uncle's parting gift, he "dupe[s]" (*M*, 107) her out of the money. Maria laments that it was "a sum sufficient to supply my own wants, and to enable me to pursue a plan I had in view, to settle my younger brother in a respectable employment. . . . Thus did he pillage me and my family, thus frustrate all my plans of usefulness" (*M*, 107). That note, "plans of usefulness," recurs repeatedly in the novel. Maria is fully capable of financial management; tragically, although she has the desire and the ability, she lacks the power to carry out these plans. Society gives all such power to the husband, whether he is fit for the responsibility or not: "But a wife being as much a man's property as his horse, or his ass, she has nothing she can call her own. He may use any means to get at what the law considers as his, the moment his wife is in possession of it, even to the forcing of a lock, as Mr. Venables did, to search for notes in my writing-desk—and all this is done with a show of equity, because, forsooth, he is responsible for her maintenance" (*M*, 107). Further, a woman cannot *"lawfully"* keep from "the gambling, spendthrift, or beastly drunkard" (*M*, 108) her own fortune, any inheritance, or even "what she earns by her own exertions," not even to maintain herself or a child.[18] The male, meanwhile, "can rob [the wife] with impunity, even to waste publicly on a courtezan" (*M*, 108), and the law affords the wife no protection. Maria ironically suggests that when such laws were formed, part of the legal arrangement should have been that henceforth each husband "should always be wiser and more virtuous than his wife, in order to entitle him . . . to keep this idiot, or perpetual minor, for ever in bondage" (*M*, 108). Women are fully capable human beings who are as able to think as men. The terrible injustice of their legal position as "idiots" and "perpetual minor[s]" should need no comment. Wollstonecraft argues that the law gives a man the right to a woman's body and property to such an extent that the woman virtually is enslaved. Although Maria's husband had tried to "sell . . . [her] to prostitution" (*M*, 111), when Maria leaves him, even after the years of mistreatment that culminate in this final debasement, he has the legal right to make her return—or to lock her away in a madhouse, as he does. Maria passionately comments that despots are "for ever stigmatized" for ordering "even the most atrocious criminals to be chained to dead bodies" (*M*, 114), yet this is what the law does to women whose marriages are empty of all esteem and affection. The laws are inhuman, she says, that "forge adamantine fetters to bind minds together, that can never mingle in social communion" (*M*, 114).

Maria's uncle serves several narrative purposes in the novel, and one of the most important of these is to provide a nonromantic example of what Wollstonecraft means by "social communion." Maria and her uncle have much in common and love and respect each other. The reader sees Maria in constant battle first with her parents and brother and then with her husband; the good relationship she has with her uncle underscores the fact that Maria is capable of sustaining a loving tie. Since Wollstonecraft presents the uncle as a paragon of rational and moral intelligence, it is important that he agree with Maria's decision to leave her husband. He does approve, and he plans to return to take Maria and the baby—whom he plans to adopt—away from England. He "seemed to have no doubt of obliging Mr. Venables to hear reason" (*M*, 129), Maria says, presumably by making a financial settlement. This lovely plan unfortunately dies with her uncle; the third day after Maria gives birth, her brother bursts into her room to tell her that their uncle is dead. Her brother is furious that the greatest part of their uncle's wealth has been left to the child, with Maria "appoint[ed] as its guardian." Maria notes that "every step was taken to enable me to be mistress of his fortune, without putting any part of it in Mr. Venables' power. My brother came to vent his rage on me, for having, as he expressed himself, 'deprived him, my uncle's eldest nephew, of his inheritance;' though my uncle's property, the fruit of his own exertion, being all in the funds, or on landed securities, there was not a shadow of justice in the charge" (*M*, 130).[19]

Maria feels "widowed. . . by the death of [her] uncle" and mourns accordingly. For her husband she feels only repugnance, although she wishes for the joy of sharing her child with "a respectable father" (*M*, 130). She decides to leave England even without the protection of her uncle. Ever thoughtful and responsible, she carefully arranges the affairs of her father and siblings. She seems to manage capably and efficiently: "During the period necessary to prepare for a long absence, I sent a supply to pay my father's debts, and settled my brothers in eligible situations. . . . The manner in which my uncle's property was settled, prevented me from making the addition to the fortune of my surviving sister, that I could have wished; but I had prevailed on him to bequeath her two thousand pounds, and she determined to marry a lover, to whom she had been some time attached" (*M*, 132). Having taken care of everyone else, Maria readies herself for escape. By now it is clear that her husband is solely interested in getting her property away from her. His solicitor advises her to "make over to [her] husband . . . the greater part of the property [she] had at command" or he would "claim the child" (M, 132-33). She gives her husband five hundred pounds, but he does not abide by their bargain. He has her drugged, takes away the child (who subsequently dies), and interns Maria in the madhouse where we first meet her. In the madhouse itself he sends her word that for half her fortune he will let her go; she is not fooled and refuses the suggestion. The events of the story unfold quickly. The keeper of the madhouse runs off, and Jemima helps Maria and Darnford to escape. The three of them take a lodging together, with Jemima as housekeeper. Darnford learns why he had been committed—relatives had tried to keep him from claiming a fortune he had inherited—and he and Maria decide to follow the offenders to Paris. Before they can leave, however, Maria's husband commences an action against Darnford for "seduction and adultery."[20] Darnford goes to Paris, and Maria "determine[s] to remain in London till the termination of this affair" (M, 142), taking "the task of conducting Darnford's defense upon herself" (M, 145).

The last relatively complete chapter that Wollstonecraft left is the trial. As in the trial at the end of *Caleb Williams*, justice plays no part in the proceedings. Maria's impassioned defense of her conduct with Darnford and her attack on the institution of marriage in contemporary England form a fitting summary to the events of the novel. Her eloquent statement, however, is ignored by the presiding judge, who accepts the series of distortions, half-truths and lies set forth by the counsel for the plaintiff. Maria is the wife of "an indulgent husband" (M, 145), he concludes. She ran away for no cause; Darnsford prevented the peace-officers from bringing her back, and so on. Maria counters with a long, written statement describing her married life: her husband's many infidelities, her support of his deserted illegitimate child, his extortion of sums of money from her wealthy uncle, and, finally, his attempt to "barter" her to his colleague.

Maria intersperses among the particulars a damning analysis of marriage. She insists that there are many and diverse cases where a woman should and must be allowed to separate herself from her husband: "I exclaim against the laws which throw the whole weight of the yoke on the weaker shoulders, and force women, when they claim protectorship as mothers, to sign a contract, which renders them dependent on the caprice of the tyrant, whom choice or necessity has appointed to reign over them" (M, 146). After her husband tried to "barter" her for relief from his debts, Maria tells the court, she left him. Since a bequest from her uncle provided money to support herself and her child, she "destroyed the settlement" for the five thousand pounds that her husband had received with her at their marriage. She "require[d] none of [her] property to be returned to [her], nor . . . the sums extorted from [her] during six years" (*M*, 147). She had been "hunted like a criminal from place to place, though [she] contracted no debts and demanded no maintenance" (*M*, 147). When her uncle died and left her his property, she was "exposed to new persecution," and finally put in a private madhouse. Her life with her legal husband, then, was a series of disappointments and betrayals. There is nothing between them except the legal bond, a bond that Maria twice reminds the judge she had made when she was too young to know better, and which she in any case considers dissolved with the death of their child.

In contrast, she describes the relationship between herself and Darnsford, a relationship entered into freely by mature adults. She feels that her relationship with Darnsford transgresses no moral bounds. A woman, she says,

> must be allowed to consult her conscience, and regulate her conduct . . . by her own sense of right. The respect I owe to myself, demanded my strict adherence to my determination of never viewing Mr. Venables in the light of a husband, nor could it forbid me from encouraging another. If I am unfortunately united to an unprincipled man, am I for ever to be shut out from fulfilling the duties of a wife and mother?—I wish my country to approve of my conduct; but, if laws exist, made by the strong to oppress the weak, I appeal to my own sense of justice, and declare that I will not live with the individual, who has violated every moral obligation which binds man to man. [*M*, 148]

While she lived with her husband, she "never encouraged a lover" (*M*, 149); after the traps he laid "to ensnare" (*M*, 149) her, she considers herself free. Surely these arguments are remarkable, as so much of this novel is remarkable, in view of the time when Wollstonecraft is writing. She insists that morality is separate from law, and that when bad laws dictate immoral behavior, the individual—here specifically the individual woman—must act according to her own moral promptings. A husband who has "violated every moral obligation which binds man to man" has freed his wife from any obligation to him. Wollstonecraft's argument is part of the contemporary reevaluation of all relationships with authority. Holcroft, for example, makes the point in *Anna St. Ives* that it is not the biological parent but the person who does the nurturing who is to be considered a real parent;[21] along the same lines, Wollstonecraft finds that the relationship between a man and a woman must be based on the spiritual rather than the legal bonds between them. Marriage, then, "is the concern of the individuals who consent to [a] mutual association, and they ought not to be prevented from beginning, suspending, or terminating it as they please." The judge dismisses such arguments. He notes "the fallacy of letting women plead their feelings, as an excuse for the violation of the marriage-vow. For his part, he had always determined to oppose all innovation, and the new-fangled notions which incroached on the good old rules of conduct. . . . It was her duty to love and obey the man chosen by her parents and relations, who were qualified by their experience to judge better for her, than she could for herself" (M, 149). And he reverts to the theme of money: "he hoped that no Englishman would legalize adultery, by enabling the adulteress to enrich her seducer" (M, 150). Keeping the rules of marriage as they are, he says, is "evidently for the good of the whole" (M, 150).

In light of the realities of Maria's marriage, the ironies inherent in the judge's summation are overwhelming. *Maria or the Wrongs of Woman* is not well-written, subtle, or even finished as a novel, yet it is a very powerful book. It is true that Wollstonecraft implausibly piles just about every possible misfortune on her characters—but it is equally true that women were subject to any combination of these misfortunes. Wollstonecraft, like Godwin, does not soften the edges of her social criticism. She is not alone in her recognition of the wrongs society inflicts on women; Holcroft and Bage describe many of the same injustices. But they refrain from condemning their characters to the helpless dysfunction that Maria and Jemima inevitably experience. In their novels the potential damage with which society threatens women is checked by the individual woman's intelligence and strength of character teamed with the understanding of an exceptional man. As we shall see in the next chapter, Austen too is aware that women face danger because of the way society is structured, but she presents a world in which it is the woman's job to avoid those dangers. This the woman does by marrying a good man. There is some social criticism in Austen, but in comparison with the images of the Godwin circle, it is not very intense. The idealism of the radical novelists of the nineties— and the anger that attends it—in Austen gives way to a pragmatic acceptance of society and woman's role.

# SEVEN

# Jane Austen:
## *Pride and Prejudice* and *Emma*

Austen's women are ordinary women, not ideals of the good or the bad, and they find themselves in ordinary situations, growing up, courting, and marrying. The actions of these women are always seen within the perspective of common sense. Austen's images of women are less critical than those of the radical novelists who are chronologically close to her, and they are different in significant ways from those of earlier novelists as well. Austen concentrates on the norm, and that norm essentially is relative. Her heroines are not larger than life, and her villainesses may be mean and catty, but they too are never grotesques in the manner, for example, of Fielding and Richardson. Similarly, behavior in Austen novels, with rare exceptions, is measured by relative standards—behavior is more or less good, as Darcy exemplifies throughout *Pride and Prejudice*. Charlotte's married life presents another example of the refusal absolutely to label. There are no surprises in the images of women that Jane Austen gives us. Marriage is the goal of a woman's life, and if a woman plays the courtship game right, and has a little luck into the bargain, she stands a good chance of having a rather pleasant life. Almost all of the discomfort with woman's ability to function in society that writers like Defoe, Richardson, and Wollstonecraft show, and certainly the confusion about how to view women that Fielding manifests, is absent in Austen's novels. Austen assumes a rational bias in her readers. We are expected to identify with the reasonable characters in her novels— with Elizabeth Bennet in *Pride and Prejudice,* with Mr. Knightley in *Emma.* Austen's women are completely integrated into their society.

Elizabeth Bennet's walk across a muddy field from her house to Bingley's has been seen as an assertion of her self, even of her "feminism."[1] But she walks across the field, of course, not in rebellion against anything but because it is the shortest and quickest—the most logical—way to get to her sick sister Jane. So exactly do Austen's characters fit into their social grids that this small edge of Elizabeth's action that is not absolutely expected can look, even for a moment, like rebellion.[2] Austen accepts the rules of her society, and her characters play out their stories within those rules, not against them. While Austen finds it regrettable that Jane Fairfax would have to waste her life as a governess if she could not find someone to marry her, she accepts this lamentable circumstance as she accepts any other unfortunate fact of life. Austen recognizes the problem in a situation like Jane's but does not suggest that society needs to seek some answer to that problem. Similarly, she recognizes the potentially sad reality of the tenuous place someone like Miss Bates holds in society, but, again, recognizes it not as a condition subject to change but as something unfortunate—a social club foot.

All critics of Austen have noted that the novels are about marriage, and many have realized that that means the novels are about money.[3] Austen makes it clear that the way a woman makes a living is to marry a man. This is the central concern of the characters in both *Pride and Prejudice* and *Emma:* the action of the novels and the plotting of the characters revolve around marriage. Even when marriage is based on practicality rather than affection, as in the match between Charlotte Lucas and Mr. Collins, Austen does not mark the solution as clearly inappropriate. When Elizabeth visits Charlotte she does not find her miserably unhappy living with Mr. Collins; Charotte has arranged her life to make it bearable, if not exuberant, and having set up her husband in the sunny parlor so that he will be less likely to wander too often into her sitting room, she seems reasonably content.

Austen's novels focus at this level of day-to-day reality. Women get the hems of their skirts dirty, quietly shift living arrangements to produce the least friction, and make conscious and unregretted compromises. Austen's characters, busily functioning on this level, do not question the basic structure of society. Life is difficult for a woman who has not married—all women in Austen novels know that truth. Rather than question the social structure that makes this so, each woman acts so as to maximize her chances for the marriage that will stand between herself and the unfortunate condition of spinsterhood. Women in *Pride and Prejudice* and *Emma* generally seem happy. When a woman is not happy, the unhappiness usually results from her own misperception or even foolishness. Thus Emma, when she is unhappy, most often has caused her misery by her own misguided manipulations of those around her; her friend Harriet, whose unhappiness never seems very severe in any case, also is a victim of her own foolishness enhanced by Emma's misguided advice. Elizabeth Bennet is quite content most of the time, as is Emma. And like Emma, Elizabeth's unhappy moments are caused by her own failures of perception. Austen's images of women are of their daily concerns. A letter from Frank Churchill, a visit from Mr. Knightley, a snub from Darcy at a ball is important; Austen's women spend little time talking about the future or imagining themselves in it. The major exception to this mental fix is marriage: naturally, in novels that are so concerned with courtship, the characters would from time to time imagine themselves married. But these occasions are, actually, quite few. The most obvious such imagining is Elizabeth's when she visits Pemberly and thinks about how she would have felt had the estate been hers.[4]

It is impossible to speak of falling in love, courtship, and marriage in *Pride and Prejudice* without speaking of property. Significantly, Elizabeth first begins to appreciate Darcy when she actually visits Pemberly. The good taste and refinement of the place reflect the man; Elizabeth hears only good of Darcy from his housekeeper. But these aspects, salient as they are, are not the turning point: that comes when Elizabeth admires the physical estate and reflects that she could have been its mistress. The property is attractive because it is Darcy's, but it is attractive for itself as well. Dorothy Van Ghent got it just right when she emphasized the inescapable pairing in the novel of love and property beginning with its famous opening sentence: "It is a truth universally acknowledged, that a single man in possession of a good fortune, must be in want of a wife." She notes that in Austen's second sentence such a man "in the minds of the surrounding families . . . is considered as the rightful property of some one or other of their daughters." Her commentary on the beginning of *Pride and Prejudice* is worth quoting:

In this first chapter, the fundamental literary unit of the single word—"fortune," "property," "possession," "establishment," "business"—has consistently been setting up the impulsion of economic interest against those non-utilitarian interests implied by the words "feelings" and "love." The implications of the word "marriage" itself are ambivalent; for as these implications are controlled in the book, "marriage" does not mean an act of ungoverned passion (not even in Lydia's and Wickham's rash elopement does it mean this: for Wickham has his eye on a settlement by blackmail, and Lydia's infatuation is rather more with a uniform than with a man); marriage means a complex engagement between the marrying couple and society—that is, it means not only "feelings" but "property" as well. In marrying, the individual marries society as well as his mate, and "property" provides the necessary articles of this other marriage.[5]

The identification of marriage and money, particularly property, is consistent throughout *Pride and Prejudice,* and in *Emma* as well. Austen finds it not only reasonable but unavoidable to look at money matters as part of any matrimonial pairing. She objects to an overly mercenary view of marriage but not to a rational view in which the financial prospects of the partners are considered. Making a living in Austen novels often seems mysterious at best, and Austen most of the time seems to think of wealth as a fixed pool that is shared out according to marriage deals. Since this is so, the marriage dealings are extremely important. If we think about how few people in these two novels seem to make a living other than by marriage, this perspective becomes quite pronounced. The Gardiners in *Pride and Prejudice* are in trade; Mr. Weston in *Emma* was first in the militia and then found a comfortable livelihood in business. Otherwise, earning money by work seems quite chancy: Wickham does not do very well; Mr. Collins manages, but very carefully indeed plays up to Lady Catherine. For women, there is always that horrible fate of governess. People do not seem to have many options. When Lydia's marriage needs to be compensated monetarily, Mr. Bennet regrets that he does not have adequate funds to do the job himself—that he'd not been careful with his money when he was young. There is never any suggestion that he might earn some more. It is in this perspective that we must see Austen's manipulations of her characters and her comments on marriage and money: she sees the financial aspect as a perfectly reasonable, necessary, part of the marriage package. And further, for Austen money and class are closely connected. Whatever the fun Austen makes of pretensions of one sort or another, in every case the final pairings do not offend class lines. To take the most obvious example, Harriet Smith in *Emma* appropriately marries the yeoman Robert Martin.

Austen uses financial detail to delineate character; that is, a person's financial profile is part of his—or her—portrait. Although she often cloaks her references to money in irony, Austen's attention to financial detail is precise. She does not approve of the Miss Bingleys;

she remarks, with some asperity, that their wealth has convinced them that they are "in every respect entitled to think well of themselves, and meanly of others."[6] But she does not skimp on the financial description: "They were rather handsome, had been educated in one of the first private seminaries in town, had a fortune of twenty thousand pounds, were in the habit of spending more than they ought, and of associating with people of rank; and were therefore in every respect entitled to think well of themselves, and meanly of others. They were of a respectable family in the north of England; a circumstance more deeply impressed on their memories than that their brother's fortune and their own had been acquired by trade" (P, 15). And "Mr. Bingley inherited property to the amount of nearly an hundred thousand pounds from his father" (P, 15). The sums are impressive; Bingley's hundred thousand pounds is magnificent.[7] The sisters nevertheless spend more than they ought, marking them as deficient in character since clearly they should be able to live within the bounds of such a fortune. And although she is making fun of pride and prejudice, Austen finds it relevant to note the source of Bingley's fortune. Austen points to the ridiculousness of the snobbery that looks down on money earned in trade—yet Darcy, the romantic hero of her novel, indeed is possessed of old, truly aristocratic money. We will see many examples of this traditional, conservative base in Austen.[8]

Austen goes on to discuss the question of whether Bingley will purchase an estate, perhaps an odd concern in view of Bingley's relatively young age and single status; but of course Bingley's renting of the estate at this point helps to define his character. Renting is part of "the easiness of his temper" (P, 15). The same lack of conviction and resolve that allows him to be led away from Jane precludes his making the decision to buy. One of the aspects of Austen's happy ending is that Bingley indeed does purchase an estate, thus taking his proper role in the social structure. Note that here at the very beginning of the novel we know not only about Bingley's lack of an estate but about his sisters' feelings on this matter. The single Miss Bingley as well as the married Mrs. Hurst is "very anxious for his having an estate of his own" (P, 15-16). Mrs. Hurst, "who had married a man of more fashion than fortune" (P, 16), is quite happy to consider her brother's home her own when it suits her. What is worth remarking in all this is the emphasis Austen puts on these property matters. Most of what we know early in the novel about Bingley and his sisters is defined in terms of their relationship to property.

The next chapter begins on much the same note. Again Austen

first defines her characters by the source of their money and the attendant social position they occupy. Sir William Lucas "had been formerly in trade in Meryton, where he had made a tolerable fortune and risen to the honour of knighthood by an address to the King, during his mayoralty" (*P*, 18). Thus neither Lucas's money nor his title are old. Further, the impact of the latter conditioned his response to the former: "The distinction had perhaps been felt too strongly. It had given him a disgust to his business and to his residence in a small market town; and quitting them both, he had removed with his family to a house about a mile from Meryton, denominated from that period Lucas Lodge, where he could think with pleasure of his own impor- tance, and unshackled by business, occupy himself solely in being civil to all the world" (*P*, 18). The Lucas family, like the Bingley family, has been positioned carefully by Austen on a money-social position grid. It then suffices to describe Mrs. Lucas as "a very good kind of woman, not too clever to be a valuable neighbour to Mrs. Bennet" (*P*, 18). Placing the family in terms of finances and rank takes fourteen lines; two phrases suffice after that to pin down Mrs. Lucas.

The Bennet family, of course, must be defined in due course:

> Mr. Bennet's property consisted almost entirely in an estate of two thousand a year, which, unfortunately for his daughters, was entailed in default of heirs male, on a distant relation; and their mother's fortune, though ample for her situation in life, could but ill supply the deficiency of his. Her father had been an attorney in Meryton, and had left her four thousand pounds.
>
> She had a sister married to a Mr. Phillips, who had been a clerk to their father, and succeeded him in the business, and a brother settled in London in a respectable line of trade. [*P*, 28]

The entail is of central significance to the plot of the novel; because the family property will leave the Bennets upon Mr. Bennet's death, it is not just desirable but urgent for the daughters to find self-supporting husbands. Although there is no indication that Mr. Bennet himself has any job, others in the family have had professions. Mrs. Bennet's father had been an attorney, and obviously had been reasonably successful, to leave her four thousand pounds. Her sister's husband, Mr. Phillips, had gone from clerk to succeeding her father; finally, there is the brother, whom we later realize to be Mr. Gardiner, who is in a "respectable" line of trade. Each relative is carefully affixed to the financial map.

Marriage and making a living first come together in a more than theoretical way in the unlikely person of Mr. Collins. The Bennet estate, in the absence of a male heir, is entailed on Mr. Collins. There had been some sort of family feud between Mr. Collins's father and the elder Bennets, but, Mr. Collins's father having died, Mr. Collins feels free to make it up. He is in a financial position to marry, having been given a decent living by "the Right Honourable Lady Catherine de Bourgh, widow of Sir Lewis de Bourgh, whose bounty and beneficence has preferred me to the valuable rectory of this parish" (*P*, 62-63), he writes to Mr. Bennet. So situated—that is, in possession of a comfortable living—Mr. Collins is ready to make amends to the Bennet family. Lady Catherine has told him to marry, and he thinks it would be kind to take one of the Bennet girls whom he will one day disinherit. Mr. Collins, then, suggests marriage as a means of righting a financial wrong. We could assume that Austen contemptuously dismisses the view that marriage is a financial transaction—Mr. Collins is, after all, a certified twit—if it were not for Miss Charlotte Lucas, Elizabeth's close friend.

> Having now a good house and very sufficient income, [Mr. Collins] intended to marry; and in seeking a reconciliation with the Longbourn family he had a wife in view, as he meant to chuse one of the daughters, if he found them as handsome and amiable as they were represented by common report. This was his plan of amends—of atonement—for inheriting their father's estate; and he thought it an excellent one, full of eligibility and suitableness, and excessively generous and disinterested on his own part. [*P*, 70]

He settles on Jane, only because she is the eldest daughter; when Mrs. Bennet tells him that Jane is likely soon to be engaged, he switches to Elizabeth. Most aspects of his proposal have to do with financial matters.

> "My reasons for marrying are, first, that I think it a right thing for every clergyman in easy circumstances . . . to set the example of marriage in his parish. Secondly, that I am convinced it will add very greatly to my happiness; and thirdly—which perhaps I ought to have mentioned earlier, that it is the particular advice and recommendation of the very noble lady whom I have the honour of calling patroness. . . . [S]he said, 'Mr. Collins, you must marry. A clergyman like you must marry.—Chuse properly . . . let her be an active, useful sort of person,

not brought up high, but able to make a small income go a good way.'"
[*P*, 105-6]

Mr. Collins, as part of his proposal, notes to Elizabeth that

> To fortune I am perfectly indifferent, and shall make no demand of that
> nature on your father, since I am well aware that it could not be complied
> with; and that one thousand pounds in the 4 per cents. which will not be
> yours till after your mother's decease, is all that you may ever be entitled to.
> On that head, therefore, I shall be uniformly silent; and you may assure
> yourself that no ungenerous reproach shall ever pass my lips when we are
> married. [*P*, 106]

Elizabeth rejects such terms; Charlotte accepts them.

Austen's description of Mr. Collins presents a man of mean understanding and little warmth:

> Mr. Collins was not a sensible man, and the deficiency of nature had been
> but little assisted by education or society; the greatest part of his life having
> been spent under the guidance of an illiterate and miserly father. . . . A
> fortunate chance had recommended him to Lady Catherine de Bourgh
> when the living of Hunsford was vacant; and the respect which he felt for
> her high rank, and his veneration for her as his patroness, mingling with a
> very good opinion of himself, of his authority as a clergyman, and his rights
> as a rector, made him altogether a mixture of pride and obsequiousness,
> self-importance and humility. [*P*, 70]

With no illusions, Charlotte takes this man as her husband. Charlotte
accepts his proposal of marriage without any games, for "the stupidity
with which he was favoured by nature, must guard his courtship from
any charm that could make a woman wish for its continuance; and
Miss Lucas, who accepted him solely from the pure and disinterested
desire of an establishment, cared not how soon that establishment
were gained" (*P*, 122). What is Austen showing us with the Collins-
Lucas match? It is tempting to react as Elizabeth does and assume that
Charlotte is wrong to sell herself in this way. But Jane, who often is
quietly wiser than Elizabeth, sees the matter differently: "Jane con-
fessed herself a little surprised at the match; but she said less of her
astonishment than of her earnest desire for their happiness; nor could
Elizabeth persuade her to consider it as improbable" (*P*, 127). Charlotte
herself feels the same way.

Her reflections were in general satisfactory. Mr. Collins to be sure was neither sensible nor agreeable; his society was irksome, and his attachment to her must be imaginary. But still he would be her husband.—Without thinking highly either of men or of matrimony, marriage had always been her object; it was the only honourable provision for well-educated young women of small fortune, and however uncertain of giving happiness, must be their pleasantest preservative from want. This preservative she had now obtained; and at the age of twenty-seven, without having ever been handsome, she felt all the good luck of it. [*P*, 122-23]

As she explains to Elizabeth, " 'I am not romantic you know. I never was. I ask only a comfortable home; and considering Mr. Collins's character, connections, and situation in life, I am convinced that my chance of happiness with him is as fair, as most people can boast on entering the marriage state' " (*P*, 125).[9] And indeed, when Elizabeth visits Charlotte she finds her friend quite comfortable. Charlotte arranges the routine so as to minimize where possible her contact with her husband. She does her part in playing up to Lady de Bourgh, and she seems, in general, reasonably content. This option of marrying for a situation only would not work for Elizabeth, nor even for the much more compliant Jane, but it seems adequate for someone with Charlotte's temperament and outlook. That Austen does not show us a miserably unhappy Charlotte repenting her mercenary leap into marriage is significant. Similarly, later in the novel Austen makes it clear that although Lydia's marriage to Wickham is unfortunate, not to have the marriage, as in Charlotte's case also, would be still more unfortunate. Marriage almost always represents a happy ending of sorts in *Pride and Prejudice* and *Emma*.

The clearly financial paradigm of the Collins-Lucas marriage is the first pairing we have in *Pride and Prejudice*. The other three, Jane's, Elizabeth's, and Lydia's, all have important financial components. The most obvious case is Lydia's: Wickham simply strikes a financial deal, demanding specific remuneration in return for which he marries Lydia. It is Wickham's callous use of blackmail and his abnegation of responsibility that offend Austen, not merely the fact that Wickham seeks some sort of financial base from his wife as wives often do from their husbands. A financial settlement for Lydia is not Wickham's first attempt to attain money by marriage. We remember that early in their acquaintance Wickham had singled out Elizabeth herself for preference. The embryonic courtship does not find enough to nourish it, however, and the relationship miscarries:

His apparent partiality had subsided, his attentions were over, he was the admirer of some one else. Elizabeth was watchful enough to see it all, but she could see it and write of it without material pain. Her heart had been but slightly touched, and her vanity was satisfied with believing that *she* would have been his only choice, had fortune permitted it. The sudden acquisition of ten thousand pounds was the most remarkable charm of the young lady, to whom he was now rendering himself agreeable; but Elizabeth, less clear-sighted perhaps in his case than in Charlotte's, did not quarrel with him for his wish of independence. Nothing, on the contrary, could be more natural; and while able to suppose that it cost him a few struggles to relinquish her, she was ready to allow it a wise and desirable measure for both, and could very sincerely wish him happy. [*P*, 149-50]

Elizabeth finds it perfectly reasonable that Wickham wishes "independence" and is ready to earn it in this way.[10] Austen returns to the subject a little later when Elizabeth discusses with Mrs. Gardiner Wickham's desertion. Mrs. Gardiner teases "'what sort of girl is Miss King? I should be sorry to think our friend mercenary.'" The conversation suggests several truths about at least one step of the matrimonial dance:

> "Pray, my dear aunt, what is the difference in matrimonial affairs, between the mercenary and the prudent motive? Where does discretion end, and avarice begin? Last Christmas you were afraid of his marrying me, because it would be imprudent; and now, because he is trying to get a girl with only ten thousand pounds, you want to find out that he is mercenary. . . ."
>
> "But he paid her not the smallest attention, till her grandfather's death made her mistress of this fortune."
>
> "No—why should he? If it was not allowable for him to gain *my* affections, because I had no money, what occasion could there be for making love to a girl whom he did not care about, and who was equally poor?" [*P*, 153]

Elizabeth's point is not trivial: if it is imprudent for young people to marry without the means to support themselves, why is it not merely prudent for them to marry with the financial issue in mind? Later on Elizabeth reassesses her evaluation of Wickham in the light of Darcy's letter: "[Wickham's] attentions to Miss King were now the consequence of views solely and hatefully mercenary; and the mediocrity of her fortune proved no longer the moderation of his wishes, but his eagerness to grasp at any thing" (*P*, 207). Elizabeth comments on the "mediocrity" of Miss King's fortune, suggesting that she—and Austen—rates fortunes by size, and that indeed Wickham's courtship of Miss King might be assessed in terms of the moderation of his wishes. All along the continuum of fortune/wishes is the implicit suggestion that at some point interest in fortune is common sense, and on either side of that mark interest shades either into greed or desperation. Austen's depiction of these considerations of Elizabeth surely suggests that Austen sees the financial compatibility of the partners as at least as valid as an intellectual, physical, or temperamental fit. Presumably it is perfectly reasonable to consider money; only the purely mercenary consideration disgusts.

Against this backdrop the financial details of the Darcy and Bingley matches take on substantive defining functions. All marriages in *Pride and Prejudice* are seen in terms of financial detail, not just those of the protagonists. Discussions about suitors, or about men and women of marriageable age, repeatedly come back to financial matters. Very early in the novel Charlotte Lucas says of Darcy that his pride " 'does not offend *me* so much as pride often does, because there is an excuse for it. One cannot wonder that so very fine a young man, with family, fortune, every thing in his favour, should think highly of himself. If I may so express it, he has a *right* to be proud' " (*P*, 20). When Elizabeth talks with Colonel Fitzwilliam about Darcy, Fitzwilliam comments in much the same tone: " 'He likes to have his own way very well. . . . But so do we all. It is only that he has better means of having it than many others, because he is rich, and many others are poor' " (*P*, 183). The point here is not whether Darcy indeed has the right to be unpleasant because he is rich—Austen of course assumes not—but that in each of these evaluations his wealth importantly characterizes him as a person. By not very subtle extension, his wealth also characterizes him as a suitor. Fitzwilliam makes the connection explicit when he continues the conversation with Elizabeth:

> "I speak feelingly. A younger son, you know, must be inured to self-denial and dependence."
>
> "In my opinion, the younger son of an Earl can know very little of either. Now, seriously, what have you ever known of self-denial and dependence? When have you been prevented by want of money from going wherever you chose, or procuring any thing you had a fancy for?"
>
> "These are home questions—and perhaps I cannot say that I have experienced many hardships of that nature. But in matters of greater weight, I may suffer from the want of money. Younger sons cannot marry where they like."
>
> "Unless they like women of fortune, which I think they very often do."

"Our habits of expence make us too dependant, and there are not many
in my rank of life who can afford to marry wthout some attention to
money."

. . . "And pray, what is the usual price of an Earl's younger son?
Unless the elder brother is very sickly, I suppose you would not ask above
fifty thousand pounds." [P, 183-84]

This banter underscores a significant point: Darcy and Bingley are free
to marry whom they choose, even fortuneless girls like Elizabeth and
Jane, because they are financially independent. Fitzwilliam and Elizabeth would not make a good match, as Elizabeth realizes. Elizabeth
casually must have considered him, but she feels no pain when he
leaves the neighborhood: "Colonel Fitzwilliam had made it clear that
he had no intentions at all, and agreeable as he was, she did not mean
to be unhappy about him" (P, 188). This is the context in which Darcy's
proposal comes. "While settling this point [her feelings about Colonel
Fitzwilliam's leaving], she was suddenly roused by the sound of the
door bell" (P, 188).

Darcy's proposal is famous for the infelicity of its phrasing. His
powerful reservations about Elizabeth's family make him almost incapable of proposing at all, and when he does approach Elizabeth it is in
such terms that she is barely capable of a civil response. " 'In vain have I
struggled,' " Darcy laments to her. " 'It will not do. My feelings will not
be repressed. You must allow me to tell you how ardently I admire you
and love you' " (P, 189). Austen wryly comments: "His sense of her
inferiority—of its being a degradation—of the family obstacles which
judgment had always opposed to inclination, were dwelt on with a
warmth which seemed due to the consequence he was wounding, but
was very unlikely to recommend his suit" (P, 189). Darcy is shocked
when Elizabeth rejects him, and he angrily demands her reasons; " 'I
might as well enquire,' " she responds, " 'why with so evident a design
of offending and insulting me, you chose to tell me that you liked me
against your will, against your reason, and even against your character?' " (P, 190). His answer is significant: "disguise of every sort is my
abhorrence. Nor am I ashamed of the feelings I related. They were
natural and just. Could you expect me to rejoice in the inferiority of
your connection? To congratulate myself on the hope of relations,
whose condition in life is so decidedly beneath my own?" (P, 192).
Although Elizabeth is justified in her anger at Darcy's enunciation of
these perceptions, Darcy is not unjust in his analysis of Elizabeth's
family situation. Elizabeth does not, even to herself, dispute the ac-

curacy of Darcy's assessment of her relatives; on numerous occasions Elizabeth herself cringes at the antics of her mother, younger sisters, and even her father. Darcy learns to put up with Elizabeth's family, but Austen does not suggest that he was wrong about them. Money and good breeding are involved here, and it would have been helpful—although given the eventual outcome joining Elizabeth and Darcy it was not necessary—for Elizabeth's family to have had one or the other. Darcy's acceptance of the Gardiners correctly has been seen as a mark of his diminished pride, but we must look carefully at Austen's terms. The Gardiners are very well bred, and they seem to have plenty of money. They are not aristocrats, but aristocratic forbears in Austen novels are always far less important than ready cash. It is not often remarked, I think, that the two heroes, essentially equal as marital prizes, are both rich but are not both of aristocratic lineage. It is Elizabeth who on several occasions makes the assumption that Darcy's objections to her family stem from "her having one uncle who was a country attorney, and another who was in business in London" (P, 186). Actually, Darcy quite explicitly states the source of his reservations: " 'The situation of your mother's family, though objectionable, was nothing in comparison of that total want of propriety so frequently, so almost uniformly betrayed by herself, by your three younger sisters, and occasionally even by your father' " (P, 198). Elizabeth recognizes the truth of his remarks. "When she came to that part of the letter in which her family were mentioned, in terms of such mortifying, yet merited reproach, her sense of shame was severe. The justice of the charge struck her too forcibly for denial" (P, 208-9). Darcy's hesitation in choosing Elizabeth, then, is not based on rank or fortune but on the behavior of her family. He is free to ignore problems of lineage or fortune just because he has both.

Actually, except for the ridiculous conversation when Lady Catherine de Bourgh intrudes upon Elizabeth, social class draws little attention in the discussions of marriage in *Pride and Prejudice*. On the other hand, money in all cases is seen as a central concern in these passages. When Darcy explains the circumstances of his family's relationship with Wickham and Wickham's parents, he explains that Wickham had to be supported at school and then at Cambridge by Darcy's family because "his own father, always poor from the extravagance of his wife, would have been unable to give him a gentleman's education" (P, 200).[11] Wickham himself clearly cannot manage money, for he is always in debt. His solution to the financial problem, as we have seen, is to attempt to marry money. But whereas the women in the novel treat the matter gingerly, Wickham's approach is direct. Wickham first tries for an heiress, but his seduction of Darcy's exceedingly rich fifteen-year-old sister is foiled by the child herself when she confesses to her brother. Wickham's next object is Miss King, a young lady of much more moderate means; she rejects him. Finally, he successfully uses Lydia's giddy decision to run away with him to blackmail her friends. Wickham clearly is a reprobate. Charlotte is not, even though she accepts Mr. Collins solely to gain an establishment, but her decision also seems less than admirable. The best case is to marry money but to marry for love of the man, as Jane and Elizabeth do. Austen never suggests that it would be romantic for two people without money to marry each other.

Numbers are important. Austen refers time and again to exact figures. Darcy tells Elizabeth that "'Mr. Wickham's chief object was unquestionably my sister's fortune, which is thirty thousand pounds'" (P, 202). When Wickham resigned the living that Darcy's father had left him, he "'accepted in return three thousand pounds'" (P, 201), which Elizabeth, in considering Darcy's letter, notes is "so considerable a sum" (P, 205). Even the silly Mrs. Bennet is aware of relative outlays, checking with Elizabeth about the Collinses' way of life and mode of housekeeping: "'A great deal of good management, depend upon it. Yes, yes. *They* will take care not to outrun their income. *They* will never be distressed for money'" (P, 228). Everything in the Lydia-Wickham marriage revolves around money. Mr. Bennet's initial miscalculation in allowing Lydia to go to Brighton is that "'she is luckily too poor to be an object of prey to any body'" (P, 232). Although Wickham—knowing Lydia has no fortune—does not set out to seduce her, he is ready to take her when Darcy arranges that she will bring a substantial payoff. As the truth about Darcy's part in the wedding emerges, it becomes clear that Wickham was looking simply for the best deal he could get. Not satisfied with what he thought he could extort from Mr. Bennet, "'Wickham still cherished the hope of more effectually making his fortune by marriage, in some other country'" (P, 323). Darcy makes him a generous proposal. Elizabeth learns the details from her aunt Gardiner: "'His debts are to be paid, amounting, I believe, to considerably more than a thousand pounds, another thousand in addition to her own settled upon *her*, and his commission purchased'" (P, 324).

The other prospective husbands, Bingley and Darcy, are themselves rich, and while it is important that the couples are compatible, the wealth of each man is not unimportant as an aspect of his charm.

This element is particularly obvious in Darcy's case. After all Elizabeth's negative comments about him, her family is shocked when she announces her seemingly sudden change of heart. Elizabeth fears that her family's dislike of Darcy is such that even "all his fortune and consequence" (P, 372) might not be able to overcome their dislike. Later, when the lovers decide that Darcy will break the news to Mr. Bennet and Elizabeth will tell her mother, Elizabeth again doubts "whether all his wealth and grandeur would be enough to overcome [her mother's] abhorrence of the man" (P, 375). Mr. Bennet, although he does not like Darcy and tries to warn his daughter away from him, gives his consent to the marriage, for, he admits to Elizabeth, " 'He is the kind of man, indeed, to whom I should never dare refuse any thing, which he condescended to ask' " (P, 376). In other words, Darcy's wealth and prestige buy him Mr. Bennet's acceptance, if not approbation. That Mr. Bennet is speaking of Darcy's wealth and not some trait of character in this remark we know from his comment to Elizabeth: " 'He is rich, to be sure, and you may have more fine clothes and fine carriages than Jane. But will they make you happy?' " (P, 376). Mr. Bennet accepts Darcy because of his wealth but with reservations; Mrs. Bennet accepts him for the same reason—and with no reservations at all.

> "Good gracious! Lord bless me! only think! dear me! Mr. Darcy! Who would have thought it! And is it really true? Oh! my sweetest Lizzy! how rich and how great you will be! What pin-money, what jewels, what carriages you will have! Jane's is nothing to it—nothing at all. I am so pleased—so happy. Such a charming man!—so handsome! so tall!—Oh, my dear Lizzy! pray apologise for my having disliked him so much before. I hope he will overlook it. Dear, dear Lizzy. A house in town! Every thing that is charming! Three daughters married! Ten thousand a year! Oh, Lord!" [P, 378]

Mrs. Bennet never considers what marriage might mean beyond pin money and carriages. The marriage of the senior Bennets is presented in precise detail. Although Austen talks a great deal in *Pride and Prejudice* about what a good marriage involves, in this novel she pays rather a great deal of attention to the imperfect unions. We understand that a good marriage is almost precisely the opposite of the Bennets'. Mr. Bennet is the thinking partner in the marriage, and only he suffers in it. Mrs. Bennet's idea of happiness in marriage simply is being married. Too stupid even to perceive her husband's lack of respect for her, she lives unaware of any imperfection other than the financial problem of the entail. Of her relationship with Mr. Bennet she does not think at all. Her view is manifest in her earliest remarks. A young man has entered the neighborhood. Not yet knowing anything about him, she wants him as a husband for one of her daughters. A little later, still not having met Bingley, she tells her husband that " 'If I can but see one of my daughters happily settled at Netherfield . . . I shall have nothing to wish for' " (P, 9). When Mr. Collins announces his intention to find a wife—any wife—among the Bennet girls, Mrs. Bennet is delighted. No matter how obnoxiously he acts, she would give him any one of her daughters. When Mrs. Lucas has the privilege of selling Charlotte to Mr. Collins, Mrs. Bennet can barely contain her disappointment. Once Lydia and Wickham are officially married, Lydia becomes the favorite daughter because she is the only married one. Mrs. Bennet does not worry about her new son-in-law's dissolute character, nor about the couple's compatibility. When Jane marries Bingley, Mrs. Bennet is perfectly happy; as we have just seen, when Elizabeth announces that she will marry Darcy, Mrs. Bennet is ecstatic, forgetting entirely her dislike of the man. Mrs. Bennet's satisfaction with marriage, her own or her daughters', is not contingent on who or what the marriage partner is. Austen shows that this is in large part also society's view: after all, in the face of Wickham's documented bad character, everyone, even Jane and Elizabeth, still hopes that he can be persuaded to marry Lydia. And Lydia, the most like her mother of the five daughters, sees nothing of Wickham's character and absolutely lords it over her sisters as Mrs. Wickham.

Mr. Bennet, Jane, and Elizabeth voice Austen's sentiments: marriage ideally is a matter of companionship, compatibility, understanding, and, very important, of mutual respect. Mr. Bennet's marriage fails painfully on all these counts. Austen's portrait of this marriage, so carefully wrought, brilliantly depicts a marriage of name but not of spirit. The Bennets live in the same house, but they share no ideals. The earliest interaction between the two, the very famous conversation in which Mrs. Bennet tries to get her husband to introduce the family to the new young bachelor in the neighborhood, usually is seen essentially as a comic introduction to the novel's theme of women and marriage. It is that, but it also very precisely defines the relationship between the elder Bennets. Austen in this scene has perfect pitch: Mr. Bennet amuses himself at the expense of his wife, and Mrs. Bennet is quite unaware that she is the butt of a joke. The reserve between them comes entirely from him; incapable of subtlety either of feeling or discernment, Mrs. Bennet doesn't notice her husband's stance. "Mr. Bennet was so odd a mixture of quick parts, sarcastic humour, reserve, and caprice, that the experience of three and twenty years had been insufficient to make his wife understand his character. *Her* mind was less difficult to develop. She was a woman of mean understanding, little information, and uncertain temper" (*P*, 5). Twenty-three years of marriage between such an ill-matched pair results in much the same sort of arrangement that Charlotte and Mr. Collins have: a managed coexistence, with the sensitive and reasonable partner simply accepting the arrangement for whatever he, or she, has decided to take from the marriage; interestingly, for both Mr. Bennet and for Charlotte this seems to translate into having an establishment. Knowing his own situation, Mr. Bennet views Charlotte's acceptance of Mr. Collins with ironic distain; "such [emotions] as he did experience [on hearing that Charlotte would marry Mr. Collins] he pronounced to be of a most agreeable sort; for it gratified him, he said, to discover that Charlotte Lucas, whom he had been used to think tolerably sensible, was as foolish as his wife, and more foolish than his daughter!" (*P*, 127). At every turn he makes fun of his wife. When it seems that Jane has been " 'crossed in love' " by Bingley, Mr. Bennet teases Elizabeth that she too should find someone to jilt her, for " 'it is a comfort to think that whatever of that kind may befal you, you have an affectionate mother who will always make the most of it' " (*P*, 137-38). He takes a detached amusement in his wife's failings; Austen comments that that is all he finds in his marriage. Austen's description of the Bennet marriage and of Elizabeth's reaction to her father's attitudes in his marriage is masterful.

> Had Elizabeth's opinion been all drawn from her own family, she could not have formed a very pleasing picture of conjugal felicity or domestic comfort. Her father captivated by youth and beauty, and that appearance of good humour, which youth and beauty generally give, had married a woman whose weak understanding and illiberal mind, had very early in their marriage put an end to all real affection for her. Respect, esteem, and confidence, had vanished for ever; and all his views of domestic happiness were overthrown. But Mr. Bennet was not of a disposition to seek comfort for the disappointment which his own imprudence had brought on, in any of those pleasures which too often console the unfortunate for their folly or their vice. He was fond of the country and of books; and from these tastes had arisen his principal enjoyments. To his wife he was very little otherwise indebted, than as her ignorance and folly had contributed to his amusement. This is not the sort of happiness which

a man would in general wish to owe to his wife; but where other powers of entertainment are wanting, the true philosopher will derive benefit from such as are given.

Elizabeth, however, had never been blind to the impropriety of her father's behaviour as a husband. She had always seen it with pain; but respecting his abilities, and grateful for his affectionate treatment of herself, she endeavoured to forget what she could not overlook, and to banish from her thoughts that continual breach of conjugal obligation and decorum which, in exposing his wife to the contempt of her own children, was so highly reprehensible. [P, 236]

"Respect, esteem, and confidence" for Austen are the center of a good marriage, and Austen emphasizes that it is the "weak understanding and illiberal mind" of Mrs. Bennet that doom the marriage. Elizabeth objects to her father's open contempt of her mother in front of the children, but she cannot disagree with his feelings. When Jane announces her own marriage, Mr. Bennet is very satisfied: " 'I have great pleasure in thinking you will be so happily settled. I have not a doubt of your doing very well together. Your tempers are by no means unlike. You are each of you so complying, that nothing will ever be resolved on; so easy, that every servant will cheat you; and so generous, that you will always exceed your income' " (P, 348). But he has fears for Elizabeth when she announces that she wants to marry Darcy.

"Lizzy, . . . I have given him my consent. . . . I now give it to *you*, if you are resolved on having him. But let me advise you to think better of it. I know your disposition, Lizzy. I know that you could be neither happy nor respectable, unless you truly esteemed your husband; unless you looked up to him as a superior. Your lively talents would place you in the greatest danger in an unequal marriage. You could scarcely escape discredit and misery. My child, let me not have the grief of seeing *you* unable to respect your partner in life. You know not what you are about." [P, 376]

There are two aspects of Mr. Bennet's statement that deserve attention. The first is what he sees as the center of marriage: being able " 'to respect your partner in life.' " Clearly, having never been able to respect *his* partner, this emphasis shows both perception and real affection for the daughter he wants to save from such an empty relationship. Mr. Bennet's views here on what makes a good marriage are Austen's: there is no indication that we are to find any part of his speech less than reasonable and just. So that his comments, particularly in light of recent attempts of feminist criticism to see Austen as a kind of prefeminist, are particularly significant. Mr. Bennet insists to Elizabeth that " 'you could be neither happy nor respectable, unless you truly esteemed your husband; unless you looked up to him as a superior.' " He goes on, " 'Your lively talents would place you in the greatest danger in an unequal marriage.' " Mr. Bennet's implication here is that "equality" in a marriage means that the woman looks up to her husband "as a superior." Austen seems oblivious to the contradiction in the terms of Mr. Bennet's statement. The other marriage that we see in some detail in *Pride and Prejudice* is the Collinses'. There will be no friendship in this marriage, as there is not in the Bennet marriage, and for quite the same reason: one partner cannot respect the other. Here Austen is markedly evenhanded—in one marriage it is the female who is empty-headed, in the other, the male. And, interestingly, in both cases the idiotic partner has no sense that anything is wrong. Mr. Collins, indeed, thinks that his is a marriage made in heaven: " 'My dear Charlotte and I have but one mind and one way of thinking. There is in every thing a most remarkable resemblance of character and ideas between us. We seem to have been designed for each other' " (*P*, 216). Austen tells us in *Pride and Prejudice* that the marriages of Jane and Elizabeth will be happy, but she does not do much in the way of showing her reader a happy, functioning marriage. Mr. and Mrs. Gardiner seem content, but there is little detail about their life together.

The quest for marriage partners informs the plot movement of the novel; the friendships between and among the characters is the stable base from which these explorations set out. While the plot of each novel revolves around pairing off sets of characters, the most basic personal interactions take place between friends. This pattern is most obvious in *Pride and Prejudice*, but it is marked in *Emma* too, where both threads merge: Emma's best friend—and finally the object of her marital quest—is Mr. Knightley. In *Pride and Prejudice* friendships are basically same-sex relationships; Darcy's friendship with Bingley is a long-term bond, and Elizabeth's friendship with Jane is simply the central relationship in her life. The relationship between the sisters, in fact, is by far the most detailed in the novel.

Elizabeth and Jane share a deep commitment to each other. Austen draws a very full, and very beautiful, relationship between the sisters, and this is her most positive contribution, I think, to the early novel's images of women.[12] There are many extended depictions of female friendship in the early English novel. I have examined several of them: Moll and her "governess," Amy and Roxana, Amelia and Mrs. Atkinson, and, of course, Clarissa and Anna. All of these relationships are limited in some way, either by a mutual dependence for practical survival or by a clear inequality between the partners. But between Elizabeth and Jane there is both equality and unbounded affection. Without portraying either of the women as a paragon, Austen depicts their friendship as ideal. Between Darcy and Bingley the relationship is slanted toward Darcy, but between the two sisters there exists an unflawed friendship. Austen, then, quietly suggests that great friendship can be a female preserve.

The bond between Jane and Elizabeth is completely unselfish. When Elizabeth visits her sick sister at Bingley's, she truly is anxious about Jane's health. Elizabeth spends as much time as she can with Jane in her room, joining the company below only because she feels that, for the sake of politeness, she must. As the Bingley sisters note with disapproval, Elizabeth does not care how she looks to the assembled company; her warmth toward Jane is remarked with much favor, incidentally, by both Darcy and Bingley. When Jane falls in love with Bingley, even before Jane herself is quite conscious of her feelings, Elizabeth shares Jane's hope—and her pain. Elizabeth's feelings about Darcy for a long time are conditioned essentially by her perception that he has persuaded Bingley to lose interest in Jane. For Elizabeth there is no contest between the very eligible Darcy and Jane: friendship for her sister clearly comes first. Elizabeth worries about Jane's hurt even though Jane herself makes light of her disappointment about Bingley's leaving Netherfield Park. When Jane goes off to be with the Gardiners, Elizabeth is ill at ease until she can see for herself how Jane manages her disappointment.

Jane is the first person with whom Elizabeth wants to share any experience or feeling. She must discuss her shock at Charlotte's accepting Mr. Collins. " 'My dear Jane, Mr. Collins is a conceited, pompous, narrow-minded, silly man; you know he is, as well as I do; and you must feel, as well as I do, that the woman who marries him, cannot have a proper way of thinking. You shall not defend her, though it is Charlotte Lucas. You shall not, for the sake of one individual, change the meaning of principle and integrity, nor endeavour to persuade yourself or me, that selfishness is prudence, and insensibility of danger, security for happiness' " (P, 135-36). After her visit to Charlotte, during the course of which Darcy has approached her, Elizabeth can hardly wait to tell Jane about "Mr. Darcy's proposals" (P, 217). And when she finally can tell Jane about Darcy's letter—and about her new perception of him—Elizabeth warmly admits to Jane how much she needed to talk to and be comforted by her. " 'I was very uncomfortable, I may say unhappy. And with no one to speak to, of what I felt, no Jane to comfort me and say that I had not been so very weak and vain and nonsensical as I knew I had! Oh! how I wanted you!' " (P, 226). The attachment between the sisters is equal. Jane earnestly discusses her own feelings, and when finally Jane and Bingley reach an understanding, "Jane could have no reserves from Elizabeth, where confidence would give pleasure; and instantly embracing her, acknowledged, with the liveliest emotion, that she was the happiest creature in the world" (P, 346). The depth of the relationship between the two women is obvious when Elizabeth tells Jane that she has decided to marry Darcy. In view of all Elizabeth's earlier remarks about Darcy, Jane is understandably surprised by her sister's announcement. And she is very worried. Jane's concern is that Elizabeth might be making a mistake: " 'forgive the question—are you quite certain that you can be happy with him?' " (P, 373), she asks. And again, " 'And do you really love him quite well enough? Oh, Lizzy! do any thing rather than marry without affection. Are you quite sure that you feel what you ought to do?' " (P, 373). Darcy's rather obvious advantages as a husband, his wealth, his position, these do not impress Jane. She needs to be sure that Elizabeth will find contentment and fulfillment in her marriage. Only when Jane has been satisfied on these points does she settle down for "half the night spent in conversation" (P, 374). The friendship drawn by Austen is complete: she clearly intends it as a paradigm of what friendship should be. The sisters are not identical in their personalities. Elizabeth is the more outgoing of the two, but neither sister dominates the relationship. It is clear that we are meant to remark these traits, for Austen makes a point of referring to the inequality of the friendship between Darcy and Bingley in which Darcy is obviously the dominant force; as Elizabeth ironically notes, "Mr. Bingley had been a most delightful friend [to Darcy]; so easily guided that his worth was invaluable" (P, 371).

Elizabeth's friendship with Mrs. Gardiner is similar to her friendship with Jane in its affection, mutual concern, and ease of comprehension. After everything is settled with Darcy, Elizabeth "was almost ashamed to find, that her uncle and aunt had already lost three days of happiness" (P, 382). She writes to them in one of the most charming passages of the novel:

"I would have thanked you before, my dear aunt, as I ought to have done, for your long, kind, satisfactory, detail of particulars; but to say the truth, I was too cross to write. You supposed more than really existed. But *now* suppose as much as you chuse; give a loose to your fancy, indulge your imagination in every possible flight which the subject will afford, and unless you believe me actually married, you cannot greatly err. You must write again very soon, and praise him a great deal more than you did in your last. I thank you, again and again, for not going to the Lakes. How could I be so silly as to wish it! Your idea of the ponies is delightful. We will go round the Park every day. I am the happiest creature in the world. Perhaps other people have said so before, but not one with such justice. I am happier even than Jane; she only smiles, I laugh. Mr. Darcy sends you all the love in the world, that he can spare from me. You are all to come to Pemberly at Christmas." [*P*, 382-83]

Significantly, the whole of the last paragraph of *Pride and Prejudice* concerns the Gardiners:

With the Gardiners, they were always on the most intimate terms. Darcy, as well as Elizabeth, really loved them; and they were both ever sensible of the warmest gratitude towards the persons who, by bringing her into Derbyshire, had been the means of uniting them. [*P*, 388]

One of the most salient points Austen makes about friendship is that it is part of marriage, but not only between the married pair. Contributing to the strength of both Elizabeth's and Jane's marriages will be the sharing of friendship among all the partners as well as among selected family members. No one is going to get very close to Lady Catherine, but it will be a support to the relationship between Elizabeth and Darcy that they have a shared regard for the Gardiners. When there is not a shared regard, Austen shows us, friendship suffers. Elizabeth, whose girlhood friendship with Charlotte had been quite close, finds it impossible to maintain the same relationship after Charlotte has joined herself to Mr. Collins. The correspondence between the girls after Charlotte's wedding "was as regular and frequent as it had ever been; that it should be equally unreserved was impossible. Elizabeth could never address her without feeling that all the comfort of intimacy was over, and, though determined not to slacken as a correspondent, it was for the sake of what had been, rather than what was" (*P*, 146). Elizabeth's visit to her old friend goes off in the same style of polite, but not meaningful, discourse.

Elizabeth's relationship with Mrs. Bennet never had much of friendship in it, although there is affection. Embarrassed by her mother, Elizabeth nevertheless is angered by her father's open contempt for his wife's understanding. Elizabeth wants her mother's approbation, but with her mother she is most worried as usual "that her manner would be equally ill adapted to do credit to her sense" and Elizabeth "could no more bear that Mr. Darcy should hear the first raptures of her joy, than the first vehemence of her disapprobation" (P, 375). Her worry about her father is quite different, and when Darcy follows Mr. Bennet to the library to tell him of the engagement, Elizabeth's "agitation [is] extreme" (P, 375). She is not afraid that her father will withhold his approval but that "he was going to be made unhappy, and that it should be through her means, that *she*, his favourite child, should be distressing him by her choice" (P, 375). If Elizabeth shares friendship with one of her parents, clearly it is her father. In terms of the traditions of the English novel before Austen, Elizabeth's preference for her father is not surprising. Relatively few important novels in the century describe in detail a mother-daughter relationship, and of these fewer still present positive relationships. The male mentor/father, on the other hand, is considerably more common; Mr. Villars in Burney's *Evelina* is an obvious example of such a friend. Curiously, even in novels that center on female characters, mother-daughter relationships seem essentially unimportant. Thus, in *Emma* Austen entirely omits the mother from the cast.

While Austen's subject matter is the same in *Emma* as in *Pride and Prejudice*, her emphasis shifts. Marriage is still the unmarried woman's goal, and the status quo remains, in essence, just fine. But in discussing society, and specifically marriage, Austen's emphasis in *Emma* is more on class than on money.[13] I think this is so because unlike in the earlier book, the protagonist of *Emma* is herself rich. The neatness of *Emma*'s plot diplays itself not alone in creating couples, but in making matches that are appropriate in terms of social classes. This sort of fit seems so natural to Austen that she can play within the concept of class, moving pieces of her human puzzle around—Harriet and Mr. Elton, for example, as a theoretical pair—and finally come back to a perfectly tidy solution. Although in some technical ways *Emma* has been seen as a more polished novel, in terms of social perspectives it is even less adventurous than *Pride and Prejudice*—which itself, as we have seen, accepts the social grid of Austen's milieu with a minimum of questions. The images of felicity in *Emma* are very traditional. Ideally, the man should be the marriage partner who brings most to the marriage in terms of class, wealth, and wisdom. Where this is not the case, problems abound; when this pattern orders the relationship, married life brings comfort. Unlike in

*Pride and Prejudice,* in *Emma* Austen does present several excellent partnerships, giving us at the outset the marriages of Miss Taylor and Isabella. In the discussion of Mr. Weston's first marriage Austen quickly sketches the discomforts of a union where the "favor" is all on the wife's side.

The first chapter of *Emma* examines in some detail the marriage of Emma's governess Miss Taylor to Mr. Weston. This marriage, along with the marriage of Isabella, Emma's elder sister, serves as the model of what marriage should be. Both present pleasant but not romanticized pictures. Austen describes the prospect for Miss Taylor's married life: "The event had every promise of happiness. . . . Mr. Weston was a man of unexceptionable character, easy fortune, suitable age and pleasant manners."[14] He was "a good-humoured, pleasant, [and] excellent man" (*E,* 8). This delightful man provides for her "a house of her own" (*E,* 8), that is, an establishment of her own. Austen emphasizes here, as in *Pride and Prejudice,* the economic and social base of the marriage. Mr. Knightley, always Austen's voice, insists to Emma that "the marriage is to Miss Taylor's advantage; [Emma] knows how very acceptable it must be at Miss Taylor's time of life to be settled in a home of her own, and how important to her to be secure of a comfortable provision. . . . Every friend of Miss Taylor must be glad to have her so happily married" (*E,* 11). This is not complaint about the hard fate of the woman who must marry to survive. Austen's comment assesses reality—surely it *is* nice that Miss Taylor has married and will have a pleasant establishment and a loving family of her own rather than being part of someone else's household: it is common sense that one's own establishment is to be preferred to someone else's. Miss Taylor has been in Emma's family for sixteen years; it would have been a pleasant enough period. She has been treated like a family member, and, clearly, she has not been under any pressure to seek a new employer. Emma is twenty-one when the story opens, so that Miss Taylor cannot truly have been employed as a governess for some years. And Miss Taylor has not married merely to be married; repeatedly, we are told what a good, "straight-forward, open-hearted man" (*E,* 13) Mr. Weston is.

Austen documents the social reality that marriage is a matter of class ties and that favor largely is bestowed by the relatively higher class person. This is what all the byplay with Harriet and Mr. Martin is about: when Emma thinks that Harriet is of a higher social class than Mr. Martin, she wants Harriet to marry "better." Mr. Knightley sees that Emma is wrong, but his is not the voice of democratic intermarriage: he simply sees that the boarder Harriet is not likely to be of a better class than the yeoman Robert Martin and that the couple indeed are well suited. It should be noted that Harriet in truth does belong to an appropriate class for Robert Martin. The importance of relative class position is shown clearly in the two marriages of Mr. Weston. His first marriage was to a woman who felt that she was of higher class than her spouse. He was "born of a respectable family, which for the last two or three generations had been rising into gentility and property. He had received a good education, . . . [had succeeded] early in life to a small independence, . . . and had satisfied an active cheerful mind and social temper by entering into the militia" (E, 15). Miss Churchill was "of a great Yorkshire family" (E, 15), and her brother and sister-in-law were much against the match.

> Miss Churchill, however, being of age, and with the full command of her fortune—though her fortune bore no proportion to the family-estate— was not to be dissuaded from the marriage, and it took place to the infinite mortification of Mr. and Mrs. Churchill, who threw her off with due decorum. It was an unsuitable connection, and did not produce much happiness. Mrs. Weston ought to have found more in it, for she had a husband whose warm heart and sweet temper made him think every thing due to her in return for the great goodness of being in love with him; but though she had one sort of spirit, she had not the best. She had resolution enough to pursue her own will in spite of her brother, but not enough to refrain from unreasonable regrets at that brother's unreasonable anger, nor from missing the luxuries of her former home. They lived beyond their income, but still it was nothing in comparison of Enscombe: she did not cease to love her husband, but she wanted at once to be the wife of Captain Weston, and Miss Churchill of Enscombe. Captain Weston, who had been considered, especially by the Churchills, as making such an amazing match, was proved to have much the worst of the bargain; for when his wife died after a three years' marriage, he was rather a poorer man than at first, and with a child to maintain. [E, 15-16]

This "unsuitable connection" does not produce much happiness. Note that although Miss Churchill feels that she has condescended in marrying him, her fortune is not great; certainly she leaves Mr. Weston in poorer rather than better financial circumstances when she dies. Nevertheless, because of her social status, Mr. Weston perceives that his wife has honored him in their marriage. The nature of the perceived favor is characterized in the description of Mr. Weston's second marriage:

between useful occupation and the pleasures of society, the next eighteen
or twenty years of his life passed cheerfully away. He had, by that time,
realized an easy competence—enough to secure the purchase of a little
estate adjoining Highbury, which he had always longed for—enough to
marry a woman as portionless even as Miss Taylor, and to live according
to the wishes of his own friendly and social disposition. . . . He had made
his fortune, bought his house, and obtained his wife; and was beginning a
new period of existence with every probability of greater happiness than
in any yet passed through. He had never been an unhappy man; his own
temper had secured him from that, even in his first marriage; but his
second must shew him how delightful a well-judging and truly amiable
woman could be, and must give him the pleasantest proof of its being a
great deal better to chuse than to be chosen, to excite gratitude than to feel
it. [E, 16-17]

Austen ironically notes that Mr. Weston is so attentive to his first wife
because of the favor she had done him in marrying him, but in the
description of the second marriage her tone is straightforward. It is
indeed more pleasant "to chuse than to be chosen, to excite gratitude
than to feel it," and Mr. Weston is in this position now. Austen
emphasizes that Mr. Weston's role has been reversed from that in his
earlier marriage. Since it is the relative social and financial capital that a
person brings to marriage rather than the sex of the partner that
determines whether he or she is the "giver," men are as vulnerable as
women. Austen's reference in the very next paragraph to the Churchill
aunt underscores this truth: "The aunt was a capricious woman, and
governed her husband entirely" (E, 17). In Austen novels, men stand
as much chance of problems in marriage as women. But in general
being married is desirable, and the basis of a good marriage is an easy
companionship such as that between Miss Taylor and Mr. Weston.
"She felt herself a most fortunate woman; and she had lived long
enough to know how fortunate she might well be thought" (E, 18). She
is "at Randalls in the centre of every domestic comfort" (E, 19), and
goes home from visits "attended by her pleasant husband to a carriage
of her own" (E, 19).

Austen insists that in a good marriage the partners must be socially
and educationally similar; if one mate has more to give, especially in
terms of material endowment, it is preferable that the fortune come
from the man. Education in this context denotes breeding and wisdom
more than book or professional knowledge. All of Austen's happy
marriages work out along such lines. Mr. Weston's second marriage,
Austen tells us explicitly, is more successful than his first because he

and Miss Taylor are matched in social and intellectual class, and, additionally, he has more to give than she does. Mrs. Elton and Mr. Elton see the world through much the same eyes, and so will Harriet and Robert Martin. Austen makes fun of class lines and class snobbery, but she arranges her matches so that they conform to those lines. This is not a pattern unique to Austen. Even a radical like Robert Bage, having pretended all through *Hermsprong* that his hero is plebeian, finally reveals Hermsprong's aristocratic origins so that when hero and heroine wed, the marriage is strictly within class lines. Fanny Burney had earlier done exactly the same thing in *Evelina*, where the supposedly middle-class heroine is revealed as an aristocrat before she marries the lord. This impulse of the authors to prescribe marriage within as opposed to across class lines itself spans the conservative-liberal spectrum. Thomas Holcroft, in this connection, deserves a good deal of credit for being able to imagine differently: in *Anna St. Ives* the heroine is an aristocrat and her beloved is the son of the steward of the family estate. At the end of the novel, no mysterious circumstances surrounding anyone's birth have been discovered; Anna is still an aristocrat and Frank still is not. And they will marry. But such a leap of the imagination, even in fiction, is rare.

For all the fun she pokes at the concept of class, Austen never makes this leap. The match between Robert Martin and Harriet provides an instructive example. Austen satirizes Emma's ideas about the pairing, but she disproves Emma's fantasies about the elevated worth of Harriet, not about the need for equality in a marriage. Robert Martin sends "a direct proposal of marriage" (*E*, 50) to Harriet. Emma is "surprized" by its quality: "There were not merely no grammatical errors, but as a composition it would not have disgraced a gentleman; the language, though plain, was strong and unaffected, and the sentiments it conveyed very much to the credit of the writer. It was short, but expressed good sense, warm attachment, liberality, propriety, even delicacy of feeling" (*E*, 50-51). Robert Martin is a worthwhile man—rational, warm, and sensitive. The reader, in on the joke at the expense of the misguided Emma, understands that Emma's reaction to Mr. Martin's proposal is wrong. Some pages later, Mr. Knightley's endorsement of Robert Martin reinforces the reader's perception. Surely a man who "considers [Knightley] as one of his best friends" (*E*, 59) is all right. And Knightley's analysis bears this out:

He came to ask me whether I thought it would be imprudent in him to settle so early; whether I thought her too young: in short, whether I approved his

choice altogether; having some apprehension perhaps of her being considered . . . as in a line of society above him. I was very much pleased with all
that he said. I never hear better sense from any one than Robert Martin. He
always speaks to the purpose; open, straight forward, and very well judg-
ing. He told me every thing; his circumstances and plans, and what they all
proposed doing in the event of his marriage. He is an excellent young man,
both as son and brother. I had no hesitation in advising him to marry. He
proved to me that he could afford it; and that being the case, I was convinced he could not do better. [*E*, 59]

We now are sure that Robert Martin is thoughtful, prudent, and financially capable of taking on a wife. When Emma says that Harriet
has rejected the proposal, Mr. Knightley becomes angry. Emma argues
that Robert Martin is not Harriet's equal. Mr. Knightley does *not*
respond that equality has nothing to do with love, or that equality does
not matter in making a match. He analyzes the relative merits of Mr.
Martin and Harriet:

"Not Harriet's equal!" exclaimed Mr. Knightley loudly and warmly; and
with calmer asperity, added, a few moments afterwards, "No, he is not her
equal indeed, for he is as much her superior in sense as in situation. Emma,
your infatuation about that girl blinds you. What are Harriet Smith's claims,
either of birth, nature or education, to any connection higher than Robert
Martin? She is the natural daughter of nobody knows whom, with probably
no settled provision at all, and certainly no respectable relations. She is
known only as parlour-boarder at a common school. She is not a sensible
girl, nor a girl of any information. She has been taught nothing useful, and
is too young and too simple to have acquired any thing herself. At her age
she can have no experience, and with her little wit, is not very likely ever to
have any that can avail her. She is pretty, and she is good tempered, and
that is all. My only scruple in advising the match was on his account, as
being beneath his deserts, and a bad connection for him. I felt, that as to
fortune, in all probability he might do much better; and that as to a rational
companion or useful helpmate, he could not do worse." [*E*, 61]

Austen's argument never has been the democratic one that class does
not matter; she argues, somewhat less liberally, that *within* any class
there are very worthy people. Robert Martin, in a sense, is as good as
Mr. Knightley, but in a different category. Mr. Knightley does not say
that Harriet should not mind going down in class—he says that she
has no "claims, either of birth, nature or education, to any connection
higher than Robert Martin." Robert Martin, on the other hand, could
probably "do much better" in terms of fortune. Mr. Knightley does not

see anything wrong with this kind of arithmetic: he recounts it as a fact of life, neither good nor bad in itself. Compare, for example, his analysis of Robert Martin's and Elton's situations:

> "Elton is a very good sort of man, and a very respectable vicar of Highbury, but not at all likely to make an imprudent match. He knows the value of a good income as well as anybody. Elton may talk sentimentally, but he will act rationally. He is as well acquainted with his own claims, as you can be with Harriet's. He knows that he is a very handsome young man, and a great favourite wherever he goes; and from his general way of talking in unreserved moments, when there are only men present, I am convinced that he does not mean to throw himself away. I have heard him speak with great animation of a large family of young ladies that his sisters are intimate with, who have all twenty thousand pounds apiece." [E, 66]

And, indeed, faced with Emma's plot to join him with Harriet, Elton is "affronted" (E, 131). " 'Every body has their level: but as for myself, I am not, I think, quite so much at a loss. I need not so totally despair of an equal alliance, as to be addressing myself to Miss Smith!' " (E, 132). Emma, in her turn, is annoyed that he has had

> the arrogance to raise his eyes to her. . . . Perhaps it was not fair to expect him to feel how very much he was her inferior in talent, and all the elegancies of mind. The very want of such equality might prevent his perception of it; but he must know that in fortune and consequence she was greatly his superior. He must know that the Woodhouses had been settled for several generations at Hartfield, the younger branch of a very ancient family—and that the Eltons were nobody. The landed property of Hartfield certainly was inconsiderable, being but a sort of notch in the Donwell Abbey estate, to which all the rest of Highbury belonged; but their fortune, from other sources, was such as to make them scarcely secondary to Donwell Abbey itself, in every other kind of consequence; and the Woodhouses had long held a high place in the consideration of the neighbourhood which Mr. Elton had first entered not two years ago, to make his way as he could, without any alliances but in trade, or any thing to recommend him to notice but his situation and his civility. [E, 135-36]

Austen has some fun with this idea of mutual jockeying—but she *does* marry Emma to Knightley: Hartfield to Donwell Abbey. She is sure to emphasize, at the end of the story, that "Harriet's parentage became known. She proved to be the daughter of a tradesman, rich enough to afford her the comfortable maintenance which had ever been her's, and decent enough to have always wished for concealment.—Such was the blood of gentility which Emma had formerly been so ready to vouch for!" (*E*, 481-82). Emma was wrong not in that she thought class important but that she had so badly misjudged Harriet's niche. Austen's thinking about class, as about many matters, is essentially commonsensical. It should be emphasized that common sense is to some degree dependent on time and place, and that certain of Austen's rules about marriage present problems to some modern readers. As we have seen, Austen believes that marriages are best made between people of similar class and wealth, and if there are differences, the best arrangement is that the greater position belong to the man; in addition, the man should be the greater in intellectual and experiential wealth as well. Mr. Knightley is not an ogre because he has always treated Emma paternally and there is every indication that he will continue to be her mentor. He is clearly the book's hero, as Darcy is in *Pride and Prejudice.*

But outside of marriage, class rules need not be so rigorously observed; to observe them rigorously, in fact, is both inconvenient and silly. This it seems to me is the point of the episode of the Coles and their dinner party. "The Coles had been settled some years in Highbury, and were very good sort of people . . . but, on the other hand, they were of low origin, in trade, and only moderately genteel" (*E*, 207). When they had first come "into the country" they had lived modestly and kept "little company," but the last years had brought them a substantial increase in wealth, and, with the money, they had also changed their lifestyle until "in fortune and style of living" they were "second only to the family at Hartfield" (*E*, 207). Emma begins by feeling strongly that "the regular and best families" (*E*, 207) certainly should not mix socially with the Coles, and that should she be invited to their house, "nothing should tempt *her* to go . . . and she regretted that her father's known habits would be giving her refusal less meaning than she could wish. The Coles were very respectable in their way, but they ought to be taught that it was not for them to arrange the terms on which the superior families would visit them. This lesson, she very much feared, they would receive only from herself; she had little hope of Mr. Knightley, none of Mr. Weston" (*E*, 207). Emma is wrong, and Austen mocks the snobbery of her heroine. Emma feels regret when everyone else is ready to set out for a lovely dinner party. Finally, respectfully invited, she accepts with pleasure. This is Emma early in the book when she still has many lessons to learn. Emma makes the same mistake here that she had made in her discussion with Frank about who could or could not be invited to a ball—she had felt that in Frank "of pride, indeed, there was, perhaps, scarcely enough;

his indifference to a confusion of rank, bordered too much on inelegance of mind" (E, 198) because Frank had argued that "so many good-looking houses as he saw around him" had to be able to provide enough suitable people for a ball. Even after it was explained to him who the different people were, "he was still unwilling to admit that the inconvenience of such a mixture would be any thing, or that there would be the smallest difficulty in every body's returning into their proper place the next morning" (E, 198). Emma is wrong again—of course there are enough people for a ball, people are worthy even if of different class or rank, and so on. I think we generally dismiss the part about "every body's returning into their proper place the next morning," but it seems to me that this is Austen's point: people will mix for an evening and then, properly, separate into their social groupings again.

These incidents both take place in the first half of the book. It is instructive in this context to look at the discussion about Harriet in the last chapter of the novel.

> Harriet's parentage became known. She proved to be the daughter of a tradesman, rich enough to afford her the comfortable maintenance which had ever been her's, and decent enough to have always wished for concealment.—Such was the blood of gentility which Emma had formerly been so ready to vouch for!—It was likely to be as untainted, perhaps, as the blood of many a gentleman: but what a connexion had she been preparing for Mr. Knightley—or for the Churchills—or even for Mr. Elton!—The stain of illegitimacy, unbleached by nobility or wealth, would have been a stain indeed.
>
> No objection was raised on the father's side; the young man was treated liberally; it was all as it should be: and as Emma became acquainted with Robert Martin, who was now introduced at Hartfield, she fully acknowledged in him all the appearance of sense and worth which could bid fairest for her little friend. She had no doubt of Harriet's happiness with any good tempered man; but with him, and in the home he offered, there would be the hope of more, of security, stability, and improvement. She would be placed in the midst of those who loved her, and who had better sense than herself; retired enough for safety, and occupied enough for cheerfulness. She would be never led into temptation, nor left for it to find her out. She would be repectable and happy; and Emma admitted her to be the luckiest creature in the world, to have created so steady and persevering an affection in such a man;—or, if not quite the luckiest, to yield only to herself.
>
> Harriet, necessarily drawn away by her engagements with the Martins, was less and less at Hartfield; which was not to be regretted.—The intimacy

between her and Emma must sink; their friendship must change into a calmer sort of goodwill; and, fortunately, what ought to be, and must be, seemed already beginning, and in the most gradual, natural manner. [E, 481-82]

The last paragraph suggests a great deal about Austen's perspective on class and marriage. The intimacy between Emma and Harriet was never a good idea—that was one of the things Emma needed to learn. Unlike her relationship with Jane Fairfax, the association between Emma and Harriet had never been a similarity of "Birth, abilities, and education . . . marking one as an associate" (E, 421) for the other. But the implication in this last mention of Harriet is not that the relationship between Emma and Harriet will fade because they are not intellectually suited; rather, the relationship will continue to become less intimate because the two women will henceforth move in quite different social circles. Austen emphasizes the rightness of this: "fortunately, what ought to be, and must be, seemed already beginning, and in the most gradual, natural manner." Austen insists on class boundaries for marriage; in terms of other social interactions, common sense and convenience, as long as every one returns to his place next morning, may be allowed to govern. Naturally, the rules themselves carry responsibilities; that is why Emma's taunting of Miss Bates is so bad—"Were she your equal in situation," Knightley chides Emma, but "consider how far this is from being the case" (E, 375). The social code provides a structure within which people can relate to each other; that is part of the meaning of the incident at Box Hill. Most of the time, this structure smooths social interplay, and even provides a context for people like the Bates who might otherwise have no means of functioning in society. That the game comes with rules I have mentioned; in this context, I will turn in a moment to the situation of Jane Fairfax. It seems to me that Austen's point with Jane, as with the Bates, is that one must attempt to manage within the givens of society. For a girl of marriageable age, like Jane, that means finding a husband. It is unfortunate if she cannot succeed, but Austen does not attack the structure within which Jane's search must be made. Nor, it seems to me, does Austen find the situation of Mrs. and Miss Bates something to complain about.

The case of Mrs. and Miss Bates often has been misread as a strong comment against the limitations that society imposes on women. If it is that, Austen is not very convincing about it. Let us take the situation of Mrs. Bates first. Mrs. Bates is a widow, the wife of "a former vicar of

Highbury." She is "a very old lady, almost past every thing but tea and quadrille." The description finishes: "She lived with her single daughter in a very small way, and was considered with all the regard and respect which a harmless old lady, under such untoward circumstances, can excite" (*E*, 21). Mrs. Bates is not much to be pitied, but if she were to be pitied it would have to be for a combination of natural decay, that is, her very old age, and lack of money. But had her husband survived her, or had they both survived into old age, the problems of age and money would be the same. In short, Mrs. Bates's problems do not stem from the fact that she is female. The main difference between the situations of Mrs. Bates and Mr. Woodhouse is money, but the limits of Mrs. Bates's means are not caused by the fact that she is a woman. The description of Miss Bates follows that of her mother: "Her daughter enjoyed a most uncommon degree of popularity for a woman neither young, handsome, rich, nor married" (*E*, 21). This description has occasioned a great deal of critical attention, supposedly exemplifying Austen's social consciousness. Taken by itself, it seems to say that society normally treats women badly if they do not have the social embellishments of youth, beauty, money, and, of course, a husband. But this is only part of Austen's point, and perhaps a minor part at that. For there is more to the description: "Miss Bates stood in the very worst predicament in the world for having much of the public favour; and she had no intellectual superiority to make atonement to herself, or frighten those who might hate her, into outward respect. She had never boasted either beauty or cleverness. Her youth had passed without distinction, and her middle of life was devoted to the care of a failing mother, and the endeavour to make a small income go as far as possible" (*E*, 21). Miss Bates is not a victim— of anything. Her talents have not been wasted, and her skills have not been squandered, for Austen emphasizes that Miss Bates has never "boasted" any sort of personal or intellectual distinction. There is nothing to pity or complain about here, no implication that Miss Bates could have been quite something else. Miss Bates, on the contrary, seems to fit quite well in her world and to be happy and well thought of within it:

And yet she was a happy woman, and a woman whom no one named without good-will. It was her own universal good-will and contented temper which worked such wonders. She loved every body, was interested in every body's happiness, quick-sighted to every body's merits; thought herself a most fortunate creature, and surrounded with blessings in such an excellent mother and so many good neighbours and friends, and a home that wanted for nothing. The simplicity and cheerfulness of her nature, her contented and grateful spirit, were a recommendation to every body and a mine of felicity to herself. [E, 21]

This hardly, all in all, seems a cry of social protest. Further, when Austen introduces Mrs. Bates and Miss Bates, she introduces them as part of a set of three, with Mrs. Goddard being the third. Thus, presumably, we are to consider the three ladies as being essentially in the same category. Mrs. Goddard, however, seems to be doing very well: no possibility in her portrait for worries about social place or anything else.

Mrs. Goddard was the mistress of a School—not of a seminary, or an establishment, or any thing which professed, in long sentences of refined nonsense, to combine liberal acquirements with elegant morality upon new principles and new systems—and where young ladies for enormous pay might be screwed out of health and into vanity—but a real, honest, old-fashioned Boarding-school, where a reasonable quantity of accomplishments were sold at a reasonable price, and where girls might be sent to be out of the way and scramble themselves into a little education, without any danger of coming back prodigies. Mrs. Goddard's school was in high repute—and very deservedly; for Highbury was reckoned a particularly healthy spot. . . . She was a plain, motherly kind of woman, who had worked hard in her youth, and now thought herself entitled to the occasional holiday of a tea-visit; and having formerly owed much to Mr. Woodhouse's kindness, felt his particular claim on her to leave her neat parlour hung round with fancy-work whenever she could, and win or lose a few sixpences by his fireside. [E, 21-22]

Austen's tone here is approving; John Halperin's account of Austen's own time away at school describes a place very like this one.[15] Mrs. Goddard supports herself decently and without undue hardship. She had "worked hard in her youth" and now has a very pleasant life, with "the occasional holiday of a tea-visit" coming not all that infrequently. Mrs. Goddard and the Bates ladies function well enough in their society, and Austen does not imply that any of them are badly treated by that society.

The situation of Jane Fairfax gives us what is certainly the closest Austen comes to criticism of woman's lot. That criticism is quite tepid. I have been showing all along in this chapter that Austen in both *Pride and Prejudice* and *Emma* accepts the status quo and has her characters work not against but within the rules of her society. I want to preface my discussion of Jane Fairfax with a look at a short passage that generally goes unremarked in our reading of *Emma*. It comes just at the beginning of the novel, when Emma and her father are discussing Miss Taylor's marriage. Mr. Woodhouse in his self-absorbed way is talking about how hard it will be to get to Randalls—it is too far to walk and too short for a carriage ride. No, says Emma, there will be no problem; James will

> "always like going to Randalls, because of his daughter's being housemaid there. . . . That, was your doing, papa. You got Hannah that good place. Nobody thought of Hannah til you mentioned her—James is so obliged to you!"
>
> "I am very glad I did think of her. It was very lucky, for I would not have had poor James think himself slighted upon any account; and I am sure she will make a very good servant; she is a civil, pretty-spoken girl; I have a great opinion of her. Whenever I see her, she always curtseys and asks me how I do, in a very pretty manner; and when you have had her here to do needlework, I observe she always turns the lock of the door the right way and never bangs it. I am sure she will be an excellent servant; and it will be a great comfort to poor Miss Taylor to have somebody about her that she is used to see. Whenever James goes over to see his daughter you know, she will be hearing of us. He will be able to tell her how we all are."
>
> Emma spared no exertions to maintain this happier flow of ideas, and hoped, by the help of backgammon to get her father tolerably through the evening, and be attacked by no regrets but her own. [*E*, 8-9]

There is no comment or corrective by Austen on this discussion. Mr. Knightley enters, and the focus of the scene shifts entirely away from this interlude. But the discussion of Hannah the servant maid is, I think, useful for us as a measure of our own perspective on the much more important Jane Fairfax characterization. What is significant in this discussion about Hannah is the unquestioned assumption that some people have servants and that some people are servants. Mr. Woodhouse thinks highly of Hannah: she is "a civil, pretty-spoken girl" who politely asks him how he is and who never bangs the door. That she might have feelings or the desire to do more than be had in to do needlework, or that she might even want to live in the same house with her father, does not enter Mr. Woodhouse's mind—and we understand his lack of empathy, since already we know that above all he is self-centered. But none of this enters Emma's mind either, and none of it shows up in a comment by the author.[16] Hannah seems just fine to Mr. Woodhouse and to Emma. She also, I am suggesting, seems fine to Austen. Hannah has a social place and fits into it; we don't worry about her any farther.

Jane Fairfax does not yet have a social position; because of her lack of money and connection, her social position depends at any given moment on the people to whom she has attached herself. Emma tells Frank, for example, "I must give you a hint; . . . any want of attention to her *here* [Highbury] should be carefully avoided. You saw her with the Campbells when she was the equal of every body she mixed with, but here she is with a poor old grandmother, who has barely enough to live on. If you do not call early, it will be a slight" (*E*, 194). Jane's ultimate position in society will depend on whether she marries and the sort of husband she can snare. Obviously, being a governess as opposed to being Frank Churchill's wife is the much-to-be-avoided ending. Austen has more sympathy for a Miss Fairfax than for Hannah, but her sympathy does not extend to a statement that this social system must be changed. Remember that the beloved Miss Taylor was in a similar position. If the point of the Jane Fairfax case then is not to decry its unfairness, we must examine it in terms of what it does show about woman's task in Austen's society. Not surprisingly, the task is to marry. Being a governess sounds fairly gruesome—but of course Austen is comparing that to being a lady. Austen's clear preference, for men as well as for women, is to have so much money that money itself does not enter into any considerations. It is lovely to be Darcy or Knightley or even Mr. (and Miss) Woodhouse. Austen does not comment much on what it is to be male and in need of a living—to be a soldier perhaps, like Jane Fairfax's father, and to die in the soldiering. Such interests are outside Austen's scope.

All the details of Jane's background are given to us in one passage; at the end of the novel, in a similar passage, we get Harriet's. Harriet is "the daughter of a tradesman" (*E*, 481); Jane is "an orphan, the only child of Mrs. Bates's youngest daughter" (*E*, 163), so that "By birth she belonged to Highbury" and by birth, presumably, she deserves a higher marriage than Harriet. The Bates have very little money, and so the expectation should be "of her being taught only what very limited means could command, and growing up with no advantages of connection or improvement to be engrafted on what nature had given her in a pleasing person, good understanding, and warm-hearted, well meaning relations" (*E*, 163). Jane, however, has the good fortune to be taken up by Colonel Campbell, a man obviously richer than either the Bates or her own father; she enjoys the education of a young lady, living the same style of life as the colonel's own daughter. But the colonel does not have enough money to provide for both Jane and his daughter, and it is clear that some plan must be made for Jane's future. The plan agreed upon is to educate Jane "for educating others. . . . [By] giving her an education, he hoped to be supplying the means of respectable subsistence hereafter" (E, 164). Although Austen repeatedly mentions the excellent education Jane received, she does not give us many details.[17] That Jane learns from "Living constantly with right-minded and well-informed people," is almost all that Austen thinks we need to know. "[Jane's] heart and understanding had received every advantage of discipline and culture; and Col. Campbell's residence being in London, every lighter talent had been done full justice to, by the attendance of first-rate masters" (E, 164). At least equal attention is given to Jane's natural charms and abilities. She has "decided superiority both in beauty and acquirements" (E, 165) over the Campbell daughter, Austen emphasizes. But, the matrimonial race being no less unfair than many things in life, Miss Campbell wins out over Jane, superior accomplishments and all. Austen pointedly makes the connection between marriage and making a living: Jane and her friend "continued together with unabated regard . . . till the marriage of Miss Campbell, who by that chance, that luck which so often defies anticipation in matrimonial affairs, giving attraction to what is moderate rather than to what is superior, engaged the affections of Mr. Dixon, a young man, rich and agreeable, almost as soon as they were acquainted; and was eligibly and happily settled, while Jane Fairfax had yet her bread to earn" (E, 165).

These remarks about Jane's education, and most importantly about Jane's losing out to Miss Campbell's "moderate" attractions in the marriage lottery, precede the comments that lately have earned so much attention about the horrors of life as a governess. The remarks surely are pointed and bitter: "With the fortitude of a devoted noviciate, she had resolved at one-and-twenty to complete the sacrifice, and retire from all the pleasures of life, of rational intercourse, equal society, peace and hope, to penance and mortification for ever" (E, 165). A little later, Austen adds that taking on such a job "require[s] something more than human perfection of body and mind to be discharged with tolerable comfort" (E, 166). The sharpness of these comments, however, must be taken in context, and that context is the sad reality that Jane deserved Mr. Dixon more than Miss Campbell did. Austen's emphasis is at least as much on Jane's need to marry as on the horrors of governessing; if the marriage game were fairer, Jane would not have any problem. The objective is to find a fit mate for Jane. Emma suspects Miss Campbell's Mr. Dixon was once in the picture; Mrs. Weston suggests that Mr. Knightley might "give Jane . . . a respectable home" (E, 225).

This caveat having been made, we must not minimize the strength of Austen's statement, with Jane, about the urgency of the unprovided female's need to marry. Austen is a realist, but not a polemicist, and her view is unburnished here as elsewhere: marriage for Jane is the difference between a life of misery and a life of happiness. The misery of the governess's life is underscored not just by Jane's comments but by the fact that the only person who actively promotes this solution is Mrs. Elton, who repeatedly tries to find suitable positions for Jane and to push her into accepting them.[18] Jane's reaction to these favors is to put off the moment as long as possible: " 'When I am quite determined as to the time, I am not at all afraid of being long unemployed. There are places in town, offices, where inquiry would soon produce something—Offices for the sale—not quite of human flesh—but of human intellect' " (E, 300). Equally striking are the comments on woman's position that Jane's situation elicits even from the self-satisfied Emma. Since these all come rather late in the book, they serve to show a certain degree of maturity in Emma's outlook as well as to comment on the realities of a woman's life. Emma ponders, for example, "the contrast between Mrs. Churchill's importance in the world, and Jane Fairfax's; . . . one was every thing, the other nothing—and she sat musing on the difference of woman's destiny" (E, 384). All this is changed as soon as Jane is to marry Frank: "Her days of insignificance and evil were over.—She would soon be well, and happy, and prosperous" (E, 403). Remarkably, having watched Jane come so close to the brink, this becomes not the romantic but simply the pragmatic view.

Thus we come back to marriage, the delineation of which occupies so striking a place in the novel. The fact that marriage is of such vital importance to a woman does not mean that it is undertaken just as a practical matter. The marriage relationship itself in *Emma* repeatedly is shown to be tender, loving, and satisfying for both partners. I have discussed the early pictures of marriage in the book, Isabella and John Knightley and Miss Taylor and Mr. Weston. These images are reinforced toward the end of the novel by views into the future of the newly marrying pairs, Harriet and Robert Martin, Jane and Frank Churchill, and of course Emma and Mr. Knightley. Emma's own image of marriage is that of being "the first, the dearest, the friend, the wife to whom he look[s] for all the best blessings of existence" (E,

422-23); poor Emma finds this picture a torture when she mistakenly imagines Harriet with Mr. Knightley, but Austen surely has this definition in mind when she speaks, in the very last words of the novel, of "the perfect happiness of the union" (*E*, 484) between Knightley and Emma. Knightley's own definition of conjugal felicity pours out when he comments on Frank's good fortune in finding and winning Jane:

> "He is a most fortunate man! . . . So early in life—at three and twenty—a period when, if a man chooses a wife, he generally chooses ill. At three and twenty to have drawn such a prize!—What years of felicity that man, in all human calculation, has before him!—Assured of the love of such a woman—the disinterested love, for Jane Fairfax's character vouches for her disinterestedness; every thing in his favour,—equality of situation—I mean, as regards society, and all the habits and manners that are important; equality in every point but one—and that one, since the purity of her heart is not to be doubted, such as must increase his felicity, for it will be his to bestow the only advantages she wants.—A man would always wish to give a woman a better home than the one he takes her from; and he who can do it, where there is no doubt of *her* regard, must, I think, be the happiest of mortals.—Frank Churchill is, indeed, the favourite of fortune. Every thing turns out for his good.—He meets with a young woman at a watering-place, gains her affection, cannot even weary her by negligent treatment—and had he and all his family sought round the world for a perfect wife for him, they could not have found her superior." [*E*, 428]

Mr. Knightley clearly is right, and Frank himself is fully aware of Jane's excellence and patience, of the "kindness and favour [he has] met with" (*E*, 439). Mr. Knightley and Emma will be equally happy: "It was all right, all open, all equal. No sacrifice on any side worth the name. It was a union of the highest promise of felicity in itself, and without one real, rational difficulty to oppose or delay it" (*E*, 468). And of Emma, with Harriet happily paired off with Robert Martin, "The joy, the gratitude, the exquisite delight of her sensations may be imagined. The sole grievance and alloy thus removed in the prospect of Harriet's welfare, she was really in danger of becoming too happy for security.—What had she to wish for? Nothing, but to grow more worthy of him, whose intentions and judgment had been ever so superior to her own. Nothing, but that the lessons of her past folly might teach her humility and circumspection in future" (*E*, 475).

Marriage brings joy, comfort, and real companionship. And these advantages may be fairly well counted on as long as the common sense guidelines of like interests, like education, and like background are followed. For Austen, class is one of the primary ordering devices of society; class distinctions do not keep people separated, but on the contrary they help people to move in society with the least friction possible. Mr. Knightley and Robert Martin get along well and there is mutual admiration between them, but each needs the other to be in his respective place. This is what Knightley means when, trying to please Emma, he tells her that [Robert Martin's] "sense and good principles would delight you.—As far as the man is concerned, you could not wish your friend in better hands. His rank in society I would alter if I could; which is saying a great deal I assure you, Emma.—You laugh at me about William Larkins; but I could quite as ill spare Robert Martin" (*E*, 472-73). The relationship between Mr. Knightley and Robert Martin is good for both of them. Marriages also work well when the respective and relative positions are appropriate, and by the end of the novel Austen has worked out the puzzle so that each piece is in place. The neatness of a Harriet marrying with a Robert and an Emma with a Mr. Knightley is philosophical; in Austen's world, such pairing by class and background, which for Austen are nearly synonymous, is a manifestation of rationality. Jane Austen does not see her world as perfect—Jane Fairfax comes perilously close to becoming part of the slave trade of the mind—but it is very ordered. Austen presents a world with rules; she presents players attempting to act within those rules. Most of the time, adherence to the rules leads to a fairly happy ending.

# EIGHT

# Conclusion

Next to the great ball, what makes the most noise is the marriage of an old Maid that lives in this street, without a portion To a Man of £7,000 per Annum and they say £40,000 in ready money. Her Equipage and Liverys outshine any body's in Town. He has presented her with £3,000 in Jewells and never was man more smitten with these Charms, that [had] lain invisible this forty year.

Lady Mary Wortley Montague
to Mrs. Frances Hewet
Feb. 13, 1710

When as an old woman Lady Mary Wortley Montague read *Clarissa*, she wrote to her daughter that "This Richardson is a strange fellow. I heartily despise him, and eagerly read him, nay, sob over his works in a most scandalous manner. The first two tomes of Clarissa touched me, as being very resembling to my maiden days."[1] Lady Mary's courtship has all the elements of the Richardsonian drama. She corresponds with Edward Wortley Montague against her father's wishes; her father learns about the courtship, sends her to the country to get her out of the way of temptation, and makes it clear that all she can expect from him if she marries against his will is a relatively paltry annuity of four hundred pounds.[2] Finally, father determines on a marriage partner for Lady Mary and makes all the plans for a wedding, including, as in *Clarissa*, ordering expensive clothes for the bride-to-be. There are elements of *Tom Jones* too—Lady Mary and Wortley plan an elopement, and her father tries to foil the plan by removing Lady Mary to another town. Wortley sets off in pursuit but cannot quite catch up with her, or so he thinks. Actually, each unknown to the other, the lovers spend the night in the same inn. Wortley and Lady Mary finally do manage to evade pursuit and to marry, showing that parental despotism and financial transactions are irrelevant to the course of romantic love.

Not quite. It is worth noting in this real-life romantic adventure how much concern each of the lovers shows for financial matters. A large proportion of their correspondence deals with the financial aspects of their possible marriage, and many of their numerous disagreements revolve around monetary questions. Each lover remarks on what he or she stands to lose financially by marrying the other, and each jockeys for a more remunerative position. Wortley is a most reluctant suitor, and his reluctance stems directly from the fact that he will lose Lady Mary's fortune if they marry without parental consent. He asks Lady Mary repeatedly if she cannot find some way to bring her father around. She tells Wortley over and over that her father will not consent to a marriage unless Wortley agrees to her father's terms; if Wortley does not commit himself in any case, she tells him, she is going to end the relationship. Lady Mary's father, Lord Dorchester, insists that Wortley's estate be entailed on the first son. Wortley refuses, claiming that he cannot immediately so burden his estate, and in turn he is rejected by Lord Dorchester as a suitor for Lady Mary. Continuing to correspond clandestinely with his beloved, the ardent suitor, as Robert Halsband picks up the plot, "tried to discover her father's exact financial terms, especially the size of her dowry. She denied knowing it: 'People in my way are sold like slaves; and I cannot tell what price my master will put on me.' Like a cautious business man Wortley did not wish to commit himself until he knew the price, and he again asked her. He even calculated for her how her father and brother could raise her dowry to £25,000, but then fearfully wondered whether his impertinence might raise the settlement demanded of himself."[3] While Wortley continued to worry about losing her dowry, Lord Dorchester accepted a suitor for her, the Honourable Clotworthy Skeffington, whose marriage contract provided for an allowance of £500 a year as pin money and £1,200 a year if he died. Lady Mary uses his offer to negotiate with Wortley.

This outline only suggests the depth of the financial discussions between Lady Mary and her beau. Of the more than one hundred letters and notes that represent the courtship period in Halsband's edition of the collected letters, a third talk about financial matters. Most of these are not casual references but detailed discussions about money.

Wortley badgers Lady Mary to tell him what her father will give her, and he simply will not believe her when she says she does not know.

> I am far from being resolv'd to break off but I own I am not yet determin'd to close the bargain, nor do I know what woud close it. I think it coud not suddenly be done were both of us and all concern'd for us agreed. I was told before I went abroad your money was to be raisd by the Marriage of your brother; that may, for ought I know, be near, but I have not heard it is over. My affairs will, I believe, oblige me to engage my estate for a considerable sum. It may, indeed, be clear again in two months and I be the richer for doing this. But I did not know it woud be so when I treated, nor did I mention it. So that it seems as if neither side were ready to finish. Matters of this sort shoud not be long in Agitation, and till there is a prospect of ending speedily, it is better to be quiet, most certainly not to engage. If you think it will be well taken in me to enquire of the person I spoke with how the affairs of your family now are, I will go to him. Perhaps I may before I have your answer. My own opinion at present is to do so, tho I am sure no offer whatever has bin rejected or kept back on my account, for I never appeard satisfy'd with the demands that were made, and only said as every civil body shou'd do in such a case, that when I came to town I woud desire again to know what was expected. . . . I yet think it not unlikely for us to agree and that in less than two months. If it is not before the Spring, I take it for certain it will never be. [c. Nov. 17, 1710]

Wortley is even more explicit in his next letter.

> But is it not wonderful you are ignorant what the terms are on which you are to be disposd of? Was you ever free in any other family where discourses of that kind did not make up a great part of the Conversation? Those you have to do with cannot set a low value on themselves and must set a very high one upon you, and cannot have thought on this subject less than others. I shoud hope you might find out some way to know what is intended. I will, if I can, delay giving an answer till I hear from you again, and desire you will lay no stress upon any thing I say at present. [Nov. 21, 1710]

Lady Mary, with well-deserved annoyance, begins her answering letter abruptly, with the acerbic comment that "I confesse women very seldom speak truth, but it is not utterly impossible, and with all sincerity, I assure you, I know no more of my own Affairs than a perfect stranger, nor am I capable of returning to you any other answer than I have allready done" (c. Nov. 22, 1710). Within a few days Wortley is writing again:

If £60,000 shoud be added to the estate of your family (as I hear it will) the
giving £20,000 or £25,000 out of it for portions is a very trifle. I am sure it is
advantageous to those that do it for money they don't want and this is very
much for their honour. How can any one suppose less will be done where
there is an estate already too big? Can it be thought a great estate suffers if
£40,000 be added to it instead of £50,000? The taking from the land so much
in present as you two want, tho the greatest part of this fortune shoud not
be receiv'd immediatly, can be no less even in the point of money. For what
you now cost is certainly more than the interest of 2 very large portions. If
your father and brother joyn in this it may easily be done and surely a
brother cant take it ill to hear such a thing mention'd, or, if he shou'd, how
easy is it to get a friend to discourse the case with both of 'em and I am
convinc'd it woud easily be granted. [c. Nov. 24, 1710]

Each answering letter talks about terms and settlements. The lovers
discuss in detail their individual financial status, the terms her father
may or may not agree to, and their own feelings about the other's
responses to these financial questions. Both Wortley and Lady Mary
show irritation not simply with her father but with each other. Financial matters take a central place in Wortley's courtship; they are certainly not peripheral to Lady Mary's concerns. In fact, quite often she
either implicitly or explicitly defends whatever decisions her father
wishes to take. "You'll think me Mad," she tells Wortley sweetly, "but
tis indifferent to me whither I have £10,000 or £50,000, and shall never
quarrel with my family by pretending to direct in the Matter" (c. Nov.
27, 1710). She's not interested in money, she tells him, and she really is
"as sensible as you your selfe can be of the Generosity, which claims
the sincerest proceeding on my side. Perhaps there is no other man
that would take a woman under these disadvantages." But, she gently
chides, "On the other side, consider a little whither there are manny
other Women that would think as I do. The Man my familly would
marry me to, is resolv'd to live in London. Tis my own fault if I do not
(of the humour he is) make him allways think whatever I please. If he
dies, I shall have £1,200 per Annum rent charge; if he lives I shall enjoy
every pleasure of Life, those of Love excepted" (Aug. 6, 1712). In
another letter some days later she protests, "I know not one action of
[my life] that ever prov'd me Mercenary" and then goes on

I think there cannot be a greater proof of the contrary than treating with
you, where I am to depend entirely on your generosity, at the same time
that I have settle'd on me £300 per Annum pin money and a considerable
jointure in another place, not to reckon that I may have by his temper what

command of his Estate I please; and with you I have nothing to pretend to. I do not however make a Merit of this to you. Money is very little to me because all beyond necessarys I do not value that is to [be] purchas'd by it. If the man propos'd to me had £10,000 per Annum and I was sure to dispose of it all, I should act just as I do. [Aug. 12, 1712]

Wortley is the more insistent of the two in his discussions about the financial basis of their possible union, but Lady Mary, even in her protestations, shows a keen awareness not just of the issues involved but of the sacrifices she as well as Wortley is called on to make. From the young couple's letters it is clear that the financial aspects of their marriage are in themselves of interest; their discussions do not center only on her father's demands. Wortley wants a dowry with her; the reality of her dowry is part of, not separable from, her charm.

The images we have seen in the fiction leap out of these real-life letters. Lady Mary's correspondence with Wortley is forbidden. Her father chooses a mate for her, and we find Lady Mary, using almost exactly Clarissa's words, begging simply to be allowed to remain single.[4] And yet the emphases are not Richardson's; Lady Mary almost seems to work with her family. In *Clarissa* the young woman is deprived of all viable options, her virginity essentially her only capital in a mercenary exchange. Lady Mary's letters show us the same minuet from another angle. The financial aspects of the transaction are still markedly center stage, but the woman is not the helpless victim portrayed by Richardson. Financial status, in Richardson's novel the concern only of the family, often enough is a focus of the woman herself, as we see when we look not just at Lady Mary's correspondence—which provides such a remarkable example of a contemporary courtship—but at many of the fictions of the eighteenth century as well. One of the major themes of the eighteenth-century English novel, as I have argued, is its focus on women and money. I have shown that the money scenes, connections, and analyses—such as the detailed explorations of finance in *Moll Flanders* and *Roxana*—are not accidental or peripheral but represent a major theme of the novelists as they depict female characters.

In life and in fiction, women not surprisingly evidence an interest in money that is quite the same as men's. It is, for example, as Lady Mary's correspondence shows, not only parents who are fascinated by money; a woman marrying for money may not be acting solely at her parents' behest. Sarah Fielding in *David Simple* wryly explores this possibility with Miss Nanny Johnson, who throws away the hero,

David, for a coach and six. Nanny's father, aware that David might make a promising husband for one of his daughters, invites David home; in a short time, David becomes attracted to Nanny. Mr. Johnson oversees the courtship: "The Girl was commanded by her Father, if Mr. *David* made any Addresses to her, to receive them in such a manner, as to fix him hers."[5] Young Miss Johnson obediently charms David and within three months David "asked her Father's Consent, which was easily obtained" (*DS*, I, 45).

But Sarah Fielding is not presenting a case of parental despotism, nor even of a particularly obedient female child. Nanny herself warns David not to seem too anxious to have her, "for she was certain her Father designed, if he found he loved her enough to take her on any Terms, to save some of her Fortune to add to her Sister's" (*DS*, I, 46). The courtship runs smoothly. In the meantime, however, the elder sister accepts a very rich suitor who, in turn, one day brings a guest to dinner at the Johnson house. This Mr. Nokes, an ugly, deformed, but exceedingly rich old man, shows interest in the younger daughter, now just on the verge of being married to David. Mr. Johnson wants his daughter to quit David and accept the addresses of her new admirer. The old man himself, Fielding notes, "was not afraid of being refused, for he had Money enough to have bought a Lady of much higher Rank" (*DS*, I, 51). Mr. Johnson tells Nanny that "as she had hitherto been a very obedient Girl, he hoped she would still continue so" (*DS*, I, 51). He admits that he had encouraged her to accept David "because at that time he appeared to be a very advantageous Match for her; but now when a better offered, she would, he said, be certainly in the right to take the Man she could get most by; otherwise she must walk on foot, while her Sister rode in her Coach" (*DS*, I, 51-52). And then he leaves her to think about her choice.

Miss Johnson agonizes. The depiction of her indecision within our context is fascinating. The course of Nanny's ruminations provides a marvelous counterbalance to the clichés of paternalistic oppression that exist in eighteenth-century novels and that exist with even greater frequency in some modern criticism. Nanny Johnson's unhappiness is not caused by her father, for, as we have seen, her father does not insist that she accept Mr. Nokes; he merely presents her options and his own preference, leaving the decision to her. We already know the extent of her loyalty to her father: we have seen her tutoring David to be sure that he bargains effectively for her dowry. Nanny's agony is inherent in her own dilemma, for she wants the wealth that comes with Mr. Nokes and the happiness of being with David. She retreats to her room in hysterical tears and pours out her troubles to her friend Miss Betty Trusty—who does not see any problem. Mr. Johnson is imposing "unreasonable Commands" (*DS*, I, 53), she tells Nanny, and it is no sin to ignore them. But you don't understand, Nanny says, "I am not troubling my head, either about the *Sin*, or my *Father*; but the height of my Distress lies in not knowing my own Mind: if I could once find that out, I should be easy enough. I am so divided, by the Desire of Riches on the one hand; and by my Honour, and the Man I like on the other, that there is such a struggle in my Mind, I am almost distracted" (*DS*, I, 53). Nanny cannot bear the thought of her sister driving around in "her Coach and Six, while I take up with a Hack, or at best with a Coach and Pair" (*DS*, I, 55). Should she give up "all Thoughts of being a *great Woman*" (*DS*, I, 55), she wonders, lamenting to her friend that "if I should neglect this Opportunity of making my Fortune, every Woman whom I see supported in Grandeur, will make me mad, to think I had it once in my power to have been as great as her" (*DS*, I, 56-57). She just cannot decide what to do. David, overhearing her soul searchings, saves her the choosing. He leaves, and Nanny marries the peevish and infirm old man.

Nanny is no one's victim but her own. Sarah Fielding's inversion of the Parental Despotism formula suggests that even as early as 1744 that formulation had come to seem hackneyed. As in Lady Mary's courtship, the intransigent parent is only one element of the drama and often not the deciding one.[6] As so many of the novels show, Defoe's, Henry Fielding's, and Austen's among them, no matter how much parents may interfere, they are not necessarily the deciding players in courtship games. In *David Simple*, Nanny has no excuse for her choice except her own ill judgment. Nanny's ordinariness is made manifest. She is not especially greedy nor exceptionally vain, Fielding insists; had she not been faced with the choice between the two suitors, she would have married David and "exulted in her own Happiness, and been the first to have blamed any other Woman, for giving up the Pleasure of having the Man she loved, for any Advantage of Fortune; and would have thought it utterly impossible for her ever to have been tempted to such an Action. . . . For to talk of a Temptation at a distance, and to feel it present, are two such very different things, that every body can resist the one, and very few People the other" (*DS*, I, 58-59).

Richardson's Pamela, like his Clarissa, is of course beyond temptation: she never for a moment considers giving in to the blandishments of her very rich master. But her awareness of money, in terms both of goods and currency, defines her character from the first pages of her story. I do not want to enter here into the debate about whether Pamela sells *herself*; I do want to point out the obvious accounting in the novel, particularly in the earliest letters. Pamela often appears to define virtue in terms of the giving of presents—both her old mistress and her new young master wear an aspect of the angelic when they give gifts. The early letters deal largely with gifts, both those given to Pamela and those she gives to her parents. In the first letter of the novel Pamela blesses her new young master, "and pray with me, my dear Father and Mother, for God to bless him: For he has given Mourning and a Year's Wages to all my Lady's Servants; and I having no Wages as yet . . . gave me with his own Hand Four golden Guineas, besides lesser Money, which were in my old Lady's Pocket when she dy'd."[7] Those four guineas thread through twenty letters as Pamela's parents worry about using the money, are reassured by Pamela ("Pray make use of the Money; you may now do it safely" [*P*, 29]), do use a part, and worry about giving it back. Finally Pamela writes to her parents, "Don't trouble yourself, now I think of it, about the Four Guineas, nor borrow to make them up; for they were given me, with some Silver, as I told you, as a Perquisite, being what my Lady had about her when she dy'd; and, as I hope for no other Wages, I am so vain as to think I have deserv'd them in the fourteen Months, since my Lady's Death" (*P*, 53). The guineas, like Pamela's clothes, act as a kind of financial barometer, measuring the degree of danger to be perceived for the heroine. Pamela's clothes help define her moral status: when she uses her savings to outfit herself once more according to her rank, rather than dressing in the silks and other presents that she has from her master, we know that Pamela's virtue will triumph. The listing of items, with the attendant estimates of their worth, recurs in letter after letter. Her master has given her "a Suit of my old Lady's Cloaths, and half a Dozen of her Shifts, and Six fine Handkerchiefs, and Three of her Cambrick Aprons, and Four Holland ones: The Cloaths are fine Silks, and too rich and too good for me, to be sure. I wish it was no Affront to him to make Money of them, and send it to you: it would do me more good" (*P*, 30), she writes to her parents. In her next letter, "my Master gave me more fine Things. He call'd me up to my old Lady's Closet, and pulling out her Drawers, he gave me Two Suits of fine *Flanders* lac'd Headcloths, Three Pair of fine Silk Shoes, two hardly the worse, and just fit for me; for my old Lady had a very little Foot; and several Ribbands and Topknots of all Colours, and Four Pair of fine white Cotton Stockens, and Three Pair of fine Silk ones; and Two Pair of rich

Stays, and a Pair of rich Silver Buckles in one Pair of the Shoes" (*P*, 31). When her master first offers his improper addresses, Pamela considers whether she should run away but is perplexed about how she should take her things with her. And when she makes more final plans to leave, she is truly confused about the property problem, even calling on Mrs. Jervis to help her to decide which things she can in good conscience take with her: she divides her goods into three bundles, her lady's presents, her master's presents, and the things she had from before or has bought herself. She is so precise that she accounts for the shoelaces from two old pairs of shoes.

Pamela's attention to the listing of what she has, both in money and in goods, is typical of many eighteenth-century heroines. Not as typical, and so unsubtle as to shade into the comic, are her repeated ejaculations that she "can be content with Rags and Poverty, and Bread and Water" (*P*, 28). "[H]ow easy a Choice Poverty and Honesty is" (*P*, 43), she says, and "I can so contentedly return to my Poverty again, and think it less Disgrace to be oblig'd to wear Rags, and live upon Rye-bread and Water, as I use to do, than to be a Harlot to the greatest Man in the World" (*P*, 49). Pamela's awareness of the prices of things colors her descriptions not only of goods but of virtues. Like many eighteenth-century female characters, Pamela often talks about her virtue as if there is a slash mark after it: virtue/money. Despite her repeated and insistent declarations that wealth is unimportant to her, she is always conscious of it. As I have shown, this awareness of money and its implications for a successful adjustment into society is a recurring theme in those novels of the eighteenth century that look seriously at their female characters.[8] I have argued elsewhere[9] that eighteenth-century novels often present in fairly straightforward fashion many of the most vital concerns of the day. Surely, as we look at the images from Defoe to Austen, the representation of women's connections to financial concerns fits this pattern.

Peter Earle recently has documented the degree to which women in late seventeenth- and early eighteenth-century England were active in the London financial scene. He finds that, either as spinsters in control of the money they earned and inherited or as widows, women controlled a good deal of wealth. Some of this money was in businesses that the women themselves managed, but much of it was in investments and mortgages. He sums up: "The . . . point that is obvious . . . is the enormous importance of women, particularly widows, in the London investment markets. Women must have owned a sizeable proportion of the London housing stock (or at least of the long leases of that stock) and a woman as landlady must have been a common experience. . . . Women, too, played a vital role in the provision of loan capital through the bond and mortgage markets, one man's accumulation of business capital being realized by his widow to provide another man with that vital loan which would enable him to build up his business in his turn."[10] Defoe's images of Roxana building her fortune through investment, of her worrying over the per cents in her mortgages, are images that for his readers simply would have reflected what they saw around them. Similarly in the early pages of the novel, Roxana being set up as a landlady also would have reflected the experience of Defoe's early audience, for whom renting from a woman would have been quite usual. And Moll's analysis of the marriage market, that "the market is against our sex just now," precisely reflects the economic and demographic facts: "an imbalance must be noted between the numbers of men and women in London . . . reflected both in a surplus of spinsters to bachelors and of widows to widowers. This female surplus was aggravated by a lack of enthusiasm on the part of many men to marry in a world where the financial benefits of bachelorhood and the easy availability of alternative sources of sexual gratification and of housekeepers made single life an attractive option."[11] The patterns Earle points out are reflected in novels throughout the century: the age difference between Emma and Mr. Knightley, for example, is quite usual in the middle and upper classes.[12]

The eighteenth-century English novel shows women very much engaged with their society. Somehow we have come to think of women in these novels as essentially sheltered from the world beyond their families, but this perception simply does not stand up to scrutiny.[13] The women in the radical novels of the nineties concern themselves with a wide range of social issues and act upon their social theories just as the men do. It is easy in these radical novels to see the interplay between society and the individual woman; my point is that this interplay is explored by novelists from Defoe to Austen. We cannot ignore that connection without distorting the novels. Thus, to return once more to the example of Defoe's heroines, to assume that Defoe's depiction of their business dealings is somehow peripheral to his characterizations is to ignore the shape of his craft.

There are other patterns too that need to be noted, all of them suggesting that eighteenth-century novelists generally represented a world in which women were seen to function with relative success. For one thing, most of the thematic omissions I have noted in these novels—the lack of discussion of education in any formal sense, the general lack of descriptions of work or profession—is the same for both sexes. Characters are not defined by profession in these early novels, and education has not yet come to vie with class as a determinant of social position. Conversely, for both men and women class is a significant aspect of characterization throughout our period. Sexual codes surely are important, but they are not as strict as the Richardsonian model assumes. In general, it is the sentimental heroine who finds the step beyond the hearth to be fatal; in other novels, women most often get about quite safely. In fact, as we have seen, these women as a group seem remarkably sturdy. Even the most battered of them, Jemima, shows extraordinary resiliency.

Finally, I want to call attention to one more theme that runs through these novels. There has been much discussion in recent years, built on the perceptive work in Janet Todd's *Women's Friendship in Literature*,[14] of the role of women's friendship—meaning a friendship between women—in the English novel. We essentially, and sadly, have ignored a theme at least as significant, that is, the depictions of friendships between women and men. An obvious case is the relationship between Knightley and Emma, which within the critical, especially the feminist, perspective has dwindled into a mentor-pupil relationship that merely extends the parent-child pattern that delimits Emma before her marriage. This is a neat formula, but not an entirely true one. Knightley does indeed function as Emma's mentor, but this does not exclude the reality of an abiding friendship between them. Women friends often function as mentors to each other, as Clarissa does to Anna and Jane to Elizabeth, and of course this relationship can be part of a friendship between a man and a woman as well. The depiction of the friendship between Emma and Knightley is one of the most charming aspects of Austen's novel.[15]

All of the novelists I have studied in this book, with the obvious exception of Richardson, depict female-male friendships. Moll shares friendship with Jemmy just as she does with her female friend the governess. As I have shown, if anyone is the "mentor" in the relationship between Moll and Jemmy, it is Moll. One of the remarkable aspects of Defoe's characterization of Moll and Jemmy is that many of the traditional assumptions governing male-female relationships are turned around—Moll is the stronger figure, Moll is the better organizer, Moll is the real breadwinner. And neither Jemmy nor Moll has any trouble with all this. It is clear that they like each other and take pleasure in each other's company. Fielding does not depict female-male friendship in *Tom Jones,* where as I have suggested most of the images of women are stereotypes, but in *Amelia* the friendship between Amelia and Booth defines them both. Like Moll and Jemmy, Amelia and Booth truly like each other and take pleasure in each other's company. They want to be together; they need to share experiences with each other. By any definition, it seems to me (in a book that devotes a good deal of attention to the concept of friendship), Fielding carefully delineates the friendship between his protagonists. Both Defoe and Fielding take female-male friendship as a normal human bond, and neither comments explicitly about these aspects of their characterizations.

The radical novelists, whose novels are constructed as polemical pieces and who comment explicitly on so many social topics, do emphasize their depiction of female-male friendship. Anna and Frank are first friends, then lovers. Hermsprong and Maria are never lovers but enjoy a delightful friendship. In *Nature and Art* Inchbald insists on the friendship between Henry and Rebecca, contrasting their relationship explicitly with that of William and Hannah, and implicitly with the relationships of the older couples, William and Lady Clementina and Lord and Lady Bendham. As backdrop to all of these relationships stands the failed bond between the brothers William and Henry. For Inchbald, then, gender is irrelevant to the validity of friendship. This is much the same tack taken by Wollstonecraft, whose lovers, Maria and Darnford, also begin as friends responding to the marginal notations in literary works they share. Jane Austen in *Pride and Prejudice* highlights same-sex friendship in her delineations of the relationships between Darcy and Bingley and, most important, between Elizabeth and Jane. The bond between the sisters is based in limitless affection, real joy in each other's company, and an intense need to share experience. We have the sense, in the scene in which Elizabeth finally confesses her love for Darcy to Jane, that until she could share with her sister the wonder of her new feelings, Elizabeth's falling in love did not have closure. Elizabeth will be very happy with Darcy, but the basic friendship of her life will be with her sister. In *Emma* precisely this sort of friendship defines the relationship between Emma and Knightley.

Austen's depiction of Emma and Knightley is delightfully subtle, drawn in large part by implicit comparisons with other relationships that are enthusiastically embraced by Emma only to be discarded as she grows beyond them. In *Emma,* Austen shows that a match in age and sex does not in itself provide an adequate basis for friendship and that friendship is based on mutuality of interest and outlook rather than on gender. Emma's closest friend for most of the novel is Harriet Smith; this typically adolescent relationship withers, not really even a little mourned, as Emma comes to understand more about the girl's limitations. In terms of a match of interests, social class, sex, and age, Emma should be friends with Jane Fairfax—but as Austen so marvelously lets us see, the spark of unforced liking just is not there. It is her bond with Knightley that continues to develop as Emma matures; their relationship does grow into a romantic, i.e., sexual, one, but it begins with and is based on their friendship. When Emma goes to Knightley to find support and affirmation of her self and her perceptions, she does so in much the same spirit that animates Elizabeth's need for Jane.

I began by suggesting that the images of women in eighteenth-century English novels are essentially positive. Most novelists take as their heroines capable human beings whose stories end happily, as in *Pride and Prejudice* and *Emma*, largely because of their own good sense. Novelists from Defoe to Austen depict women engaged with society rather than cloistered from it. The involvement with financial matters is a reflection of this engagement, as is the women's awareness in so many of the novels of a wide spectrum of social issues. The friendships that women have with each other define them, and so do the friendships that they have with men, for their involvement with men on this level reflects human involvement that goes far beyond the patriarchal prison into which modern criticism sometimes has forced the characters. This is our fault, not the novelists', for they are drawing not victims but functioning people. In novel after novel men and women are seen as equally capable human beings—in some novels, like *Moll Flanders*, women arguably are more capable. This perspective usually is simply implicitly assumed; occasionally, as in *Anna St. Ives*, it is made explicit. Faith in the female character does not vary according to the gender of the novelist. The truism says that historians always like to have the important things happen in their respective periods; it is safe to make the same assumption about critics. For those of us who study the novel, much that was important did happen in the eighteenth century. The evolving form from the first made assumptions about the characterization of women that assured the careful depiction of women as part of society. That this seems so natural to us is owing to the skill of those extraordinary writers; we so much take for granted the tradition the eighteenth-century English novel began that we must stop to think if we are to notice that it could have been different.

# Notes

## Chapter 1. Introduction

1. Thus it seems to me that both recent waves of feminist criticism have distorted the focus of these novels by placing their emphasis on the victimization of women: the first wave (Gilbert and Gubar) saw women destroyed by their victimization; more recent feminist criticism (Poovey, Auerbach, Spacks) argues that it was somehow productive. I have found that the novels for the most part are not depicting women as victims but rather show women functioning, and functioning fairly well, in a society that is not always kind to their male counterparts either.

2. Claudia L. Johnson, *Jane Austen: Women, Politics, and the Novel* (Chicago: Univ. of Chicago Press, 1988). A very perceptive analysis of feminist criticism and its readings of Austen is Julia Prewitt Brown's review essay "The Feminist Depreciation of Austen: A Polemical Reading" in *Novel* (Spring 1990): 303-13.

3. John J. Richetti, *Defoe's Narratives: Situations and Structures* (Oxford: Clarendon, 1975), 195, describes Roxana as "androgynous"; David Blewett, "Introduction" to *Roxana, The Fortunate Mistress* (Penguin: Middlesex, England, 1982), 17-22, details what he sees as her increasingly severe mental illness.

4. Jane Austen, *Emma*, ed. R.W. Chapman (Oxford: Clarendon, 1926), 21.

5. Janet Todd, *Women's Friendship in Literature* (New York: Columbia Univ. Press, 1980), 403-4.

6. Keith M. May, *Characters of Women in Narrative Literature* (New York: St. Martins, 1981), 55.

7. It is not a new observation that the period from the 1760s to the 1790s does not continue the development of the novel that the preceding decades had brought; the powerful lines of Defoe, Richardson, and Fielding are followed by what Frederick R. Karl aptly labels "a series of minor efforts: the novel of sensibility, the Gothic romance, [and] the novel of sentiment" (*The Nineteenth Century British Novel* [New York: Farrar, Straus and Giroux, 1966], 8).

The images of women in these novels, like other aspects of the works, are distorted to fit the plot and pathos requirements of the form—in all, this period holds relatively little of interest in a study such as mine. Only Fanny Burney's *Evelina*, 1778, comes as an exception, with its bright focus on the coming of age of the initially naive yet intelligent young heroine.

8. In their lack of emphasis on virginity and chastity the novels are reflecting social realities. E.A. Wrigley, of the London School of Economics and the Cambridge Group for the History of Population and Social Structure, notes that "At the start of the 'long' eighteenth century fewer than a tenth of all first births were illegitimate; before its end the proportion had risen to a quarter and a further quarter of all first births were prenuptially conceived" (*Past and Present: A Journal of Historical Studies* 98 [Feb. 1983]: 132-33). These figures suggest a society much less concerned with a woman's sexual experience than we might have assumed; if fully 50 percent of the births by the end of the century were conceived before marriage, such sexual activity surely did not carry social ostracism. Further, half of these women did marry before the child was born, again suggesting that the obvious proof of having had sex before marriage did not make women unmarriageable.

9. Probably the best known of these American novels is *The Coquette* by Hannah W. Foster. I discuss a number of early American novels and their use of the seduction theme in "The American Novel of Seduction, being an explanation of the omission of the sex act in *The Scarlet Letter* and other matters," *The Nathaniel Hawthorne Journal* (1978).

10. Patricia Spacks, "Every Woman Is At Heart a Rake," *ECS* 8 (1974): 46.

11. Todd, 407-9.

12. There is still a great deal of research to be done on the topic of women and work in eighteenth-century England. Peter Earle has made a fascinating beginning in "The female labour market in London in the late seventeenth and early eighteenth centuries," *Economic History Review* 2nd ser. (1989); in studying the depositions of female witnesses before three sets of London courts he found that "only 28 per cent of the sample mentioned no employment for which they received payment" (337). The majority of these women worked in "women's occupations," especially as servants, in nursing, or in occupations related to textiles such as making and mending clothes, needlework, etc. He finds that many of these women's occupations were "casual, intermittent, or seasonal" and few "except servants and those running shops or vitualling outlets would have expected to be employed the whole year through" (342); this work, "much of it of a casual nature and none of it organized by gilds or livery companies" (342), not surprisingly was considerably less well paid than most of the "male" trades. As Earle notes, it is understandable that prostitution as a means of making a living does not appear in the depositions.

13. A sampling of the most recent scholarship in this area includes many books on individual authors as well as studies of the period focusing in some way on women or women's contributions. Studies of individual authors include John J. Richetti's *Daniel Defoe* (Boston: Twayne, 1987); Paula R. Backscheider's *Daniel Defoe: Ambition and Innovation* (Lexington: Univ. Press of Kentucky, 1986); Jocelyn Harris's *Samuel Richardson* (Cambridge, Mass.: Cam-

bridge Univ. Press, 1987); Elizabeth Bergen Brophy's *Samuel Richardson* (Boston: Twayne, 1987); and Margaret Anne Doody's *Frances Burney: The Life in the Works* (New Brunswick, N.J.: Rutgers Univ. Press, 1988). More general studies include Janet Todd's *Sensibility: An Introduction* (London and New York: Methuen, 1986) and *The Sign of Angellica* (New York: Columbia Univ. Press, 1989); Terry Castle's *Masquerade and Civilization: The Carnivalesque in Eighteenth-Century English Culture and Fiction* (Stanford: Stanford Univ. Press, 1986); and Nancy Armstrong's *Desire and Domestic Fiction: A Political History of the Novel* (New York and Oxford: Oxford Univ. Press, 1987). This significant outpouring represents only part of the abundance of the last few years.

14. Paul Hunter, *Before Novels: The Cultural Contexts of Eighteenth-Century English Fiction* (New York: Norton, 1990), 5, astutely argues against critical approaches that "blur" rather than elucidate texts. "In spite of the popularity of New Historicism, widespread interest generally in all kinds of cultural issues, and the present lively debates about origins, ahistoricism remains a powerful force in literary studies. Ultimately it is a threat to the very idea of literary history, and its premises are directly contrary to the aims, assumptions, and methods that I engage here. Sometimes disguised as 'theory' and often flying under the flags of formalism, structuralism, post-structuralism, narratology, myth criticism, or even reader response criticism, ahistoricism finds friendly cover wherever it can and boldly blurs distinctions rather than sharpening them."

## Chapter 2. Daniel Defoe: *Moll Flanders* and *Roxana*

1. Daniel Defoe, *The Fortunes and Misfortunes of the Famous Moll Flanders*, ed. George Starr (New York: Oxford, 1987; rpt., 1971), 1. All further references are to this edition.

2. The whole question of intentional or unintentional irony for many years has been a major critical focus in discussions of Defoe, most importantly in the work of Ian Watt and Wayne Booth. But I think that the debate about Defoe's use of irony, while in some ways very helpful in defining our readings, in an important sense for a long time made it difficult to accept Defoe simply at his word—that is, naked of any sort of irony.

3. Ian Watt, *The Rise of the Novel: Studies in Defoe, Richardson and Fielding* (Berkeley: Univ. of California Press, 1967), 131.

4. The situation here is exactly paralleled in Defoe's last novel when Roxana hesitates in choosing between starvation and becoming the merchant's mistress; in context, Roxana's lamentations too represent a false morality.

5. Defoe talks at length about woman-as-investor in *Roxana* also. This theme of woman and her investments is not unique to Defoe. Clarissa mentions *her* investments in Richardson's novel, and Fielding makes explicit reference to the importance of the female investor in *The True Patriot*. Angela J. Smallwood in *Fielding and the Woman Question* (New York: St. Martin's, 1989), 37, notes that "In the second number of *The True Patriot* published during the Jacobite campaign of 1745, Fielding appeals seriously and directly to women

readers. He points out the genuinely political role they will be fulfilling by leaving their investments in the public funds and thus maintaining the strength of the government: '[T]ho' they are not intitled to the Glory of fighting for their Country, nor can decently enter into Associations for the Support of the Government; yet those of them whose Fortunes are in the Funds, may be intitled to some share of Merit, by contributing all that lies in their power to keep up the Credit of those Funds which were originally raised for its Support.'"

6. Defoe's later novel, *Roxana,* actually shows the descent into total poverty; we see Roxana and her children reduced to the point of virtual starvation.

7. For example, Juliet McMaster, "The Equation of Love and Money in *Moll Flanders,* " *Studies in the Novel* 2 (1970): 142, says that Moll "is by vocation rather than necessity a prostitute and a thief."

8. Lois A Chaber, "Matriarchal Mirror: Women and Capital in *Moll Flanders,* " *PMLA* (Mar. 1982): 14, comments that "one structural device unifying diverse episodes in *Moll Flanders* is the incremental identification of the putatively 'legitimate' world and the criminal one it so self-righteously punishes. When Moll informs us in a digression of the way the Newgate jailors used 'nightfliers,' prisoners allowed out at night to steal so that their betters could claim the rewards for the stolen goods the next day, ambiguous syntax collapses the distinction between the organizers and their instruments, relocating *all* the guilt in the jailors, who 'restore for a reward what *they* had stolen the evening before' [emphasis added]. . . . Defoe conflates apparently disparate roles—those of the victim and the victimizer, the criminal and the citizen—by casting Moll, despite her errant ways, as his legitimate spokeswoman."

9. Moll has done well; these particular goods would be considerably more valuable than a modern reader might assume. For some suggestion of the worth of such items see Richard B. Schwartz's *Daily Life in Johnson's London* (Madison: Univ. of Wisconsin Press, 1983), 47-48.

10. Maximillian E. Novak, *Economics and the Fiction of Daniel Defoe* (Berkeley: Univ. of California Press, 1962), 100-101, compares Moll's "honest Clark" who dies of despair when his business fails to Jemmy and concludes that Defoe finds Jemmy by far the more admirable character. "There is no question that Defoe was suggesting that dishonesty is preferable to despair. In times of difficulty, he argued, many a tradesman does things which he later repents, but it is better to act and repent than despair and die. Crusoe, Moll, and Defoe's other heroes and heroines never despair. Honest and good as Moll's fifth husband is, he does not face life with the bravery of Moll's Lancashire husband, who greets failure as a challenge and prefers stealing to starving."

11. John J. Richetti, *Daniel Defoe* (Boston: Twayne, 1987), 85-86, points to a very similar situation in *Colonel Jack:* Jack's past "saves him, for he has discovered among his indentured servants his faithless first wife, now repentant and still desirable, made wise by misfortunes. In a sequence too complicated for exact summary, she talks him out of his panic and devises a plan of escape.

While she goes to London to see about a pardon, Jack embarks on the first of what is eventually a series of fabulously successful smuggling voyages into the Spanish Caribbean." Thus in *Colonel Jack*, as in *Moll Flanders* and *Roxana*, woman is portrayed as capable and in control.

Richetti also notes (86) the structure and language of these voyages, which in our context take on special interest; Jack sounds very like Moll and Roxana. Richetti says that "From the point of view of narrative economy and coherence, these voyages are [unnecessary]. And yet Defoe takes special care to explain in some detail just how Jack gets around the ban on non-Spanish imports into Cuba and Mexico. Jack's narrative virtually turns into a bill of lading and a ledger, as cargoes are itemized and profits added up: 'The chief of the cargo we bought here was fine English broad cloth, serges, drugets, Norwich stuffs, bays, says, and all kinds of woollen manufactures, as also linnen of all sorts, a very great quantity, and near a thousand pounds in fine silks of several sorts. . . . I clear'd in these three months five and twenty thousand pounds sterling in ready money.' Defoe seems to take particular delight in showing how Jack transforms his initial capture by the Spaniards off Cuba into large profits. At the very end, on his last trading voyage [Jack has realized a profit of] '8570 pieces of eight . . . so that I was indeed, still very rich, all things consider'd.' "

12. Michael Shinagel in *Daniel Defoe and Middle-Class Gentility* (Cambridge, Mass: Harvard Univ. Press, 1968) misses the point of Moll's active engineering of her prosperity when he says of her setting-up in America that "Fortunately . . . they have some money with them and Moll has prosperous relatives in the colonies" (159). As I have shown, Moll leaves no financial aspect of this voyage to "fortune," and it is not rich relatives but careful planning that stocks her plantation.

13. For Defoe, Moll's emphasis throughout the novel on her economic self is positive and appropriate. Ian Watt is right: "There is certainly nothing in *Moll Flanders* which clearly indicates that Defoe sees the story differently from the heroine" (122). Why then do modern readers have trouble with this aspect of the book? "The answer would seem to be a matter not of literary criticism but of social history. We cannot today believe that so intelligent a man as Defoe should have viewed either his heroine's economic attitudes or her pious protestations with anything other than derision. Defoe's other writings, however, do not support this belief. . . . [Defoe] was not ashamed to make economic self-interest his major premise about human life; he did not think such a premise conflicted either with social or religious values; nor did his age" (127).

14. Paula R. Backscheider, *Daniel Defoe: His Life* (Baltimore: Johns Hopkins Univ. Press, 1989), 487-88, finds that with regard to the transportation episode, "The experience of Moll Flanders is authentically rendered. . . . Defoe presents transportation as both opportunity and the means to break an addictive pattern." Backscheider provides a valuable history of criminal transportation and the laws that governed it. See pages 485ff.

15. Moll seems to be completely unaware that she could well have been the servant rather than the lady of the house. It is interesting that Moll takes it for granted that she needs servants, and she has no fellow feeling for people

whose state in life might well have been her own. Later on, she buys more servants and seems very satisfied with her bargain when one of the females seven months later delivers a little "extra" she picked up on the ship.

16. Richetti, 113, finds that "Defoe's originality lies precisely in Roxana's oscillations and defining inconsistencies as she relives her life in the telling of it. Her story has an eddying motion in which regret and repentance pull her down even as pleasure and affluence bear her up. And yet, *Roxana* is more than a whirlpool of episodes and incidents. It has a narrative pattern, a unified plot more coherent than Defoe had ever managed."

17. *Roxana, The Fortunate Mistress*, ed. and introd. by David Blewett (Middlesex, England: Penguin, 1982), 42-43. All further references are to this edition.

18. *Feminism in Eighteenth-Century England* (Urbana: Univ. of Illinois Press, 1882), 68. Rogers says that "Roxana's claim that she would have been happy if she had kept her chastity 'tho' I had perish'd of meer Hunger; for, without question, a Woman ought rather to die, than to prostitute her Virtue and Honour' is surely to be read ironically. It is better to become a nice man's mistress than to starve." She notes that "Moll too repeatedly finds herself in a position where she must choose between morality and survival. . . . As long as they live as respectable women, Moll and Roxana are passive victims." Novak, *Economics and the Fiction of Daniel Defoe*, sees the novels in much the same way: "Moll's primary concern, although by no means her only one, is to live as well as she can in an environment often unfriendly to survival. She becomes a mistress and a prostitute in the same manner that Roxana becomes first a mistress and then a courtesan. When faced by genuine poverty, they have little choice between starvation or survival through sin" (97).

19. David Blewett effectively summarizes the legal issues involving contemporary divorce, but I disagree with his conclusion that Defoe takes Roxana's position here. Blewett notes that "Neither wilful desertion nor adultery was an adequate ground for divorce. Moreover, Canon 107 of the 1604 canons of the Church of England forbids remarriage after separation or divorce, even of the innocent party. Many Puritan (and some Anglican) divines, however, argued that the innocent party ought to be allowed to sue for divorce and to remarry (as was briefly the case when the Cromwellian Marriage Act of 1653 was in force), and there is evidence that among the Puritans private (i.e., extra-legal) divorce existed and that remarriage took place. In the debate . . . Roxana accurately represents Defoe's own conservative attitude to divorce and remarriage" (*R*, p. 385, note 44).

20. Susan Moller Okin's "Patriarchy and Married Women's Property in England: Questions About Some Current Views," *ECS* (Winter 1983-84), gives a very good overview of the married woman's lack of property rights. She finds that "in general throughout the century women's fortunes were normally given, along with their persons, to their husbands" (132-33). For all the details about how the law operated with regard to women and property, see Susan Staves's *Married Women's Separate Property in England, 1660-1883* (Cambridge, Mass.: Harvard Univ. Press, 1990), *passim*.

21. The accounting deals not just with material things. When after a year

and a half with the prince Roxana becomes pregnant, she notes that there would not be much trouble about raising such a child, for while to maintain a bastard under normal circumstances the father must in effect steal from the patrimony of his legitimate chldren, in the case of "Great Men," they

> are deliver'd from this Burthen, because they are always furnish'd to supply the Expence of their Out-of the-Way Offspring, by making little Assignments upon the Bank of *Lyons,* or the Town-House of *Paris,* and settling those sums, to be receiv'd for the Maintenance of such Expence as they see Cause.
>
> Thus, in the Case of this Child of mine, while he and I convers'd, there was no need to make any Appointment, as an Appennage, or Maintenance for the Child, or its Nurse; for he supplied me more than sufficiently for all those things; but afterward, when Time, and a particular Circumstance, put an End to our conversing together . . . I found he appointed the Children a settled Allowance, by an Assignment of annual Rent, upon the Bank of *Lyons,* which was sufficient for bringing them handsomely, tho' privately, up in the World; in that not in a Manner unworthy of their Father's Blood. [*R,* 116]

22. Compare Anna's description of Clarissa: "You may take notice of the admirable facility she had in learning languages: that she read with great ease both Italian and French, and could hold a conversation in either, though she was not fond of doing so" (*Clarissa* [New York: Viking Penguin, 1985], 1468).

23. Shinagel suggests that this passage shows that Roxana's "wealth has become so much of an obsession that it rules all her thoughts and she cannot act like a woman because of it" (183), but I see no evidence that this is Defoe's meaning. Rather, it seems to me that Roxana—and Defoe with her—is luxuriating in the awareness of her financial capability. But critics often have been made uncomfortable by Roxana as a businessperson. Blewett, "Introduction," *passim,* like Shinagel, finds her essentially mad. Richetti repeatedly uses the formulation that she "seems an effectively androgynous character" (*Daniel Defoe,* 107); see also his *Defoe's Narratives: Situations and Structures* (Oxford: Clarendon, 1975), 195. Backscheider, "Defoe's Women: Snares and Prey," *Studies in Eighteenth-Century Culture* 5 (1976), uses the same formulation: Moll and Roxana only prosper when they become "Men-women" (106). With regard to Roxana, Backscheider finds that "What characteristics she has that are not vain are masculine," which Backscheider defines as "common-sensical rather than polished" (*Daniel Defoe: Ambition and Innovation* [Lexington: Univ. Press of Kentucky, 1986], 184). I would argue that Defoe's point is just the opposite: Roxana is both female and effective. Thus it is that Roxana comments, "I knew no Reason the Men had to engross the whole Liberty of the Race, and make the Women, not withstanding any desparity of Fortune, be subject to the Laws of Marriage; . . . it was my Misfortune to be a Woman, but I was resolv'd it shou'd not be made worse by the Sex; and seeing Liberty seem'd to be the Men's Property, I wou'd be a *Man-Woman;* for as I was born free, I wou'd die so" (*R,* 212).

24. James Sutherland notes in *Daniel Defoe: A Critical Study* (Cambridge, Mass.: Harvard Univ. Press, 1971), 175, that Defoe's attitude about women is quite liberal; Katherine Rogers's "The Feminism of Daniel Defoe" in *Women in*

*the Eighteenth Century and Other Essays* (Sarasota, Fla.: A.M. Hakkert, 1975), studies that liberalism in some detail.

25. Lady Mary Wortley Montagu uses virtually the same words to describe what she sees as the admirable situation of contemporary Turkish women. She explains in a letter to her sister that the Turkish costume, which effectually conceals the identity of the woman enclosed within it, because of the anonymity it provides allows Turkish women a great deal more freedom than English women enjoy. In any case, she notes, "Neither have they much to apprehend from the resentment of their Husbands, those ladys that are rich having all their money in their own hands, which they take with 'em upon a divorce with an addition which he is oblig'd to give 'em. Upon the Whole, I look upon the Turkish Women as the only free people in the Empire" (*The Complete Letters of Lady Mary Wortley Montagu*, vol. I, ed. Robert Halsband [Oxford: Clarendon, 1965], 329). Lady Mary's implication, of course, is that the woman's control of her own money provides safety for her under all conditions, even should an infidelity be discovered.

Perhaps of equal interest in a discussion of *Roxana*, in the same letter Lady Mary, living in Turkey as the wife of England's ambassador to that country, describes her own Turkish dress:

> I beleive you would be of my Opinion that 'tis admirably becoming. . . .
> The first peice of my dresse is a pair of drawers, very full, that reach to my shoes and conceal the legs more modestly than your Petticoats. They are of a thin rose colour damask brocaded with silver flowers, my shoes of white kid Leather embroidier'd with Gold. Over this hangs my Smock of a fine white silk Gause edg'd with Embroidiery. This smock has wide sleeves hanging halfe way down the Arm and is clos'd at the Neck with a diamond button, but the shape and colour of the bosom very well to be distinguish'd through it. The Antery is a wastcoat made close to the shape, of white and Gold Damask, with very long sleeves falling back and fringed with deep Gold fringe, and should have Diamond or pearl Buttons. My Caftan of the same stuff with my Drawers is a robe exactly fited to my shape and reaching to my feet, with very long strait falling sleeves. Over this is the Girdle of about 4 fingers broad, which all that can afford have entirely of Diamonds or other precious stones. . . . The Curdee is a loose Robe they throw off or put on according to the Weather, being of a rich Brocade (mine is green and Gold) either lin'd with Ermine or Sables. [326]

Backscheider, *Ambition and Innovation*, 187 and 197, and other critics have suggested that Roxana's Turkish dress somehow signals her immorality, but I see no evidence of this implication. Surely Lady Mary's fascination with and pleasure in her exotic outfit, seemingly quite similar to Roxana's responses, do not have anything sinister about them. We might note that the respectable Lady Mary twice sat for portraits in her Turkish dress. Halsband, *The Life of Lady Mary Wortley Montagu* (New York: Oxford Univ. Press, 1960), tells us that Alexander Pope commissioned one of the paintings, which hung in his "best room fronting the Thames . . . for the rest of his life," and Lady Mary herself ordered a full-length portrait in her Turkish dress. Further, Halsband remarks that "Her fame was fortified by the publication of a print showing her wearing a Turkish dress and holding a book. [It was] entitled 'Lady M-y W-r-t-l-y M-nt-g-e The Female Traveller'" (98-100).

26. Blewett, p. 387, note 69, explains that "In order to insure against loss of the bill of exchange in the mail, the drawer of the bill provided several copies (known as a 'set'), payment of any one of which cancelled the others."

27. Rogers, 8-9.

28. Shinagel, 186. Blewitt notes that Roxana talks about investment returns of "no less than 6 *l.* per Cent" and remarks that "the usual rate of interest at this time, 5 per cent, was what Defoe considered fair." He concludes from this that "Clayton's various investment schemes were probably not meant to sound either admirable or honest" (p. 393, note 180). Novak, *Economics*, 131-32, also suggests that Clayton is meant to be a negative figure. But since Defoe goes into so much detail in these investment passages, with no indication in the text that the strategies presented are anything but reliable, it seems to me that on this issue Shinagel makes the more convincing case.

29. Shinagel, 186-87; see also Maximillian E. Novak, *Realism, Myth and History in Defoe's Fiction* (Lincoln and London: Univ. of Nebraska Press, 1983), 106. Both Percy G. Adams, *Travel Literature and the Evolution of the Novel* (Lexington: Univ. Press of Kentucky, 1983), and Paul Hunter, *Before Novels: The Cultural Contexts of Eighteenth-Century Fiction* (New York: Norton, 1990), emphasize that contemporary readers enjoyed and expected the didactic parts of the writing. Adams convincingly argues that the mix of "fiction" and "fact" found in early novels, and especially in the novels of Defoe, is a function of the novel's development from the very popular literature of travel; it was travel literature's habit, on any number of pretexts, to mix proportions of fiction and fact. See Adams's third chapter, "The Truth-Lie Dichotomy," especially pp. 93ff. Hunter finds that modern readers have trouble with the didactic parts of texts because our tastes are different from those of earlier readers: "historical evidence suggests that many real eighteenth-century readers seem actually to have enjoyed the tones and intentions of the texts their culture characteristically produced, even though to take such a pleasure in being told what to do— sometimes even in being harangued or harassed to do it—bears no relationship to any idea of pleasure that we in our time honor" (227).

30. Compare, for example, this passage from Henry Brooke's *The Fool of Quality* (London: Edward Johnson, 1776), I, 99-102.

I am sensible that the gentlemen of large landed properties are apt to look upon themselves as the pillars of the state, and to consider their interests and the interest of the nation, as very little beholden to or dependent on trade; tho' the fact is, that those very gentlemen would lose nine parts in ten of their returns, and the nation nine tenths of her yearly revenues, if industry and the arts (promoted as I said by commerce) did not raise the products of lands to tenfold their natural value. The manufacturer, on the other hand, depends on the landed interests for nothing save the materials of his craft; and the merchant is wholly independent of all lands, or, rather, he is the general patron thereof. I must further observe . . . that this beneficent profession is by no means confined to individuals. . . . Large societies of men, nay, mighty nations, may and have been merchants. When societies incorporate for such a worthy purpose, they are formed as a foetus within the womb of the mother, a constitution within the general state or constitution; their particular laws and regulations ought, always, to be conformable to those of the national system, and, in that case, such corporations greatly conduce to the peace and good order of cities and large towns, and to the general power and prosperity of the nation. . . . Avarice . . . may pile; robbery may plunder; new mines may be opened . . . conquerors may win kingdoms; but all such means of acquiring riches are transient and determinable; while industry and commerce are the natural, the living, the never-failing fountain, from whence the wealth of this world can alone be taught to flow.

And *The Fool of Quality* is a children's book!

31. Thus Novak says that in the ending of the book Roxana's success "is offset by her final misery" (100); Sutherland talks of *Roxana* having "got out of hand" (206), and Shinagel says that "the story by this time is no longer controlled by Defoe . . . he cannot even bring himself to finish the novel satisfactorily" (192).

32. Shinagel finds that these scenes with Roxana, Amy, and the landlord "suggest, in short, that Defoe no longer was able to control his imagination" (194); Novak notes that Roxana's pairing of Amy and the landlord makes Roxana "the only protagonist in Defoe's fiction who intentionally forces evil on another character" (105). Both of these observations are just: Roxana's actions here are inexcusable, and, in the context of the book as a whole, inexplicable—that is, they do not fit into a coherent scheme of the novel. Defoe seems to have toyed with sensationalizing his novel, but except for these scenes did not in fact continue this line. This also would explain why he leaves unclear Roxana's involvement with the *possible* murder of her daughter; obviously, if Roxana were to be actively or actually involved with such a murder, the sensational aspects of the book would be far more prominent. Sutherland notes (209) that Defoe separates Roxana from the death of her daughter. Hunter's discussion of "the novel's engagement with taboos" is useful in this context. He notes that

from the beginning the novel involved itself with forbidden, repressed, or secret arenas of human activity, as well as those private recesses of the human mind, will, and appetite that produce them. . . . The novel implicitly claims that we do not have to move beyond the annals of ordinary existence to discover events that are strange and conduct that is 'irrational,' unlikely, or weird. In the familiar world of ordinary people, the novel claims, there is plenty. Taking advantage of its commitment to novelty means for the novel not a flight into enchantment or romance, but rather an admission that human nature involves more variety than classical and neoclassical theorists had admitted. The individual, the eccentric, the bizarre, and even the unique all have a place in novels almost by definition, yet the early novel concentrates not on true extremes . . . but rather on people who slip beyond the norm and test the social fabric. Here are murderers, thieves, rapists, those who commit incest, and those who father bastards or malidentified offspring; and here are victims who receive the violence or are drawn into disruptive or confused behavior of their own. But even when acts are horrible or characters heinous, the novel finds ways to comprehend them without violating our sense that we are reading about recognizable people in a world we know. [35-37]

33. This is a significant amount of money; remember that when Roxana arranges with her husband to keep their estates separate, she insists that he take the interest on her money—£2000—to use for all their annual household expenses.

34. Richetti, *Daniel Defoe*, 86, remarks in the context of his discussion of *Colonel Jack* that "For many modern readers of Defoe what does ring true is the inconsistent and thereby authentic personality of the storyteller, whose confusion about the causes of behavior is part of the truth the narrative delivers." This is surely true about Roxana. When the character is confused about the causes of his or her behavior, the critic may be tempted to impose an order on the text, but in such cases the order is just not there. Thus Roxana can be right at times, as in her discussions about woman and the "money in her own hand," and very wrong at others.

## Chapter 3. Samuel Richardson: *Clarissa*

1. Jerry Beasley, in *Novels of the 1740s* (Athens: Univ. of Georgia Press, 1982) provides the most intensive reading of *Clarissa* as Christian narrative, subtitling his chapter on Richardson's novels "Pamela *and* Clarissa: *Fiction as Devotional Literature.*" For Beasley, *Clarissa* "is finally about the heroine's spiritual life" (151). Beasley finds that "*Clarissa* looks hard at the world, refuses to allegorize it as susceptible to goodness, and finds it finally depraved almost beyond redemption. . . . In a world largely defined by the character of Lovelace, the only safe place for the goodness of a Clarissa is heaven itself, where she goes to meet her bridegroom, Christ, in a union signifying the beginning of eternal and unthreatened bliss" (148). Margaret Anne Doody insists that "it is important to understand Richardson as a Christian artist, his emphasis upon spiritual life a Christian theme. For Richardson, the love of God is a natural passion" (*A Natural Passion: A Study of the Novels of Samuel Richardson* [Oxford: Clarendon, 1974], 153). Carol Houlihan Flynn's *Samuel Richardson: A Man of Letters* (Princeton: Princeton Univ. Press, 1982) also at least in part sees the novel in the tradition of Christian allegory; see pages 21ff.

2. R.F. Brissenden in *Virtue in Distress: Studies in the Novel of Sentiment from Richardson to Sade* (New York: Harper and Row, 1974), 161, remarks that "*Clarissa*, however, is not an allegory, an eighteenth-century morality play. It is a novel," as if the point must be emphasized.

3. Samuel Richardson, *Clarissa, or the History of a Young Lady* (New York: Penguin, 1985), 41. All further references to the novel are to this edition.

4. The same effect of course can be accomplished by marrying Solmes—thus withdrawing herself from the equation.

5. Brissendon, 164, notes that "Richardson had originally intended to call the novel *The Lady's Legacy*. The root of the trouble in the Harlowe family is the decision by Clarissa's grandfather to bestow the bulk of his estate on her, rather than on his son . . . or his grandson." He discusses (164-65) the financial thinking of Clarissa's family, pointing to "the complicated game of social-climbing chess played by [its] ambitious members." Janet Todd, in *Women's Friendship in Literature* (New York: Columbia Univ. Press, 1980), points to Clarissa as representing "the middle class against an unfamilial and libertine nobility" and notes "the conflicting demands of a bourgeois femaleness in the novel" (306).

6. Rachel Brownstein, "An Examplar to Her Sex: Richardson's Clarissa," *Yale Review* 67 (1977), discusses the house imagery in *Clarissa* at length; see particularly pages 30-31. One interesting connection she makes is between eighteenth-century houses and clothing, both, as she notes, "formidable enclosures."

7. Todd, 65, finds that "Money, the male instrument, cannot bring peace or legitimate power to a woman" in *Clarissa*. For Defoe, as my previous chapter shows, money is not a "male instrument."

8. *The Rape of Clarissa* (Minneapolis: Univ. of Minnesota Press, 1982), 16.

9. Terry Castle's observation on this subject is wonderful: "It does not occur to [Richardson], obviously, that a female reader—even a moderately pious one—might not necessarily take an unalloyed pleasure in seeing one of her sex made over into a decomposing emblem of martyred Christian womanhood, or respond wholly favorably to that equation between sexual violation and death which he seems unconsciously to have accepted as a given" (*Clarissa's Ciphers: Meaning and Disruption in Richardson's "Clarissa"* [Ithaca: Cornell Univ. Press, 1982], 173).

10. Todd's discussion of *Clarissa* in *Women's Friendship in Literature* is particularly valuable to students of the novel; note also Katharine Rogers's perceptive comments in *Feminism in Eighteenth-Century England* (Urbana: Univ. of Illinois Press, 1982). Rogers finds that Richardson's respect for female friendship is linked to his respect for female intelligence: "Richardson demonstrated his confidence in women's capacity for friendship and in the quality of their minds. The noble friendship in *Clarissa* is that of the women, not the men; Part II of *Pamela* and all of *Sir Charles Grandison* are filled with similar friendships between women attracted by each other's minds and uninfluenced by sexual jealousy. The friendship between Clarissa and Anna is the most significant and satisfying relationship in their lives. Anna admires Clarissa without envy and illustrates in her friend's troubles the reckless generosity that Lovelace restricted to the 'nobler Sex.' Disproving his sneer, she is ready for Clarissa's sake to jeopardize her all-important reputation, by going to London with her disgraced friend" (129-30).

11. Brissenden, 163, observes that Richardson states this focus clearly: "Richardson argues in his *Postscript*" that the altercations between Clarissa and her family " 'are the Foundation of the whole.' "

12. One of the most cogent discussions of the legal status of women in the eighteenth century remains Erna Reiss's *Rights and Duties of Englishwomen: A Study of Law and Public Opinion* (Manchester: Sherratt & Hughes, 1934). I recommend all of her first chapter, and especially pp. 20ff with regard to "Woman as Owner of Property." A more easily available study of women's property rights is Susan Okin's excellent article "Patriarchy and Married Women's Property in England: Questions on Some Current Views" *ECS* 17 (1983-84): 121-38. The most recent examination of these issues, although at some points perhaps too technical to be useful to most readers, is Susan Staves's *Married Women's Separate Property in England, 1660-1833* (Cambridge, Mass.: Harvard Univ. Press, 1990).

13. Reiss, 20.

14. J. Paul Hunter has recently argued (" Some Notes on Readers and the Beginnings of the English Novel" in *Anticipations of the Enlightenment in England, France, and Germany* [Philadelphia: Univ. of Pennsylvania Press, 1987]) that the "rising middle class" paradigm for the novel is a partially false one. "Like many clichés, the statement that the novel is a middle-class form developed for middle-class readers is partly true, but enormously misleading" (261). Hunter emphasizes the youthfulness of the novel's readers, rather than their financial status; for these readers, the novel becomes a kind of how-to manual for living and doing well in society. This refinement on the model underscores the conduct manual intention of a novel such as *Clarissa.*

15. Brownstein, 33, tells us that Richardson wrote to his own family members although they were living in the same house.

16. Brownstein finds that "Clarissa's clothing is her armor. . . . Clothing gives Clarissa actual power as well as the useful illusion of it." Lovelace can reduce Clarissa to tears when he catches her unclothed; "when formally clothed, she rebukes her tormentor with dignity." Brownstein also reminds us that Clarissa's clothes "are extraordinarily expensive for a middle-class young girl living quietly in the country" (32).

17. Doody analyzes at some length critical discussions of " 'prurience,' pornography, and sadism" in *Clarissa,* only to dismiss all such insights as, at most, "discomfort . . . felt more by male than female critics" (" Popular Narrative," 94). But these currents in the novel cannot be dismissed; there is indeed a stream of prurience in *Clarissa* that is bound up inextricably with Richardson's presentation of Clarissa's character.

18. Flynn notes that "Lovelace . . . recognizes the revenge mixed with Clarissa's forgiveness," and, about Clarissa's revenge on her parents, Flynn suggests that "In her death, Clarissa lives out the child's fantasy of revenge through suicide, the fantasy of the grieving parents mourning the child they have mistreated" (44).

19. Fanny Burney's *Evelina* and most of Austen's novels, to name just some of the more obvious examples, center around the awkward problems caused by class mobility.

20. *The Fool of Quality; or, the History of Henry Earl of Moreland,* vol. I (London: Edward Johnson, 1776), 176.

21. Richard B. Schwartz in *Daily Life in Johnson's London* (Madison: Univ. of

Wisconsin Press, 1983) provides some convincing suggestions about modern equivalents for the value of goods in the eighteenth century. See especially pp. 44-54.

22. Mrs. Harlowe has been the object of much critical attention. Doody says that some of the scenes between Clarissa and her mother are "perverse . . . as the mother loves and betrays and tries to blackmail her daughter" (*Popular Narrative*, 94-95). In *A Natural Passion* Doody analyzes in detail the character of Mrs. Harlowe, finding her "a likeable character of good but weak intentions . . . who has no real will of her own" (102-3). Brissenden finds her much more obviously evil: "Whether Richardson realizes it or not, Mrs. Sinclair is really Mrs. Harlowe in another form—the nightmare vision of the mother figure (significantly she becomes *physically* more brutal, repulsive and frightening as the book goes on). Mrs Harlowe, by conniving at the scheme to sell her daughter to Solmes, exhibits the morality of a whore-monger" (81). But Brownstein's analysis is, I think, the most interesting: "One of Clarissa's more fascinating relationships is with her mother: she is determined to be different from her mother and afraid she is like her. Mrs. Harlowe, as Clarissa sees her, has been bludgeoned by a tyrannical husband into becoming a tyrant herself; by nonresistance to evil, she has done evil, in a sense more than her husband has, because her collusion in the pressures on her daughter hurts Clarissa more than anyone else's. Clarissa has expected her father to behave like a tyrant; of her mother she expected more, and in her mother she is therefore more disappointed" (53).

23. This complaint, that sons learn to be tyrants from their fathers and then exert their power over the females in the household, especially over their sisters, is made throughout the century. Wollstonecraft presents precisely this pattern in Maria's story in *Maria or The Wrongs of Woman*.

24. There is of course the view emphasized by many critics that Clarissa has a strong impulse of heterosexual sensuality that she represses (Brownstein, 35) and that Lovelace "provokes" (Flynn, 91). This view assumes that Clarissa cannot recognize her own feelings and that the reader must understand Clarissa's motivations even though they are not made explicit in the text. But since everything else in the novel is so explicit—is stated and reiterated—I find such a method of reading this particular novel less than convincing. Clarissa has no problem expressing her feelings about anyone other than Lovelace, after all. I agree, then, with Katharine Rogers: "Clarissa longs to settle in a single life, in which she could 'defy the [male] Sex'" (132).

25. See also p. 155. Uncle Antony tells Clarissa "I know that you may love him if you will. I had a good mind to bid you hate him; then, perhaps, you'd like him the better: for I have always found a most horrid romantic perverseness in your sex. To *do* and to *love* what you should not, is meat, drink, and vesture to you all."

26. Thus Belford reports to Lovelace about the image worn at Clarissa's breast: "She has just now given from her bosom, where she always wore it, a miniature picture set in gold of Miss Howe" (1357).

27. Brownstein, 38, reminds us that *Clarissa* is "at the beginning of a long tradition of English novels about love between ladies and gentlemen

who do not work." The argument could be made that the female life Richardson chronicles with such approbation would be the norm for virtuous girls of certain classes. There are two points to be made here. One, even if the young woman portrayed does not see the emptiness of such an existence, a reader can be dismayed that the author himself presents such "days" as fully worthwhile; the second, related point is that, as more and more recent research has been showing, women indeed were doing more with their time than the Clarissa model suggests. See for example Marilyn L. Williamson's *Raising Their Voices: British Women Writers, 1650-1750* (Detroit: Wayne State Univ. Press, 1990).

28. Doody in *A Natural Passion,* 171, suggests a "galloping consumption" and concedes that Clarissa's illness "is certainly a trifle mysterious." Flynn notes that "[a]fter nineteen years of excellent health, hardy Clarissa sickens and dies. We never learn the nature of her illness, only its unavoidable fatality. Clarissa continually makes sure that she cannot be accused of suicide, [but her protestations are unconvincing]. Clarissa seeks death not only to please her family but to please herself, to escape from the demands of life" (39). Flynn's discussion of Clarissa's death provides a lucid analysis of Richardson's death scenes; rather than avoiding the issue of how Clarissa manages to die, Flynn unambiguously calls Clarissa's death a suicide (41).

29. "I knew I was right, said the doctor. A love case, Mr. Goddard! A love case, Mr Belford! There is one person in the world who can do her more service than all the faculty.

Mr Goddard said he had apprehended her disorder was in her mind; and had treated her accordingly" (1081-82).

See also p. 1127: "Her apothecary came in. He advised her to the air . . . and he gave it as the doctor's opinion, as well as his own, that she would recover if she herself desired to recover, and would use the means."

30. Although attempts have been made to separate *Clarissa* from the long line of Compromised Virgin novels, *Clarissa* clearly is part of this tradition. In a novel that has a tragic denouement, the girl's decision to leave home without her parents' consent usually leads irrevocably to her demise. That is, the act of running away, stepping into a coach, signals her fall. Other, less subtle renderings of this pattern make the relationship between leaving "home" and being instantly "lost" explicit. For example, in Susanah Rowson's *Charlotte Temple* (New Haven: College and Univ. Press, 1964), 82, young Charlotte ventures out of her boarding school to meet her lover, Montraville, who convinces her to run away with him. Her loss of consciousness represents her destruction.

> "Alas! my torn heart!" said Charlotte, "how shall I act?"
> "Let me direct you," said Montraville, lifting her into the chaise.
> "Oh! my dear, forsaken parents!" cried Charlotte.
> The chaise drove off. She shrieked, and fainted into the arms of her betrayer.

Chapter 4. Henry Fielding: *Tom Jones* and *Amelia*

1. Martin Battestin, "General Introduction," Henry Fielding's *Amelia* (Middletown, Conn. : Wesleyan Univ. Press, 1983), xi. All further references are to this edition.

2. John Richetti's essay on "Voice and Gender in Eighteenth-Century Fiction: Haywood to Burney," *Studies in the Novel* 19:3 (Fall 1987) examines a number of issues relating to limitations on the female voice in the eighteenth-century novel; his observations on Fielding are particularly apt. See especially pp. 264ff.

3. Henry Fielding. *The History of Tom Jones*, ed. Martin Battestin, two vol. (Oxford: Wesleyan Univ. Press, 1975), I, 40. All further references are to this edition.

4. In *The Brink of All We Hate: English Satires on Women, 1660-1750* (Lexington: Univ. Press of Kentucky, 1984), Felicity Nussbaum defines five categories of stereotype in Restoration and eighteenth-century drama and poetry: "the most compelling of the myths [are] the permissive female or whore, the powerful Amazon, [and] the angel" (4). Although she does not deal with novels, her argument is largely applicable to Fielding.

5. Claude Rawson, in *Henry Fielding and the Augustan Ideal Under Stress* (London: Routledge and Kegan Paul, 1972), finds much significance in the portrait of Blear-eyed Moll, seeing in it basically a "charged formulaic interplay between startling incongruity and the order it subverts" (80-81). He reminds us that this "type of grotesque portrait is an old one, looking back to many hags and bawds in Martial and Juvenal, in medieval allegorists and in Ben Jonson" (80).

6. Henry Fielding, *Joseph Andrews*, ed. Martin Battestin (Middletown, Conn.: Wesleyan Univ. Press, 1967), 32. All further references are to this edition.

7. Janet Todd's discussion of the "bleak picture of female relationships in [Fielding's] fiction" is excellent. See particularly pages 332ff. of *Women's Friendship in Literature* (New York: Columbia Univ. Press, 1980).

8. Todd, 333, notes of this passage that "the lengthy list of [Miss Mathews'] forbears—Dalila, Jezebel, and the like—leaves no doubt that Fielding is presenting his female monster, and it does not surprise when the woman emerges powerful, sexual, and predatory."

9. Henry Fielding, "Preface," *The Adventures of David Simple* by Sarah Fielding (New York: Garland, 1974), iv.

10. Lawrence Stone, *The Family, Sex and Marriage in England 1500-1800* (New York: Harper and Row, 1977), 656.

11. Robert Alter, *Fielding and the Nature of the Novel* (Cambridge: Harvard Univ. Press, 1968), 141.

12. Trent's pandering of his wife to his Lordship in return for "a good round Sum" (*A*, 471) sufficient to set them both up in grand style defines not only the debasement of marriage but also the corruption Fielding talks about in so many contexts with regard to the upper classes. George Sherburn's two seminal essays on Fielding, "Fielding's *Amelia*: An Interpretation," *ELH* 3

(1936), and "Fielding's Social Outlook," *Philological Quarterly* 35:1 (1956), both talk about Fielding's concerns with aristocratic corruption; see also my *Social Protest in the Eighteenth-Century English Novel* (Columbus: Ohio State Univ. Press, 1985), 26ff.

13. Mrs. Atkinson was Mrs. Bennet before she married the sergeant. Her earlier history includes managing to become "polluted" by a wretch whom she allowed to seduce her even though she was happily married; she then "pollutes" her husband, who turns against her in horror and soon dies. She is also a learned lady; it is significant that Fielding chooses to give Mrs. Atkinson, the only woman in the novel with any claim to learning, this background!

14. "Preface," to *David Simple*, vii and viii.

15. "Preface" to *David Simple*, viii. Richetti, in "Voice and Gender," notes of Fielding's comments in this preface that "Such masculine praise is implicitly, traditionally condescending. . . . What Sarah Fielding lacks and what she compensates for by the force of her natural genius is quite simply everything normally required of a writer: art, learning, and experience. . . . It is worth noting that a few years later in *Tom Jones* Fielding describes learning and 'conversation' (worldly experience 'with all ranks and degrees of men') as essential supplements to the 'genius' required of the 'historian.' In effect, Fielding places his sister's novel within the secondary categories of women's writing: it is a 'romance' and is therefore not to be judged by the highest literary standards; it is a book whose minor stylistic deficiencies (visible only to discerning male judges) do not detract from its profoundly insightful but essentially instinctive or at least relatively untutored nature" (264).

16. On the subject of women and learning, Felicity Nussbaum notes that "when women look like men or act like men, it 'unsexes the ladies,' a phrase often applied to women who sought education in Restoration or eighteenth-century England. . . . Capable of corrupting other women with her ideas, the learned lady becomes a pervasive metaphor for the unnatural woman who refuses to perform the natural functions of her sex and who actively usurps the functions of the male sex" (43).

17. Hassall notes that Fielding manages to "filter . . . off the bathos which threatens [the] description [of Sophia], and leaves the unpretentious and charming excellence of Sophia entire. She is thus lifted to a plane above the comic world of the rest of the novel (19-20).

18. Richard Dircks talks of Sophia's "instinctive" understanding of life (*Henry Fielding* [Boston: Twayne, 1983], 88); although the point he is making is rather different from mine, I think his phrase points up what I mean, for I would use the word instinctive here as opposed to learned.

19. See, for example, John Middleton Murry "In Defence of Fielding," in *Unprofessional Essays* (London: Jonathan Cape, 1956), 38; reprinted as "Fielding's 'Sexual Ethic' in *Tom Jones*" in *Fielding: A Collection of Critical Essays*, ed. Ronald Paulson (Englewood Cliffs, N.J.: Prentice Hall, 1962), 97; J. Paul Hunter, *Occasional Form: Henry Fielding and the Chains of Circumstance* (Baltimore: Johns Hopkins Univ. Press, 1975), 169; Anthony J. Hassall, *Henry*

*Fielding's Tom Jones* (Sydney: Sydney Univ. Press, 1979), 18; Jerry Beasley, *Novels of the 1740s* (Athens: Univ. of Georgia Press, 1982), 199.

20. Dircks notes that "Fielding's characterization of women often lacks sharp definition, and, unlike his portraits of men, his sense of female life seldom penetrates beyond the surface of their actions. Often, they seem to exist merely as foils to the evolution of the characters of the men with whom they interact in the fable." His discussion of women in the novels of Fielding is most perceptive; see pages 115ff.

21. William Empson, in an amazingly insensitive comment on this passage, notes merely that "Fielding disapproved of women who argue, [and] indeed makes Allworthy praise Sophia for never doing it." *"Tom Jones," The Kenyon Review* 20 (Spring 1958): 236. Reprinted in *Fielding: A Collection of Critical Essays* (Englewood Cliffs: Prentice Hall, 1962), 136.

22. Walter Allen in *The English Novel: A Short Critical History* (New York: Dutton, 1954), comments that "Fielding, it has become a cliché of criticism, was a 'man's man,' and his heroines are the women of a man's man. Sophia Western is scarcely likely to satisfy a feminist." This remark, unusually perceptive for a critic writing in the 1950s, is then undercut by the more usual praise for Sophia herself. "But she is anything but a doll, and her behavior shows that she is neither stupid nor passive; reading of her, we are convinced equally of her beauty, her goodness, and her generosity of spirit. . . . The mainspring of her life, unless conscience is outraged, is a gracious obedience" (58-59).

23. Todd, 333.

24. Patricia Meyer Spacks, "Female Changelessness; or, What Do Women Want?" *Studies In The Novel* 19:3 (Fall 1987): 280.

25. Claude Rawson, *Henry Fielding and the Augustan Ideal Under Stress* (London: Routledge and Kegan Paul, 1972), 96-97.

26. Nussbaum, 4-5. Nussbaum points out that Addison's *Spectator* 15 (17 March 1711)

> reflects the expectations of the age: *"Aurelia,* tho' a Woman of Great Quality, delights in the Privacy of a Country Life, and passes away a great part of her Time in her Own Walks and Gardens. Her Husband, who is her Bosom Friend, and Companion in her Solitudes, has been in Love with her ever since he knew her. They both abound with good Sense, consummate Virtue, and a mutual esteem; and are a perpetual Entertainment to one another. Their Family is under so regular an Oeconomy, in its Hours of Devotion and Repast, Employment and Diversion, that it looks like a little Common-Wealth within it self."

27. Nussbaum, 5.

28. Henry Fielding. *The Life of Mr. Jonathan Wild the Great* (London: A. Millar, 1754), 262-63.

Chapter 5. The Male Radical Novelists: Thomas Holcroft: *Anna St. Ives*; William
Godwin: *Caleb Williams*; Robert Bage: *Hermsprong*

1. J.M.S. Tompkins in *The Popular Novel in England 1770-1800* (Lincoln:
Univ. of Nebraska Press, 1961; orig. pub. 1932), 301-2, comments with charm
and insight about *Anna St. Ives* that it "is by no means a good book; . . . yet
there is a peculiar sweetness in it. Holcroft's young people take up poses of
angular heroism . . . and hold them in the face of ridicule and danger; at the
end of the book we are still far from the millenium, but two or three crusted
Tories have been shaken in their prejudices, and a brilliant, selfish young man
has begun to think. It is a white book and not entirely silly."
2. Thomas Holcroft, *Anna St. Ives* (London: Oxford Univ. Press, 1970),
464. All further references are to this edition.
3. Allene Gregory in *The French Revolution and the English Novel* (New
York: G.P. Putnam's Sons, 1915), 70, comments "Anna's social idealism is
heaven-high above the prudence of Clarissa as a controlling virtue. Moreover,
Anna and Frank are much less enhaloed by the author than their prototypes in
Richardson." Gregory's classic study remains one of the best accounts of the
novel in this period.
4. Anna's comment about marrying sounds a little like Clarissa in the
reluctance it suggests, but the similarity is misleading, for Anna really does like
men and very much loves Frank. Except for her hesitation about her duty to
society, she does want to marry him.
5. In the *Memoirs of the Late Thomas Holcroft* (London: Longman, Hurst,
etc., 1816) William Hazlitt quotes from a letter to a friend written by Holcroft in
February, 1790: " 'The great object I have in view, is not the obtaining of riches,
but the power of employing my time according to the bent of my genius, in the
performance of some works which shall remain when I am no more—works
that will promote the general good. This is a purpose I have so strongly at
heart, that I would with pleasure sacrifice ease, peace, health, and life for its
accomplishment. . . . It has been my pursuit for years, and you are my witness, I have never relaxed, never been discouraged by disappointment, to
which indeed I hold men of real strength to be superior.' " Hazlitt goes on to
comment, "A clearer picture cannot be given of the motives from which the
writer appears to have engaged in and prosecuted his task—the regard of good
men hereafter, and a wish to promote the general welfare of mankind, by
diffusing a system of more just and enlightened principles of action" (II, 103-4).
Hazlitt notes admiringly that Holcroft "believed that truth had a natural
superiority over error, if it could only be heard; that if once discovered, it must,
being left to itself, soon spread and triumph; and that the art of printing would
not only accelerate this effect, but would prevent those accidents, which had
rendered the moral and intellectual progress of mankind hitherto so slow,
irregular, and uncertain" (II, 122-23). Holcroft maintained this viewpoint even
after the turbulent political events of the mid-nineties: in his diary entry for
November 14, 1798, he recounts a recent conversation. Someone had asked
him "if the universal defection had not made me turn aristocrat. I answered,
that I supposed my principles to be founded in truth, that is, in experience and

fact: that I continued to believe in the perfectibility of man, which the blunders and passions of ignorance might apparently delay, but could not prevent; and that the only change of opinion I had undergone was, that political revolutions are not so well calculated to better man's condition, as during a certain period I, with almost all the thinking men in Europe, had been led to suppose" (III, 64-65). Hazlitt's detailed and sympathetic analysis of *Anna St. Ives* (II, 106-33) is well worth reading.

6. Holcroft, to his credit, does not at the end of the novel change Frank's rank or parentage; Frank remains the son of a steward, while Anna of course remains an aristocrat. In *Hermsprong,* however, Bage only pretends that his lovers are not of the same rank: Hermsprong as the rightful heir to Lord Grondale's estate is a fitting partner for Caroline.

7. Gregory remarks that "We who criticize Holcroft's heroes for their tendency to preach need not plume ourselves upon any special discernment; Holcroft was perfectly capable of criticizing himself with greater discernment than his opponents have ever shown. Godwin, having neither imagination nor humour, caricatures his own theories unconsciously. Holcroft had both, and some knowledge of the world to boot. His faith in the ultimate triumph of social idealism was so deep and serene that he could afford to laugh at the well-meaning tiresomeness of himself and his fellow idealists," as he does, Gregory suggests, in Coke Clifton's letters describing the grand speeches of Anna and Frank (64-65).

8. In Godwin's next novel, *Fleetwood,* the blameless Mary is driven from her home by the increasingly insane Fleetwood; although Mary has done nothing to deserve Fleetwood's suspicion that she is deceiving him, he indulges his fantasy and destroys his family. In *Mandeville,* again, the exemplary Henrietta is hounded by her mad brother Mandeville, who cannot bear the idea that she is to marry his supposed enemy Clifford. Godwin's last two novels, *Cloudesley* and *Deloraine,* similarly are peopled by exemplary women who are victimized by the damaged men around them.

9. William Godwin, *Caleb Williams* (London: Oxford Univ. Press, 1970), 38. All further references are to this edition.

10. Godwin's resistance to domestic sentiment is remarked by C. Kegan Paul in *William Godwin: His Friends and Contemporaries* (New York: AMS Press, 1970; reprinted from the edition of London: 1876): "The marriage [of Wollstonecraft and Godwin] itself took place at Old St Pancras Church on March 29th, 1797. . . . Godwin takes no notice whatever of it in his diary" (I, 234).

11. William Godwin, *St. Leon: A Tale of the Sixteenth Century* (New York: Arno, 1972; reprint edition of London: Henry Colburn and Richard Bentley, 1831), 40-41. All further references are to this edition.

12. Gregory, 100, dryly summarizes the action: "Marguerite arrives at the critical moment to wind up her husband's affairs for him while he indulges in a fit of insanity."

13. Robert Bage, *Hermsprong; or, Man as He Is Not* (Oxford: Oxford Univ. Press, 1985), 26. All further references are to this edition.

14. Harriet's "virtue" is only marginally compromised here; in other of his novels Bage's challenge to the definition of female virtue as sexual innocence is

much more explicit. Gary Kelly in *The English Jacobin Novel, 1780-1805* (Oxford: Clarendon, 1976), 40, remarks that Bage "seems, like the other English Jacobins, to have believed strongly in the equality of women," and part of that view, evident in several of Bage's novels, is a disemphasis on sexual purity. The story of Kitty Ross in *Barham Downs*, for example, shows that though a woman is seduced, she may later "earn her right to reclaim the title of virtuous woman" (42). Tompkins had earlier noted much the same thing: "Some allusion has . . . been made to Bage's fearless dealings with the virtue of his heroines. His books were full of shocks for the conventional. A girl who has been ravished becomes the happy wife of another man; militant Clarissas defend themselves with sarcastic and resolved vigour; another young woman, chaste in mind, yet determines out of gratitude to become the mistress of the man who has preserved her from death, while vivacious girls claim the right to think, talk, and even jest about sex, since it is their prime concern. . . . Critics who cried haro at this relaxation of discipline, did not always notice that it is made possible by Bage's belief in the strength of will and faculty of mental growth in women" (202-3).

15. Lord Grondale deserves no respect from Caroline; a man of low morals and no talent, as Kelly remarks, he "is a complete monster . . . associated with political corruption and tyrannical attitudes to domestic and public affairs. Caroline Campinet's intention to obey him at all costs is opposed by Miss Fluart, who controls Lord Grondale by teasing him, as Bage perhaps hoped to control oppression by his humour and satire" (47). Kelly finds that the "rather hackneyed issue [of filial duty and parental oppression] is in itself given new impetus and wider relevance by Bage, because he treats parental oppression of romantic lovers as a domestic variety of the same tyranny that led to persecution of individuals such as Wilkes at home, and the American colonists abroad" (46).

16. Mrs. Merrick and Caroline, about to be pulled over the edge of a cliff by their runaway horse, are saved by Hermsprong's fortunate presence at the scene. This accidental encounter serves to introduce the hero to the heroine, and to the reader as well.

17. Marilyn Butler, *Jane Austen and the War of Ideas* (Oxford: Clarendon, 1987), 84, notes that "The reader cannot help feeling conned when he discovers that Hermsprong, Caroline's rational choice, the man of no name, is really (in the worst manner of conventional plotting) the long-lost Sir Charles Campinet." She finds that Caroline herself in some significant areas "adopts the approved stance of the eighteenth-century heroine," and saves her highest praise for Maria: "What Maria Fluart does that her friend the conventional heroine does not do is to speak her mind with freedom. The reader comes to look for and to value a style in conversation which reveals liberty of mind. Hermsprong and Maria Fluart have the manner to perfection" (82-83).

Chapter 6. The Female Radical Novelists: Elizabeth Inchbald: *Nature and Art*;
Mary Wollstonecraft: *Maria or the Wrongs of Woman*

1. Some recent feminist criticism has distorted the picture by suggesting
that *Nature and Art* is solely about the seduction and subsequent destruction of
the young girl Hannah (Jane Spencer, *The Rise of the Woman Novelist* [Oxford:
Basil Blackwell, 1986], 130). But Hannah's story is only one of many subplots in
the novel.

2. Elizabeth Inchbald, *Nature and Art*, 2 vol. (London: G.G. and J. Robinson, 1797), I, 26-29. All further references are to this edition.

3. Jane Austen, *Emma*, ed. R.W. Chapman (London: Oxford Univ.
Press, 1926), 461.

4. Mary Wollstonecraft, *Maria or The Wrongs of Woman* (New York: Norton, 1975), 24. All further references are to this edition.

5. C. Kegan Paul in *William Godwin: His Friends and Contemporaries* (New
York: AMS Press, 1970; reprinted from the edition of 1876, London) notes the
similarities between Maria's story and the real-life situation of Mary
Wollstonecraft's sister Eliza. "Eliza Wollstonecraft had married a Mr Bishop,
but the marriage had proved from the first an unhappy one. It is more than
probable there were faults on both sides. All the Wollstonecraft sisters were
enthusiastic, excitable, and hasty-tempered, apt to exaggerate trifles, sensitive
to magnify inattention into slights, and slights into studied insults. All had bad
health of a kind which is especially trying to the nerves, and Eliza had in excess
the family temperament and constitution. . . . Yet with all this there can be no
doubt that Bishop was a man of furious violence, and from the letters which
remain it would seem that many of the painful scenes in Mary's unfinished
novel, 'The Wrongs of Woman,' are simple transcriptions of what she had
known or even witnessed in her sister's married life" (I, 164).

6. The parallels with Falkland's hounding of Caleb from place to place as
Caleb attempts to escape from his former master are pronounced. Gary Kelly
notes the close relationship between *Maria* and *Caleb Williams*, especially in
terms of form: "Godwin's novel provided her with a pattern for the *exposé* of
legal oppression and 'the modes of domestic and unrecorded despotism.'"
"Introduction," *Mary, A Fiction and The Wrongs of Woman* (London: Oxford
Univ. Press, 1976), xvi-xvii.

7. For discussion of the husband's legal right to restrict the physical
liberty of his wife see Erna Reiss, *Rights and Duties of Englishwomen: A Study in
Law and Public Opinion* (Manchester, England: Sherratt and Hughes, 1934), 7,
38, and 45.

8. Inchbald here is talking about men and employment; later, with
Hannah, she makes the same point about women. She is more impartial on this
point than Wollstonecraft, seeing the lack of even marginal employment as a
social problem rather than a problem of discrimination by gender.

9. Samuel Johnson's famous review of *A Free Inquiry* answers Jenyns's
argument with passionate logic. He compares the relative insensitivity of the
poor to the "vexations" of the rich to the anguish of a "malefactor who ceases to
feel the cords that bind him when the pincers are tearing his flesh." I discuss

Inchbald's strange turn at the end of *Nature and Art* more fully in *Social Protest in the Eighteenth-Century English Novel* (Columbus: Ohio State Univ. Press, 1985), 195-201; Johnson's review is most readily available in Richard B. Schwartz's *Samuel Johnson and the Problem of Evil* (Madison: Univ. of Wisconsin Press, 1975).

10. The scandal of public institutions which are run for private profit—and the obvious conflict of interest that this arrangement ensures—is a topic of frequent complaint not only in Wollstonecraft's circle but also earlier in the century. John Gay in *The Beggar's Opera*, Henry Fielding in *Amelia*, and Godwin in *Caleb Williams* all detail the corruptions of a penal system run along these lines of private gain.

11. Forty pounds seems quite a good wage for such a position. In July of 1787 Wollstonecraft reports to George Blood that she has been offered a post as governess: "Forty pounds a year was the terms mentioned to me, and half of that sum I could spare to discharge my debts, and afterwards to assist Eliza" (Kegan Paul, I, 183-14). Earlier (January, 1784), she had noted that she and her sister "With economy . . . can live on a guinea a week, and that we can with ease earn" (Kegan Paul, I, 171). Wollstonecraft's struggle to support not only herself but her sister continued for years. By November of 1788 she has found a more amenable way to make a living than selling herself as governess: "Mr Johnson, whose uncommon kindness, I believe, has saved me from despair and vexation . . . assures me that if I exert my talents in writing I may support myself in a comfortable way. I am then going to be the first of a new genus; I tremble at the attempt, yet if I fail *I* only suffer, and should I succeed my dear girls [Eliza and Everina] will ever in sickness have a home, and a refuge, where for a few months in the year they may forget the cares that disturb the rest" (Kegan Paul, I, 191-92). In *The Wrongs of Woman*, one of Maria's primary reasons for marrying, of course, is to provide a refuge for her sister.

12. Moira Ferguson, "Introduction," *Maria or The Wrongs of Woman* (New York: Norton, 1975), 8.

13. The idea that the parent may not be the best educator of the child is a familiar one in the novels of the eighteenth century. In Henry Brooke's *The Fool of Quality* the child is taken away from his parents to be educated because it is clear that the parents, in this case aristocrats, could not do the job properly. Among Wollstonecraft's contemporaries, Holcroft and Bage also suggest that the parent often is not the best preceptor. For a fuller discussion of this topic see my "Redefining the Filial Tie: Eighteenth-Century English Novelists from Brooke to Bage" *Etudes Anglaises* (Jan.-Mar. 1985).

14. Godwin makes a very similar argument about society misshaping human beings in their ability to relate to each other in *Caleb Williams*. Even Falkland becomes a monster, we remember.

15. Compare Maria's plaint with Mary Shelley's account of William Godwin's view of marriage: "He was very averse to marriage. . . . When he concocted a code of morals in 'Political Justice,' he warmly opposed a system which exacted a promise to be kept to the end of life, in spite of every alteration of circumstance and of feeling" (Kegan Paul, I, 161).

16. We can follow a similar chain of events in the life of Mary's sister Eliza;

Mary's letters to Everina Wollstonecraft recount her indecision about helping Eliza to escape from her marriage, the actual running away, and the terrifying aftermath.

[December 1783]. "I don't know what to do. Poor Eliza's situation almost turns my brain. I can't stay and see this continual misery, and to leave her to bear it by herself without any one to comfort her, is still more distressing. I would do anything to rescue her from her present situation. . . . In this case something desperate must be determined on. . . . I am convinced that [leaving] is the only expedient to save Bess, and she declares that she had rather be a teacher than stay here. I must again repeat it, you must be secret; nothing can be done till she leaves the house" (Kegan Paul, I, 167).

[January 1784]. "Here we are, Everina; but my trembling hand will scarce let me tell you so. Bess is much more composed than I expected her to be; but to make my trial still more dreadful, I was afraid in the coach she was going to have one of her flights, for she bit her wedding-ring to pieces. When I can recollect myself, I'll send you particulars; but, at present, my heart beats time with every carriage that rolls by, and a knocking at the door almost throws me into a fit. I hope B. [Eliza's husband Mr. Bishop] will not discover us, for I could sooner face a lion; yet the door never opens, but I expect to see him panting for breath. Ask Ned how we are to behave if he should find us out, for Bess is determined not to return. Can he force her?—But I'll not suppose it, yet I can think of nothing else" (Kegan Paul, I, 169).

[Sunday Afternoon January 1784]. "Your welcome letter arrived just now, and we thank you for sending it so soon. Your account of B. does not surprise me, as I am convinced that, to gratify the ruling passion, he could command all the rest. The plea of the child occurred to me, and it was the most rational thing he could complain of. I know he will tell a plausible tale, and the generality will pity him and blame me; but, however, if we can snatch Bess from extreme wretchedness, what reason shall we have to rejoice. It was, indeed, a very disagreeable affair; and if we had stayed a day or two longer, I believe it would never have been effected. For Bess's mind was so harassed with the fear of being discovered, and the thought of leaving the child, that she could not have stood it long. I suppose B. told you how we escaped; there was full as much good luck as good management in it. As to Bess, she was so terrified, that she lost all presence of mind, and would have done anything. I took a second coach, to prevent his tracing us. Well, all this may serve to talk about and laugh at when we meet, but it was no laughing matter at the time. Bess is tolerably well; she cannot help sighing about little Mary, whom she tenderly loved; and on this score I both love and pity her" (Kegan Paul, I, 169-70).

17. In *Tom Jones* Fielding has Mrs. Fitzpatrick comment on the difference between the public and private personae of a man—she notes that only the wife or daughter gets to see the less attractive side of what may be in public eyes a quite attractive person. But Fielding stops far short of the physical detail that makes the reader recoil in disgust from the sloven a woman may meet across the breakfast table.

With respect to realism, Wollstonecraft is quite unlike other eighteenth-century novelists, except perhaps for Godwin in the prison scenes of *Caleb Williams*. Wollstonecraft uses detailed description in her novel, as opposed to merely naming complaints: recall, for example, Jemima's account of her life trying to make a living over a wash tub. The sharpness of Wollstonecraft's images, whether in descriptions of poor or middle-class life, is an important stylistic contribution to the novel form.

18. Maria's first landlady after she leaves Mr. Venables is an example of a working woman whose husband steals her wages and abuses her in the bargain: the landlady " 'toiled from morning till night; yet her husband would rob the till, and take away the money reserved for paying bills; and, returning home drunk, he would beat her if she chanced to offend him, though she had a child at the breast' " (*M*, 120). Subtlety not being the strongest point of Wollstonecraft's novel, this tale is followed a few pages later by a quite similar story (*M*, 126-28) of another landlady whose husband repeatedly takes and loses her earnings, dropping her over and over again to the bottom of the economic ladder, and returning to steal her earnings each time she painfully rises once more.

Reiss, 11-12, notes that if a husband deserted his wife, "her property remained in his possession, even the property which she had earned during such desertion; he could come back at any moment and insist on the resumption of cohabitation. . . . She could . . . pledge his credit, but where no credit was to be obtained a woman had no alternative but the workhouse unless she could earn her own living, and under such circumstances her earnings would be paid to him if he chose to claim them."

19. The angry assumption by Maria's brother that Maria somehow has cheated him echoes Clarissa's brother on the topic of his inheritance. Note the bitterness of the recrimination in both cases.

20. Reiss, 8, explains that a "man had the right to sue and to claim damages from any one who deprived him of the services and society of his wife, whether by causing her an injury or by enticing her away from him and harbouring her against his will. He could bring an action against the man with whom his wife committed adultery."

21. The hero, Frank, considers the father of his friend Oliver Trenchard to be his true father, for while Mr. Trenchard helped him to gain an education and thus to mature morally, his own father, Abimelech Henley, "kept [him] in ignorance as much as was in his power" (London: Oxford Univ. Press, 1970), 8.

Chapter 7. Jane Austen: *Pride and Prejudice* and *Emma*

1. The varying perspectives of critical comment on Austen are commensurate with the explosion of critical analyses of the author and her novels. Needless to say, each school of criticism has its own "Jane;" Alistair Duckworth, in his very thoughtful essay "Jane Austen and the Conflict of Interpretations" in *Jane Austen: New Perspectives*, ed. Janet Todd (New York: Holmes and Meier, 1983), somewhat ruefully tries to make sense of them—there are, among others, the Chicago, the Marxist, the Freudian, the feminist, the histor-

ical criticisms—but he finally, it seems to me, having made clear his own historical viewpoint, agrees to differ. His essay makes a valuable starting point for a survey of the (relatively) current points of view about Austen. An earlier and equally valuable review of the then current modes is Marilyn Butler's introduction to her own discussion of Austen in her classic *Jane Austen and the War of Ideas* (Oxford: Clarendon, 1976).

2. Claudia L. Johnson's comment in "A 'Sweet Face as White as Death': Jane Austen and the Politics of Female Sensibility," *Novel* 22:2 (Winter 1989): 164, is typical of this response: "Elizabeth Bennet's shamelessly athletic run through the muddy countryside implicates and overrules politically charged subtexts about female propriety."

3. Sandra M. Gilbert and Susan Gubar, *The Madwoman in the Attic* (New Haven: Yale Univ. Press, 1980), 154, note that "Austen's propriety is most apparent in the overt lessons she sets out to teach in all of her mature novels. Aware that male superiority is far more than a fiction, she always defers to the economic, social, and political power of men as she dramatizes how and why female survival depends on gaining male approval and protection. . . . [T]he happy ending of an Austen novel occurs when the girl becomes a daughter to her husband." At the other end of the critical spectrum, John Halperin, *The Life of Jane Austen* (Baltimore: Johns Hopkins Univ. Press, 1984), 21, puts the matter even more bluntly: "nor should we be surprised if her books sometimes rebuke individualistic female initiatives and imply, as they all do, that the consummation of a woman's life lies in marriage to a commanding man."

4. Carole Fabricant, "The Literature of Domestic Tourism and the Public Consumption of Private Property" in *The New Eighteenth Century*, ed. Felicity Nussbaum and Laura Brown (New York: Methuen, 1987), places Elizabeth's visit to Pemberly within the context of English domestic tourism. She reminds us that country house touring in England was very popular and that there was a "widespread dissemination" of literature recording it, all of which serves as background for the passages in *Pride and Prejudice*. Like Marilyn Butler (*War of Ideas*, 215), Fabricant notes that "the disposition of [Darcy's] house and grounds, and the enthusiastic testimonial of his fiercely loyal housekeeper, constitute an extremely effective advertisement for the values and way of life of its owner" (255). It is significant that the tour Elizabeth takes with the Gardiners would have been a quite usual outing for people of their class and interests; Elizabeth's appearance at Pemberly is not a mere plot contrivance. Fabricant's examination of the social role of domestic tourism is fascinating.

5. Dorothy Van Ghent, *The English Novel* (New York: Holt, Rinehart and Winston, 1953), 102.

6. Jane Austen, *Pride and Prejudice*, ed. R.W. Chapman (Oxford: Oxford Univ. Press, 1926), 15. All further references in the text are to this edition.

7. The historian David Spring, "Interpreters of Jane Austen's Social World" in *Jane Austen: New Perspectives*, does an excellent job of helping the modern reader to make sense of Austen's numbers:

> Aristocratic landowners, having more money, had more to spend. A few had a
> great deal more to spend, as much as £100,000 of gross income annually. To

appreciate what a very great deal this was, remember that in the first decade of the nineteenth century a skilled worker with a family to support would have been fortunate to enjoy an annual income of £100, an unskilled worker of £40. Even the lowest annual income of an aristocratic landowner was something like £5000 to £10,000, Mrs. Bennet's measurement of the lordly life. . . . The gentry had less money to spend—although relative to the income of a working man, even modest gentry incomes were still impressive, probably on a level with the income of a large town merchant and exceeding the incomes of most professional men. A modest gentry income was something like £1,000 to £2,000 a year. It was Mr. Bennet's income in *Pride and Prejudice*. . . . To the unpleasant but aristocratic Lady Catherine de Bourgh, even Mr. Bennet's Longbourn with its £2,000 a year was scarcely adequate: deficient in park, servants, and whatever else was needed to impose on the imaginations of social inferiors. [58]

Spring defines the terms "aristocrat" and "gentry" in terms of what "Jane Austen called 'style of living,' that is . . . how they spent their money" (58). It should be noted that the £20,000 and £100,000 figures for the Bingleys signify not annual income but the amounts of their inheritance.

8. Marilyn Butler makes a very strong argument for Austen as a conservative writer. The purpose of her study, Butler says, "is to show that [Austen's] manner as a novelist is broadly that of the conservative Christian moralist of the 1790s" (*War of Ideas*, 165). She finds that "In this period of deep partisan feeling, the form of a novel is decisive. . . . The action through which the central character passes tends to reflect an ideal progress: either he is freed from social pressure, like Bage's heroes, and Maria Edgeworth's, or he is schooled in accepting it, like Jane West's and Jane Austen's. The plots of Jane Austen's six novels begin in the conservative camp and, very significantly, remain in it. She may experiment by placing her heroine in a different role in relation to the key process of self-discovery. The action itself remains essentially the same, a single all-revealing fable through which she reflects the individual's life in society. The unyielding scepticism about the individual conveyed by that plot suggests that she is innately . . . orthodox" (293). Butler's reading is reaffirmed by Alistair Duckworth, "Conflict of Interpretations," 45.

9. Halperin explores this perspective on Charlotte's marriage to Mr. Collins at some length, seeing a large measure of Austen's own experience in her depiction of Charlotte's reactions. See especially pages 53-54.

10. Butler comments that "Elizabeth's readiness to condemn Charlotte operates more as a means of throwing light on her own wavering judgement than as an insight into marriage-in-society: for the next time we hear of the subject is in relation to Wickham, whose plans for a prudent marriage to Miss King Elizabeth is so inconsistently ready to condone" (214).

11. It is worth noting the remark about the wife's "extravagance." Austen is quite aware of the wrongs women can do to men, and high on this list is financial harm. Mrs. Bennet is very good at helping to squander the limited resources of the Bennet family, and in *Emma* Austen gives us the example of

Mr. Weston, whose financial health was seriously compromised by his first wife.

12. Claudia L. Johnson in *Jane Austen: Women Politics and the Novel* (Chicago: Univ. of Chicago Press, 1988) observes that we should not take for granted Austen's endowing of her female characters with "a moral life," that, in fact, "the extent to which women have or ought to have moral lives in the same way men have moral lives was very hotly and accessibly debated in Austen's time." She notes Lionel Trilling's comment that "Emma Woodhouse was remarkable for having 'a moral life as a man has a moral life' " (xxiii). I would make the same observation for both Elizabeth and Jane in *Pride and Prejudice*.

13. Tony Tanner, *Jane Austen* (Cambridge: Harvard Univ. Press, 1986), 180, defines this focus somewhat differently: "I just want to note the significance of the fact that Emma is rich—in money. It is not property, which for Jane Austen always carried distinct responsibilities and patterns of behavior with it—or should do. Unlike money, property supplied a specific agenda of duties, actions and rewards. The danger of money, on the other hand, was that not only did it not provide any pedigree: it conferred no specific obligations. Always 'circulating,' it was as uncertain in origin as it was indeterminate in application. It embodied no entelechy and was teleologically morally neutral—and indifferent. Anyone could be a 'do-anything' with it. Emma is unique among Jane Austen's heroines in that she is rich enough to think that she does not need a marriage with a proper man—with property—in order to exist properly in society. . . . Her apparent freedom based on financial independence is thus not only deeply ambiguous but carries with it a latent double danger: she can delude herself and she can toy and tamper with other peoples' relationships. She of course does both."

14. Jane Austen, *Emma*, ed. R. W. Chapman (Oxford: Oxford Univ. Press, 1926), 6. All further references are to this edition.

15. Halperin, 25-26.

16. Arnold Kettle, *An Introduction to the English Novel* (New York: Harper and Row, 1951), 99, comments "the question at issue is not Jane Austen's failure to suggest a *solution* to the problem of class divisions but her apparent failure to notice the *existence* of the problem. . . . The values and standards of the Hartfield world are based on the assumption that it is right and proper for a minority of the community to live at the expense of the majority."

17. Discussions of female education, especially in view of the youth of so many of the major figures in Austen's novel, are quite few and always very general. Emma arranges reading lists for herself that she never gets around to going through (*E*, 23); she attempts to improve Harriet's mind "by a great deal of useful reading and conversation," but these views "had never yet led to more than a few first chapters, and the intention of going on to-morrow" (*E*, 46). The paucity of Austen's comment on the subject of female education should be compared with Thomas Holcroft and Mary Wollstonecraft on the same topic: here as elsewhere Austen's conservative outlook is reflected in her emphases. Nancy Armstrong in *Desire and Domestic Fiction* (New York and Oxford: Oxford Univ. Press, 1987), p. 275, note 7, finds that when Austen does

talk about the education of women, it is almost always within a negative context: "In every one of Austen's novels . . . there is an explicit attack on female education."

18. See for example pp. 299-300, 359, and 379ff.


## Chapter 8. Conclusion

1. Robert Halsband, *The Life of Lady Mary Wortley Montagu* (New York: Oxford Univ. Press, 1960), 28.

2. Lady Mary Wortley Montague, *The Complete Letters of Lady Mary Wortley Montague*, 3 vol. (Oxford: Clarendon, 1965), I, 160.

3. *Life*, 16.

4. *Letters*, I, 134.

5. Sarah Fielding, *The Adventures of David Simple*, 2 vol. (New York: Garland, 1974), I, 44. All further references are to this edition.

6. Peter Earle, *The Making of the English Middle Class* (Berkeley: Univ. of California Press, 1989), 186ff, notes that there were "a number of factors tending to minimize the significance of parental consent to marriages" and comments, further, that there is much evidence, especially in wills, to suggest that fathers were not as harsh in fact as we might assume from some of the novels.

7. Samuel Richardson, *Pamela* (Boston: Houghton Mifflin, 1971), 25-26. All further references are to this edition.

8. D. Grant Campbell, "Fashionable Suicide: Conspicuous Consumption and the Collapse of Credit in Frances Burney's *Cecilia*," *Studies in Eighteenth-Century Culture*, vol. 20, 1990, notes the financial theme as the center of Burney's *Cecilia*; as with the novels I have discussed, he finds that recognizing this focus markedly changes our reading of the novel. See especially pp. 132-33.

9. *Social Protest in the Eighteenth-Century English Novel* (Columbus: Ohio State Univ. Press, 1985), 9 and 120.

10. Earle, 173-74. Earle's discussion of women in business is also fascinating; he finds that women were a surprisingly significant presence in the business world. "Fire insurance records indicate that [businesses run by women] were some 5 to 10 per cent of all businesses in London" (173).

11. Earle, 184.

12. Ibid., 184-85.

13. Marilyn Butler in her preface to the reissue of *Jane Austen and the War of Ideas* (Oxford: Clarendon, 1987), xiv, notes of her own work that she "aimed to show, by the use of many examples, that the practices of novelists in the late eighteenth century were less aesthetic, less separate from society, than modern critics are in the habit of insisting on."

14. New York: Columbia Univ. Press, 1980.

15. The age difference between Emma and Knightley, which for some readers makes him seem to slip easily into the slot formerly occupied by Emma's father, should be seen within the social and economic patterns defined above.

# Index